55
50¢

I

M

Al

[xi]

L I S T   O F   P L A T E S

Books by RUTH MOORE

THE COIL OF LIFE

(1961)

THE EARTH WE LIVE ON

(1956)

CHARLES DARWIN

(1955)

MAN, TIME, AND FOSSILS

(1953)

THESE ARE BORZOI BOOKS,

PUBLISHED IN NEW YORK BY ALFRED A. KNOPF

THE COIL OF LIFE

THE COIL
OF LIFE

*The Story of the Great Discoveries
in the Life Sciences*

by RUTH MOORE

Drawings by PATRICIA M. JACKSON

NEW YORK   ALFRED A. KNOPF   1962

L. C. catalog card number: 60–14459

66- 7267

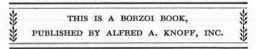

THIS IS A BORZOI BOOK,
PUBLISHED BY ALFRED A. KNOPF, INC.

PUBLISHED FEBRUARY 17, 1962
SECOND PRINTING, AUGUST 1962

I am fearfully and wonderfully made.

PSALM 139, 14

PREFACE

THE HIDDEN CONTINENT OF LIFE is seldom explored by the non-biologist. Even those closest to this infinite matter have complained that it is an "impenetrable jungle." And yet in it lies the explanation of all that we are—our appearance, our diversity, our similarity, our continuity—and there is nothing of greater fascination or importance than the deciphering of nature's fine, orderly packing of all the determinants of life into the extremely tiny coil of DNA, and into its wrappings, the chromosome, the cell, the organs, and the body.

The discovery of the role of DNA and its drawing together of all the life sciences has at long last made it possible for the layman to approach the subject of life, and to aspire to an understanding of the amazing knowledge science is gaining of it. It was this that emboldened me to undertake this book.

I wish to express my most sincere thanks to the scientists who were so kind as to open their material to me, and to read and criticize the various parts of this book. At a considerable cost in time to themselves and, in some cases, to their staffs, they have given me invaluable help. In thanking them for this generous assistance, I do not want to imply that they are responsible for what I have written. The words of praise and appraisal, the emphasis, and selection are mine. With this clearance, I should like to thank Dr. George Wells Beadle, Dr. F. H. C. Crick, Dr. Heinz Fraenkel-Conrat, Dr. Ernest F. Gale, Dr. David E. Green, Dr. Alfred Day Hershey, Dr. Mahlon B. Hoagland, Dr. H. E. Huxley, Dr. Vernon M. Ingram, Dr. Arthur Kornberg, Dr. Joshua Lederberg, Dr. Daniel Mazia, Dr. A. A. Moscona, Dr. Herman J. Muller, Dr. Severo Ochoa and Peter Lengyel, Dr. Linus Pauling, Dr. S. Meryl

Rose, Dr. Frederick Sanger, Dr. Albert Szent-Györgyi, and Dr. J. Herbert Taylor.

For the historial material, and much of the contemporary, I have drawn constantly on the Crerar Library in Chicago. I wish to express my appreciation for the library's services, and fine collections.

I also want to thank the Chicago *Sun-Times* for granting me a leave of absence to work on this book. Time, and the kind of encouragement I have received from "the paper" and its executive editor, Mr. Larry S. Fanning, are essential.

A note of this kind cannot end without a particular and special word of appreciation to my editor, Mr. Harold Strauss, editor-in-chief of Alfred A. Knopf, Inc., and his associates. Their guidance is brilliant, their support unfailing.

RUTH MOORE

Chicago
July 1960

CONTENTS

I. THE BASE OF LIFE

II. UP FROM THE BASE OF LIFE

A LOOK AHEAD

AT A FEW rare moments in the history of a science, understanding takes a long leap forward. So it is now in the sciences of life, the sciences that seek to explain the form, the functioning, and the diversity of life. New discoveries have suddenly enlarged and altered much that was known before.[1]

After more than two hundred years of searching and questioning, the base of life has been found. It is a tiny coil of matter, in structure a spiral staircase. In it lies the master plan for all that we are and the thread of continuity from the beginning of life. Here in an infinitely small bit of substance are encompassed all the likenesses and differences of the living world, and the uniqueness of the more than two billion people of this globe, and of the earth's myriads of animals, plants, and micro-organisms.

Science, having now reached the base, can take a new approach to the immense problems of life. Always before, each new finding only compelled the scientist and the world generally to ask what lay below the newly found surface and made it what it was.

No sooner did men begin to understand the relationship of the "vital organs"—the heart, the brain—to the life and well-being of their fellow men than they had to ask why these mysterious organs performed as they did. Then it was learned that the organs were made up of tissues. But still the answer was not found. What were the tissues? What determined their form and structure? The search at this point had to turn from the

---

[1] I once made a similar observation about the science of evolution. It applies so strikingly to the other life sciences that I repeat it here.

visible to the invisible, and from the tangible to the intangibly small that could be detected only with a microscope. In time it became apparent that the tissues and the organs and the individual were products of the cells, the little "boxes" that formed the underlying substance of them all.

But still this was not the base. The cell was a complex organ in itself, and something within it determined what it must be. The search had to go deeper again. A series of brilliant discoveries tracked the determinative factor, the shaping agent, to the chromosomes, little threads of matter within the nucleus of the cell, and to some manifest if undetectable units arranged in linear order along the chromosome. The units could even be changed by the chance hit of radiation. And yet the true control of life in all its form and content had not yet been found. Something deeper, something still unknown, something invisible even to the first electron microscopes directed the formation of the 1,000,000,000,000,000 specialized cells of the adult human being and carried on life.

When the long-sought basis of bases was found in the 1950's, it came as a complete surprise. Almost no one had suspected that the bottles of a gummy white powder which sat on the shelves of many laboratories could be the veritable stuff of life. But in its natural state in the cell, the powder bearing the formidable name of deoxyribonucleic acid, or DNA, was the foundation, the ultimate determiner. The proofs came from strange sources—from the behavior of a bacterium that causes pneumonia and of a virus that invades bacteria. But what was true in bacteria and the virus was true for all the rest of the living world. The source had been found.

This time science did not have to dig deeper. Though great and intractable problems remained—for science was far from solving the complexities of life—a firm base was at last available. Questions could be put in new terms, and science could begin to work, as nature works, from the beginning upward.

In very short order other major discoveries followed:

A simple elegant way in which the four varying "steps" in the DNA "spiral staircase" could invariably produce the twenty amino acids that produce the proteins that constitute the muscles, the skin, and the general body structure;

The structure of the proteins;

A wholly unsuspected world in the little drop of jelly that surrounds the nucleus of the cell, and in it the site of the protein factories and of the power plants of the cell;

The secret of how and why we move.

These were fundamental things, and the view of living things was nearly revolutionized in a very few years.

But this sudden leap forward in the solution of some of the most elemental problems of life was possible only because of what had gone before. It rested upon Lavoisier's proving, through his discovery that breathing is a combustion, that the body is governed by physical laws; upon Wohler's showing that the secretions of the body were not mystical substances, but compounds makable by man; upon Bichat's finding of the tissues; upon Pasteur's proof that life is not created spontaneously; upon Buchner's demonstration that a ferment can occur without the participation of the cell; upon Fischer's demonstrating that proteins are chains of matter; upon Roux's and Driesch's opening of a glimpse into the miracle of development; and upon Mendel's and DeVries's showing that heredity is controlled by independent units passed along from parent to offspring. And there was much more.

The search took many routes. It was the study of air which drew Lavoisier into his discoveries about breathing. The work was so vast and unfathomable that many sciences sprang up to specialize in phases of it. Among them were biochemistry, biophysics, genetics, cytology, embryology, biology, physiology.

Only now, with the discovery of DNA, are all beginning for the first time to converge. All have come down to the same marvelous molecule; all, in the words of Sewall Wright, former president of the International Congress of Genetics, are at last being "bound into one coherent whole." Many of the various concepts of the past must be reinterpreted in terms of DNA.

And now too some of the great principles of life are becoming newly simple and understandable. The tortuous complexities that gave biochemistry and some of the other life sciences their formidable reputations remain and must be dealt with by the scientist, but much about the base and organization of life is becoming comprehensible to the non-scientist. Increasing knowledge is showing unexpected simplicity and order in the hidden mazes of living things. And it is creating a new context, a context that places the human race in a different light. Few human beings familiar with the new findings will ever again look upon themselves and their fellow men in the same terms as in the past.

Some of the great break-through discoveries have already been honored by Nobel prizes. Many highly technical reports have appeared in scientific journals, and the magazine *Scientific American* has published excellent explanatory articles. But still the findings that are altering the whole view of life are relatively unknown. In many cases there has not been time for them to spread far, for they are very new. Nor have they been brought together in one comprehensive scientific book. It is not surprising that they have not yet become, as they must, a part of the thinking and knowledge of almost everyone.

It is this story, the story of the great discoveries that are changing much of the former view and concept of life, that this book will attempt to tell.

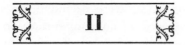

II

LAVOISIER:
THE FLAME OF LIFE

O N A CLEAR summer day in 1772 when the sun shone bright in the noonday Paris sky, the great Tschirnhausen burning glass was hauled out into the Jardin de l'Infante. This was the formal garden that stretched from the Louvre to the banks of the Seine.

Members of the Académie Royale des Sciences who had come to witness some singular experiments gathered around the lumbering, top-heavy apparatus. Antoine Laurent Lavoisier, the experimenter, mounted the low, wheeled platform, put on dark glasses, and began to turn the big thirty-three-inch lens full to the sun. He set a smaller lens that shortened the focus and brought an immense heat to bear upon a hollowed-out Paris paving stone that held—a diamond.

The heat was intense. A few of the elegantly dressed spectators thought that they saw a tiny wisp of smoke. And then the diamond had disappeared. It was gone; the hard, brilliant stone, the miraculous gem of the Middle Ages, had "burned" or been "destroyed" by the heat as completely as though it had been a drop of pure water.

Formidable, formidable! It was a startling and incredible thing to happen before one's eyes, even when one was expecting it. The group was at least partly prepared for this dramatic opening of the experiment, for the Grand Duke of Tuscany in his studies of the curative "atmospheres" or "emanations" of precious stones had demonstrated this peculiarity of the diamond some years before.

But more was to come. Maillard the jeweler had argued before the academy that diamonds "burned" only when they were heated in the air. If air were excluded, he said, the stones would not be destroyed by any temperature. So certain was the jeweler of his contention that he offered to furnish three diamonds for a test. Could he be right? An experiment was carried

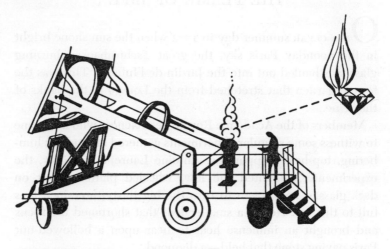

A burning glass. In its concentrated heat even the diamond "burned." Experiments with the glass opened the way to a wide exploration of life. This glass was used by Lavoisier and is similar to the great Tschirnhausen.

out according to Maillard's instructions and the diamonds came through unfazed. Debate and interest in the academy ran even higher; what could be the meaning of this inexplicable phenomenon? Why should the presence or absence of air affect the combustion of the hard, impermeable gem? It was all that was talked about.

At this point Lavoisier, one of the young members of the academy, proposed with his characteristic thoroughness that no conclusions be drawn until the diamonds had been tested with the greatest possible heat. He pointed out that a heat far surpassing that of the best of furnaces could be obtained by use of the academy's long-neglected Tschirnhausen burning lens. The great glass had been presented to the academy some sixty years before, but through most of the years since had been sitting unused in the collection of apparatus. The academy at once recognized the value of Lavoisier's proposal and asked him to undertake the experiment.

The day had arrived. The scientists and nobles who had come to watch drew closer again. Maillard's diamonds were placed in a clay pipe filled with powdered charcoal, and the pipe was doubly sealed in a double crucible. Lavoisier placed it on the focus and turned the heat of the sun full upon it. The sun burned down.

At the right moment Lavoisier turned the great glass away. He broke the seals. He poured out the charcoal, and there against its soft blackness sparkled the diamonds. They were undimmed, as brilliant and weighty as ever, completely unaffected by the inferno of heat to which they had been subjected.

Air! Then air was the determinative factor in the burning of the diamond, and what thoughtful man, especially if he had the scientist's inquiring mind, could avoid asking if air were the determinative, essential factor in all combustion? It was this question—about the relation of "elemental," ethereal, insubstantial air to burning, to the earth's most solid materials, and to living things—which would in the end upset all that men then believed about the elements around them and about their own bodies and being.

The study of air would lead Lavoisier and other scientists into an undreamed-of exploration of the nature of physical things and of the processes of life. It was a strange and improbable road to the still unrealized goal of the understanding of life, but it was the road that would be taken.

• • •

Lavoisier unquestionably was equipped to make some great contribution to the world. The man destined to turn the study of matter and of life away from the tortuousness of alchemy and into the course of today was born at Paris on August 26, 1743.

His father was a well-to-do lawyer; his mother, Emilie Punctis, a lawyer's daughter. After the death of Mme Lavoisier in 1748, M. Lavoisier took his five-year-old son and younger daughter to live in the Punctis home. Both Mme Punctis and her daughter Constance gave them all a single-hearted devotion.

From the substantial Punctis house, Lavoisier had only a short walk across the Pont Neuf to his school, the Collège Mazarin. The college, with its imposing semicircle of buildings facing the Seine and the Louvre, conducted what was generally considered the best school in France, and young Antoine Lavoisier was soon winning most of its top prizes. He thought that he might become a writer. It was not an idle dream, for even as a schoolboy this gifted child wrote with unusual clarity and logic. In 1760 he won the second prize in rhetoric in the *concours général,* a competition for all the schools of France. During his senior year, however, he attended lectures on science as part of his course in philosophy. From that point on, his interest in science was unflagging and foremost, although never exclusive or pre-emptive.

Since there had been several generations of lawyers on both sides of the family, Lavoisier willingly entered the school of law. On the other hand, his family did not oppose, but encouraged, his growing interest in science. His law courses were arranged so that he could go on with his scientific studies.

Lavoisier always had a sure instinct for the right scientific decision and procedure. He managed to study with four of the leading scientists of France: the Abbé Nicolas Louis de Lacaille, the astronomer and mathematician who had calculated the circumference of the earth; Bernard de Jussieu, the botanist then applying the Linnaean classifications to the plants in the garden of the Trianon; Guillaume François Rouelle, demonstrator in chemistry at the Jardin du Roi and renowned for his work on salts; and Jean Etienne Guettard, the geologist who had proved that the quiet mountains of Auvergne were in truth extinct volcanoes, and had thus taught men to study the earth itself for the explanations of its forms and mysteries.

Guettard had found that rock formations were not haphazardly scattered about, but often continued across the country for miles and even across the borders of other states. He hammered at the scientific bodies of France until he was authorized to undertake the geological mapping of the country. For this work he needed a student assistant. The exacting, plain-spoken geologist had little patience with the average student, but Lavoisier was an exception. He invited the young law student-scientist to accompany him on his expedition of 1763.

After the trip Lavoisier submitted his first *mémoire*, or paper, to the Académie Royale des Sciences. It was an outgrowth of his work with Guettard: a carefully developed study of gypsum. By exact weighing of his materials, he demonstrated that gypsum loses water when it is heated and converted into plaster of Paris, and that when water is taken up again there is a recrystallization that causes the material to set and solidify. Lavoisier said he would not speculate on the cause of this effect; speculation was out of place in the science of chemistry.

Not long after this, Lavoisier won first prize in an academy-sponsored competition for the best means of lighting the streets of a large city at night. He had made a thorough study of illumination, even living for six weeks in a darkened room to make his eyes sensitive to small differences in the intensity of light. And he had gone into every phase of lamp structure and costs. No one else was even cited in the class of competitors who had applied the principles of physics and mathematics to the problem, and Lavoisier received a gold medal from the King. The *Journal des Savants* commented: "This flattering distinction for so young an author, of which there is no previous instance in the academy, has greatly pleased the public." Lavoisier was twenty-three.

And he was off on another tour with Guettard, one that produced a distinguished series of geological maps and several more *mémoires* for the academy.

At twenty-five Lavoisier had submitted four *mémoires* to the academy, in addition to winning the gold medal. His friends felt that he should be a member and worked for his election. It was nearly unprecedented for a scientist to be elected at so early an age, but it was almost as though his choice were an inevitability, rather than an unusual recognition of a prodigy.

The academy met twice a week in the old Louvre to hear and discuss scientific reports. It was also charged with making whatever practical studies the state might require, whether of street lighting, aerostatic machines (balloons), the water supply, the improved production of gunpowder, or the state of prisons. From the moment of his election in 1768, Lavoisier was deep in all of the work of the academy and wrote a large share of its reports.

For Lavoisier his election to the academy was a turning point. At the same time he took another decisive and ultimately fateful step. Both to protect a sizable fortune that he had inherited from his mother and to assure himself of an occupation that would leave much of his time free for science and public duties, Lavoisier bought a one-third membership in the Tax Farm. The farm was the semi-official tax-collection body of France; it earned a reputedly rich income by the collection of all taxes for the king and state, and it was no more beloved than tax-collection agencies usually are. Lavoisier's scientific colleagues, nonplused at his choice of a business, consoled themselves: "At least the dinners he gives us will be all the better."

Paris at this time faced a serious water problem. The water drawn from the Seine and distributed by barrel was no longer sufficient or safe. The academy was asked to determine what should be done, and the study was assigned to Lavoisier. Aside from the problem of supply, the question was how the purity of water could be ascertained.

From the time of the Greeks, the world had accepted water as one of the four elements—the others were air, fire, and earth. It was also believed that water was transmutable into earth. But if this were true, how could water be purified? Lavoisier decided to experiment. "I wish to speak of facts," he explained.

He began with a review of what had been done in the past. Two major proofs had been offered of the transmutability of water and earth: (1) plants had grown from pure water, and (2) a deposit of earth was left after repeated distillations of water in glass vessels.

In 1648 Jean Baptiste van Helmont had performed the experiment that convinced the world of the first proposition. It was regarded as definitive.

Helmont put two hundred pounds of dried earth in a tub and planted a five-pound willow tree in it. Through the next five years he watered the tree only with distilled or rain water, and even placed a covering over the tub to prevent any dust from settling in it.

"Five years being finished," he wrote, "the tree sprung from thence did weigh 169 pounds and about three ounces. . . . At length I again dried the earth of the Vessel and there were found the same 200 pounds wanting about two ounces. Therefore did 164 pounds of Wood, Barks, and Roots arise out of water only."

Lavoisier, with his analytical mind, quickly saw the fallacies in the Helmont argument. The tree had also contained resins, oils, and other substances. Had water also been transmuted into these substances? And Lavoisier felt certain that if the tree had been reduced to its elements, very little earth would have been recovered. He pointed out too that the Reverend Stephen Hales, the scientist, had demonstrated that plants take in air through their leaves. The first transmutability argument could be disposed of.

The young chemist determined to put the second, the residue theory, to the most rigorous test. He obtained a "pelican" (a vessel with curving handles that suggested the neck of a pelican), filled it with water that had been eight times distilled, and weighed it on one of the supersensitive balances that he had had made to order. For 101 days thereafter he kept the water at a little less than the boiling point. At first no visible change occurred. Only at the end of about thirty days, when his hopes were beginning to run low, did some little flecks of material appear in the water. Presently they sank to the bottom of the pelican and stayed there. On the 101st day Lavoisier halted the experiment and allowed his apparatus to cool. Anxiously he put the pelican and its contents on his scales. After a hundred days of continuous distillation there was only a quarter of a grain's change in weight. But "earth" clearly had been produced.

Was it genuine "earth" or was it possible that the hot water had dissolved some of the glass of the pelican? The vessel had lost 17.4 grains in weight.

Next Lavoisier weighed the "earth," the flecks that had appeared. It tipped the balance at 4.9 grains, and when the water was evaporated and its solid contents were weighed in their turn, they yielded another 15.5 grains. This was 3 grains more than the pelican had lost, but the extra weight could easily be accounted for in the additional handling of the water. Unquestionably no earth had come from the water; the "earth" was a product of the dissolution of the glass. Soon afterward Carl Wilhelm Scheele analyzed the residual material and found that it was made up of silicon, potash, and chalk, the materials of glass.

Far from proving the transmutability of water into earth, distillation demonstrated that no transmutation takes place. Water no more changed into earth than silver into gold. The ancient faith in the four elements did not yield immediately to this devastating blow, but Lavoisier had raised questions that ultimately would destroy it and open the way to modern science and the modern understanding of the world. And he had learned many of the techniques he would use.

It was at about this same time that the academy was engaged in the great diamond debate. After the dramatic demonstration with the Tschirnhausen burning glass, Lavoisier conducted seventeen other experiments with precious stones. Certainly the diamond did not burn unless air was present, but when it was, all indications were that the diamond's burning was true combustion. Basic questions of why and how had been raised, and Lavoisier saw clearly that a wide study of combustion would be required.

Hales had reported that phosphorus absorbs air when it burns. Lavoisier, in September 1772, obtained supplies of the highly inflammable phosphorus and of sulphur, and went to work to test the Hales report. On November 1, two months later, he sent a sealed note to the academy with instructions that it was not not to be read until he authorized its release. In burning a pound of sulphur, he had obtained far more than a pound of its combustion product, vitriolic acid.

Science and men generally believed without question that when anything burned, the fire element in it escaped, as flame and light quite visibly did. And to the degree that the fire element—or phlogiston, as it was called—was lost in burning, so much, it was argued, would the material be reduced in weight.

But something was wrong. Lavoisier, weighing his sulphur and phosphorus before and after burning, saw that the contrary was true. Instead of a loss of weight, burning produced an increase in weight.

"This discovery which I have established by experiments and that I regard as decisive, has led me to think that what is observed in the combustion of sulphur and phosphorus may well take place in the case of all substances that gain in weight by combustion and calcination, and I am persuaded that the increase in weight of metallic calces is due to the same cause," said Lavoisier in his sealed note.

Lavoisier strongly suspected that the increase in weight occurred because air was absorbed. An experiment confirmed this conjecture. In a closed vessel containing some charcoal, Lavoisier heated the calx of lead—the material produced by the burning of lead. As it went back into metallic lead a volume of air a thousand times greater than the quantity of the calx was given off. Weight increased when air was taken in; it decreased when air was liberated. The demonstration was complete.

It was a revolutionary finding, a proof that again shook time-hallowed beliefs and contradicted all that men thought that they saw with their own eyes. Under the circumstances Lavoisier considered it best not to announce his findings until he could confirm them with a long and thorough series of experiments. In the meantime, he wanted to secure his claim to a discovery that he knew was of the utmost importance. The sealed note solved his problem. When it was read to the academy in 1773, many other experiments had underwritten his original conclusions.

The more Lavoisier studied the problem of air, the more basic it seemed to him. Others had observed that "common air" is released from seemingly solid substances and had reported that it was sometimes "contaminated." The great Scottish chemist Joseph Black was convinced, however, that something more than contamination was involved. The "air" given off in the burning of charcoal, in respiration, and in fermentation was so different from the air we breathe that a mouse could not live in it and a candle was immediately extinguished. Black suggested that it be called "fixed air"—it was later to be named carbon dioxide.

He also discovered that it could easily be identified by running it through limewater. It turned the clear liquid into a milky one.

Black made one remarkable large-scale test of this theory that "fixed air" is produced by breathing. He rigged up a test apparatus over a vent in the roof of a church where fifteen hundred people were attending a continuous ten-hour service. The "air" that came through the spiracle soon clouded limewater. So, he saw, fixed air was produced by the respiration of a large group.

Lavoisier was both impressed with these results and dissatisfied. On February 20, 1773, he noted in his laboratory record: "All the experiments made so far fall short of a complete body of doctrine." The work that had been done seemed to him like separate links in a great chain. Only a few had so far been joined. "An immense series of experiments remains to be made in order to produce a continuous whole," he wrote.

Lavoisier determined to repeat "with added safeguards" all the work that had been done, to study the "air" given off by as many substances as possible, and to investigate the nature of the air absorbed in combustion.

"It is established," he said, "that fixed air shows properties very different from those of common air. Indeed, it kills the animals that breathe it; whilst the other is necessary and essential to their preservation. . . . These differences will be exhibited to their full extent. . . . The importance of the end in view prompts me to undertake all this work, which seems to be destined to bring about a revolution in physics and in chemistry."

The old system was collapsing, but few scientists in such a situation have so deliberately set out to build a new one. Their names, most notably, are Newton, Darwin, Einstein—and Lavoisier.

Only the most careful planning and scheduling made such a huge undertaking possible for Lavoisier. The constant assistance of his wife counted too.

Two years before, in November 1771, Lavoisier had married fourteen-year-old Marie Paulze, the daughter of his fellow tax-farmer Jacques Paulze and the grandniece of the Abbé Terray, France's all-powerful controller general of finance. The abbé had proposed shortly before to marry his grandniece, then thirteen, to a fifty-year-old courtier with an ancient title. The abbé had it in his power to ruin his nephew financially if Paulze refused to consent to the marriage. Despite the danger to himself, Paulze determined to avert the unsuitable union. To circumvent it, he proposed a marriage of his young daughter and his highly regarded twenty-eight-year-old colleague Lavoisier.

From the beginning the marriage was a remarkably successful and happy one. Marie Lavoisier at once began to work with her husband in the laboratory. A table was set up for her only a few feet away from any experiment in progress, and she made expert drawings of the apparatus and occasionally of the whole laboratory scene. To perfect her technique, she studied with the painter Jacques Louis David. Many of the entries in the meticulously kept Lavoisier laboratory notebooks are in her hand. In addition, she learned English in order to translate scientific reports for her husband's use. Her translation of Kirwan's *Essay on Phlogiston* was published and widely circulated in France. She also was a gracious hostess and made the Lavoisier dinners famed in social and scientific circles.

To carry out the long series of combustion and air experiments that he was planning and at the same time to take an active part in the work of the academy and the Tax Farm, Lavoisier set up a carefully plotted working schedule. From six to nine o'clock in the morning and from seven to ten in the evening he and Mme Lavoisier worked in the laboratory. In addition, each Friday was set aside entirely for science. If an important experiment was to be performed, Lavoisier frequently invited some of his colleagues from the academy to be present and assist him. They remained for dinner, continuing the discussions of the day, and always dwelled on what the work meant in terms of the general concepts of chemistry.

As Lavoisier made one experiment after another, he began to suspect that it was not the common air that combined with substances during combustion, but some "elastic fluid"—later to be called a gas—that was contained in the air. Another experiment with the big Tschirnhausen was particularly persuasive.

He directed the sun's heat onto three drachms of lead. It melted instantly, and the intent audience watching saw a whitish vapor arising and a thin yellow stratum of "calx" forming on the lead. All of this happened in the first five minutes. Lavoisier kept the lead in focus for a full half-hour, but the "calcination" proceeded no further.

"There exists in the atmosphere an elastic fluid of a particular kind which is mixed with the air," said Lavoisier. "It is at the instant when the quantity of this fluid contained in the receiver is consumed that the calcination can no longer take place."

A whole new concept of air was beginning to take form. But Lavoisier also had to study the "airs and elastic fluids" disengaged from effervescent mixtures and in metallic reductions.

He placed a sparrow in a jar of "elastic fluid" disengaged from chalk. The bird scarcely reached the bottom of the jar before it fell on its side in convulsions. Lavoisier snatched it out. It had been in the invisible material for only a quarter of a minute, but it was dying.

"Without knowing exactly of what use respiration is to animals," wrote Lavoisier, "we at least know that this function is so essential to their existence that they must very soon perish if their lungs are not inflated almost every moment by the elastic fluids that compose our atmosphere."

Lavoisier did not spare himself in these experiments. He leaned over a vessel containing what was then called hepar of sulphur and took a deep breath. An insupportable weight seemed to press against his chest. He wrenched open the door of his laboratory and lurched into the garden. Supporting himself against a wall, he gasped for air. Only after a struggle did he succeed in breathing again. All the remainder of the day he felt physically uneasy. "There was a weight in my head that I cannot easily describe," he said.

The whole situation was puzzling.

"Nothing as yet enables us to decide whether the fixable part of the vapor given off by effervescing mixtures and metallic reduction is a substance essentially different from air, or whether it is air itself to which something has been added or from which something has been subtracted," Lavoisier wrote. "Prudence demands that we suspend our judgment at present on this subject."

Lavoisier felt that this work, baffling as it was, should be formally reported, and he decided to present it to the public as a collection of essays. His book, called *Opuscules physiques et chymiques,* or *Physical and Chemical Essays,* was published in January 1774. Copies were sent to scientists everywhere, and the work was greeted with enthusiasm for its new and rigorous use of the balance and measurement, as well as for its chemical insights.

Shortly afterward, in September 1774, the Reverend Joseph Priestley, one of the most distinguished figures of the era, arrived in Paris. He soon called on Lavoisier and told him of a discovery that he had made shortly before.

Priestley was then librarian to Lord Shelburne, but his duties left him time for his original and skilled chemical experimenting. He had succeeded in obtaining a twelve-inch burning glass, which he was using to heat a number of substances to high temperatures. The glass was less than a third as large as the big Tschirnhausen, but it was powerful enough to lead him to one of the greatest of all discoveries.

On a bright Monday, August 1, 1774, Priestley was working with mercury calx, the red powder produced by the heating of mercury. He put some of it into a flask, filled the flask with mercury, and inverted it in a container of mercury. Then he focused his burning glass on the red powder in the flask. As it

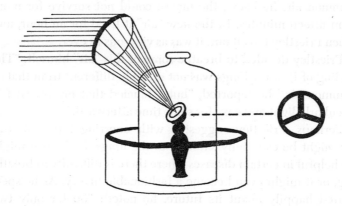

Discovery of oxygen. Priestley and Lavoisier focused a burning glass on mercury calx. Soon the flask was filled with a "strange air." A candle thrust into it burned with unreal brightness. The "strange air" was oxygen.

grew very hot, enough "air" was given off to force the mercury out of the flask. Soon Priestley had a flask full of the unknown "air." He tested some of it with water; it was insoluble. He thrust a candle into it, and, instead of dying, the flame leaped up, burning with a brightness and vigor that he had not previously seen equaled.

Priestley next tried a bit of red-hot wood. As it dropped into the strange "air," it crackled and burned with a white glow like that of hot iron.

Lavoisier was keenly interested in this report from a man whose work he deeply respected. He hurried to repeat the experiment in his own laboratory and obtained similar results.

Priestley in the meantime had returned to England and resumed his own work on the strange "air." When he applied a test he had developed for the "goodness" of air, he found to his surprise that the new air was "better" than common air. Priestley then decided to place a mouse in it. In a closed container of common air, he knew, the mouse could not survive for more than fifteen minutes. In the new "air" it lived for an hour, and when Priestley took it out, it was as vigorous as ever.

Priestley decided to breathe some of this "air" himself. "The feeling of it in my lungs was not sensibly different from that of common air," he reported, "but I fancied that my breast felt peculiarly light and easy for some time afterward."

Perhaps, Priestley suggested with unerring foresight, this air might be especially salutary to the lungs. Perhaps it might be helpful in certain diseases where there is difficulty in breathing, or it might even become a fashionable luxury. As he speculated happily about its future, he noted: "So far only two mice and myself have had the privilege of breathing it."

Priestley decided that this salutary air was probably a pure or dephlogisticated air, an air that had somehow been freed of the phlogiston that, according to current belief, filled the common air up to the point of saturation.

To Lavoisier this explanation of the new air seemed unsatisfactory. He went on working with it, seeking more and more precision. On one occasion the Duc de La Rochefoucauld, Trudaine, and Montigny watched, enthralled, the amazing effects produced by the new air.

"All of this convinced me," Lavoisier reported to the academy in 1775, "that this was not only common air but that it was even more respirable, more combustible, and consequently more pure than even the air in which we live."

And then he continued: "It seems to me to be proved that

the principle which combines with metals during their calcination and which occasions the augmentation of their weight is nothing but an exceedingly pure portion of the air which surrounds us. . . ."

This did not differ greatly from what Priestley had said, except that Lavoisier omitted the phlogiston theory. Actually he had rejected it, though he was not then ready for a public attack against it. It was also significant that he spoke of the new gas as an exceedingly pure *portion* of the air.

Lavoisier continued with his experiments. In one of them he found that the "portion" of the air which combined with metals was a little heavier than common air.

Increasingly Lavoisier was convinced that only a segment of the air combined with metals. If this were true, the common air was not a single, indivisible element, as the world had always believed; rather, it was made up of two very different constituents—one of them highly respirable and the other a substance that alone could not maintain either a flame or life.

In reflecting on his experiments in the light of this revolutionary insight, Lavoisier realized that mercury too absorbs only the salubrious or respirable part of the air. After this portion was taken out, the part of the air that remained was an asphyxiating substance. But he had to test and test again, to review, to go further. Nothing could be neglected or overlooked when the issues were great.

Lavoisier turned again to work with sulphur and phosphorus. In burning, phosphorus combined with the purest part of the air to form an acid of phosphorus; and sulphur formed vitriolic acid. Lavoisier analyzed both acids. His hunch was confirmed. More than half the weight of each was made up of what he then called "eminently respirable air."

But what, then, was the nature of the two "fluids" that made up the air upon which all living things depend? This was the essential, the pressing problem.

Lavoisier again placed some mercury in a retort and heated

it for twelve days. As the mercury evaporated, the usual red particles began to swim on its surface and the volume of air in the flask decreased. By the most exact measurements, Lavoisier saw that the air decreased by about one sixth of its volume. The five sixths that remained was not fit for combustion or respiration. It extinguished a lighted taper as quickly as though the candle had been plunged into water.

Lavoisier was finding a clue even to the proportions of the two kinds of air. But he had to complete his demonstration.

He placed forty-five grains of the red particles in a small retort with a bulb for receiving any liquid or gas that might be produced. The retort was placed in a furnace. As both retort and its contents glowed red with the heat, the red matter began to decrease in bulk. In a few minutes it disappeared completely. At the same time, forty-one grains of liquid mercury and seven to eight cubic inches of what Lavoisier still called "elastic fluid" collected in the remainder of the apparatus.

Anxiously Lavoisier turned some of the gas into a tube about one inch in diameter. He again introduced the lighted taper, and this time it burned with "dazzling splendor." Charcoal, which ordinarily is quietly consumed, burned with a loud crackle and sparkle and threw out such a brilliant light that the experimenters had to shield their eyes. They were exuberant. The salubrious portion of the air had been recovered!

But the experiment was not yet complete. If his reasoning were right, Lavoisier knew, the respirable air and the non-respirable should re-combine into the common air from which they had come.

As the tension mounted, Lavoisier combined the forty-two cubic inches of non-respirable air left from the first experiment with the eight cubic inches of respirable air that he had obtained in the reheating of the calx. And he had common air! Common air had been taken apart and put together again.

Priestly also had performed this historic experiment, and C. W. Scheele was soon to do it. Lavoisier, however, was the only one to understand and correctly interpret what had happened. To Priestley the new air had been only common air freed of its contaminants. It was left to Lavoisier to show an incredulous world that air, the ever-present, the base, the given, was not an element but principally a mixture of two elements, one of which he would soon name oxygen. The other would later be called nitrogen.

Endless new questions were raised; whole new horizons were opened as Lavoisier pushed on with the achievement of making air "by borrowing the materials of which it is formed from the different kingdoms of nature." He found he could "borrow" the materials from a number of different kingdoms, including the living.

Lavoisier dissolved animal substances in nitric acid. A great quantity of gas was disengaged, gas that quickly smothered a flame or took the life of an animal. Its character was thus established, and when Lavoisier mixed seventy-three parts of this gas with twenty-seven parts of oxygen, he again produced common air.

In his experiments Lavoisier also saw that the air issuing from the lungs was no more charged with the imaginary phlogiston than was the common air; it was "fixed air." He also recognized that the change air underwent in the lungs was similar to the change it underwent in the burning of charcoal. This suggested the nearly incredible theory that breathing was a form of combustion. In 1777 Lavoisier laid this startling theory before the academy. Combustion and respiration, he suggested, are "acts of the same order."

Until the men of the eighteenth century began their research on air, the role of respiration in the functioning of the living organism was an unknown. Living things obviously were dependent on air, but what went on below the surface no one knew. One well-known eighteenth-century textbook, Haller's *Elements of Physiology*, defined respiration as a force "adjuvant"—subsidiary—to circulation. Haller maintained that

breathing was the force that compressed the blood in the abdomen, drove it into the arteries, and sent it more rapidly into
the heart. For the eighteenth century, respiration was thus a
mechanical act. Lavoisier was saying that it was a chemical
reaction, a combustion.

In reporting this momentous conclusion to the academy,
Lavoisier again was cautious: "Now the portion of eminently
respirable air contained in the air of the atmosphere is converted into a chalky, vaporous acid in passing through the
viscera. On the one hand eminently respirable air is absorbed,
and on the other, the lung reconstitutes in its place a portion
of chalky acid vapor almost equal in volume."

This still only outlined what might take place; it was only a
pinpoint opening to a great undiscovered world. How could
this problem so near and yet so inaccessible be studied? Lavoisier knew well that heat was set free in the conversion of
charcoal into fixed air. Was it also possible, he asked, that heat
might be set free in the production of fixed air in the lungs,
and—an even more exciting possibility—could it be that the
heat created in this process maintained the heat of the body
and kept it at its constant temperature regardless of the
warmth or coldness of the environment?

Even to study the heat that Lavoisier thought might be given
off by respiration posed formidable difficulties. However, some
earlier work of Black's had developed a technique that might
be adaptable. It was a method of measuring heat by the
amount of ice melted.

The great Scottish chemist had worked it out as he studied
the puzzling melting of ice. Why did ice and snow melt slowly?
Why, when the earth warmed in the spring, did not all the
snow and ice melt at the same moment and deluge the earth?
Why was there a thaw? Black suspected that it was because
snow and ice in melting absorb large quantities of heat.

But the problem became even more curious as Black started
to study it. The temperature of a glass of ice and water re-

mained constant at the melting point of ice as long as any ice remained in the glass; no thermometer could show that the water was absorbing enough heat to melt the ice. Only when all the ice was gone did the temperature of the water rise to that of the room.

To try to solve this enigma, Black put five ounces of water into two vials. He froze the water in one tube and cooled the other to thirty-three degrees, one degree above freezing. Both were then placed in a warm room. The temperature of the cooled water rose in half an hour to forty degrees. As Black put it, enough heat "entered" to raise the temperature of the water seven degrees. The heat's rate of entry was thus marked at seven degrees in a half-hour.

The ice in the other vial melted slowly. It took ten and a half hours to reach the forty-degree temperature, or twenty-one half-hours, and therefore twenty-one times as long. Multiplying twenty-one by seven, Black calculated that 147 degrees of heat had been used in raising the temperature of the water from thirty-two degrees to forty. If the eight degrees were subtracted, 139 degrees of heat had been absorbed by the ice.

Black's work offered a way to measure heat, but an apparatus had to be devised for using it. Lavoisier enlisted the aid of his friend, the noted mathematician, the Marquis Pierre Simon de Laplace, and together they developed the calorimeter. Theoretically, they would have had only to hollow out a block of ice and see how much ice was melted by anything placed inside. Since this would have been inconvenient and inexact, they designed a cage surrounded by two compartments that could be filled with ice. The outer compartment was packed with ice to prevent the ice in the middle container from being affected by heat from the surrounding air. When the melted water from the middle ice-filled cavity was collected and weighed, it gave an exact measurement of the amount of heat given off by anything in the central cage. With this instrument, the two scientists began a long and ingenious series of experiments that not only laid the foundations of thermochemistry but also contributed significantly toward explaining the functioning of the human body.

The scientists put a guinea pig in the central cage and surrounded it with ice. In ten hours the little animal gave off

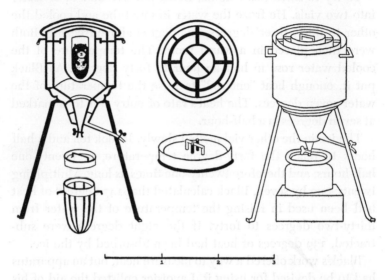

The calorimeter. Lavoisier placed a guinea pig in the central cage and filled the surrounding compartments with ice. Some of the ice melted, but the guinea pig did not turn cold, as did inanimate objects. Its body heat was replenished. The experiment indicated to Lavoisier that "respiration is a combustion" and warms the body.

enough heat to melt thirteen ounces of ice. And yet when it was removed from its icy imprisonment, its body heat was as high as when it had been placed in the cage. Somehow its bodily heat must have been renewed. Otherwise, its initial heat would have been dissipated, and the little animal would have been taken from the calorimeter as cold as the inanimate bodies the scientists had cooled in numerous other experiments.

"His vital functions constantly restored the heat that he communicated to his environment," said Lavoisier. "The quantity of ice melted therefore represents the amount of heat renewed in the same time by the vital functions of the guinea pig."

To prove the significance of this point took subtle reasoning and more experiments. These were not secrets that Nature yielded readily.

Lavoisier had previously determined exactly how much fixed air was given off by a guinea pig in a period of ten hours. It was 224 grains. He had also found by experiment how much ice was melted by the formation of 224 grains of fixed air from the combustion of charcoal. It was ten and a half ounces. Actually the guinea pig had melted thirteen ounces of ice rather than ten and a half, but Lavoisier and Laplace knew that their techniques were not perfect. They considered that the figures were in good agreement.

The amount of ice melted in the production of a given amount of fixed air was about the same whether the producer was guinea pig or charcoal.

Lavoisier concluded: "Respiration is therefore a combustion, certainly very slow, but nevertheless entirely similar to that of charcoal. It takes place in the interior of the lungs without creating any sensible light because the matter of fire, having been set free, is at once absorbed by the moisture of these organs. The heat developed in this combustion is communicated to the blood which is passing through the lungs and from which it spreads through the whole animal system.

"Thus the air that we breathe serves two purposes, both of which are equally necessary for our preservation. It takes away from the blood its base of fixed air, an excess of which would be very harmful, and the heat that this combination sets free in the lungs makes up for the continual loss of heat to the atmosphere and surrounding bodies."

Later research was to show that the conversion of oxygen

into carbon dioxide does not occur in the lungs. But the role of oxygen was established, and for the first time it was conclusively demonstrated that respiration is far more than a mechanical ventilation of the lungs. It was a chemical phenomenon; the breath of life and the warmth were a strange, invisible combination of chemical reactions.

"One can conclude without resort to hypothesis," said Lavoisier, "that the conservation of animal heat is due in great part to the changing of pure air into fixed air by respiration."

By 1783 Lavoisier thus had developed the general theory of combustion, had shown that air is not an element but is made up primarily of oxygen and nitrogen, and had demonstrated that a form of combustion produces and maintains the warmth of living things.

In all of this Lavoisier had actually been rejecting the theory of phlogiston, the idea that combustion was produced by the escape of the element fire. He had nevertheless refrained from a direct attack. The most illustrious scientists of the day, Priestley, Henry Cavendish, Richard Kirwan, Scheele, Antoine Fourcroy, and Claude Berthollet, still held to the old theory of phlogiston when Lavoisier decided in 1783 that he must take the question before the academy.

"It is time for me to speak out plainly in a more precise and formal manner about an opinion which I look upon as an error that is fatal to chemistry and seems greatly to have delayed its progress," he told its members.

Chemists, Lavoisier said, had made phlogiston a vague principle. "Sometimes it has weight, sometimes not; sometimes it is free fire, sometimes it is fire combined with earth; sometimes it passes through the pores of vessels, sometimes these are impenetrable to it. It explains at once causticity and non-causticity; transparency and opacity; color and the absence of color. It is a veritable Proteus that changes its form at every instant."

Set forth thus, the stark contradictions of the old theory had to be recognized.

"It is time to lead chemistry back to a stricter way of thinking," Lavoisier continued. "It is time to strip the facts with which this science is daily enriched of the additions of rationality and prejudice, to distinguish what is fact and observation from what is system and hypothesis, and in short to mark out, as it were, the limits that chemical knowledge has reached, so that those who come after us may set out from that point and confidently go forward to the advancement of science."

Lavoisier brilliantly summarized the facts about combustion:

1. There is true combustion only when the combustible body is surrounded by and in contact with oxygen. In any other kind of air, burning bodies are at once extinguished.

2. In every combustion there is an absorption of the oxygen in the air.

3. There is an increase in the weight of the body that is burned, and it is exactly equal to the weight of the air absorbed.

4. There is an evolution of light and heat.

Phlogiston, said Lavoisier, speaking with a fire of his own, is imaginary. "I do not expect that my ideas will be adopted at once," he concluded. "The human mind inclines to one way of thinking and those who have looked at Nature from a certain point of view during a part of their lives adopt new views only with difficulty; it is for time therefore to confirm or reject the opinion that I have advanced."

The academy was stirred. "He seized Stahl limb for limb and did not let go until he had torn him to pieces," said Fourcroy, telling of this devastating analysis.

Fourcroy had not exaggerated; Lavoisier's facts had demolished Georg Ernst Stahl, the leading advocate of phlogiston. Lavoisier was entirely right, however, about the acceptance of the bold new doctrine he was proposing. The human mind is difficult to change, and there were troublesome questions still unanswered.

If combustion were a union with oxygen, how was the burning of "inflammable air"—the air evolved when metals were dissolved in acids, later to be named hydrogen—to be explained? It burned, but there was no proof that it combined with oxygen in doing so. This was a weakness in Lavoisier's argument.

Some years earlier Pierre Joseph Macquer had noticed that a few drops of a clear fluid formed when he held a piece of porcelain in a burning jet of inflammable air. Priestley later had discovered that when he exploded a mixture of common and inflammable air in a closed vessel, a "dew" fogged the glass. Cavendish had gone a little further; he had learned that such an explosion reduced the volume of the common air by one fifth, and had decided that the one fifth of the common air and the inflammable air had condensed into the dew. He continued his work until he had collected 135 grains of the unidentified moisture. It had no taste, no smell, and it left no sediment when it evaporated; in short, said Cavendish, "it seemed pure water."

It was pure water.

When this became certain, Cavendish postulated that the water formed because both the common air and the inflammable air contained moisture.

In June 1783 Charles Blagden, assistant to Cavendish, went to Paris and of course called at the arsenal—Lavoisier had become director of the Gunpowder Commission and had established a fine laboratory in his house at the arsenal. Lavoisier listened incredulously to the report of what Cavendish had found. It seemed impossible that the combustion of inflammable air and common air could yield water. He had thought— all his experiments indicated—that any combination with oxygen produced an acid. But, if Blagden were correct, it offered a solution to his problem. Would Blagden assist him in repeating the experiment?

The next day, with Blagden present, Lavoisier and Laplace hastily reproduced the Cavendish apparatus and set off the electric spark that exploded the mixture of "airs." Water was formed "in a very pure state." Lavoisier hastened to the academy to report the surprising result.

Water had always been regarded as another of the elements, a fixed and final part of the universe, a thing beyond man's compounding. Now Lavoisier glimpsed another possibility. Again he knew that every proof would be required. If, as he suspected, water was not wrung from moisture-filled gases but

Water is not an element. Lavoisier passed steam over a heated gun barrel filled with iron filings. The receiver bottle filled with an "inflammable air" that Lavoisier later named hydrogen—the generative principle of water. Water, then, was made up of hydrogen and oxygen.

was a veritable compound of "inflammable air" and oxygen, it should be possible to decompose water into these two gases and then to reconstitute it.

In the arsenal laboratory Lavoisier filled a retort with distilled water and placed it over a laboratory furnace. A tube led from it into a gun barrel filled with iron filings. Another tube led from the gun barrel to a bottle ready to collect any gases that might be given off. Fires were lighted under the retort and the gun barrel. As steam from the water passed over the red-hot iron filings its oxygen was abstracted by the hot iron—

a calx or rust of iron was formed, and the receiver bottle filled with a gas. The gas was inflammable air.

Lavoisier held a lighted taper at the mouth of a bottle of the inflammable air. It burned gently, first at the neck of the bottle, and then inside as the external air made its way in. So inflammable air's power of burning was merely the power of decomposing air and "carrying off" its oxygen. It did not burn unless in contact with common air or oxygen.

A public session of the academy was called on November 12, 1783. In the presence of a distinguished audience, Lavoisier spoke: "Water, besides oxygen, contains another element." Later Lavoisier gave the other element, "inflammable air," the name that seemed to him wholly appropriate—hydrogen, or the "generative principle of water."

Water, then, was no more an element than air; it was on the contrary made up of two substances, hydrogen and oxygen— H_2O. The cycle was complete, and so this time was the defeat of the ancient order.

A few of the advocates of phlogiston stayed with their element of fire, but the French chemists soon came around. Berthollet announced his conversion at a meeting of the academy on August 6, 1775. The great triumph came, however, when Joseph Black began to teach the new system. That for Lavoisier was the real victory and accolade.

The French chemists had been restive for some time about the disordered jungle of chemistry. The only terms they had were those which had come down through the centuries and through alchemy, and these were a motley collection—"vitriol of Venus," "salt of alembroth," "butter of arsenic," "flowers of zinc." The French group decided that the nomenclature had to be reformed.

Lavoisier, with his clarity of mind and appreciation of the problem, was assigned the main responsibility. He liked to quote the Abbé de Condillac to the group: "We think only through the medium of words. The art of reasoning is nothing more than a language well arranged."

As Lavoisier worked on the new nomenclature, he soon found, he explained, that the undertaking "transformed itself without my being able to prevent it, into a treatise on the elements of chemistry." To remake the language of chemistry meant establishing a new philosophy and reorganizing the science. "It is now time," he said, "to rid chemistry of every kind of impediment that delays its advance. . . . I have imposed on myself the law of never advancing but from the known to the unknown, of drawing no conclusions that do not derive immediately from experiments and observations."

In the first part of his book Lavoisier laid the foundations of modern chemistry. The four elements that had come down from the Greek philosophers of course had to be discarded, but in their place there had to be a new list of elements as experiments revealed them, and a nomenclature that would indicate not only what they were but the ideas they represented.

Lavoisier understood clearly what he was doing: "If by the term elements we mean to express those simple and indivisible atoms of which matter is composed, it is extremely probable we know nothing at all about them; but if we apply the term elements or principles of bodies to express our idea of the last point to which analysis is capable of reaching, we admit as elements all the substances into which we are able to reduce bodies by decomposition."

"In the natural order of ideas," Lavoisier used the name of the class or genus to express a quality common to a large number of "individuals"; the name of the "species" to express a quality peculiar to "certain individuals." Each acid, for example, was compounded of two substances that Lavoisier's work indicated were elements. One, oxygen, constituting the acidity, was common to all; the other was different in each case. Thus the acid created by the combination of oxygen—the common element—with sulphur was named sulphuric acid, and an acid

made up of the same materials but with less oxygen, sulphur-
ous acid.[1] The salts, on the same principle, were named sul-
phates and sulphites.

So too the "calces" of metals contained a principle common
to them all and a principle peculiar to each. The "calces"
were renamed oxides. Thus the old names martial ethiops, col-

*An alchemist's laboratory. Chemistry as a science did not develop
until the time of Lavoisier.*

cothar, and rust of iron became simple black, red, and yellow
oxide of iron. The red part of the blood, lymph, and most of the
bodily secretions were oxides, Lavoisier pointed out.

Lavoisier also showed that animal and vegetable materials
were formed of compound groupings of hydrogen, carbon,

[1] The modern chemist would add that an acid is created by a combination of these elements with water and hydrogen evolved from the
water

and oxygen. In emphasizing this combination of carbon groups —or radicals, as they are called today—with oxygen, Lavoisier was opening the way for the development of organic chemistry.

It was an extraordinary thing—from one vegetable oxide, the sweet juice of grapes, came carbonic-acid gas (the bubbles of champagne) and alcohol. A sweet body was thus converted into two completely different substances, one combustible and one non-combustible.

Lavoisier, with his habitual careful weighing of all materials, had long known that nothing was lost when one body was converted into another. But, studying fermentation as he worked on the *Traité*, he defined the law that lay behind this hard-to-grasp spectacle: "We may lay down as an incontestable axiom that in all the operations of art and nature nothing is created. An equal quantity of matter exists before and after experiments; the quality and quantity of the elements remain precisely the same and nothing takes place beyond change and modification in the combinations of the elements.

"Upon this principle the whole art of performing chemical experiments depends. Hence, since from the 'must' of grapes we procure alcohol and carbonic acid, I have the right to suppose that 'must' consists of carbonic acid and alcohol. I can say that 'must' of grapes = carbonic acid + alcohol."

This was the first clear statement of the law of conservation of mass or the law of the indestructibility of matter as it applied to chemical change. And Lavoisier pointed out the full implications.

"By successively supposing each of the elements in the equation unknown, we can calculate their values in succession," he explained, "and thus reciprocally verify our experiments by calculation and our calculations by experiment. I have often employed this method for correcting the first results of my experiments and to direct me in the proper road for repeating them to advantage."

Chemistry had completely left behind the abracadabra of

alchemy. And Lavoisier had done for chemistry what Newton in the *Principia* had done for physics. Acceptance was inescapable, and the revolution that Lavoisier had foreseen and set out to accomplish "came to pass."

But another revolution also was coming to pass. France was bankrupt and her people were stirring against oppression and inequality. As a member of the Tax Farm, as a constant consultant of the state, and as a friend and associate of the liberals who were fitfully brought into the government to stave off disaster, Lavoisier exerted a strong influence for reform.

When Louis XVI yielded to popular pressure for provincial assemblies, Lavoisier was elected to the Assembly of Orléanais. His father had purchased an estate and a title of nobility for him at Fréchines.

"It was Lavoisier who did everything, who inspired everything, who was everywhere," said Léonce de Lavergne. When the nobles balked at a system of taxation which Lavoisier proposed, he told them: "Today the nation is too enlightened not to know that its duty is to act in the interests of the majority, that if exceptions are to be allowed in favor of any class of citizens, particularly with regard to taxes, they can be made only in favor of the poor. Inequality of taxation cannot be tolerated except at the expense of the rich." Lavoisier also fought for a system that would give the third estate (commoners) double representation and thus equality with the clergy and nobility.

In 1789, the same year the *Traité* was published, Lavoisier also drafted proposals for the abolition of illegal processes of arrest and imprisonment, for reform of the civil and criminal codes, for a system of social insurance against old age and poverty, and for a national system of education. But these wise provisions that might have changed the course of history were not adopted.

On July 12 of the same year rioters stormed through the streets of Paris. Two days later the Bastille fell and the roar of revolution filled Lavoisier's laboratory, for his home in the Petit Arsenal adjoined that ancient fortress and symbol of political oppression. Three weeks later false rumors that gunpowder was being shipped out of Paris sent the mob against the arsenal itself, and Lavoisier narrowly escaped death.

The National Assembly had taken over the government of Paris, but was not yet entirely extremist. Lavoisier and many of his colleagues at the academy were elected to membership, and Lavoisier, who was increasingly being relied upon to solve the desperate financial problems of France, was made governor of the Discount Bank. The National Assembly pushed through a series of drastic reforms.

On February 5, 1790, Lavoisier wrote to his friend Benjamin Franklin, telling him the chemical news and adding: "It would be well to give you news of our revolution; we look upon it as over, and well and irrevocably completed."

As the new government attempted to function with some degree of order, Lavoisier also had to work out the technicalities of the paper money issued by the assembly. He prepared a report on import duties for the committee on taxes, and he was directed to develop a process to protect gun barrels against rust, to experiment with hospital hygiene, and to assist in the development of a new system of weights and measures.

With all of these demands on his time and in all the agonizing upheaval of revolution, Lavoisier turned to one of the most profound and untouched of problems—the chemistry of the human body. Few had even attempted to study the processes that underlay and controlled the outward physical manifestations that men knew.

Lavoisier had continued to worry about the difference between the amount of ice the guinea pig melted in the calorimeter and the lesser amount of ice melted by the production of carbon dioxide from charcoal. In the one case it was thirteen ounces and in the other, ten and a half. The two were close enough, as he had reported to the academy, to indicate that the animate and inanimate processes were the same. But was that two-and-a-half-ounce difference due to experimental error, as he had at first thought? In the meanwhile some of his other experiments had indicated that the amount of oxygen consumed in breathing was not entirely accounted for by the amount of fixed air produced. Lavoisier found evidence that part of the missing oxygen combined with hydrogen to form water. Perhaps this was a clue to the puzzling difference. Here obviously were matters of the first importance. To assist him in making a thorough study of the whole process of human respiration, Lavoisier took as his aide Armand Séguin, a young man of twenty.

The two chemists repeated the guinea-pig experiment with added safeguards. They still could find no experimental error. It looked as though the additional heat were produced by the formation of water. Somehow part of the oxygen combined with hydrogen. Lavoisier reported to the academy that the heat of experimental animals was a dual thing, partly produced by the combination of oxygen with carbon, and partly created by the combination of the remainder of the oxygen with the hydrogen of the blood.

Were the strange heat-making processes also going on in the human body? Séguin volunteered to serve as the subject for finding out.

But how could such a thing be studied? There was no apparatus, no precedent to guide them. However, experiments with the guinea pigs had suggested one approach. Although the guinea pig used the same amount of oxygen whether it was given pure oxygen or common air, its consumption of oxygen went up when it moved around. Here was a way to get at their problem. They would study the human consumption of oxygen at rest, at work, during fasting, digestion, and under other circumstances. Here was a variable, a tool with which to work.

A mask was developed to fit over Séguin's face. A five-foot tube carried oxygen from a glass balloon to the young chemist.

Assistants rushed around keeping the apparatus in working order while Mme Lavoisier, elegant in flowing skirts and an elaborately curled coiffure, sat at a table taking down figures and making notations. She also sketched the scene and thus fortunately preserved it for posterity—if she had not, it would have been lost, for the full reports of the experiments were never to be finished.

Even in the beginning the work began to reveal much about the amazingly adjustable chemical processes of respiration. For hours before the experiment began, Séguin ate nothing. If the room was then cooled, he consumed more oxygen than if it were warm. A fasting man in a cool room needed more oxygen. But if Séguin ate a full meal before the experiment began, his consumption of oxygen increased still more, half as much again.

The effect of work had to be determined. Beneath the table at which Séguin sat they rigged up a treadle. He pressed it steadily while Lavoisier measured his oxygen consumption. In other experiments Séguin lifted a fifteen-pound weight during the fifteen minutes of the test. The work he performed was the equivalent of raising the fifteen pounds to a height of 650 feet. At work, Séguin consumed nearly three times as much oxygen as at rest. And when he worked the treadle or lifted the weight following a good meal, he used almost four times as much oxygen.

Lavoisier stood beside his assistant, taking his pulse and temperature. Although Séguin's pulse increased, his temperature remained almost constant.

Cold, warmth, digestion all affected the rate of oxygen consumption. At last some light was being shed on how the human body adapts itself to the range of requirements to which it is subjected, and a way was developed to measure what is known today as the basal metabolism. By breathing, by taking in and consuming varying amounts of oxygen, we attain the steady warmth that gives us a large degree of independence of the climate around us.

"We can establish the following proposition," said Lavoisier in his *mémoire* on heat. "The conservation of heat is due, for the most part, to the heat that is produced by the combination of the pure air animals breathe with the base of fixed air which their blood furnishes." Or, as he said in the conclusion of the same report: "One can conclude directly without hypothesis that it is the changing of pure air into fixed air by respiration that largely conserves animal heat."

Lavoisier was a philosopher as well as an experimentalist, and a man of literary imagination as well as a scientist. As he saw this strange relation between breathing and heat, he remarked with obvious pleasure: "One would say that the analogy between respiration and combustion has not escaped the poets, or rather the philosophers of antiquity whose interpreters they were. The fire stolen from heaven, the fire of Prometheus, is not merely an ingenious poetical idea; it is a faithful picture of the operations of Nature, at least for animals that breathe; we can therefore say with the ancients that the flame of life is lit at the instant when the child draws its first breath and that it is extinguished only at death.

"When we consider these remarkable anticipations, we are sometimes tempted to think that the ancients actually penetrated farther than we suppose into the sanctuary of knowledge, and that fable is indeed only an allegory under which they hid the great truths of medicine and physics."

Other philosophical considerations also were involved in this work that Lavoisier was doing. When Séguin had been at physical or mental work, he had consumed more oxygen. "Observations of this kind lead us to compare different expenditures of strength between which there would seem to be no relationship," said Lavoisier. "We could ascertain, for instance, the number of pounds in weight that are equivalent to the efforts of a man who delivers an oration or of a musician who plays an instrument. We could even evaluate the mechanical effort in the work of the philosopher when he is reflecting, and of the man of letters when he is writing, of the musician when he is composing.

"These tasks considered to be purely intellectual have nevertheless in them something physical and material which allows us, according to the relationship that we have established, to compare them to those of the laboring man. It is therefore not without reason that the French language has united under the common definition of *travail* the efforts of the mind with those of the body, the *travail* of the study and the *travail* of the hired servant."

The cries of "equality" that filled the streets had an entirely different tenor and meaning. Far from being completed, as Lavoisier had written Franklin, the revolution was moving forward with gathering violence. Inflammatory journals denounced any who deviated in any degree from the impassioned extremes of their writers. Lavoisier was a chief target of one of them, *Ami du peuple,* edited by Jean Paul Marat. Marat was a fanatic who at one time had aspired to be a scientist and had written a book maintaining that he had made visible the element of fire. In presenting it to the academy, Lavoisier had dismissed it with a few scornful words that Marat never forgot.

On January 27, 1791, *Ami du peuple* attacked Lavoisier: "I denounce you the Coryphaeus—the leader of the chorus of charlatans, Sieur Lavoisier, son of a land grabber, apprentice-chemist, pupil of the Genevan stock jobber, Tax Farmer, Commissioner of Gunpowder and Saltpeter, Governor of the Discount Bank, Secretary to the King, Member of the Academy of Sciences."

In the midst of this strain and turmoil Lavoisier continued his scientific work, and completed for the National Assembly a study of the territorial wealth of France. It proposed a modern system of taxation, based on the first reliable statistics ever compiled on where the wealth of the realm lay. Like other moderate recommendations, it was ignored.

The worsening financial crisis was blamed not on the lack of a fair system of taxation but on the alleged crimes of the Tax Farm. "Make the robbers disgorge," shouted the infuriated mass. On March 20 the Tax Farm was abolished. After twenty-three years Lavoisier lost his post, his investment, and the laboratory he had established in his official residence at the arsenal. The laboratory had no equal in France.

Lavoisier resigned most of his other paid offices and attempted to devote himself solely to scientific work. It was too late. The Jacobins were in control, and with the guillotining of the King on January 21, 1793, the Terror was beginning.

Lavoisier saw close friends and associates arrested and sent to the guillotine. The tragedy was close and immediate, and yet he still tried to serve his country. At the request of the Bureau of Consultation of Arts and Crafts, he worked out a plan for a national system of free primary education for all children, as a "duty society owes to the child."

At grave risk to himself, Lavoisier also continued to fight to save the academy. Despite the constant attacks on the academy and the associations of its members, it was commissioned to make many studies for the state. Lavoisier reminded the state of its need for such services, and particularly for the great project of developing a new system of weights and measures. Lavoisier was the mainstay, the reliance of the academy and its members as the society of which it was a part went down in blood and agony.

On November 24, 1794, the arrest of the Farmers General was ordered. Four days later Lavoisier gave himself up and joined his father-in-law, Paulze, in the Port Libre prison. The tax-farmers were ordered to prepare their accounts for inspection—an inspection that ultimately would show that their profits had been moderate. But at the time no showing mattered. On May 7 the entire group was taken before the Revolutionary Tribunal. Death was the sentence.

The tumbrels were waiting. They rolled across the Pont Neuf, which Lavoisier had crossed so frequently as a boy on his way to school, past the Academy of Sciences, and on to the Place de la Révolution.

While Lavoisier was forced to watch, his father-in-law went to his death on the guillotine. Lavoisier was next. And thus one of the greatest of all French scientists died on May 8, 1794.

"Only a moment to cut off that head," cried Joseph Louis Lagrange, "and a hundred years may not give us another like it."

Only a year and a half later, but in another era, the Lycée des Arts honored the memory of Lavoisier at a public ceremony. The great hall was draped in black, and around it stood columns, each bearing the title of a Lavoisier discovery. As a hundred choristers sang, a black-clad audience watched the dedication of a bust of Lavoisier. It was crowned with the laurel of the immortals.

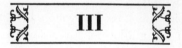

III

BICHAT: TISSUES

THE LEARNED and skilled surgeons of the last quarter of the eighteenth century argued that the heart, the stomach, and the other organs were the all-important "machines" of the human body.

Each had its own "vital properties," sacred properties that were inborn and a part of the life that was beyond man's understanding or inquiry. Doctors and anatomists might minutely and skillfully describe the heart and the characteristics that distinguished its vital properties from the vital properties of other organs. But, with a few exceptions, no one attempted to ask of what the heart and the other organs were constituted, or what made them function, or why they did not function when there was death. In a sense, such questions were unthinkable, for the presence or absence of life was itself the whole explanation.

Harvey's discovery of the circulation of the blood and Lavoisier's proof that breathing and the vital warmth of the body are an operation of physical principles did not quickly shake this faith in life as a mystic whole.

In view of this dogma and the detailed knowledge of the appearance of the organs, young Marie François Bichat felt hesitant about suggesting that science would have to look deeper for the causes of death, illness, and health, and that it would have to study the tissues of which the organs were formed.

In the preface of his book that forced—or, rather, persuaded —science to a new view, Bichat pleaded with the savants to excuse him for undertaking a treatise in a field where what had been done undoubtedly surpassed what remained to be accomplished. Bichat was a modest genius.

Though Bichat was in error or excessively humble in balancing past against future, he was seldom in error about what he did or where he was going. He was born at Thoirette on November 11, 1771. Even when he was a child, it was clear to all those around him that he was rarely gifted. While he took the top prizes in mathematics and Latin at school, he delved on his own into the study of plants and animals.

His father was a physician, and as soon as it was possible, Bichat went to Lyons to study medicine with the famous Dr. Marc Antoine Petit. During his first year there study was difficult, for mobs swept through the streets in the early frenzy of the French Revolution. During his second year, work was all but impossible even for one with Bichat's ability to concentrate. The city was besieged by revolutionary forces, and when the hospital in which the students worked ran up a black flag in an appeal to the attackers to spare it, the signal was either misinterpreted or ignored. The bombardment was intensified. Famine set in and in the end forced the surrender of the city. But even then there was no mercy or peace. Hundreds of the defenders were shot to death on the edge of a grave that had been dug for them. Bichat had to leave.

The young student arrived in Paris in 1793 and quickly attached himself to the group around Pierre Joseph Desault, chief physician of the Paris Hôtel-Dieu and one of the most noted of French physicians. At the conclusion of each of the professor's lectures a student was chosen to review what had been said. The report was given at a later gathering of the class at which an assistant professor presided. About a month after Bichat's arrival, the student who had been selected for the review was forced to cancel his appearance, and Bichat volunteered to take his place.

As the young—he was then twenty-two—newcomer from Lyons spoke, the usual small shuffling ceased; the students listened in an extraordinary silence. Bichat finished and the silence held for another moment. Then came wild applause and cheers. His presentation had been so exact and brilliant it seemed that of a professor rather than a student.

Desault was quickly informed of the unusual happening. Up to that time he had scarcely been aware of Bichat's presence in his classes. His interest aroused, he sent for the remarkable student. As Bichat talked, Desault was so impressed that he soon made him his assistant and began to treat him almost as a son.

From this time on, Bichat worked closely with the chief physician, accompanying him on his rounds and assisting him at operations. At night he also was at Desault's hand, aiding him in his research. Little spare time remained for Bichat, but in that narrow margin he began his own program of dissection. When Desault died in 1795, his twenty-four-year-old assistant took over much of his work, and, as a labor of affection and gratitude, also undertook to publish Desault's research.

As Bichat visited his patients at the hospital, he was struck by the accuracy of an observation made by another well-known physician, Philippe Pinel. Pinel had pointed out that the same kind of lesions often occurred in the membranes of different organs. Could it be, Bichat asked, that the membranes were similar even though they belonged to different organs and different parts of the body? And could it be that disease was an alteration of the tissue of an organ?

Bichat could find no answer to his question in the annals of surgery or medicine. The anatomists of the past had applied themselves to describing as minutely as possible the over-all characteristics and appearances of the major organs. Only a few had sought to penetrate further. Among the few was the great Italian Marcello Malpighi, who had described some of the glands and had discovered the capillaries in the lung of the frog. Another physician, Fallopius, had timidly tried to classify the tissues of the organs according to their origin, their warmth or coldness, their dryness or moistness. But such attempts at analysis had seemed beside the point. Both physiology and physics were preoccupied with the relation of the organs to the "vital principle," soul, or governing principle, as it was variously called.

Bichat was convinced that there was only one place to look for his answer. That was in a detailed study of the human and animal body. He had a dank, odorous laboratory in the depths of the hospital, and there he began a systematic examination of every tissue in the body. Each tissue in turn was subjected to heat, air, water, acids, alkalis, and neutral salts. Bichat dried them, macerated them, and let them putrefy to study their different textures. Oddly enough, he did not make use of the microscope, the one instrument that could have helped him the most. He was familiar with it, for he spoke of its importance in studying the unseeable, but he did not employ it.

By 1800 Bichat, then only twenty-nine, had his basic answer.

"When we study a function we must consider the complicated organ which performs it," he wrote, "but if we would be instructed in the properties and life of that organ we must absolutely resolve it into its constituent parts."

As he resolved the organs into their constituent parts, Bichat found twenty-one tissues, distributed throughout the body and entering into the composition of other tissues.

As he listed them, they were: (1) the cellular membrane; (2) the nerves of animal life; (3) the nerves of organic life; (4) the arteries; (5) the veins; (6) the exhalants; (7) the absorbants and glands; (8) the bones; (9) the medulla; (10) cartilage; (11) muscular fiber; (12) fibrocartilaginous tissue; (13) muscles of organic life; (14) those of animal life; (15) the mucous membrane; (16) the serous; (17) the synovial; (18) the glands; (19) the dermis; (20) the epidermis; (21) the cutis or deeper layer of the skin.

"Such are the real organized elements of our frame," said Bichat. These were the tissues of which the body was made; they were the reality underlying appearances.

Bichat had to argue for this way of looking at the human body. It was "only of late," he pointed out, that science had recognized that it had to study causes as well as the phenomena "which are the effects." But, he said, it was this attention to causes and what lay deeper which had carried both physics and chemistry forward.

Newton had been the first to discover the basic principles that underlay those aspects of the universe which men knew so well. "Let us thank the immortal Newton," said Bichat. "He first discovered the secret of the Creator; namely, the simplicity of causes united with multiplicity of effects."

It had been the same in chemistry. Lavoisier and others had found the elements that made up the familiar compounds. "And just as chemistry has its simple bodies, which by various combinations form the compound ones, so anatomy has its simple tissues which by their combinations form the organs," Bichat continued. Furthermore, he emphasized, the nature of the parts was not altered by being blended together, any more than chemical elements were changed by uniting in a compound.

Bichat strongly defended his plan of examining the single tissues "of our component parts." "It rests," he said, "on undeniable ground and I trust it will exercise a wide and powerful influence over physiology as well as on the practice of physics."

As Bichat dissected, he found that the same simple tissue might be spread out in a membrane, contracted into a tube, or gathered into a bundle of fibers. For example, the nervous tissue took the form of a membrane in the retina and of cords in the nerves. Form did not change its nature.

But each tissue was distinctive, and each had its peculiar "mode of action." "The whole theory of secretion, exhalation, absorption, and nutrition is founded on this principle," explained Bichat. "Blood is a common reservoir, from which every tissue borrows and chooses its materials according to the degree of its sensibility and appropriates them to itself, retaining or rejecting them subsequently."

From this argument, it followed that the prevailing emphasis on the peculiar life of each organ would have to be changed to an emphasis on the life of the simple tissues.

Bichat offered some striking illustrations to prove his point. The stomach is composed of serous, organic, muscular, and mucous tissues and is furnished with arteries and veins. "If we take a confused and general view of the peculiar life of the stomach," he said, "it will be utterly impossible to form a correct and precise idea of it. In fact, the mucous surface is so different from the serous and both so distinct from the muscular that we could form no clear judgment of them by confounding them in one general consideration. It is the same with the intestines, bladder, and uterus, etc. . . . If we do not distinguish the fabric of the tissues that form these complicated organs, the term 'peculiar life' will offer vague and uncertain ideas."

It was the observation that the same kind of lesion often occurred in different organs which led Bichat into his study of tissues. As he developed the principle, he found additional confirmation of it in disease. In every organ composed of many tissues, he pointed out, one tissue might be impaired without any disorder occurring in the others. Indeed, this was generally the case.

Bichat analyzed each of the principal organs on these grounds. In the eye a single membrane was often diseased while others continued healthy. The substance of the heart was often without a single blemish while the pericardium was badly diseased.

The publication of the treatise on membranes in 1800 focused medical attention on Bichat. His book was so explicit, and based on such a prodigious actual examination of the structures of the body, that medicine had almost nothing to say. For once a revolutionary change in the whole study of the body was accepted with relatively little opposition, and in most cases enthusiastically.

After the publication of the *Treatise on Tissues* a whole new approach to anatomy was inescapable. Bichat went to work immediately on a *General Anatomy*.

All the while his duties had increased. His classes were crowded with students—in his usual modesty he had not foreseen that so many would want to study with him and had not requested quarters large enough to accommodate them.

But he could never accumulate enough facts about the human body. In one winter Bichat studied the bodies of more than six hundred persons who died at the Hôtel-Dieu. His writing had to be done late at night. But when he began to write, Bichat knew exactly what he wanted to say. It was said that he did almost no rewriting or revising. Only his health held him back. It was not good, and he was required to rest for several months after what was called a hemorrhage of the lungs.

But in 1801 his *Anatomie générale Appliquée à la physiologie et à la médicine* appeared. He then plunged on into work on a *Descriptive Anatomy* and succeeded in completing two volumes.

One evening as he left the autopsy room and its fetid airs, the young physician fell on the stairs. Although he at first seemed to recover from the effects of the fall, a fever developed and he died fourteen days later. The man who had rebuilt physiology and the approach to life was dead in 1802 at the age of thirty.

Napoleon had recently been named First Consul, and the sad news was quickly relayed to him: "Bichat has died on a battlefield that numbers many victims. No man in so brief a time has done so many things so well."

Napoleon, as well as the medical profession, recognized the loss to France. More than five hundred students followed Bichat's body to the grave, and ten days after his death a marble plaque was dedicated to him and to his master Desault.

It was erected by their fellow physicians to express their gratitude for the services the two men had rendered to the science whose domain they had so notably enlarged.

In the eulogy with which French medicine said farewell and formalized the record for posterity, the eulogist spoke particularly to the students: "Let Bichat be at the same time your guide and model. He has shown what one can do in but a little while. What an example for you young men who are pursuing the same career! You are witnesses of the regret that he carried with him, of the tears which he has caused to flow, and of his triumphs; take him for an example. Be as he was, active and hard-working, patient and zealous. Time adds nothing to glory, and with genius and work, thirty years of life suffice to render one's name immortal."

Thirty years also had sufficed to show that if life was to be understood, it would not be enough to examine the physical principles underlying appearances; it would be necessary to look deeper, into the tissues that make up all living bodies. The great pursuit moved from surface, to principle, to tissue.

WOHLER AND LIEBIG:
MAKABLE BY MAN

IN THE SAME YEAR that Bichat published his *Treatise on Tissues*—1800—and forced the world to recognize that the heart and other organs were not mystical entities, another scientist was born who would carry on the attack on mysticism in the study of living things. He would show that the fluids of the body were compounds made up of the same prosaic materials as other matter.

It was not that scientists had failed up to this time to examine the fluids of the body, the blood, the saliva, the urine. They had studied these substances carefully, and on occasion had used them awesomely. But all knew without question that they were the product of the vital forces that animated all living things. They were part of the mysterious working of life itself, and thus beyond the "making" and probably the understanding of man. There was no attempt at analysis or synthesis, for why should man attempt what no man could do?

Young Friedrich Wohler was not undertaking this impossibility of impossibilities when he achieved it. He was simply pursuing the study of chemistry and seeking the answer to questions posed by his curious mind at the time he made one of the great break-through discoveries.

Wohler had always been curious about the natural world around him. As a boy in the village of Eschersheim he watched the armies of Napoleon marching through, but the collection and trading of minerals interested him far more than military pomp. A friend of his father's gave him the use of his chemical laboratory and library and perhaps determined the direction the youngster's interest would take. Another friend gave him an old furnace in which he could build roaring fires and melt down anything that came to hand.

Medicine seemed to be the field for a young man with such interests, and without much question Wohler enrolled at the University of Marburg to study for his degree. He soon set up a little chemical laboratory in his room and when he should have been engaged in his medical studies often worked in it. He took up the unusual pursuit of studying some of the waste products of the human body. With a little experimentation he succeeded in separating the clear colorless crystals of urea from the urine. They were slender, four-sided, dull-pointed prisms. Medicine was well acquainted with them.

But neither medicine nor chemistry had ever succeeded in making the cyanogen iodide that Wohler put together in his college quarters. It was something new. Wohler wrote up his discovery and reported it to his professors. His initiative, however, brought only criticism. Why was he wasting his time on chemistry when he should have been studying medicine?

Wohler decided to leave Marburg and go to Heidelberg, where he could study under the famed physician and chemist Leopold Gmelin. He did well there and took his degree in Medicine, Surgery, and Midwifery. To complete his training, he was about to leave on a round of European hospitals. But Gmelin had been so impressed by his work and skill in chemistry that he urged him instead to go on with the study of chemistry. He suggested that he apply for admission to the laboratory of the greatest chemist of the day, Johann Jakob Berzelius of Sweden, the man who had ascertained the weight of the elements.

Wohler tremblingly wrote to the noted chemist at Uppsala. A gracious answer came back promptly: "Anyone who has studied chemistry under the direction of Leopold Gmelin has very little to learn from me, but I cannot forgo the pleasure of making your personal acquaintance. You may come whenever it is agreeable to you."

Excited and eager, Wohler left at once for Sweden. It seemed unbearable to him when he could not book an immediate passage and was forced to wait for six weeks at Lübeck. To make use of the wasting time, he looked up a friend and through his good offices obtained the use of a laboratory. While he waited for the boat, he tried to work out a method of producing large quantities of the violently active metal potassium. The English chemist Humphry Davy had recently isolated it.

Wohler finally arrived at Uppsala at night and impatiently waited for the morning. At the first possible moment he hurried to Berzelius's home. "With a beating heart I stood before Berzelius's door and rang the bell," he later related. "The door was opened by a well-dressed, portly, and vigorous man. It was Berzelius himself. As he led me into the laboratory I was in a dream."

The laboratory through which the great chemist showed him could not have been plainer or more sparsely equipped. In one of the two rooms stood two common deal tables. Berzelius worked at one, and the other was intended for Wohler. Neither of the rooms had a furnace or gas service.

"On one of the walls were a few cupboards for reagents," said Wohler. "In the middle was a mercury trough, whilst a glass blower's torch stood on the hearth. In addition there was a sink with an earthenware cistern and tap and, standing over a wooden tub there, the despotic Anna, the cook who had to clean the apparatus every day.

"In the other room were the balances and some cupboards containing instruments and close by a workshop fitted with a lathe. In the neighboring kitchen, in which Anna prepared the meals, was a small but seldom used furnace and the sand bath."

Berzelius decided that his new student needed experience in laboratory techniques and put him to making mineralogical analyses. Wohler threw himself into his first assignment and finished it in the shortest possible time. He hurried to show his results to Berzelius. The Swedish master looked at him a little ruefully. "Doctor, that was quick, but bad." Wohler learned the lesson well. He became one of the calmest and most careful of workers. One of the men who worked with him in later years said that he started no experiment without the fullest reflection and that he guarded against drawing any conclusions until he had completed the most rigorous testing and felt that all errors would have revealed themselves.

If Berzelius slowed down his overeager young assistant, he encouraged him to continue the study of cyanic acid which he had started at Marburg. Wohler thought that it might be interesting to combine the cyanic acid with ammonia. He expected that the combination would yield an inorganic salt with a base similar to that in some vegetables. The test seemed well worth trying.

Wohler put his materials together and carried them through several preliminary steps. He then boiled away the water in his compound. Some white crystals were left behind. They were about an inch long—slender, four-sided, dull-pointed prisms. They could not have been much further from the salt he expected to see, and, in fact, they looked exactly like the crystals of urea. Wohler could not mistake the resemblance; he knew the urea crystals too well. And yet that was preposterous, impossible. Wohler repeated the experiment time and again, and every time he obtained the puzzling crystals. He could not publicly claim that he, a twenty-eight-year-old unknown medical graduate, had produced in a test tube a substance that could be created only by the vital forces of life.

Wohler was not so bold or presumptuous, although there is every indication that he knew what he had accomplished. He recognized that he had to be absolutely sure before making a report that would overturn a base of established belief. In 1824 he merely published his analysis of the cyanates. It demonstrated that ammonium cyanate was made up of four different elements—one atom of carbon, one of oxygen, two of nitrogen, and four of hydrogen. As it happened, this was enough to produce results almost as unexpected as those he had obtained in the test tube.

One year earlier another young German chemist, Justus von Liebig, had published a paper on the explosive fulminates. He had been fascinated by them since as a boy he had watched an itinerant fireworks maker turn them into firecrackers. At every chance, as he grew older, Liebig studied his dangerous hobby. In 1823, while he was completing his chemical studies in the laboratory of Joseph Gay-Lussac in Paris, he finally worked out the composition of fulminic acid. It was made up of one atom of carbon, one of oxygen, two of nitrogen, and four of hydrogen. And this was the report he published in the *Annales de chimie,* edited by Gay-Lussac.

When Wohler submitted his paper on the cyanates to the *Annales,* Gay-Lussac immediately noticed that the formula Wohler gave for cyanic acid was the same as that Liebig had arrived at for fulminic acid. It was incredible, bewildering. The blue fulminates were so different from the white crystalline cyanates that they could not have been confused. Gay-Lussac could see no way in which either of the men could have been mistaken about his materials; both were careful workers. Under the circumstances, a hoax also was unthinkable.

Liebig was an impetuous young fellow and quick to anger if he thought he had been wronged. But this time, instead of hurling accusations, he repeated Wohler's experiment. To his astonishment, he obtained the same results. The two utterly different compounds were in truth identical, and both men had been right in their analyses. But this strange coincidence meant that chemistry would have to face up to a disturbing question: was it possible for the same elements to combine in the same proportions and yet form wholly dissimilar products? If so, it was contrary to all known principles.

Guy-Lussac readily accepted the undeniable. He pointed out that the contradiction might be explained if one assumed that the different elements combined in different patterns in the two substances and thus made them different. To Berzelius this at first seemed an impossibility. But as he checked and re-checked the experiments, he could no longer doubt. He then named the phenomenon isomerism, and so it is known to this day. The way in which the four elements were linked made all the difference. A shift in order and arrangement of even the same elements affected the outcome as materially as, for example, the shifting of the order and relationship of four letters of the alphabet—say, s. t. o. p. In one order the four letters form the word STOP; in another, the totally different word POST. The difference is great, though the elements are the same.

Later, substances were found which formed dozens of isomers. In fact, the phenomenon goes far toward explaining the more than half a million carbon compounds that have now been identified and that make up the field of organic chemistry, the chemistry of life.

At the very outset of their careers the two young chemists had made a major discovery. They were anxious to meet, and did soon after both returned to Germany. Liebig was appointed professor of chemistry at the University of Giessen—a post the famous Alexander von Humboldt secured for him—and Wohler came back to teach in the city trade school of Berlin.

Wohler lost no time in resuming his work with his "peculiar white crystalline substance." Again as he mixed ammonia and cyanic acid he obtained the crystals that he was increasingly convinced were urea. They passed every test he could devise, but one test in particular was decisive.

Wohler poured a little nitric acid on the long white crystals. In a short time glistening scales floated in his test tube. He put the scales through several re-crystallizations and, after neutralizing them again, was able to extract his original substance. Urea behaved in exactly the same way when subjected to exactly the same treatment.

"The similarity to urea in behavior induced me to carry out comparative experiments with completely pure urea isolated from urine, from which it was plainly apparent that urea and this crystalline cyanate of ammonia, if one can so call it, are completely identical compounds," said Wohler.

He could no longer question. The slender crystals that formed when he added ammonia to cyanic acid were urea. Wohler now flatly said so in a paper published in 1828: "Research gave the unexpected result that by the combination of cyanic acid and ammonia urea is formed, a fact that is the more noteworthy, inasmuch as it furnishes an example of the artificial production of an organic, indeed of a so-called animal substance."

Some of Wohler's true jubilance shone through in his letter to Berzelius: "I must now tell you that I can make urea without calling on my kidneys and indeed without the aid of animal, be it man or dog. Ammonium cyanate is urea."

An impassable gulf had been passed. An ancient article of faith had been shattered and, more than this, a whole philosophy that rested upon it—the placing of man in a separate, unreachable category—had been altered from that moment on. A quiet-humored scientist had done what it was firmly believed that no man would ever do.

It is true that Lavoisier and Laplace had shown that the production of animal heat was a combustion. Others had observed the presence of hydrochloric acid in the stomach, and Wohler himself had seen that when organic salts passed through the human body they were converted into carbonates, the very substances that would have been formed had they been consumed in combustion. But still this was not converting a few pinches of chemicals into a product of the body.

Wohler said none of this. He did not go into the far-reaching implications of his work or announce a new theory of life. He simply stated a fact. It was a fact that he had submitted to every possible test and that anyone could verify by repeating his experiments. Actually, it admitted of no difference of opinion, and no storm of dissent was aroused.

Berzelius, for all of his convictions about the impossibility of producing an organic material in the laboratory, was not a man to resist incontestable fact or to fail to grasp its potentialities.

He hastened to congratulate the young man he had so warmly welcomed to his laboratory only a few years earlier. And he included praise for another feat of Wohler's. The year before Wohler had succeeded in isolating and producing aluminum.

"Like precious gems—aluminum and artificial urea—two very different things coming so close together—have been woven into your laurel wreath. You have certainly made an important and magnificent discovery and I cannot find words to describe my pleasure at learning about it."

What particularly struck the Swedish master was the change that turned two inorganic chemicals into urea. Berzelius had of course verified the action himself. "It is quite remarkable how the salt-like character completely vanishes when the acid and ammonia combine," he said. "Future theorists will certainly find this a very illuminating fact."

Actually, it was not necessary to wait for the future. Berzelius himself understood basically what was happening. "This is an example," he wrote, "that shows how compounds containing the same relative number of atoms of the elements can differ in their chemical properties, because of the different relation of the simple atoms to one another in a compound atom."

Arrangement mattered mightily. Berzelius had first glimpsed its importance when Wohler's and Liebig's work with cyanic and fulminic acid had shown that a different arrangement of the atoms could turn the same materials into substances as different as the blue acid and the firecracker explosive. Here was another proof of what occurred when one pattern was disarranged—in this case by the heat of boiling—and shifted into another pattern. You came out with something as different as urea.

But Berzelius could not have foreseen what an almost unlimited bonanza this insight would open up. By altering the placement of a chemical element or a group of elements, by knowingly moving a molecule from one position to a different one, modern chemists have produced thousands of new products ranging from nylon to new drugs and plastics. By a little additional rearranging they have made their new materials harder or softer, impervious or absorbent, solid or fluffy, or specifically directed as need might dictate. Incalculable possibilities have been developed by work with structure.

But still this was only a part of the new worlds opened by the making of urea. Liebig saw it clearly: "The extraordinary and to some extent inexplicable production of urea without the assistance of the vital functions . . . must be considered one of the discoveries with which a new era in science has commenced. There are many bodies similar to urea, all of which will probably at a future period be produced by artificial means."

If urea could be produced in the laboratory, so might other substances formed in plants and animals. The crystals that formed in Wohler's test tube did not indicate exactly how this could be done, but they raised every hope that the scientific work of the future would reveal the means. Scientists were no longer barred by an insurmountable barrier from even hoping that they could duplicate and understand natural substances. Chemistry could move into biology.

Despite Liebig's pointing up of this momentous consequence of Wohler's work and his wholehearted praise of it, certain other phases of their research seemed to put them into conflict. Some colleagues were implying that one would disprove the other. Wohler was not happy about it.

In 1829 he decided upon some counteraction. "It must be some wicked demon that again and again imperceptibly brings us into collision by means of our work and tries to make the chemical public believe that we purposely seek the apples of discord," he wrote to Liebig. "But I think he is not going to succeed.

"If you are so minded, we might for the fun of it undertake some chemical work together in order that the result might be known under our joint names. Of course you would work in Giessen and I in Berlin. When we are agreed upon the plan, we could communicate with each other from time to time as to its progress. I leave the choice of subject entirely to you."

The impetuous Liebig was as quick to respond to warmth and friendship as he was to fight if he felt an issue were involved. He delightedly accepted Wohler's offer, and it was the start of a lifetime of close friendship and collaboration. They were soon to work even more closely together than either could have anticipated.

In 1832 Wohler's young wife died. Distraught and inconsolable, he went to his friend Liebig, who persuaded him to immerse himself in their research. As they worked side by side in the laboratory, Wohler gradually found surcease.

At this time the two chemists decided to study oil of bitter almonds, an oil made from a variety of almond that had earlier attracted the interest of the French chemists. They exposed a dish of the volatile material to the air. In a very short time the oily fluid had turned into the beautifully crystalline substance known as benzoic acid. The transformation was almost as striking as when Wohler evaporated cyanic acid and ammonia and obtained urea. It again seemed like chemical legerdemain.

The two men marveled at how such a product could arise "from bodies apparently so different." They at once began an intensive investigation of the intriguing phenomenon, for they were convinced that through great good fortune they had happened upon another rare "inlet" into "the dark province of organic nature." Wohler also told Liebig that he thought of the possibilities opened by the dramatic change in the oil as a "point of light" to guide them further into the unknown.

They made the inlet a deep one, for they were a balanced, perceptive team of researchers. "In me," said Liebig, "the predominating inclination was to seek out the points of resemblance in the behavior of bodies or their compounds. He [Wohler] possesses an unparalleled facility in perceiving their differences. Acuteness of observation was combined in him with an artistic dexterity and ingeniousness in discovering new means and methods of research or analysis."

Why did a fluid oil turn into fixed, precise crystals? This was the question the two men put to themselves.

They soon found the explanation; Wohler insisted that it was an "easy explanation." The oil absorbed one atom of oxygen from the air and lost one of hydrogen, and suddenly it was benzoic acid. The acid was formed by "simple oxidation."

At this point Wohler had to return to the teaching post at Cassel to which he had been appointed shortly before his wife's death. He sadly missed the daily association with Liebig. "I am back here again in my darkened solitude," he wrote to his friend. "How happy was I that we could work together face to face. The days that I spent with you slipped by like hours and I count them among my happiest."

Although Wohler and Liebig were now forced to return to their first plan of collaboration at a distance, they pushed on with their studies of the oil of bitter almonds.

Hour upon hour of the most exacting work in the laboratory showed them that the oil was made up of one atom of hydrogen and a group of atoms that they always found linked together. The composition of the group was unvarying—fourteen atoms of carbon, ten of hydrogen, and two of oxygen.

They put the group through every test either of them could think of, and it remained intact. And they found the same tight little group in other substances too. It retained its form no matter how the atoms about it might shift. It was something like finding a nugget on a beach, a nugget that would retain its form amid all the grains around it.

Wohler and Liebig named the group a radical. It was a term Guy de Morveau had first used in 1787. Lavoisier also had suggested the existence of radicals or linked groups of atoms in organic substances, and Gay-Lussac had further pointed up the possibility of their existence. But Wohler and Liebig clearly demonstrated for the first time that such a group could remain intact through a series of reactions. Here was one highly important element of order in the bewildering complexity of organic compounds. Here also was proof of a connection between the properties of substances and the radicals they contained. It was truly an "inlet" into organic chemistry.

Wohler and Liebig had begun to edit the journal that later was to become known as the *Annalen der Chemie und Pharmazie*, and they published their report in it.

"Reviewing and collecting together the reactions described in the present essay, we find that they all group around one single compound, which does not change its nature and composition in all its combining with other bodies," they wrote. "This stability, this consequence of the phenomenon, induced us to consider that body as a compound base and therefore to propose for it a peculiar name, i.e., benzoyl."

Berzelius was immediately informed of the new find and conclusions. The Swedish chemist again was greatly pleased by this new achievement of his former student. More than this, he proposed a simpler designation for it than benzoyl. His note on the designation was attached to the original Wohler-and-Liebig essay.

"The results consequent upon your examination of the oil of bitter almonds are the most important that vegetable chemistry has thus far received, and promise to diffuse an unexpected light over this part of science," said Berzelius. He suggested that whenever science might learn with certainty of the existence of groups of atoms which "combine after the manner of simple bodies" they should be designated "by a peculiar sign." In that way, he noted, the idea of the combination could be clearly expressed and conveyed to the reader.

He illustrated his meaning: Benzoyl might be identified by the symbol Bz. Then oil of bitter almonds, made up of benzoyl plus an atom of hydrogen, would become BzH, and so with other benzoyl compounds.

In 1836 the academically important post of professor of chemistry at Göttingen became vacant. Both Wohler and Liebig were considered, but Wohler was chosen, and in the same year took up the position that he would hold for almost half a century. Liebig's only reaction was to rejoice in the selection of his friend. The two went on working together as before.

Not long after going to Göttingen, Wohler made a finding that interested him. He dashed off a note to Liebig: "I am like a hen which has laid an egg and straightaway sets up a great cackling. I have this morning found how bitter oil of almonds containing prussic acid may be obtained from amygdalin, and would propose that we jointly undertake the further investigation of the matter."

They did, and were led into a study of uric acid, another organic compound present in small amounts in urine. And that led them on to other organic compounds.

By 1838 they were ready to publish their new findings. They had added no fewer than sixteen new substances to the list of organic compounds that could be "made" in the laboratory. The two chemists could no longer hesitate to acknowledge the real meaning and significance of their work.

"The philosophy of chemistry must draw the conclusion," they said, "that the synthesis of all non-living organic compounds must be looked upon not merely as probable but as certain of ultimate achievement.

"Sugar, salicin, morphine, will be artificially prepared. As yet we are ignorant of the road by which this will be reached, since the proximate constitutions required for building up these substances are not known to us, but these the progress of science cannot fail to reveal."

Others had been willing to make the same predictions earlier, but the men who had made the predictions possible were certain when they spoke. They proved the most accurate of prophets.

From this time on, Liebig was drawn in another direction. Why, he asked, could not some of the new organic chemicals be used to restore fertility to the soil? The idea was greeted with disdain. How, the critics asked, could a few chemicals do what could only be done by manures and other natural fertilizers? This in itself was enough to stir Liebig to action. In 1840 he took a barren piece of land near Giessen and fed it only with his mineral fertilizers. Soon the plants there were flourishing as few others. This was the beginning of agricultural chemistry.

But Liebig was not altogether happy about his digression into the land and its chemistry. "I feel as though I were a deserter," he wrote to Wohler, "a renegade who has forsaken his religion. I have left the highway of science and my endeavors to be of some use to physiology and agriculture are like rolling the stone of Sisyphus—it always falls back on my head, and I sometimes despair of being able to make the ground firm."

But Wohler too was deserting basic research on the materials of life. As he glimpsed the boundless possibilities of organic chemistry, he also realized its equally limitless complexities. No sooner did he work out the chemical composition of benzoyl than he was forced to ask why the atoms combined as they did, and he was no nearer to the ultimate explanation than when he began. It was frustrating.

"Organic chemistry nowadays almost drives me mad," Wohler complained to Liebig. "To me it appears like a primeval tropical forest full of the most remarkable things, a dreadful endless jungle into which one does not dare to enter for there seems no way out."

Other problems claimed his attention and were more promising. It was easy for Wohler to give more attention again to his work with minerals. The process by which he obtained the pure white powder aluminum was used until mass production came in during the twentieth century. Wohler then succeeded in isolating two other new elements, beryllium and yttrium, and narrowly missed being the first to discover vanadium.

He was analyzing a lead mineral that a friend had sent him from Mexico. Before he could finish the work, he became ill and was unable to go on. He sent one of his specimens to Berzelius, tagging it with a question mark. In the meanwhile N. G. Sefstrom announced the discovery of vanadium.

Berzelius replied with a fable: "In the remote regions of the North there dwells the Goddess Vanadis, beautiful and lovely. One day there was a knock on her door. The goddess was weary and thought she would wait to see if the knock would be repeated, but there was no repetition. The goddess ran to the window to look at the retreating figure. 'Ah,' she said to herself, 'it is that fellow Wohler.' A short time after there was another knock, but this time so persistent and energetic that the goddess went herself to open the door. It was Sefstrom, and thus it was that he discovered vanadium. Your specimen is, in fact, oxide of vanadium. But the chemist who has invented a way for the artificial production of an organic body can well afford to forgo all claims to the discovery of a new metal, for it would be possible to discover ten unknown elements with the expenditure of so much genius."

Wohler also became a famous teacher. The same good will and modesty about his own abilities which drew friends to him attracted students from all around the world. The famed master would pull up a stool in the laboratory and help the newest and least advanced. He could also laugh when the tables were turned on him. Edgar F. Smith, who later became a well-known American chemist, was warned just before he had to appear before Wohler for his doctor's examination that Wohler had asked other candidates about platinum. Smith spent part of the night committing to memory twelve pages in which Wohler dealt with the subject. On the dread day of the examination, Wohler, as predicted, asked the question, and Smith began to recite. After a few minutes Wohler stopped him, thanked him, and complimented him on his knowledge.

After receiving his Ph.D., Smith paid the customary call on each professor. Wohler again congratulated him on his answer to the platinum question, adding that the answer was not only correct but couched in perfect language. Smith felt he had to confess. "I replied," he later related, "that it was not my language that I used but his." Wohler took it as a great joke and was delighted with the tale.

After their urea report, Wohler and Liebig did little more work together, although they remained the closest of friends. Wohler frequently intervened to persuade the hotheaded Liebig, then at the University of Munich, not to involve himself in scientific disputes. Liebig was then engaged in a running battle with famed Louis Pasteur.

"To make war against Marchand, or indeed anyone else, brings no contentment and is of little use to science," Wohler wrote on one of these occasions. "Imagine that it is the year 1900 and that we are both dissolved into carbonic acid, water, and ammonia and our ashes, it may be, are part of the bones of some dog that has despoiled our graves. Who will care then whether we have lived in peace or anger; who will think then of your polemics, or of the sacrifice of your health and peace of mind for science? Nobody. But your good ideas, the new facts you have discovered, these, sifted from all that is immaterial, will be known and remembered for all time. But why should I advise the lion to eat sugar?"

Liebig could never resist the gentle persuasion and humor

of such a letter. He would moderate, if he did not abandon, any dispute in which he was becoming embroiled. With the passing of the years he valued even more the friendship with Wohler and the scientific co-operation for which it stood. By 1871, when his health was poor and he felt his days were limited, he sent Wohler his usual New Year greeting and added: "Even when we are dead and have long been dust, may the bonds which have united us ever keep us both in the remembrance of man as a not too frequent example of two men who were faithful without envy and ill feelings; who wrestled and strove in the same arena and were ever firmly knit in friendship." Liebig died in 1873.

Wohler lived almost another ten years, to the full age of eighty-three. His death came on September 23, 1882.

The wishes of both men were to be realized. They have been remembered as two scientists who chose friendship and co-operation rather than conflict. It would have been easy for them to dissipate their energies in quarreling. Instead, they produced findings that changed the course of science. At long last, men could productively study life and living things. Wohler and Liebig had opened the way.

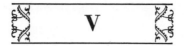

SCHLEIDEN AND SCHWANN:
THE CELL

*Each adds a little to our knowledge
of Nature and from all the facts assembled arises grandeur.*

ARISTOTLE

Perhaps only a part of the unseen reality and strangeness that lay below the surface had been discovered by Bichat. If the organs were made up of tissues, was it possible that the tissues were composed of some more fundamental unit? Men of curiosity were constrained to wonder. And yet the discovery, when it finally came almost a third of a century later, was arrived at almost by indirection. The truth was largely unimaginable. It could not be put together out of the elements that men knew; it was beyond experience. Men might imagine gods and gnomes and unicorns, but who, other than a few visionaries, could dream that the body was made up of cells and organisms too small to be seen by the eyes, or felt by the hands, or apprehended in any other way by the senses?

The evidence of the cell had to be stumbled upon and pieced together over a period of nearly two hundred years. It was not until 1838 that two German scientists, Matthias Jacob Schleiden and Theodor Schwann, carried the work a little further and mobilized the facts so convincingly that men recognized that a new hidden unit had been discovered and a new direction taken.

Until the last years of the sixteenth century there was no way to look below the surface or beneath the structures laid bare by the scalpel. Only then did the Dutch spectacle-makers find that they could adjust two lenses in such a way as to enlarge an object under observation.

The great William Harvey (1578–1667) made use of his "perspicullum" to watch the beat of the hearts of wasps and flies. But almost another half-century passed before anyone began to use the microscope, as it was then named, to make a systematic study of the products of the body and of the general world of nature.

The microscope, with its ingenious arrangement of lenses and its ability to "overcome the infirmities of the senses," was exactly the kind of device to interest Robert Hooke (1635–1703).

Hooke had been born on the Isle of Wight on July 18, 1635. Orphaned at the age of eight, and sickly, he was apprenticed to the painter Sir Peter Lely. Only a small inheritance, to which he tenaciously clung, made it possible for him to enter Oxford when he was eighteen.

At Oxford in the 1650's was a group of young men interested in experimenting with the seemingly chaotic and unpredictable things that made up their environment, whether a pump to lift water or the movement of the planets. They were curious about many matters that had always been taken for granted. Among the group was the dashing Robert Boyle, fourteenth child of the "great" Earl of Cork. He engaged the poor and ugly but adroit young Hooke as his assistant. Hooke designed and built the air pump that is described in Boyle's first book, and he may have had more than a casual hand in the formulation of Boyle's law.

Pumps, springs, everything mechanical fascinated eighteen-year-old Hooke. He conceived the idea of using a spring to control the oscillation of a balance wheel in a watch, and he thus turned the erratic timepiece of the past into a precision instrument. He also seems to have developed the spiral spring, although he was soon involved in an acrimonious and continuing dispute—one of his many—to prove it.

Hooke was not the most agreeable of men, but there was no denying his inventiveness and originality. In 1662, when the Royal Society was chartered, Hooke was named its curator. It was his duty to produce "three or four considerable experiments" for each of the weekly meetings.

For one of them the hard-worked curator brought in his own, improved compound microscope. To twentieth-century eyes it resembles a small fire-extinguisher. A nozzle-like lens was attached to a cylinder elaborately ornamented with scrollwork. To light an object under examination, a candle was set up nearby and its light concentrated on the object by means of a reflector and a small convex-plano lens.

"By the help of the microscope," Hooke told the royal fellows, "there is nothing so small as to escape our inquiry."

He predicted to his willing though skeptical audience that it was probable, or at least not improbable, that by working with the microscope science might discover the composition of bodies, the various textures of "their matter," and perhaps even the manner of their "inward motion."

Hooke beamed his candle on the stinging hairs of a nettle, on the head of a fly, on the tufted gnat, on the edge of a knife, on the beard of a wild oat, and on hundreds of other specimens.

Among them was cork—common enough, certainly, and yet remarkably able to hold air in a bottle "without suffering the least bubble to pass" and quite "unapt to suck or drink in water."

One day Hooke sharpened his penknife until it was "as keen as a razor" and cut off a "good clear piece" of cork. This left the surface very smooth. He placed the smooth surface under the microscope and, moving it a little this way and that, thought that he could perceive it to be "a little porous." He could not be sure, although its lightness and springiness made porosity likely.

Hooke thought that with "further diligence" he could somehow make the cork structure more discernible. He took his sharpened knife and cut a very thin slice from the surface. The sliver seemed quite white, so he put it on a black object plate. "And casting the light on it with a deep plano-convex

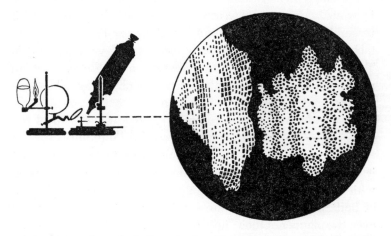

Discovery of the cell. When Hooke placed thin slices of cork under his microscope, he saw that they were made up of "an infinite company of small Boxes or Bladders of Air"—cells.

glass," said Hooke, "I could exceedingly plainly perceive it all to be perforated and porous, much like a Honeycomb."

The pores that sprang into view were regular and yet not completely regular; they also varied about as those in the honeycomb did. The similarity went even further. The cork had "very little solid substance in comparison to the empty cavity that was contain'd between the *Interstitia* (or walls, as I may so call them). The walls or partitions were near as thin in proportion to their pores as those thin films of wax in a honeycomb are to theirs."

"Next," said Hooke, naming for all time the fundamental unit of living matter, the cork was like honeycomb "in that those pores, or cells, were not deep but consisted of a great many little Boxes. . . .

"I no sooner discern'd these (which were indeed the first microscopic pores I ever saw, and perhaps that were ever seen, for I had not met with any Writer or Person, that had made any mention of them before this) but me thought I had with the discovery of them, presently hinted to me the true and intelligible reason of all the *Phaenomena of Cork*."

Hooke bent over his honeycomb of cells. With a skillful hand he drew them from two different points of view, the one showing a fabric of little square compartments, the newly named cells, and the other looking down on them so that the cavities seemed rounder and their orderly arrangement in ranks or series was not visible. He put the two drawings side by side, labeling one "A" and the other "B," and set them off dramatically against a dark circular background. His apprenticeship to Lely had not been wasted.

If Hooke did not foresee the full implication of his epochal discovery, he understood well that it was important and promising. What he was seeing suggested the answer to the problem that had drawn him into the investigation of cork—why it floated and held air in a bottle so well. It seemed apparent that the cells were filled with air that was "perfectly enclosed" in each of the distinct little boxes.

"It seems very plain why neither the Water, nor any other Air can easily insinuate itself into them, since there is already within them an *intus existens*, and consequently, why the pieces of Cork become so good floats for Nets and stopples for Viols, or other close vessels," he explained.

The microscope showed that the whole mass was nothing but "an infinite company of small Boxes or Bladders of Air."

The air could be compressed, and that was why cork made such an excellent stopple and held so tight. Hooke was never known for his physical strength, for he constantly suffered from what today's physicians interpret as chronically inflamed sinuses, but he took several pieces of cork and squeezed them as hard as he could. He was able to "condense it into less than a twentieth part of its usual dimensions neer the Earth" simply by the use of his hands and without the aid of any "forcing Engine, such as Racks, Leavers, Wheels, Pullies, or the like."

Hooke divided off several lines of cork pores and counted them. There were usually about sixty of the small cells end to end in an eighteenth of an inch.

Not a brilliant mathematician, Hooke was unable to work out the curvilinear motions of the planets and thus in his planetary studies he lost eternal fame to his rival Isaac Newton. But he had no difficulty with common arithmetic. There were more than 1,000 cells to an inch, and more than a million— 1,166,400 to be exact—in a square inch, and 1,259,721,000 in a cubic inch.

Hooke was startled. It was incredible, a thing that could not have been believed if the microscope had not established it by ocular demonstration.

And these stupefyingly numerous little cells were not peculiar to cork. Other vegetables, Hooke found, had the same compartmented structure, and in some of them the cells were even smaller than in cork. Hooke examined the pith of the elder and the pulp or pith of the "cany" stalks of such vegetables as "carrets, daucus, Bur-docks, teasel, fearn and several kinds of reed." Even the pith that filled the stalk of a feather had the same cellular texture or "schematisme."

The cells that Hooke was examining so eagerly were completely walled. And yet he saw that the juices must pass in and out through their seemingly solid partitions, for the cells of living things were filled with juices while intact cells in charred material were "empty of everything but Air."

How could this be? How could matter pass through the unbroken walls? Hooke decided to seek for the passage. He blew on the cells, hoping to force out their contents. This produced no results. Could it be that the vegetable pores had valves, like those of the animal heart, that might give passage "to the contain'd fluid juices one way and shut themselves, and impede the passage of such liquids back again?" Try as he would, Hooke could find no valves. His failure to discover the entry and exit did not mean, he hastened to add, that Nature did not have some kind of a contrivance "to bring her designs and ends to pass." With a better microscope he was hopeful that it could be found.

Hooke reported his observations on cork and a gamut of other things, ranging up to the craters on the moon, in a book that he called the *Micrographia or Some Physiological Descriptions of Minute Bodies Made by Magnifying Glasses with Observations and Inquiries Thereupon*. It was dedicated to the King—"I do most humbly lay this small present at your Majesties Royal feet"—and published in 1665.

The book aroused intense interest, even at a time when any attention at all might have seemed impossible. In 1665 the Great Plague was at its dread peak and people were dying by the thousands. The next year London was swept by the Great Fire. And yet amid all the ravages of disease and flame, the invisible had become visible, and the revelation was a startling one. Samuel Pepys sat up until two o'clock in the morning reading the *Micrographia*. He called it "the most ingenious book that ever I read in my whole life."

Hooke was only twenty-nine, but his reputation was established. And so was the cell. Men knew at last that beneath everything they saw lay tiny cells or compartments.

Other men of science and curiosity were becoming interested in the newfangled instrument that let men see things that always before had been "buried from their eyes." Pepys, no scientist but not a man to miss anything new going on about him, paid five pounds for one of the instruments, which he noted was "a great price for a curious bauble."

In 1673, eight years after the *Micrographia* had been published, the Royal Society received a letter from one of its Dutch correspondents, Reinier de Graaf. "I am writing to tell you," he said, "that a certain most ingenious person here, named Leeuwenhoek has devised microscopes which far surpass those which we have hitherto seen. . . ."

De Graaf enclosed a letter from the "ingenious" Leeuwenhoek. It indeed more than merited the adjective, for it described some unusual microscopic observations on mold, on the sting, mouth parts, and eyes of the bee, and on the louse. The Royal Society was sufficiently impressed to invite Leeuwenhoek to send them any further observations he might make.

Anton van Leeuwenhoek (1632–1723) had not been brought up for such scientific activity and formal correspondence. His only training was as a draper. And when he began to make the fine microscopes of which De Graaf wrote, he was busy at the dual and unrelated occupations of selling ribbons and buttons and seeing to the proper maintenance of the town hall. He was chamberlain to the burgomasters, a post that made him responsible for the laying of fires in the towered Delft town hall and keeping it neat and tidy.

The Delft draper and custodian was at the same time a man of rare curiosity, persistence, and confidence. When he began to make microscopes—in actuality they were magnifying glasses—he not only ground his own lenses to a new perfection, but even extracted the gold and silver in which he mounted some of the plates.

Leeuwenhoek felt overwhelmed at the notice of the Royal Society of London, certainly one of the world's most distinguished bodies of philosophers, as they were then called. He knew none of the Latin in which he should properly have addressed so learned a body. Nevertheless, Leeuwenhoek sent along some of his drawings of the bee and explained in his non-literary Dutch: "I beg that those Gentlemen to whose notice these may come please to bear in mind that my observations and thoughts are the outcome of my own unaided impulse and curiosity alone; for beside myself in our town there be no philosophers who practice this art; so pray take not amiss my poor pen and the liberty I have taken in setting down my random notions."

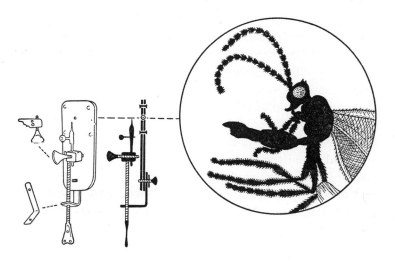

Leeuwenhoek's microscope and one of the "little animals" he saw on its pinpoint.

Leeuwenhoek was forty-one and had already made dozens of microscopes. Instead of changing his specimens, he kept them fixed under his lens and made additional microscopes for viewing the vast and varied array that he wanted to study. Perhaps making a new instrument was as easy as gluing an object to the point of a needle and getting it before his glass.

The next year Leeuwenhoek was walking beside a lake near Delft when he noticed trailing clouds of green stuff in the wa-

ter. The country folk said that the growth was produced by
the dew each summer. Leeuwenhoek collected a little bit of
the slimy green and mounted it under his microscope.

Green streaks that wound about almost like serpents leaped
out at him; there also were many small round green globules,
and among them were little "animalcules," some roundish and
some oval.

"On the last two," said Leeuwenhoek, "I saw two little legs
near the head and two little fins at the hindmost end of the
body. . . . And the motion of most of these animalcules in the
water was so swift and so various, upwards, downwards and
round about, that 'twas wonderful to see: and I judge that
some of the little creatures were about a thousand times
smaller than the smallest ones [mites] that I have ever yet
seen upon the rind of cheese, in wheaten flour, mould and the
like."

Neither the jungles of Africa nor the imaginings of mythol-
ogy could equal the fantastic forms and behavior of the little
monsters that swarmed, tumbled, and writhed in this drop of
pond water. Leeuwenhoek stared in disbelief at his first sight
of the one-celled animals that were later to be classified as
members of the phylum Protozoa. But he was not suffering
from illusions: they did not vanish with a blink of the eye;
they were as real as his microscope. Was it possible that other
water could conceal the same kind of outlandish creatures?

In September 1675 Leeuwenhoek happened to take a look
at some rain water that had been standing for a few days in
a container lined with Delft blue glaze. The water too was
full of little animals, astoundingly little ones. What could they
be compared to? What measurement could convey even an
idea of their minuteness? About the smallest animal of which
Leeuwenhoek could think, an animal even smaller than the
cheese and other mites, was the water flea that Jan Swammer-
dam had portrayed and studied. It was just large enough to be
seen with the naked eye. His animals, Leeuwenhoek calcu-

lated, were about ten thousand times smaller than the barely visible water flea.

Leeuwenhoek studied his animalcules day after day. He could describe their behavior as clearly as he could that of his cat.

"When these animalcules bestirred themselves, they sometimes stuck out two little horns which were continually moved, after the fashion of a horse's ears. The part between these little horns was flat, their body being roundish, save only that it ran somewhat to a point at the hind end; at which pointed end it had a tail, near four times as long as the whole body, and looking as thick when viewed through the microscope as a spider's web. At the end of this tail there was a pellet, of the bigness of one of the globules of the body; and this tail I could now perceive to be used by them for their movements in very clear water.

"These little animals were the most wretched creatures that I have ever seen; for when, with the pellet they did but hit on any particles or little filaments (of which there are many in the water, especially if it hath but stood some days), they stuck intangled in them; and they pulled their body out into an oval and did struggle by strongly stretching themselves to get their tail loose; whereby their whole body then sprang back towards the pellet of the tail, and their tails then coiled up serpent-wise, after the fashion of a copper or iron wire that, having been wound close around a round stick, and then taken off, kept all its windings.

"This motion of stretching out and pulling together the tail continued; and I have seen several hundred animalcules caught fast by one another in a few filaments, lying within the compass of a coarse grain of sand." [1]

Other equally remarkable animals flashed through the drop

---

[1] Undoubtedly vorticella, one-celled ciliated animals with bell-shaped bodies. Leeuwenhoek did not see that the tails might be stalks, and thus he thought the animals were trying to break out of an entanglement.

of water. Some waved "incredibly thin little feet or legs"—
Leeuwenhoek's description of the hairlike appendages that are
now called cilia. Others, about twice as long as they were
broad, sometimes stood still "twirling themselves round as
'twere, with a swiftness such as you see in a whip-top a-spin-
ning." And there were innumerable others, some monstrous in
size as compared to the tiniest ones.

Leeuwenhoek was not a man to speculate, but he did ask
essential questions. Where did this freakish menagerie come
from? Did the animalcules come down from the sky with the
rain?

On the 26th of May 1676 a heavy rain fell in Delft. During
a brief let-up Leeuwenhoek took a clean glass and caught
some of the water as it came off his slate roof. He hurried in
with it and put a drop under his microscope. A few animals
swam about in it, but Leeuwenhoek, in thinking hard about it,
realized that they might have been bred in his leaden gutters.

The rain was continuing, so the careful Dutchman carried
a large porcelain dish into his courtyard and sat it on a tub
high enough to prevent any mud from splashing into it. He
collected some more water. This time he found no animals,
though there were a lot of earthy particles in this water. Then
the animals did not rain down from the skies.

But keep the water a few days, or let the wind ruffle it,
and Leeuwenhoek found as many as a thousand animals in a
drop, "a-wallowing on their back as well as their belly, and
all a-rolling." The animals turned up in river water, in sea water, and even in the cold palatable water that Leeuwenhoek
drew from the fifteen-foot well in his yard. And they swarmed
in pepper water.

Leeuwenhoek chanced upon the last. In the course of trying
everything under his microscope, he decided to have a look at
pepper. He had always wondered what caused the "hotness
or power whereby pepper affects the tongue." It was difficult
to work with dry grains, so he put some to soak. About three

weeks later when he got around to having a look at the mixture, the sight was flabbergasting. The pepper water fairly
teemed with such a multitude of animals as he had not seen
before. Among them were some extremely thin little tubes, infinitely smaller than the smallest of the animalcules. Leeuwenhoek was looking at bacteria, although he did not know or
suspect that he was seeing for the first time the invisible group
that can do both untold ill and good to man. Leeuwenhoek
only marveled at the size and number of the rods. They out-
numbered many times the six to eight thousand animalcules
in a drop of water.

A full report on this newly discovered world and all its wonders had to be dispatched to the Royal Society. Leeuwenhoek
had his laboratory notes copied out in a fine hand on seventeen folio pages and sent them off to London.

The effect was sensational. As many animals in a few drops
of water as there were on the earth! Another world lying con-
cealed in the universe that men had always known! The society was staggered. Leeuwenhoek's work bore all the marks
of exactitude, but what he was saying went beyond what anyone could accept without the most rigorous proof. Leeuwenhoek was requested to supply more data, and Hooke, who had
been made secretary of the society in 1677, was asked to see
if he himself, as a man who had worked with microscopes,
could confirm the fantastic report from Holland.

Hooke's microscope had been neglected for several years,
"I having been by other urgent occupations diverted," but he
quickly got it out and made up some pepper water as Leeuwenhoek had done. And there were the animals in all their
multitudes and their freakishness.

"It seems very wonderfull," Hooke told the society, "that
there should be such an infinite number of animalls in soe im-
perceptible a quantity of matter; that these animalls should be
soe perfectly shaped and indeed with such curious organs of
motion as to be able to move nimbly, to turne, stay, accelerate

& retard their progresse at pleasure. And it was not less surprising to find that these were gygantick monsters in comparison to a lesser sort which almost filled the water."

Thus Hooke confirmed Leeuwenhoek's discovery of both the
protozoa and bacteria, although neither knew the strange new
population in these still unthought-of terms.

People anxiously flocked to see the marvel, among them His
Majesty Charles II, the founder and patron of the Royal Society. Hooke was also asked to demonstrate the animals before a formal session of the society. The experiments that he
set up for the meetings of November 1 and 8, 1677, ran into
difficulties, but at the next weekly meeting, on November 15,
with the aid of a better microscope and thinner glass pipes to
contain the drop of pepper water, all went well. Sir Christo-
pher Wren and others named to a special committee saw and
affirmed that the little animals were swimming to and fro, exactly as Leeuwenhoek had said. The unlettered Dutchman
had made one of the greatest of discoveries. This was evident
even then.

Leeuwenhoek did not rest on this dazzling affirmation. If
the animalcules were present in all water except that which
had just fallen from the heavens, perhaps they also lodged in
the human body. Leeuwenhoek reasoned that if they were in
the body, they would find their way to the mouth.

Each morning all through his life he had rubbed his teeth
with salt and cleaned them with a toothpick. Nevertheless
when he examined his teeth with a magnifying glass he found
around them a little white matter "as thick as 'twere batter."
He scraped off a bit and mixed it with rain water in which
there were no animalcules, and with a little spittle.

As his candle lighted up his microscopic slide, the sight
made Leeuwenhoek, with all of his experience, start. Some
very little animals were "prettily amoving" through his witch's
brew of a mixture. The biggest and longest shot through the

drop like a pike (the fish). Another kind hovered together like a swarm of gnats. And if these specimens, from teeth as "clean and white as falleth to the lot of few men," were numerous and swift, they were as nothing compared to the myriad that inhabited a specimen Leeuwenhoek obtained from an old man who had never cleaned his teeth.

The human mouth was alive with animalcules, Leeuwenhoek reported to the Royal Society. He did not assume that the wriggling, somersaulting little animals that he found in the mouth and later in the wastes of the body were harmful. They were there, and Leeuwenhoek was satisfied to give explicit, unforgettable accounts and descriptions of them.

The Royal Society wanted to honor its prodigious correspondent. Leeuwenhoek was unanimously elected a fellow, and the society voted to send him his suitably inscribed diploma in a silver box. To increase its grandeur, the society voted at a later meeting to have its arms engraved on the box.

It was the greatest of honors. Leeuwenhoek was all but overwhelmed. He accepted, gratefully pledging the society that for the "singular favour" they had shown him, he would strive with all his might and main all through his life to make himself worthy of the honor and privilege. Universities might thereafter denounce him and the common folks might swear he was a conjuror who made people see what was not there, but from that time on, as a fellow of the Royal Society of London—not a mere foreign member—he was fortified against all assaults.

Word of the wonders the Dutch shopkeeper was disclosing spread everywhere, and Leeuwenhoek was besieged by visitors begging for a look at the fabulous little beasts. Peter the Great of Russia, on a visit to the Netherlands in 1698, sailed down the canal to Delft to see for himself. Two gentlemen of his retinue were dispatched to bid Leeuwenhoek to bring his incomparable magnifying glass to one of the Tsar's ships. The

Tsar spent more than two hours peering through the Dutchman's revealing microscope and thus saw another of Leeuwenhoek's most famous sights.

In the tail of a little fish stuck into one of the tiny viewing tubes, the Dutch custodian showed his royal visitor the circulation of blood in the capillary vessels. By demonstrating how the blood went from the arteries to the veins, Leeuwenhoek confirmed the observation of the Italian scientist Marcello Malpighi and completed the theory of circulation developed by William Harvey some fifty-five years before.

In the tail of a little fish, stuck into a "viewing tube" by Leeuwenhoek, the Tsar of Russia saw blood circulating in the capillaries.

Leeuwenhoek bountifully kept his promise to continue serving the Royal Society throughout his life. In all, more than two hundred of his inimitable letters went to London. As he lay dying in 1723, in his ninety-first year, his last act was to ask a friend to translate two last letters into Latin and send them to the society. Leeuwenhoek also had prepared one final gift for the great gentlemen and philosophers who had understood and valued his work.

It was a black-and-gilt cabinet filled with his most precious microscopes, some of which he had not previously displayed to anyone. In the five drawers of the cabinet were thirteen square tin cases, each covered with black leather and holding two instruments. A letter prepared in advance to go with them explained that every one of the lenses had been "ground by myself and mounted in silver, and furthermore set in silver, almost all of them in silver that I extracted from the ore, and separated from the gold wherewith it was charged; and where-withal is writ down what object standeth before each little glass." Affixed to the needles were objects ranging from the globules of blood "from which its redness proceedeth," to a thin slice of the wood of the lime tree, "where the vessels con-veying the Sap are cut transversely," to "the organ of sight of a Flie."

More than two hundred years later, in the full perspective of history, Professor Lorande Woodruff of Yale called the Leeuwenhoek letters to the Royal Society the longest and most important series of communications that a scientific so-ciety has ever received.

Another part of the fantastically inhabited and structured universe that underlay and controlled the body and the sur-face had been revealed. It was another demonstration that men would have to look deeper, beyond the visible, for an understanding of what they are.

But when Leeuwenhoek died, there was no one to succeed him. His "secret" way of examining his helter-skelter of mate-rial had died with him, for he would reveal it to no one. Clifford Dobell, who made the modern translation of the Leeu-wenhoek letters, believes that it was a method of dark-ground illumination. Either because of a lack of comparable tech-niques and instruments, or because of a feeling that there was no point in further pursuing studies done with such superlative thoroughness, no comparable microbe hunter appeared for the next 150 years.

Science took another track; it became preoccupied with a

long debate on pre-formation—the theory that man is present in miniature in the first cell from which he springs.

But even without the impetus of another brilliant series of discoveries and with science diverted into a blind alley, there was a slow gain in the understanding of the underlying cells and animalcules and what they mean to life.

In the 1790's Jean-Baptiste-Pierre-Antoine de Monet, Chevalier de Lamarck (1744–1829) was telling his classes at the Jardin du Roi, which had only recently been renamed the Jardin des Plantes, that every living body is essentially a mass of cellular tissue.

Lamarck had been convinced of the validity of the still novel idea as he peered into his microscope trying to classify the invertebrates according to their fundamental organs. He was also attempting to work out the steps in the great progression that he believed had carried life from the simple polyp to man. Lamarck was an evolutionist—though so little heeded that no one was seriously disturbed about his unorthodox views. France, rather, was centering her agonized attention on the guillotine, which was then doing its deadly work not far from the garden.

By 1809, when he published his *Philosophie zoologique*, Lamarck was explicit about the cells: "Every living body is essentially a mass of cellular tissue in which more or less complex fluids move more or less rapidly."

In his chapter on the physical causes of life, he argued that the entire operation of Nature consists of organizing cellular tissues from the little masses of gelatinous or mucillaginous material that Nature "finds at her disposal."

Here was an important about-face. To Hooke studying his transparently thin slices of cork, the cell had seemed primarily a cavity surrounded by a wall. Lamarck saw that what mattered was the little jelly interior—the protoplasm of today—and its organization into cellular tissues.

But the emphasis generally fell on the tissues. The French

scientists had not forgotten the lessons of the young genius Bichat. And their own observations also drew them in the same direction. They generally were examining tissues, a complex of cells that brought to mind the comparisons they used, a honeycomb, lace, or foam. Aside from Lamarck's observations, not much attention was given to that "gelatinous, mucillaginous" interior of the cell.

It was precisely this interior that attracted the interest of an English scientist, Robert Brown (1773–1858). Brown was a physician who gave up the practice of medicine to devote himself to botany. Soon after this shift of careers he went off on an expedition to Australia and Tasmania. Upon his return, he was made librarian of the Linnaean Society and Curator of the British Museum. Humboldt soon labeled him "facile Princeps Botanicorum."

When Charles Darwin accepted the invitation to go on the voyage of the *Beagle,* he inevitably called on Dr. Brown to ask for his advice. On one of these visits the botanist led the young Cambridge graduate into his study and invited him to look into a microscope set up there. Darwin saw some vegetable cells and in them some marvelous moving currents of green. Darwin, who still had most of his science to learn, excitedly and innocently asked the doctor what the spectacle was. Brown stiffly answered: "That is my secret." Darwin was on the point of leaving England for five years, and yet he felt, he said in his autobiography, that Brown feared he might try to steal his discovery. Darwin considered the "first man of botany" a scientific miser.

The secretive Dr. Brown had discovered that the green stuff in plants was scarcely more still than were Leeuwenhoek's animalcules. Under the seemingly immobile surface of vegetable tissue were streaming movements of what seemed to be granular material in the plant cells.

But there was also something else. Every cell in the epidermis of orchids, the family of plants to which Brown was giving particular attention, contained a small circular spot "somewhat more opake than the membrane of the cell." Brown could even see that it was slightly convex in shape. Although it sometimes appeared to be on the surface of the cell, he recognized that it actually lay inside.

Brown, a systematic man, looked to see if the little spots would turn up in other orchid cells. They did. He discovered them in the gland and pollen cells, and in the cells of other plants. In most cases, the spot was "uncommonly distinct."

Brown accurately named the little "opake" spot—the spot that was thereafter to be recognized as the controlling, all-important core of the cell—the areola or nucleus.

The doctor's use of the word "nucleus" indicated that he had some sense of the significance of the "opake spot" and perhaps of its function. Brown, however, looked coldly upon going beyond the exact limits of observation. He wanted nothing to do with theorizing.

By this time Darwin had returned from his five-year voyage around the globe, filled with facts and theories, and asking if it all might mean that species had slowly evolved on this planet. He went again to call on the first man of botany. In fact, while he was living in London and working on the manuscript of *The Voyage of the Beagle*, he often dropped in on Brown on Sunday mornings.

Darwin always left these sessions with a feeling of frustration. He later explained: "Brown . . . seems to be chiefly remarkable for the minuteness of his observations and their perfect accuracy. He never propounded to me any large scientific view in biology. His knowledge was extraordinarily great, and much died with him, owing to his excessive fear of ever making a mistake."

Brown's book *Observations on the Organs and Mode of Fecundation in Orchidæ æ and Asclepiadeæ*, published in 1833, reported the discovery of the nucleus of the cell. That was the end of it; it had been found. Brown went no further.

In France, at about the same time, another physician who

had abandoned medicine for botany had been led into a study of the cell. Henri Dutrochet (1776–1847) started to study the baffling sensitive plant known as Mimosa pudica.

He would run his finger down the gray-green spine of the leaf and watch the leaflets close together as neatly as the fingers closing into the palm of the hand. It was a game that endlessly delighted children, but Dutrochet wanted to know why a mere touch should produce so marked a reaction in a plant.

He scraped out a bit of the plant's pith and examined it under the microscope. Like other vegetables, it was made up entirely of cellular tissues. The cells had a hexagonal shape and were disposed in a longitudinal series—a handsome pattern.

The English scientist Nehemiah Grew had compared such cellular tissues to the bubbles of foam on a fermenting liquor. But the compartments of foam are separated only by a single wall. The pith cells looked different to Dutrochet; it seemed to him that each cell had its own walls. If he could separate the cells, he reasoned, he could find out certainly.

Dutrochet tried a dozen ways to break up the cellular tissues. His problem was not their tininess so much as the firmness with which the cells held together. Perhaps acid would dissolve their adhesion.

Dutrochet placed a bit of tissue in a tube of nitric acid and plunged it into boiling water. The experiment worked like magic. The cells rapidly came apart, although one had to be careful. If the treatment was continued too long, the cells were destroyed.

With the cells separated, it was a simple matter to pick one up, place it in a drop of water, and slide it under the lens. Dutrochet's hunch had been correct: the walls were not shared like those of foam. Not at all. Each cell had its own complete wall, and when two cells adjoined there was a double wall.

Dutrochet applied his test to other vegetable tissues and to animal tissues. Sometimes the cells were assembled in long strings—fibers—but in every case when they came apart they were little walled globules.

"We may draw the conclusion," the French scientist said, "that the globular corpuscles which by their assemblage make up all the organic tissues of animals are actually globular cells of exceeding smallness. . . . They appear to be united only by a simple adhesive force. . . . Thus all tissues, all animal organs, are actually only a cellular tissue variously modified. . . ."

Dutrochet in one experiment had cut off the tail of a little fish. As it swam around in the bowl in which he kept it, a sort of aquatic mold with long green streamers developed on the wound. At the end of each of the trailing filaments was a bulbous swelling large enough to be seen by the unaided eye. Dutrochet snipped off a few filaments and studied them under his microscope. To his amazement, a host of little globules was being expelled from the lower part of the bulb and the empty compartment filled with water.

The ejection of the globules had not been caused by contraction. Dutrochet could see no narrowing in the shape of the capsule. The water, then, must have entered first and acted as a piston in driving out the globules. But how did water enter the unbreached walls? Dutrochet asked Hooke's question.

Dutrochet was well aware that the microscope can mislead an unwary observer. He considered the possibility that he might be witnessing an optical illusion; yes, that probably was it. He simply made a note of the odd phenomenon and thought little more about it. He might have forgotten it if by sheer chance he had not later seen the same thing happen on a large enough scale to be visible to the naked eye. Then it had not been an illusion.

Here was a happening that had to be further investigated. Dutrochet began to ask what kind of a force could draw water into the closed cell. The pasty transparent substance that filled cells seemed to be denser than the blood plasma that bathes the walls or is separated from them only by the extremely thin walls of the capillaries. In that case the blood plasma would continually tend to enter the cells, and this would set up two electric currents, one forcing the substances of the blood into the cells and the other bringing about a return of some of the cell substances to the blood stream. It was an illuminating insight.

Dutrochet coined the word osmosis to describe this vital transfer of materials between the cell and its environment. Although the term osmosis is now used only to refer to the passage of water in and out of the cell, Dutrochet was the first to understand the principle of the exchange. Few knew of the significant discovery or credited him with it.

Dutrochet's studies were so thorough that he began to realize the vast potentialities of the cell. Different products manufactured in that little drop of pasty stuff must account for the nearly incomprehensible diversity of living things—for their structure, their organs, their skin, their coloring, and all of their other varied traits and appearances, and for the even greater diversity of the plant kingdom. This had to be, for the physical and chemical substances secreted in the cells made up the distinctive fruits, stems, roots, leaves, and flowers in all the plants that cover the surface of the globe.

"One can scarcely conceive that such an amazing diversity of products results from the activity of a single organ—the cell," said Dutrochet. "When one compares the extreme simplicity of this organ with the extraordinary diversity of its internal powers, it becomes evident that the cell is truly the *pièce fondamentale* of the living organism."

All of this Dutrochet reported in his book *Recherches anatomiques et physiologiques sur la structure intime des animaux et des végétaux et sur leur motilité.* It was published in 1824.

In the fifty-nine years after Hooke had reported the odd little compartments in cork, cells had been found in all kinds of plant and animal tissue. The nucleus had been discovered and Dutrochet had sensed and said that the cell was the *"pièce fondamentale,"* the fundamental building block. And yet this growing knowledge of the cell was scattered. It had not been brought together with the completeness and definitiveness that would establish the cell as the universal unit of life.

This was still to come. It was awaiting the first meeting of two German scientists.

In 1837 they were introduced at a dinner party. Before the dinner ended, the two were so intent on their discussion that the rest of the company was forgotten.

The more voluble and assured of the professors, Matthias Jacob Schleiden, was expounding his views with a lawyer's force and persuasiveness—he had been a lawyer before he became a botanist. He, Schleiden explained, had been able to demonstrate that plants are composed entirely of cells and that their entire growth consists of a formation of cells within cells.

Dr. Theodor Schwann listened eagerly and put in many questions. Neither he, the great Johannes Müller, with whom he had studied, or other anatomists had been able to find a single underlying elementary particle in animal tissue. On the contrary, the elementary particles of animal matter exhibited an overwhelming variety of form. It was true that cells could be seen under the microscope, but some were of one kind and some of another. In the nervous system the elementary particle was a fiber. And none of these various forms seemed to have anything in common except that they grew by the addition of new molecules between those already existing. As Schleiden knew, Schwann continued, the anatomists had never been able to discover any rule that governed the way molecules joined together to form living particles.

And yet, if there were a single principle, if animal tissues, like Schleiden's plant tissues, were made up of cells, it would explain some of the things he—Schwann—had been seeing under his microscope that very summer.

Schwann had been investigating the ends of nerves in the tails of frog larvae. As he put tiny bits of tissue under the microscope, he saw that the Chorda dorsalis (spinal cord) had a "beautifully cellular structure." This confirmed Müller's finding that the Chorda dorsalis in fish consists entirely of separate cells. Schwann at once asked if cells would be found in other tissues, and went on to examine some cartilage corpuscles. They too were made up of cells.

"But," he explained to Schleiden, "this led to no further results."

That was the state of affairs when he met Schleiden.

"Dr. Schleiden opportunely communicated to me his excellent researches upon the origin of new cells in plants and from the nuclei within the parent cells," said Schwann. "The previously enigmatical contents of the cells of the cartilages of the frog larvae thus became clear to me; I now recognized in them young cells provided with a nucleus."

Schleiden and Schwann hurried to Schwann's laboratory. The two scientists pored over Schwann's excellent drawings of the cell structure he had seen. Schleiden pointed out the similarity of the animal and plant cells. It was striking, and yet Schwann decided upon a thorough review and additional work before coming to any conclusions.

With the zeal of the explorer who sees his goal ahead, Schwann made new slides of the Chorda dorsalis. The cells varied in size and had an irregular polyhedral shape, and each one had its own membrane. The cell walls were thin, colorless, smooth, and almost completely transparent. It was the same with the cartilage cells, no matter how closely they were examined.

"The detailed investigation of the Chorda dorsalis led us to this result," Schwann explained. "The most important phenomena of their structure and development accord with the corresponding processes in plants.

"We have thrown down a grand barrier of separation between the animal and vegetable kingdoms, viz., diversity of structure."

The elation of the two scientists shone through Schwann's words, but Schwann knew that if the world was to be persuaded, complete proof would be needed. His work had already convinced him that the tissues had their beginnings in groups of young cells. But to establish the point, he decided, it would be necessary to prove it beyond question.

Schwann chose birds' eggs as the best material to study— young, grayish-white eggs removed from the ovary. He put one on his dry object plate, pricked it with a needle, and allowed its contents to flow out. The contents consisted entirely of very pale cells of variable size. They were so small and so closely packed that they might have been taken for a granulous mass if they had not been viewed under a very revealing light. Schwann was able to show, however, that such cells subsequently become the globules of the yolk cavity.

He then took a fresh-laid hen's egg and removed a portion of the germinal membrane—a little white disk from which the embryo is formed. It was made up entirely of cells. Schwann demonstrated that after eight hours of incubation such cells gave rise to the first rudiments of the embryo.

The "primordial substance" itself was a cell, and from the moment of its origin to the formation of the tissues, development was only a multiplication of cells. In general, Schwann felt certain that he could say all tissues originate from cells.

But he knew this still would not be easily accepted. Nails, teeth, and bone derived from cells! Critics had always ridiculed the idea. To remove such doubts, Schwann decided that he would also have to trace such structures back to a cellular origin.

Schwann snipped a bit of nail from a finger of a newborn baby and divided it into longitudinal sections. The microscope showed that it was made up of layers of cells. Horny hoof tissue from the animal fetus also consisted entirely of "the most beautiful vegetable-like cells."

Feathers turned out to be another perfect example. It had always been maintained that they were "fibrous." To the naked eye they seemed to have nothing to do with the kind

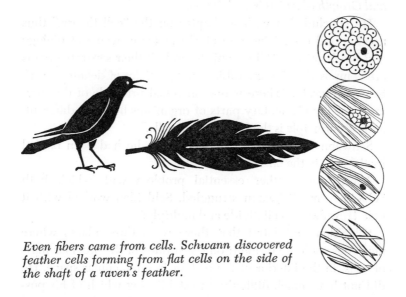

Even fibers came from cells. Schwann discovered feather cells forming from flat cells on the side of the shaft of a raven's feather.

of cell that had been seen under the microscope for well over half a century. Schwann showed that in fact feathers are formed from large flat epithelial cells from the cortex. Each one of them had a "fine" nucleus and two nucleoli. The verdict was conclusive here too—fibers came from cells.

Teeth had traditionally been classified as bone. But when Schwann examined the crown of a growing tooth under the microscope, he found it likewise composed entirely of cells.

It was the same with the muscular fibers and nerves.

Schwann could carry their generation back to cells, and could show that the nerves "bring every part of the body into connection with the central part of the nervous system by means of uninterrupted cells." It was true, then, that even the least cellular-looking parts of the body originated in cells.

This work was completed in a little less than a year, and Schwann was ready in 1839 to publish his soon to be famous *Microscopical Researches into the Accordance in the Structure and Growth of Animals and Plants.*

He concluded it with a chapter on the "cell theory," thus naming and organizing one of the major concepts of biology and biochemistry. "All organisms and all their separate organs are composed of innumerable small particles of definite form," Schwann wrote. "There is one universal principle of development for the elementary parts of organisms however different, and this principle is the formation of cells."

Schwann had come a long way since he had been baffled by the cells in the tails of frog larvae.

There was another essential problem with which both Schleiden and Schwann struggled. Schleiden worked with it first. How did the cell divide and multiply?

Schleiden postulated that there were three places where new cells could be formed: on the surface of the previous mass of cells, in the interior of the cell, or in intercellular space. He did not have much difficulty in establishing which of his possibilities was the true one. "I believe that I have demonstrated that in accordance with Nature, the entire growth of plants consists only of a formation of cells within cells," he said.

This was fine and true; time would unerringly verify it. Schleiden went wrong only when he tried to determine how the division occurred.

Schleiden held that the cell begins with a granulous mass, around which the nucleus forms as a sort of a coagulation. When the nucleus reaches its full growth, Schleiden said, a minute transparent vesicle arises on top of it, and this is the new cell. The botanist compared the new cell on the nucleus to a watch glass capping a watch.

Schwann more or less accepted this erroneous theory, or fancy, of his scientific colleague. Mitosis, or the process by which the cell divides to form two cells, was not to be discovered for many years. But Schleiden was not merely misinterpreting or failing to understand; he was inventing processes that did not occur.

Schleiden had mentioned his theory in a brief paper that he published in 1838, a year before Schwann brought out his book and reprinted Schleiden's essay at the end of it. Schleiden also emphasized that plants are built up of cells and that the embryo arises from a single cell, but his principal concern was with his theory of cell genesis, mistaken though it turned out to be.

Schleiden's error would soon be discovered and corrected, but his work and that of Schwann at last made the world aware of the cell. Perhaps their work only pulled together into a meaningful whole all the essential understandings that had been reached earlier by others; perhaps it only prompted a coalescing of knowledge. Certainly the world up to this time had not realized that the cell is the fundamental unit of living matter. Only after 1838 was it generally recognized that plants, animals, and men are compositions of cells, and that the life of the whole is a sum total of cellular life. It was an illuminating and heady concept, and one of the most fruitful ever opened to research. Men were on the way to understanding themselves.

In 1845 the Royal Society gave Schwann its highest honor, the Copley Medal. Two years later a translation of his work and Schleiden's was published in England by the Sydenham Society. In time, Schleiden and Schwann were cited in nearly all the textbooks as the founders of the cell theory. They were honored as the fathers of one of the most significant of all biological ideas, an idea that revolutionized a science.

The next hundred years proved and established the cell theory. Studying the tiny unit of life, science probed deeper into
the processes and structures that give life its form and substance and difference. By the 1930's it was clear that the cell
theory was one of the great concepts of all time, ranking, in
its total effect, only slightly behind the greatest achievements
of the nineteenth century, the laws of heredity and the theory
of evolution.

It seemed eminently fitting in 1938 that the hundredth anniversary of the cell theory should be observed with all of the
acclaim that science devotes to the centenaries of major scientific discoveries. The botanical, zoological, and historical
sections of the American Association for the Advancement of
Science joined to honor Schleiden and Schwann and to appraise the cell theory as it stood one hundred years after its
origin. The observance was called "The Cell, Its Past, Present,
and Future," and was arranged for the 1938 meeting of the
association at Richmond, Virginia. Authorities in the field
were invited to deliver addresses. Two of the most noted were
invited to speak on the honorees; Dr. John S. Karling was to
discuss the Schleiden-Schwann contribution to the cell theory,
and Dr. Edwin G. Conklin, the predecessors of Schleiden and
Schwann.

No centennial celebration ever went more thoroughly awry.

Professor Conklin began to speak. His first few words revealed to his startled audience that he had come not to praise
the men being honored, but in effect to bury their century-old
reputation.

"The cell theory in its fundamental features is older than
either Schleiden and Schwann," he began. "Their cell theory
was a special one and in important respects, an erroneous one.
There is no present biological interest in their theory and it
is amazing that we still continue to call it after them, as if they
were the sole inventors."

Conklin reviewed the work of Schleiden's and Schwann's

predecessors, Hooke, Grew, Lamarck, Brown, and others, and as he did so his outrage mounted. "So far from being the founder of the cell theory, it can truly be said that his [Schleiden's] contributions to this great theory were inferior to those of many of his predecessors. It is one of the amazing facts of scientific history that in many textbooks Schwann is called the founder of the cell theory, as if he had first discovered that all tissues of plants are composed of cells or that the cell is the universal unit of organic function as well as structure."

Conklin attributed every correct idea of Schleiden and Schwann to one of their predecessors, and flayed them not only for their errors but also for having failed to give the proper credit to earlier scientists. "I once heard a distinguished physiologist say that there are two ways to gain recognition: either brag or fight. It seems to me that Schleiden did both. I suggest that it would be more accurate as well as more becoming to strike out of our literature these personal possession tags attached to important discoveries."

Still more was to come. Karling assigned immortality and indispensability to the cell theory—"the cell concept is the concept of life, its origin, its nature, and its continuity"—and then joined Conklin in the angry attack on Schleiden and Schwann. To Karling it seemed paradoxical that "men who contributed little or nothing original" to the cell theory should have been regarded for a hundred years as its founders. The centennial, said Karling, in a reversal of the usual observance of such events, was an appropriate occasion to strip Schleiden and Schwann of the credit "erroneously" given to them.

Like Conklin, Karling reviewed the earlier work on the cell. In doing so, he readily admitted that there were gaps in the earlier insights, however brilliant they might have been. But he forgave them. Schleiden he held rigorously to account for every error and gave him only slight credit for insights that proved right.

Karling's indignation reached its peak when he came to Schleiden's error on cell formation. Fantastic! Completely erroneous! Scorn shot through Karling's words. Even Schleiden's errors were not his own. He had been too ignorant even to take the correct theories from others.

Karling also considered the possibility of banishing Schwann's name from the theory with which it had been associated for a hundred years. He decided, however, that Schwann's name should be retained although Schwann would have "to stand or fall with Schleiden because he accepted Schleiden's "false principle of cell formation." Karling's merciless summary held that the only contribution of Schleiden and Schwann was a wholly misleading one.

The audience listened stunned to this harsh destruction of the heroes it had come to honor. The secretary of the combined sections noted, with conspicuous understatement, that the session brought surprising results "bearing on Schleiden and Schwann, who up to then had generally been given most of the credit for the cell theory."

Both Karling and Conklin evidently had been influenced by a study of the development of the cell theory made some years before by John H. Gerould. Both followed Gerould very closely, although they disregarded his guidance when it came to the verdict.

Without any of the anger of Karling and Conklin, Gerould held that Schleiden "did good service" to science by emphasizing Brown's discovery of the nucleus of the cell and in stimulating his friend Schwann "in those important and epochmaking studies of the structure of animal cells that we have so long regarded as the foundations of the cell theory."

"Schwann," Gerould concluded, "added to the cell theory of Lamarck, Mirbel, and Dutrochet, guided by Brown's discovery of the nucleus, a clear-cut conception of the nature and limits of the individual animal cell. His elaborate speculative comparison between the origin and growth of cells was

founded on an erroneous belief as to the origin and development of new cells out of nucleoli but nevertheless contained
suggestions as to the nature of growth and foreshadowed some
of the more recent ideas of biochemistry and biophysics."

Few ideas in science spring pure and without debt from the
mind of any one man. The great discovery is more often a new
insight or synthesis or proof that illuminates much that has
gone before. Or it may be an explanation in terms that men
can understand and work with. Many centuries ago Aristotle
observed: "Each adds a little to our knowledge of Nature, and
from all the facts assembled arises grandeur."

This is particularly the story of the cell. Many contributed,
though Schleiden and Schwann brought the final realization
that the amazing processes going on in an infinite number of
little compartments determine the form and function of life.
Both have survived their centennial celebration, and their
names continue to be associated with one of the great achievements of their century—the cell theory. And, like all crucial
discoveries, it opened new ways to the understanding of life.

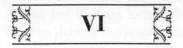

VI

PASTEUR:
LIFE IS A GERM

A CONTRADICTION in a scientific note caught the attention of young Louis Pasteur. He had not yet finished his scientific studies at the Ecole Normale Supérieure, but with growing excitement he read the note again and again.

Eilhardt Mitscherlich, the celebrated German chemist, was saying, as though there were nothing remarkable about it, that the crystals of tartaric and paratartaric acid differed in one important respect. How could that be? Pasteur half asked and half argued. Both crystals were products of the same wine-fermentation vaults, both had the same chemical composition, the same crystal shape, the same angles, the same specific gravity, the same double refraction. Therefore it was obvious to Pasteur that if a beam of light were passed through them, both should have affected it in the same way.

And yet Mitscherlich was calmly reporting that in a polarimeter, tartaric acid rotated a beam of light to the right, while paratartaric-acid crystals were optically inactive.[1] They produced no effect on the light beam.

Pasteur was an unknown, still in his twenties; Mitscherlich, a recognized authority, was discussing his own thorough studies. But Pasteur did not doubt that something was wrong with Mitscherlich's statements. If the two crystals were identical,

---

[1] Light, in passing through certain kinds of crystals or arrangements of crystals, is said to be "plane polarized." It cannot pass through a second set of crystals unless the second arrangement is in line with the first. The two sets of crystals transmit light when they are rotated into a parallel position and block it when they are not.

Natural materials rotate the plane of polarization of polarized light to either the right or the left. They are said to be optically active.

why should they affect polarized light differently? Pasteur decided immediately that there must be some undetected difference in the two and that he would find it.

For Pasteur, to see a problem meant to act. As soon as he had graduated, he began a study of the two materials. He began logically by examining the crystals themselves. He studied them not with the passing, accepting glance of most workers, but with a scrutiny that revealed their every property, and his thoroughness produced a surprising result. Pasteur detected what all others seemingly had missed: the crystals had small facets, similar to those of a crystal of quartz.

With a rush of emotion Pasteur realized tartaric acid must be asymmetrical—that it was right-handed, as a right glove is right-handed. And suppose that paratartaric acid was not asymmetrical. In that case, the latter would produce no optical effect. Pasteur hopefully thought he had discovered the difference that Mitcherlich and the other experts had overlooked.

Trembling with eagerness, he prepared the two crystals to test his newly formed postulate. The tartrate crystals were ready first. Pasteur placed them in his polarimeter and they turned the light to the right, the usual way. They were asymmetric, "right-handed," without doubt.

"I turned to examine the shape of the crystals of paratartrate," said Pasteur, "and for an instant my heart stopped beating: all the crystals also exhibited the facets of asymmetry."

Almost stunned by this discovery of handedness where he had not expected it, Pasteur unhappily bent over the confused mass of paratartrate crystals which lay before him. He began almost unthinkingly to pick out the right- and left-faceted crystals and to pile them in two separate little heaps. As he did so, another idea flashed through his agile mind.

He seized his flasks and made up an acid of the crystals in his "right" pile. As he ran a beam of light through the solution, it turned the light to the right, exactly as tartaric acid did.

Working surely but feverishly, Pasteur made up another solution of the left-faceted crystals and put it in his polarimeter. A triumph! It turned the beam of light "beautifully" to the left.

Pasteur could hardly restrain himself, although one more test had to be made. He mixed a solution containing equal weights of the "right" and "left" crystals. By all the tests, it was paratartaric acid, identical in every respect to all the known para-

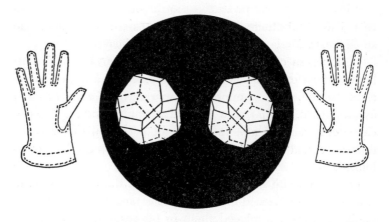

Right- and left-"handedness" in Nature. Pasteur separated crystals that were right-faceted, as a glove is right-handed, from left-faceted crystals, and thereby discovered a clue to the organization of Nature.

tartaric acid. Pasteur shone his light through it. And it was optically inactive!

The elated scientist rushed from his laboratory, colliding with one of his colleagues as he flung open the door. He threw his arms around him, shouting: "I have made a great discovery. I am so happy I am shaking all over. . . ."

The word spread with the normal speed of news. It was agreed by all that Pasteur's finding must be presented as soon as possible to the Academy of Sciences and that the Olympian

Jean Baptiste Biot was the man to make the presentation if he would consent to do so.

As a man who upheld the highest of standards in science, Biot would not even indirectly sponsor a report unless he was sure of its accuracy and value. The august, seventy-four-year-old scientist sent for the young man and directed him to repeat the experiment under his own eyes and under conditions that he would control.

When Pasteur arrived at the Biot laboratory in the Collège de France, Biot handed him a sample of paratartaric acid that he had previously analyzed and found inactive to polarized light. It produced no rotary effect. Pasteur prepared his solutions and set them to evaporate. When the crystals had separated, he returned for the critical experiment. Biot instructed him to pick out the right and left crystals and place them at his, Biot's, right and left. When this was done, Biot indicated with a gesture that he would do the rest himself. He prepared the solutions and, taking the most interesting one first, the left, put it into his apparatus. Even before he had made the complete reading he knew from the tint that there was a left orientation.

"The illustrious old man, who was visibly moved, seized me by the hand and said: 'My dear son, I love science so deeply this stirs my heart.'" Pasteur never forgot the moment or the words of the scientist he revered.

At twenty-seven Pasteur had made a discovery of outstanding importance and had won the recognition of the leading scientists of Europe.

The young scientist who had so phenomenally come to the fore had been born on December 27, 1822, in a little tannery squeezed in among the fading seventeenth-century palaces of Dôle.

A few years later his father, the tanner, settled his family in Arbois. Louis did so well in the school there that his masters insisted that he try, not for the local college, but for the "great Ecole Normale"—the Ecole Normale Supérieure founded by

Napoleon to train young men for professorships in science and letters. On his second try—he was not satisfied with his rank of fourteenth in the first examinations—Pasteur entered the famous school. The year was 1843. The young man with the fine head set so determinedly on strong shoulders was the most ardent and dedicated of students. After twelve hours of work each day in the classrooms and laboratories, his vigor was undiminished. He wanted to teach the physical sciences, but he dreamed too of the "lofty heights."

Soon after his remarkable crystal researches were announced, he was named assistant professor of chemistry at Strasbourg. He was devoting every minute to continued crystal research until he met Marie Laurent, daughter of the rector of the university. Pasteur would have believed it impossible that anything could divert him from his fascinating researches, but the thought of Marie did. He did not hesitate. He had his father make the proper and formal proposal of marriage to her father and then he put in a word for himself. His letter to her father was winningly modest: he was a young man of no property, whose only assets were "a good head, an honest heart, and my position at the university." They were married on May 29, 1849, and thereafter Pasteur had not only a devoted wife but also an unfailing aid in all the scientific undertakings and battles of his life.

Pasteur indeed had need of an understanding, co-operative wife, for he was soon back in his laboratory night and day. "I think," he wrote to a friend, "that I am on the verge of mysteries and that the veil that covers them is lifting more and more."

Behind his glittering little crystals from the distilleries Pasteur could glimpse a great and hitherto unrecognized principle of Nature. It was typical of him that he was formulating a bold hypothesis. The asymmetry, the rightness and leftness, that rotated a beam of light seemed to him a peculiar property not alone of the tartaric-acid crystals, but of life. His work correctly indicated that all organic materials, those produced by life processes, were always asymmetric; the inorganic, never.[2] Perhaps this was the true, the only sharply definable boundary between living and inert matter. Pasteur was beginning to probe into the structure of the cell and the structure of life.

His theories soared. This rightness and leftness of all natural things, he held, might be connected with the magnetic and solar forces acting upon the earth. "Life is dominated by asymmetrical action," he argued. "I can even imagine that all living species are primordially in their structure and in their external forms, functions of cosmic asymmetry."

No matter to what outermost limits his thoughts might reach, Pasteur never lost his solid grounding. Invariably he subjected his hypotheses to experiment. By experiment he would try to determine how the earth and its life had been shaped and molded. He devised a clockwork apparatus with which he hoped to reverse the direction in which solar rays fall upon plants. He was envisioning and trying to set up an artificial universe in which, in effect, the sun would rise in the west instead of the east, and living things would be subjected to a process the reverse of all that had ever been experienced before.

Pasteur felt that to reach the secret of life he would have to change the natural order within the cell. As he worked at this insuperable task, he saw that it would be necessary to start with the germ cell and modify the direction heredity had imparted to it. The cell, he pointed out, contained not only the "being" of life, but also its "becoming."

Mme Pasteur was one of the few who believed it all might be possible. She wrote to his father: "You know that the experiments he is undertaking this year will give us, if they succeed, a new Newton or a Galileo."

---

[2] Optical activity occurs only when an active product is transformed into another product without disturbing the asymmetric pattern, or when the matter is produced by a life process or by the presence of a catalyst that is itself the product of a life process.

The dream, the vision, was, of course, never to be realized. Neither did Pasteur ever wholly forget it, and it influenced his direction when other events drew him away from these wildly exalted speculations.

In 1854 Pasteur was offered the newly established chair of chemistry at Lille and an appointment as dean of the university. He was only thirty-two, an unheard-of age for assuming an academic post of such distinction.

Not long after his arrival at Lille, the father of one of his students came to consult him about the difficulties he was having with the fermentations at his distillery. It was expected that the faculty would co-operate with industry in the area, a policy wholly in accord with the views of Pasteur. Science, as Pasteur saw it, exists to make things better for people. Furthermore, Pasteur was interested; he had already started to think about fermentation.

While he had been experimenting with the crystals, he had tested some amyl alcohol, a by-product of the souring of milk, and had chanced upon another of those contradictions that he could not overlook. According to the leading chemists of the day, amyl alcohol was produced solely by the breaking down of sugar into lactic acid, a physical process that had nothing to do with life. Therefore the alcohol should not have been asymmetric.

But it was. Pasteur happily sensed another opportunity. He tested the amyl alcohol repeatedly, and each time it rotated the light of the polarimeter to the left. Pasteur was a man who faced facts as they were: if this optical activity could have been produced only in a life process, then he must assume that living organisms were involved in the fermentation. The fact that no living micro-organisms were known to participate in the process did not deter Pasteur in the least. He would discover them.

Pasteur spent days at the little distillery watching the fermentation of alcohol from the sugar beets raised around Lille.

He dipped into the vats that had spoiled and pulled up samples of the slimy gray mess that had collected in their depths. He also took samples from the healthy foaming vats.

Pasteur had only a small microscope, but he slipped a drop of the healthy brew under it. The liquid was swarming with minute globular organisms—yeasts—growing, increasing almost as he watched. He immediately jumped to the conclusion: these were the organisms responsible for the bubbling fermentation. Fermentation, then, was a living process. So he had been on the right track when he argued that amyl alcohol was produced by living organisms.

Pasteur hurried to take a look at some of the gray sludge he had collected from the sick vats. No yeasts here, but there was something else, something that he had never seen before. The drop under his microscope was filled with a moving squirming mass of little rods. Some of them moved along in strings, like a row of barges. Some of them shimmied on one spot. Pasteur scarcely could tear himself away from the sight even to eat or sleep. As he pressed on with his studies he found that the liquid from the sick vats always contained the acid of sour milk—and no alcohol. And then another of his brilliant ideas flashed through Pasteur's mind: the little rods were the organisms that produce sour milk and by getting into the wrong place they had ruined the production of alcohol from the beet juice. No one, however, had ever suggested that living organisms might be necessary to sour milk.

Pasteur knew that if he made such a report, he would run into a major scientific battle. He would have to refute Liebig and the other leading chemists of his day, and, more than this, run counter to the whole trend of his century.

Through the seventeenth and eighteenth centuries a brilliant succession of scientists—Lavoisier, Wohler, Liebig, and many others—had fought to banish the ancient belief that a mysterious "vital force" was the explanation of all natural things. Lavoisier had demonstrated that breathing was a combustion, not a vitalistic process, and Wohler had made urea, a product of the body, from simple chemicals. No mystic intervention was necessary. On the same scientific grounds, Liebig argued that only chemical action was necessary to convert beet juice into alcohol or sweet milk into sour or a pasty dough into a light palatable bread.

Liebig, of course, was not denying the presence of the yeast organisms that Leeuwenhoek had first seen and that Cagniard de la Tour had later recognized as living. He did insist that if they figured in fermentation, it was only as the producers of some substance that brought about the decomposition of sugar. Liebig could summon impressive experimental evidence to his support. He and Wohler in their work with the oil of bitter almonds had shown that amygdalin could be converted into an insoluble oil by means of a nitrogenous substance present in the skin of almonds. No living organism was necessary to accomplish this decomposition.

It had been a hard-won victory, a victory of science over shackling superstition and ignorance. If Pasteur should establish that fermentation was brought about by living organisms rather than by chemical action, it would seem a retreat to an earlier and long-disproved vitalism.

None of this stopped Pasteur. His observations and his instincts convinced him that living organisms and only living organisms could produce fermentation. It was therefore his sacred obligation to see this truth prevail. Pasteur was naturally combative and as skillful a fighter as a scientist.

Since Liebig had conceded that yeast, a living organism, might produce the substance that made sugar ferment, that battle, Pasteur considered, was half won. No one, however, had conceded that living organisms were necessary to convert sugar into lactic acid. If Pasteur could attack and destroy this citadel, the whole chemical cause would be undermined. This was exactly what he chose to do.

First of all, he would have to prove beyond even the ability of Liebig to question that the little rods were alive. But how, how could he demonstrate it? It quickly occurred to him that the unanswerable way would be to remove the rods from their natural environment and grow them independently in some new medium.

The English scientist John Tyndall compared Pasteur's problem to that of a gardener presented with a handful of granular stuff, part of it thought to be seeds, and asked what it was. He would find out by planting it. If in due time he obtained a fine crop of thistles in a bed where none had ever grown before and if he repeated the same planting fifty times and the same thistles always came up, he would be quite sure that the unknown granular material had contained at least some thistle seeds. The gardener in Tyndall's illustration would have known, however, how to plant and cultivate his unknown seeds. Pasteur had to invent microbe gardening. No one else had ever tried to raise the tiny, invisible rods, and there was no manual on how to plant and nourish them.

Pasteur first put some of the rods in a pure sugar solution. Nothing happened. They didn't grow. Perhaps they needed a richer "soil." Pasteur prepared some yeast water, put in sugar, and added a bit of chalk to keep the broth from being acid. He sprinkled this well-prepared "ground" with some of the fuzzy gray stuff from the sick vats and placed it in a good warm place to incubate. The next morning he rushed in early to see if anything had happened. The stuff in his flask was still clear. Pasteur hovered over it anxiously, and by afternoon, as he held it up to the light, he saw bubbles rising from the gray specks. A lively fermentation had begun.

Pasteur examined a drop of his ferment. It was filled with uncountable numbers of the little rods. And a drop of this material set off new fermentations.

It was not even necessary to sow the rods to get a fermentation. Pasteur had only to make up some of the "soup" of yeast, sugar, and chalk and let it stand uncovered. The next day a good lactic fermentation would be going, although a number of other organisms might also be flourishing in the rich liquid. The result, Pasteur pointed out, was similar to what you would obtain if you prepared and fertilized a plot of ground and then left it open to the chance seeding of wind and rain. Dozens of plants would spring up, and the strongest would survive. It was the same with the unseeded broth. "It soon becomes crowded with various plants and insects that are mutually harmful," said Pasteur. But plant a lactic ferment and you would reap only lactic organisms.

Pasteur hurried to tell Monsieur Bigo, the father of his student, that he had only to prevent other ferments from falling into his vats and he would have no more spoilage. He also lectured, he wrote the good news to friends, and he submitted a scholarly paper to the academy, his *Mémoire sur la fermentation appelée lactique.* Pasteur never suppressed his joy in success.

"Fermentation," said Pasteur, "is correlative with life." And yet, he admitted, the point was not "irrefutably demonstrated."

He had given science the method that would thereafter be used for microbiological research, he had shown that a specific micro-organism grown in a clear bouillon produces its own kind, and he had indicated that a tiny amount of a specific organism could ferment a disproportionate amount of material. But the big battle over life and fermentation still was in doubt.

Liebig was not overwhelmed. Yeast might be a microscopic plant, but, he repeated, it did not produce fermentation as a living agent. It acted only by liberating albuminoid (protein) materials capable of breaking down sugar into alcohol and carbon dioxide.

In the midst of all this excitement Pasteur was appointed administrator of his former school, the famed Ecole Normale, and director of its scientific studies. In the fall of 1857, only three years after arriving at Lille, the Pasteurs went on to Paris.

For all of its reputation, the *école* had no laboratory for its new scientific director. All Pasteur could find was a little hole-in-the-wall in a garret. Nevertheless, he got rid of the rats and moved in his flasks and test tubes, determined to lose no time in pushing ahead with his fermentation work.

To prove that he was right and Liebig wrong, Pasteur would have to demonstrate that it was not the presence of albuminoid materials which brought about fermentation. He would grow yeast in a liquid that had no such materials in it at all. But this was not so easily done. Pasteur struggled with one solution after another until one day he happened to notice that some ammonia salt that he had added to one batch of broth kept disappearing. Perhaps the yeasts were consuming it. Pasteur seized upon this lead. He poured distilled water and some pure sugar into a flask, added ammonia salt, and dropped in a bit of yeast.

Again there was an agonizing overnight wait. In the morning, without stopping for breakfast, Pasteur rushed to his laboratory and lifted his flask. It was fermenting. The bubbles were slowly rising, and the microscope confirmed what he saw. Alcohol had been produced. But this was the critical experiment, and Pasteur had to be certain. He spent weeks doing it over and over again. He endlessly transferred drops of the ferment from one flask to another to make certain that they would go on making alcohol. Each time the yeasts multiplied vigorously. They grew even more lustily and the fermentation was more rapid when he used young and vigorous strains.

"One cannot exaggerate the importance of these studies for the evolution of the biochemical science," said René J. Dubos, author of *Louis Pasteur: Free Lance of Science*, and himself a noted scientist. "As early as 1860 Pasteur himself pointed out that the findings made in his laboratory would permit physiologists to attack the fundamental chemical problems of life.

"The bodies of plants and animals consist of an immense number of cells, whereas in micro-organisms the living agent is reduced to the single cell level. By studying the microbila physiology therefore, it became possible to analyze the chemical phenomena which determine the function of the individual cell—the fundamental unit of life—be it that of a plant, a micro-organism, an animal, or even a man."

Pasteur was certain now. He was satisfied that his data were irrefutable, and he dropped his previous hesitancy. He turned his self-appointed task, that of convincing the world that fermentation could not occur without life, into a crusade. He made speeches and wrote papers, many of them directly challenging Liebig and those who stood with him.

Most of his colleagues were convinced. The Academy of Sciences awarded him its prize for physiology, and Jean-Baptiste Dumas—the admired Dumas, whose lectures had often brought tears to Pasteur's eyes—praised him at a meeting the next night. To great applause, Dumas called Pasteur one of the most distinguished professors of France. Pasteur described the heady scene in a letter to his father.

But still there were difficulties. Occasionally when he sowed some of the lactic rods he obtained not the sour-milk acid that he expected, but a spoiled mixture reeking with the smell of rancid butter. Pasteur spread a drop of the evil-smelling stuff on one of his slides. As he watched, he suddenly saw a little eel-like organism wriggle out from among the few half-lifeless rods and push them aside. Sometimes a number of the undulating organisms would join together and wind sinuously along. Pasteur tried in every way to suppress them; he felt, he said, that it was his duty to prevent the appearance of the little animals for fear they might be feeding on the microscopic plants that he supposed were causing the rancid ferment.

"Finally," he said, "I was struck by the coincidence which my analyses revealed between the infusoria [the eel-like animals] and the production of this acid."

It looked as though this were another fermentation produced by a living organism, but this time by an animal rather than a plant. The little animals were puzzling, though perhaps there were more kinds than one. He eagerly went on studying them. Pasteur, who saw everything, noticed one day that on the edges of his slides the little animals became inert and motionless. He turned his microscope back to the center of the drop. There they were writhing with their customary vigor. Was it possible that the air killed them? Pasteur asked incredulously. Were they congregating in the middle of the drop to get away from the air?

Pasteur had to know, he had to find out, for if this were true he would be on the verge of another momentous discovery— the discovery of a new kind of life, one not dependent on oxygen, as all life was thought to be, but actually averse to it. Lavoisier, a scientist Pasteur revered and studied closely, had established as a law that oxygen was essential to life. Pasteur was not aware that anyone since had called this principle into question. He did not know that Leeuwenhoek and Spallanzani had seen, although they had not understood, the same peculiar flight from oxygen.

When the stakes were so large, every test had to be made. Pasteur passed a current of air through a flask in which a butyric-acid fermentation was going on. Promptly the ferment was slowed or arrested. It looked again as though the wriggling little animals could not stand oxygen.

But could this be true? There was always some oxygen in liquids, and air pressed on the surface of any uncovered liquid containing the animals. Pasteur had appropriately named them vibrios. If they were killed by oxygen, how did they survive under the double exposure? Pasteur soon had the answer. The liquids also contained oxygen-breathing organisms. The latter soon used up all the oxygen in any liquid and then either settled down dead to the bottom or made their way to the surface where they could get the life-giving air. Pasteur found their remains on the bottom of his flasks. Those which reached the surface multiplied and flourished so vigorously that they formed a scum there. The expedient kept them alive and it shut oxygen away from the liquid below as effectively as though they were a sheet of glass. With the oxygen of the liquid removed and with new supplies shut out by the surface film, the oxygen haters had the airless environment they needed to survive.

It all fitted together perfectly, and yet it was startling to think of announcing that a new kind of life existed upon the earth. Pasteur decided to ask Dumas, Claude Bernard, and Antoine Balard to look over his experiments and vouch for their accuracy. "In the event the tests which I repeat before your eyes are absolutely satisfactory," he said to them, "I shall ask you to present my results to the academy."

Pasteur's demonstrations seemed flawless. But the three deeply interested observers raised a question: suppose the vessels and tubes used in the experiments contained enough oxygen to nourish the vibrios?

"If the oxygen of the air kills the butyric-acid organisms," said Pasteur, "that would be counterproof." He ran some oxygen through a flask. It killed the vibrios and dramatically underlined his point. "I believe," said Pasteur, "that my conclusions are unassailable. The butyric-acid ferment does not need oxygen for life. On the contrary, oxygen destroys it."

Pasteur proposed the name "aerobic" for life dependent on oxygen, and "anaerobic" for the newly discovered species that flourished without it.

The rank odors that rose from the butyric fermentations and their behavior closely resembled the odors and process of putrefaction. Pasteur had at first tried the ferment only with sugar and the lactate of lime. He now tested it with other matter. He made up a beef bouillon and solutions of meat macerated in water, and inoculated them with a few drops of the ferment. Soon a film had formed on the surface and nauseous odors were being given off.

Quite evidently putrefaction was only another fermentation

and there was an immediate connection between oxygen-hating microbes and decay. But this was a major problem, and investigating it would take time. Not until several years later could Pasteur find time for a full-scale effort.

Pasteur could grow vibrios with as much precision as a gardener grows roses. But he started with existing vibrios. He could not go much further unless he faced the question: where did the vibrios and the other organisms come from? Did they arise from other germs or were they created spontaneously from other material, perhaps from dead organic stuff? The problem was one of the most ancient of them all.

Aristotle had written: "Every dry body which becomes moist and every humid body which dries up breeds life." Vergil had carried the thesis a little further. Bees, he said, were bred in the putrefying entrails of a young bull. Helmont was even more sweeping: "The emanations arising from the bottom of marshes bring forth frogs, snails, leeches, herbs, and a good many other things." It was also Helmont who devised the recipe for creating mice: Take a dirty shirt and a few grains of corn. Place them in a pot and permit them to sit for twenty-one days. A lively crop of mice will be produced.

The Italian naturalist Francesco Redi cast the first general doubt on these old and honored theories. He did it by a simple experiment. To demonstrate that worms did not arise from meat, he placed a piece of net over a tray of meat. The flies, unable to get through, laid their eggs on the net. Soon the net, and not the meat, was crawling with maggots.

The old belief in spontaneous generation might not have survived this devastating experiment if it had not been for Leeuwenhoek. The multitude of tiny organisms the Dutch lens maker saw and described certainly seemed to arise spontaneously. How, otherwise, could they suddenly appear from nowhere when the grapes were ripe or someone left a bowl of milk sitting in the kitchen overnight?

The controversial questions first came to a head in the middle of the eighteenth century. In Ireland, John Needham, a Roman Catholic priest, announced that he had settled the ancient issue. He filled a flask with an "organic infusion," sealed it tight, and buried it in hot cinders. The heat, he pointed out, would kill all organisms present when the bottle was sealed. Not long after, Needham removed the flask from the cinders; it was teeming with animalcules. What more certain proof could there be that the organisms had been created spontaneously and that religion was upheld?

Needham's triumph was challenged, however, by another churchman, the Abbé Lazzaro Spallanzani of Italy. Spallanzani prepared a flask exactly as Needham had, but, instead of burying it in hot cinders, he boiled it for an hour. No animalcules whatsoever appeared in it, and the Italian scientist pointed out that his Irish confrere had simply not heated his flask hot enough to kill the organisms he had put into it. Needham was not in the least impressed. He accused Spallanzani of torturing his organic infusions, "of enfeebling or even annihilating their Vegetative Force." Spallanzani's prolonged heating had made it impossible for living creatures to generate, said Needham.

Other investigators showed that no animalcules would appear even in open flasks if the air entering them was first heated, or passed through sulphuric acid, or even filtered through cotton.

All the uncertainty and dispute boiled up again in 1858. In that year Félix Archimède Pouchet presented a paper before the French academy, reporting once again that the spontaneous-generation question was settled.

"When by meditation it became evident to me that spontaneous generation was one of the means employed by Nature for the reproduction of living things, I applied myself to discover the method by which this takes place," said Pouchet, without troubling himself about this reversal of the scientific approach. He hermetically sealed a flask of boiled water and turned it upside down in a basin of mercury. When the water was cold, he opened the flask under the mercury and introduced some oxygen and a small quantity of hay infusion that had been exposed to high temperatures. Pouchet believed that he had taken every conceivable precaution to avoid introducing living organisms into the flask—the water had been boiled, the flask was shielded from any chance entrance of air, and the hay infusion had been heated to kill its organisms. And yet within a few days Pouchet's flasks teemed with organisms. Pouchet, the respected director of the Museum of Natural History at Rouen, had produced spontaneous generation under his eye and at will.

His experiments, he told the academy, demonstrated that "animals and plants could be generated in a medium absolutely free from atmospheric air and in which therefore no germ of organic bodies could have been brought by air."

Pasteur read this with outrage. He seized his pencil and savagely underlined all the offending and questionable passages. Everything that Pasteur had done indicated that countless germs and their seeds were borne in the air: they were the motes dancing in a beam of sunlight. He could not ignore this challenge from Pouchet. "I had to form a definite opinion on the question of spontaneous generation," he explained. "These investigations are an inevitable side path of my studies of fermentations."

The difficulties nevertheless were enormous, as a hundred years and more of work testified. His friends Biot and Dumas pleaded with him not to risk his time "in such a presumptuous adventure."

Pasteur could not be stopped; his mind was made up. Near the doorkeeper's lodge at the *école* a small pavilion had been built for the architect and clerk. Pasteur wangled possession of it and converted it into a laboratory for his new crusade. The only place he could find for his drying oven was under the stairs, and to get to it he had to crawl in on his hands and knees. But for the first time he was given an assistant, and no inconvenience mattered. Pasteur was ready to study atmospheric air. His first problem was to control it.

Pasteur was convinced that the yeasts and vibrios and other organisms were carried by the air. It was clearly the air that had to be controlled. He filled flasks with sugar water and impregnated them with various infusions. He then boiled them to kill the living organisms and to drive off the air. The air was expelled through a red-hot tube. When the flasks had cooled, air could re-enter only by passing through the heated tube. Everything organic that it carried was killed by this passage. The neck of the tube was then closed by fusing. Pasteur now had an infusion in contact with oxygen, but with an oxygen devoid of everything living or organic. Despite the presence of the oxygen, which many had maintained was the essential material for spontaneous generation, no life generated in these flasks.

The careful demonstration was completed by introducing some microbes. Pasteur first collected a good supply by passing a current of air through a piece of cotton. It had long ago been shown that cotton filters out the micro-organisms of the air and holds them trapped in its tangled fibers. Pasteur first placed a piece of the life-laden cotton in the neck of his flask. Nothing happened. The liquid remained entirely clear. At the end of fifteen days—certainly time enough to show that the liquid would continue unaffected—Pasteur tilted the flask so that the bit of cotton and its germs fell into the liquid. In twenty-four hours the fluid was clouded, and waving filaments grew out of the cotton. At the end of forty-eight hours the liquid swarmed with millions of organisms.

Only when life was introduced did life appear in the flasks. The experiment was a dramatic and irreproachable one, and yet the advocates of spontaneous generation did not yield.

"By heating the air you destroy the very elements prerequisite to life," they protested.

Pasteur saw that he would have to devise some way of getting unheated "natural" air into the flasks and yet keep out the microbes. He was struggling with the problem when one day Antoine Balard dropped into the laboratory to see what was under way. Balard was a brilliant if somewhat lazy experimentalist. Instead of slaving away in his own laboratory, he delighted in watching others work, and would often reward his hosts with a suggestion that exactly solved some troublesome problem. This and his admiring enthusiasm made him a welcome visitor.

Balard watched Pasteur trying to get germ-free unheated air into his flasks. Why, he asked, don't you draw the neck of the flask out into an S curve—a swan's-neck curve? He sketched the tube. Moisture would collect in the bottom of the S and trap all entering organisms; once trapped, they could not very well fall upward into the broth. It was an inspired idea.

The swan's-neck flasks were quickly made. Pasteur filled them with the broths and boiled them, leaving the drawn-out neck open. Just as Balard had suggested, when the air began re-entering—unheated air—the microbes that it bore were trapped in the S curve. And they stayed there. The fluids in the flasks remained clear for months.

But shake the flask so that a little of its contents splashed up into the germ-laden neck, and let the liquid run back. The flask soon was cloudy and bubbly with growing micro-organisms. Or break the S neck off and permit the natural air to rush in without having to pass through a long twisty tube. Again the flask was soon swarming with microbes.

It was at last the unimpeachable demonstration. "Never will the doctrine of spontaneous generation recover from the mortal blow that this simple experiment has dealt it," Pasteur proclaimed at a crowded, applauding meeting of the Academy of Sciences.

The point had to be conceded. The air carried the germs; they did not arise spontaneously. And yet how could the air carry such a multitude of germs? Joseph Louis Gay-Lussac in

one famous experiment had shown that the must of grapes
begins to ferment as soon as it comes in contact with a few
bubbles of external air. Assuming that this was true, how could
each bubble of air contain organisms enough to ferment any
grape juice anywhere in the world or sour any bowl of milk?
If the air were so populated, Pouchet said, it would be as
"dense as iron." Pasteur answered that he was sure not all air
was equally laden with germs. He suspected that the air in
cities, where there was much stirring around and movement,

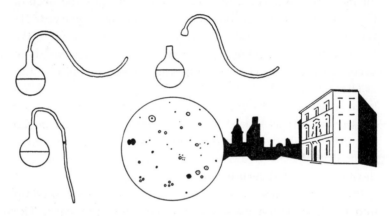

*Swan's-neck flasks and dust proved in the skilled hands of Pasteur
that all living things have parents and do not spring into being
spontaneously.* RIGHT: *The Ecole Normale Supérieure, at which
Pasteur did his work.*

was more contaminated than in the country. He would prove
it. "What will be the outcome of this giants' struggle?" asked
the *Moniteur scientifique* in April 1860.

Pasteur and his devoted assistants went to work feverishly
making flasks, this time with straight drawn-out necks, for a
great and definitive experiment. Pasteur was going to collect
air in a number of places and latitudes to prove his point.

The flasks were filled with yeast water and boiled until all the air had been driven out. At that moment the glass necks were melted with a torch and sealed. When cooled, the flasks were virtually empty of air.

On August 14, 1860, Pasteur took an armload of flasks to the courtyard of the Paris Observatory. One by one he held them high above his head—to keep them away from the dust of his clothes—and broke the necks with pincers that had just been passed through the flame of an alcohol lamp. As the glass cracked, the air rushed in with a hiss, bringing with it all the dusts carried in suspension and all the associated germs. Another lot of flasks was opened in the deep cellars of the observatory.

Pasteur put all of the resealed flasks in his oven under the stairs. The next day he crawled in a dozen times to see what was happening. Nine out of ten of the flasks opened in the clear, calm air of the cellar were transparently clear. All of the flasks broken in the dusty courtyard were alive with organisms, Pasteur happily recorded in his little laboratory notebook.

Country tests were next on his schedule. Loaded down with seventy-three of the glass flasks, Pasteur went to his old home at Arbois in the Jura Mountains. Out in a green field, well removed from any houses, he cracked open the necks of twenty flasks. Only eight became contaminated.

Pasteur was then eager to charter a balloon to test the air at higher altitudes, but was persuaded that it would be easier, if not better, to seek the heights in the mountains.

He first climbed Mount Poupet, and at an elevation of 2,760 feet opened another twenty flasks. Only five developed organic life. Delighted with this evidence that his reasoning was correct and that the air was cleaner at greater altitudes, he went on to the Alps. At Chamonix he engaged guides for a climb to the ice fields 6,500 feet up Mont Blanc. The glare of the glacier's snow was blinding, and when Pasteur lifted the flasks high above his head for the prescribed ritual of breaking, he could not see the flame for resealing them. Only by holding the lamp close to him could he manage the experiment, and that would have ruined it. Pasteur could not permit such a lapse in technique. The only solution was to remain overnight and return to the glacier before sunrise. In the half-darkness it would be possible to see the flame. Early the next day Pasteur opened and correctly sealed another twenty of the test flasks. Only one altered; all the others remained sterile.

"The higher and clearer the air, the less the dust and the fewer the microbes," Pasteur told the academy in his report on his journeys. "It seems to me that it can be affirmed that the dusts suspended in atmospheric air are the exclusive origin and the necessary condition of life in infusions."

In all the excitement over spontaneous generation, few noticed another comment: "What would be most desirable would be to push these studies far enough to prepare the road for serious research into the origin of various diseases."

Pouchet was stubborn in his conviction and refused to yield to these findings, certainly not without verifying them. He and his assistants set out upon flask-laden travels of their own. Many of the scientific bets were on Pouchet's success. "I'm afraid that the experiments you quote, M. Pasteur, will turn against you," said a writer in *La Presse*. "The world into which you wish to take us is really too fantastic. . . ."

Not to be outdone by Pasteur, the Pouchet party lugged its flasks not to a mere 6,500 feet, but to the glacier of La Maladetta at an elevation of 10,850 feet. In a deep, icy crevasse they opened them with all of the precautions prescribed by Pasteur. Their flasks, however, had been filled not with a yeast solution but with a hay infusion, and heated to the usual 212° F. And then came the vindication Pouchet had hoped for. All of the flasks revealed the development of living germs.

"The production of a new being devoid of parents, is . . . a reality," Pouchet proclaimed.

The heated travelogue debate, with its religious as well as

scientific implications, had all of France taking sides. Charges were hurled back and forth. Clergy, scientists, and officials issued statements and voiced opinions. Both sides demanded the appointment of a commission to review all the experiments and determine where the truth might lie. The Academy of Sciences was pleased to name the suggested commission. It would have gone into immediate action if Pouchet had not requested a delay.

In the meanwhile, Pasteur was invited to speak on spontaneous generation at one of the new scientific evenings the Sorbonne was presenting. On the night of April 7, 1864, the large lecture room was jammed to the last bit of standing room. Scattered among the scientists were such celebrities as Alexandre Dumas *père*, George Sand, the Princesse Mathilde, and other fashionables who had succeeded in wedging themselves in.

Quietly and almost reflectively, Pasteur invited them to face with him the great question: can living beings come into the world without having been preceded by beings similar to themselves?

The audience had just settled down to concentrate on this intriguing and philosophical query when a single beam of light shot electrifyingly through the dark. It pierced the room.

"Observe the thousands of dancing motes of dust," Pasteur commanded.

Before the eyes of his enthralled and startled company, Pasteur displayed one of the swan's-neck tubes that he had prepared four years before. Air bearing the kind of dust and germs that they had just seen teeming in the beam of light had been free to enter it, but all had been trapped by the moisture in the S curve. Behold, the liquid was limpid and transparent; no germs whatsoever grew in it.

"And therefore, gentlemen," sad Pasteur, pointing again to the swan's-neck flask, "I could say to you I have taken my drop of water from the immensity of creation, and I have taken it full of the elements appropriate to the development of inferior beings. And I wait, I watch, I question it—begging it to recommence for me the beautiful spectacle of the first creation. But it is dumb, dumb since these experiments were begun several years ago; it is dumb because I have kept from it the only thing man does not know how to produce; from the germs which float in the air, from Life, for Life is a germ and a germ is Life. Never will the doctrine of spontaneous generation recover from the mortal blow of this simple experiment."

Tumultuous applause.

"No," Pasteur concluded, "there is now no circumstance known in which it can be affirmed that microscopic beings come into the world without germs, without parents similar to themselves. Those who affirm it have been duped by illusion, blighted by errors that they either did not perceive or know how to avoid."

The evening was a triumph, and in complete confidence Pasteur pressed for action by the commission. Pouchet, for his part, weakened and backed out. The defection of his opponent did not halt Pasteur. He arrived before the commission with vans of his laboratory equipment and gave an overpowering demonstration of his experiments. The commission completely upheld him. Although it had not seen the Pouchet demonstration, it announced that the Pasteur proofs were of the most perfect exactitude.

Had Pouchet repeated his experiments before the commission, the outcome might have been different. It was later proved that if boiled flasks of hay decoction were opened anywhere in the world, they became filled with living organisms. Some years later research was to reveal the reason.

It was not that organisms spring into life in the hay infusion any more than in the yeast water, but that they had been there and had not been destroyed by ordinary boiling. While the flask remained sealed, they remained inert. When it was opened and oxygen entered, they developed rapidly. Pouchet had been entirely right about what happened, though wrong about why it happened. When some years later Pasteur learned and correctly interpreted the truth, he designed the autoclave and oven that have been used ever since to sterilize liquids and solids. "One sometimes reaches the truth by error and sometimes error by the truth," said Emile Duclaux.

Pasteur was anxious to get back to his work on fermentations; they could lead on to new understandings of the chemical processes of life. Besides, the wine industry of France, one of the props of the economy, was in trouble, and Pasteur believed fervently that it was the obligation of science to serve France and all that was important to her. "Pure science," said Pasteur, "cannot advance one step without sooner or later bringing profit to industry from the application of its precious results. No, a thousand times no, there is no category of science which can be called applied science."

Pasteur devoted several years to studying the making of wine and vinegar. In a brilliant original series of researches he taught the French wine makers how to kill the "diseases" of wine by quickly heating—pasteurizing—their wines. He saved them millions of francs. Then at the call of his friend Dumas he hurried off to the south of France to "save" the French silk industry. Again by prodigious industry in a field that was new to him—biology—he showed the silk raisers how to use biological controls to overcome the parasites that were ruining their worms. His labors were constant and wearing.

In the fall of 1868 Pasteur returned to the Ecole Normale. He was on his way to the school on the morning of October 19 when he felt a tingling in his left side. He went ahead with his work, but before the day was over he suffered a paralysis of the left side. For almost a week his life was despaired of.

Suddenly, however, he made a turn for the better. His speech cleared and he began to dictate an outline on silkworm diseases. It was definitely the turning point, the beginning of a slow recovery that left his left hand and side disabled, but did not in the least reduce his vigor or ardor.

This personal misfortune was soon followed by disaster for his beloved country. In 1870 Germany attacked, and France crumbled before the onslaught. A few months later, as the Germans besieged Paris, even the Museum of Natural History was bombarded. Pasteur, unable to serve in the armies, had fled to Arbois. As the war drew toward its close he and his wife could no longer endure their anxiety about their son, who was fighting with Bourbaki's army. Ill though Pasteur was, they set out on a grueling trip to search for the young corporal. Their relief was unlimited when they found him uninjured, though ill. Pasteur's grief at the fate of his country gave way to resolution and a stimulating anger. As the war ended he wrote to his friend and collaborator Duclaux: "My head is brimming with splendid ideas. The war has sent my brain to pasture. I am ready for new projects. . . . Poor France, my beloved country, could I only help to restore thee from thy disaster."

With Paris still too disturbed for work, Pasteur went to Clermont Ferrand to be with Duclaux, then professor of chemistry on the faculty of medical sciences there. Pasteur was dreaming of a great research institute in which a corps of dedicated scientists "would transform the world" by their discoveries. But that seemed far away. In the meantime if he could only help France . . .

Almost casually, Pasteur worked in Duclaux's laboratory on his old studies of fermentation and occasionally watched the practical application of the principles in a brewery in the nearby town of Chamalières.

And then Pasteur thought of a way in which he could make his researches serve his country. It was so much less than the transformation of the world as to seem almost ludicrous—he would discover a way to make French beer superior to the German and thus free his country from any necessity for importing the German brew. This loftily patriotic scientific investigation centering around plebeian beer was to lead him to his greatest penetration into the chemical processes of life.

Pasteur's problem was to prevent the spoiling of beer and to improve its flavor. He very shortly found this principally a matter of protecting it from the chance micro-organisms that turned it putrid or distasteful. But Pasteur found it difficult to hold himself to his chosen problem. For one thing, he did not particularly like beer and could not detect the nuances of taste that delighted the connoisseur.

"At every instant his thoughts and his actions got away from him without his being conscious of it," explained Duclaux, who was frequently working beside him.

And so it came about that while supposedly studying beer he devoted the greater part of his time to profound questions concerning the transformation of species, the origin of yeasts, and the large theoretical problems of the cell and life.

Pasteur had already proved that when he sowed a particular kind of yeast and excluded all others, he reaped that kind and no other. Vibrios produced only vibrios, exactly as cats gave birth only to cats and human beings to others of their species. And yet the principle was not irrefutably established. It was not certain that it applied to all the myriad of invisible organisms that filled the air and ground, and if one exception existed, the whole concept had to stand in doubt.

Certain organisms seemed to transform themselves into yeasts when they were submerged in sugar or other solutions. The little vinegar fungus—Mycoderma aceti—was one. Pasteur, the man who had fought for the specificity of all organisms, conceded that when it could not get air it changed into a yeast—it changed its species. At least it could produce alcohol from sugar as true yeasts did. To many this transformation appeared a remarkable case of the mutability of species for which Charles Darwin had argued in the *Origin of Species*, published a few years earlier, in 1859. If species were mutable, if they had not remained constant and unaltered since a day of creation, here was a fine example of a species change occurring almost before one's eyes.

As he worked on beer at Clermont, Pasteur decided to repeat the Mycoderma experiment. He scattered some of the fungus in small china saucers of sweetened wine and beer wort. The Mycoderma flourished on the surface, freely using the oxygen of the air to "regenerate itself and create new materials." The usual film, or mother of vinegar, formed. Pasteur submerged the film in the liquid and poured the whole mixture into a flask from which all air was excluded. Would the sudden loss of oxygen asphyxiate the Mycoderma? Would it die like any animal deprived of air? It was very rapidly clear that it definitely would not. Life continued in the submerged cells. They multiplied slowly and did not live long, it was true, but in their brief under-the-surface life span they produced alcoholic fermentation. The Mycoderma had evidently changed species; it had turned into a yeast, an alcohol-producing yeast.

"The Mycoderma, originally an aerobia—that is, a being requiring air for life and development—became after being submerged, an anaerobia, a creature which can live without air," said Pasteur. It was a little as though an animal, upon being tossed into the water, had changed into a fish, or at least behaved like a fish.

Pasteur was reluctantly convinced. Duclaux felt that under the circumstances he should assume the role of objective critic. He refused to accept the experiment as an abrupt change of species, although at times it worked so well that he hardly dared to open his mouth. Nevertheless Duclaux persisted. Perhaps the fermentation was produced by globules of yeast that had entered the air or water in the flask. Pasteur dismissed the suggestion; did he not always take all possible precautions?

It sometimes happened, though, that among the cells of Mycoderma in the bottom of the flasks the two scientists discovered some of the large spherical cells of Mucor mucedo, a mold commonly occurring in horse manure. This gave Pasteur pause.

"Since Mucor mucedo is present, although I had sown only Mycoderma vini, it must be, I said to myself, that one or several spores of this Mucor must have been introduced by the ambient air. Now if the air brings the spores of Mucor into my operation, why should it not bring the cells of yeast, particularly in my laboratory?"

Pasteur meticulously modified his procedures to suppress any possibility of yeast or germ cells falling into his mixtures. And there was then no fermentation.

"Never again did I see any yeast or any active alcoholic fermentation follow upon the submersion of the flowers of vinegar," reported the scientist. "At a time when belief in the transformation of species is so easily adopted, perhaps because it dispenses with rigorous accuracy in experimentation, it is not without interest to note that in the course of my researches on the culture of microscopic plants in a state of purity, I once had reason to believe in the transformation of one organism into another, of Mycoderma into yeast. I was then in error. . . ."

The error proved in the end to be a most fortunate one. The Mucor cells lurking in the bottom of the flasks had an interesting peculiarity.

Karl Bail had reported in 1857 that the manure mold produced long, intertwining filaments when it was grown in the air, but chains of round or oblong cells if it was submerged in a sugar solution. It so closely resembled the yeast of beer that Bail assumed that it had transformed itself into that yeast.

If Pasteur had not already discarded the transformation idea, it would have been shaken by another facet of Mucor's behavior. The short cells that fermented in the bottom of solutions recovered their long filamented form when they were again allowed to grow in the air. Certainly species did not shift

back and forth! No one could accept such a fantasy. Nevertheless, Mucor's changeability suggested another theory almost as
significant to life as grouping and the evolution of groups.

Without oxygen, Mucor behaved as a mold. With a plentiful
supply of oxygen it, like Mycoderma, became to all intents and
purposes a yeast. It had changed its mode of behavior when it
changed its environment. Could this signify a rapid adaptation
to new surroundings? Was it possible that this was the explanation of the action of all true yeasts? Whole new vistas were
opened into the behavior that underlay and explained the
phenomena of fermentation and perhaps the basic behavior of
all cells and all life. The bold idea had to be subjected to every
possible test.

Without any question, yeast grew prodigiously in the presence of air. Pasteur sowed a few cells in a shallow open saucer
of sugar water and stirred it vigorously to give the yeast all the
air it might want. Between 20 and 25 grams of yeast were produced before all the sugar—100 grams—disappeared. Almost
no alcohol was produced.

Deprive the yeast of air, though, and the results were totally
different. Pasteur submerged a few cells in the sugar liquid.
Their growth was slow and feeble. When the growth stopped,
only a trace of yeast had been produced, but 100 grams of
sugar had been converted into alcohol and carbonic acid.

What would happen if the yeast was given only a little air?
Pasteur sowed a few cells in a flask partly filled with a sugar
solution and partly with air. The yeast cells with a good supply
of air available to them grew actively. Before the action
stopped, 1.5 grams of yeast were produced and 100 grams of
sugar were changed into alcohol.

Vary the amount of air, Pasteur found, and he could exactly
control the amount of yeast or alcohol that he obtained.

Pasteur willingly faced the question his facts raised. Did the
yeast, which hungrily consumed a great amount of oxygen

when it was available, cease wanting and needing oxygen if none was to be had? Did the need to breathe cease if there was no air?

Pasteur hesitated no longer. Undoubtedly the yeast, like all other plants and animals, always needed air. But the yeast cell did not easily surrender if it was deprived of an easy supply. Instead of dying, it proceeded to take the oxygen it needed from other materials around it. It broke them down and stole their incorporated oxygen. It was not a matter of adaptation in the sense that Pasteur had thought; the yeast simply had the capability to get what it had to have, regardless of the circumstances.

"Fermentation by means of yeast appears, therefore, to be essentially connected with the property possessed by this minute cellular plant of performing its respiratory functions, somehow or other, with oxygen existing combined in sugar," Pasteur summarized.

"If we supply it with a sufficient quantity of free oxygen for the necessities of its life, nutrition and respiratory combustions—in other words, if we cause it to live after the manner of a mould . . . it ceases to be a ferment.

"On the other hand, if we deprive the yeast of air entirely, it will multiply just as if air were present, though with less activity, and under these circumstances its fermentative character will be most marked.

"Lastly, if free oxygen occurs in varying quantities, the fermentative power of the yeast may pass through all the degrees comprehended between the two extreme limits of which we have just spoken.

"It seems to us that we could not have a better proof of the direct relation that fermentation bears to life."

Fermentation was no longer an isolated, mysterious phenomenon. It was a special part of the cell's vital process of nutrition. "We can even conceive that the fermentative character may belong to every organized form," said Pasteur, "to every animal and vegetable cell." He was reaching, as he always did.

One day in the laboratory Pasteur was speculating about the universality of fermentation. Dumas, who was doing some work at the time, was highly skeptical, and a friendly argument followed.

"I'll make you a wager," said Pasteur, "that if we were to plunge a bunch of grapes into carbonic-acid gas, alcohol and carbonic acid would be immediately produced. The cells . . . would assume the function of yeast cells."

Pasteur was assuming that if oxygen was shut away from the grape cells, they, like other cells deprived of oxygen, would begin taking it from the fruit sugar around them, and, in the course of breaking down the sugar, would produce alcohol.

Dumas would not concede the point, and Pasteur immediately promised him that he would undertake the experiment.

It was toward the end of July—1872—and Pasteur gathered some fine plums in the garden of the school. He put twenty-four under a glass cylinder and filled it with carbonic-acid gas (carbon dioxide). He laid another twenty-four plums just outside the cylinder. Eight days later he removed the cylinder and compared the covered and uncovered plums. The difference was striking, "almost incredible." The uncovered plums, those exposed to the air, had ripened and were soft, sweet, watery. Those under the jar were hard and firm and had lost much of their sugar.

Pasteur crushed and distilled the hard, firm plums. They yielded 6.5 grams of alcohol, or more than one per cent of their total weight. It was just as he had predicted. When the fruit cells could not get oxygen, they took it from the sugar around them. Since all of this had taken place inside the fruit, no yeast could have been present to cause the fermentation; it was a clear case of response to anaerobic conditions.

"What better proof could we have . . . of the existence of a considerable chemical action in the interior of the fruit?" asked Pasteur. "In short, fermentation is a very general phenomenon. It is life without air."

And certainly there was life without air in animal as well as vegetable cells. "In the animal economy, oxygen gives to cells an activity from which they derive, when removed from the presence of the gas, the faculty to act in the manner of ferments," said Pasteur.

Pasteur never engaged in work with animal tissues, but with his new understanding of the functioning of the cells, he grasped the principle that governed the work of muscle.

He pointed out that an active muscle produces a volume of carbon dioxide larger than the volume of oxygen consumed during the same time. Under anaerobic conditions this was inevitable, Pasteur maintained. "The fact is not surprising according to the new theory," he explained, "since the carbon dioxide which is produced results from fermentation processes which bear no necessary relation to the quantity of oxygen consumed."

Oxygen brought into the muscle cell from the outside air would start off its action. Fuel for continuing would be drawn from other resources in the cell.

As Pasteur saw it, if the fire was larger than the initial load of fuel would have made possible, it was because other fuel was obtained. The carbon dioxide, which resulted from the combustion of carbon compounds and oxygen, was the proof. The amount of carbon dioxide produced indicated exactly the amount of combustion going on.

In short, it was the yeast phenomenon all over again. Pasteur could conclude that all living cells derive their energy from the same fundamental life processes.

"By selecting yeast and muscle to illustrate this law, he anticipated modern biochemistry, not only in one of its most far-reaching conclusions but also in its methodology, for the study of yeast and muscle physiology has provided much of our un-

derstanding of the chemistry of the metabolic process," said
Dubos.

In one way or another Pasteur hammered home his new
theme: fermentation is life without air. But a large part of his
fellow scientists still disagreed. Many of them still stood with
Liebig.

"Fermentation is not life without air," said Liebig in some of
his last laboratory notes, written shortly before his death in
1873, "for in air, as well as protected from it, alcohol can be
formed without yeast. . . . Alcohol can be produced by a soluble ferment in the absence of life."

Liebig lightly compared people who thought a living organism necessary to fermentation to the man who imagined that
the Rhine was driven by the row of water mills he saw across
the river from his home.

Pasteur answered that the conversion of one almond substance into another by a nitrogenous non-living material in
Liebig's experiments was not a "true fermentation." [3]

Both Liebig and Claude Bernard, a gentle scientist given to
deep contemplation about the meanings of science, had been
impressed by Marcellin Berthelot's discovery that yeast contains a soluble agent capable of splitting cane sugar. This agent
was later to be called an enzyme—literally "in zyme," or yeast.

At his country house at St. Julien at the time of the vintage
of 1877, Bernard began some experiments in an effort to find
this alcoholic enzyme. He crushed some grapes and observed
alcoholic fermentation in their clear juice within forty-eight
hours. He made a few brief notes on the rather crude experiment and left them in the bottom of a drawer. Berthelot found
them there, following Bernard's death, and decided to publish
them. He was pleased that they supported his own position.

Pasteur read the posthumous Bernard report on the day of
its publication. It undermined all that he had worked for years
to establish, and its coming from a man who had been his

[3] See Chapter IV.

friend and whom he had respected only made it the more intolerable. Pasteur passionately decided that Bernard must be rebutted thoroughly and immediately. "There was not a moment to lose," he said later.

In the vineyards at the end of July the germs of yeast were not yet present on the grape berry. If he covered some of the grapes with a hermetically sealed hothouse, the yeast plants could be kept away from them.

"These grapes, being crushed with all the precautions necessary not to introduce germs of yeast, will be able neither to ferment nor to make wine," Pasteur explained to his associates. "I shall give myself the pleasure of taking them to Paris, of presenting them to the academy, and of offering some clusters to those of my confreres who may still believe in the spontaneous generation of yeast."

Pasteur envisioned his campaign in every detail. He had little money, but, disregarding cost, he ordered several greenhouses. He had them shipped to a small vineyard that he owned near Arbois, and he and his staff worked feverishly to get the glass into place. To make doubly sure that no yeast would get on the grapes, he wrapped some of them in cotton.

On October 10 the grapes were ripe—those in the Pasteur greenhouses as well as those outside. Pasteur confidently gathered his harvest.

"Today, after a multitude of trials," he said, "it has been impossible for me to obtain a single time the alcoholic yeast fermentation from clusters covered with cotton, and as for the uncovered clusters on the same vines, I have only a single case of fermentation by a yeast."

Pasteur then crushed some of the grapes that had grown outside in the full sun and air. The juice soon was full of the bubbles of fermentation.

Elated by the success of his experiment, Pasteur detached some more of his cotton-covered grapes and, as he had dreamed of doing, carried them triumphantly back to Paris.

Members of the academy were free to try to get any fermentation from them. This was of course impossible, and Bernard's
inconclusive little experiment was discredited. Pasteur had
demonstrated once more that fermentation was dependent on
the presence of living yeast.

And yet the doubts could not be stilled, and would not be
as long as the chemical act that decomposed sugar was unknown.

Berthelot made this clear. "From the work of M. Cagniard
de la Tour and even more from that of M. Pasteur, it has been
proved that yeast consists of a mycodermic plant. I consider
that this plant does not act on sugar through a physiological
action but merely by means of ferments which it is able to secrete, just as germinating barley secretes diastase, almonds
secrete elumsin, the animal pancreas secretes pancreatin, and
the stomach secretes pepsin. . . ."

All of Pasteur's success was attributed to his sowing of the
organisms that produced the ferments. Pasteur himself did not
neglect the possibility that substances acting independently of
the cell might produce fermentation. He made a number of
unsuccessful attempts to extract a fermentative principle from
the living yeast.

"If I am asked what is the nature of the chemical act
whereby sugar is decomposed and what is its real cause, I
reply that I am completely ignorant of it," he said readily.

In time chemistry was to find that such changes occur in the
presence of minute amounts of substances called catalysts.
Those produced by living cells are called enzymes. Liebig's
oil of bitter almonds was changed by an enzyme obtainable
from either living or dead cells in the skin of almonds.

As James Bryant Conant, chemist and former president of
Harvard University, observed: "It is no trick to bring about
such changes without the presence of living organisms. The
change from sugar to alcohol or from sugar to lactic acid, how-

ever and all of Pasteur's other 'true fermentations' are brought about by enzymes that under usual conditions do not leave the living cell. Therefore for these changes to occur the cell must be alive and vigorous, for only under these conditions will the sugar penetrate the living cell and be transformed by the intracellular enzymes into the products (alcohol or lactic acid) that leak back into solution." The noted chemist was examining the question of who was right, Pasteur or Liebig and Bernard. His answer was neither and both. And that is the verdict of history.

Another matter was claiming Pasteur's attention. The hothouses he had erected at Arbois to keep the yeasts away from his test grapes had protected them from those germs "as Europe is protected from the cholera and plague by quarantines." The tightly sealed glasshouses had not, however, kept out some Mucor organisms. Since the Mucor parasites were present in the ground throughout the year, they were lodged under the hothouse and easily made their way to the grapes. It struck Pasteur that a number of common contagious diseases might be like the Mucor. They were "in," and all the quarantines therefore were ineffective against them.

Pasteur was moving in a new direction. In 1879 he had already begun his studies of anthrax and chicken cholera. "Can we not assume by analogy that someday simple preventive measures will end those scourges that suddenly ravage and terrorize whole populations?" he asked.

"These few lines form the introduction to a new life," wrote Duclaux, who knew him so well. "They form the connecting links between the old labors and the new. . . . I should be very much astonished if the reader has not noted their resolute manner of expression and their prophetic tone."

All of the basic knowledge that Pasteur had acquired was brought to bear upon the glorious task of conquering the diseases that ravaged men and animals. The foundation, as he regarded it, was well laid. One triumph followed upon another.

The microbes that cause boils were discovered, and the little "strings of beads"—streptococcus—that produce childbirth fever.

Pasteur's finding of the rods of anthrax and the celebrated field trials at Melun followed. To the world it seemed a modern-day miracle. Sheep that had received the Pasteur vaccine were inoculated with anthrax, but were unaffected. They grazed contentedly in the trial compound. The non-vaccinated lay dead.

The sweeping excitement of this day was rivaled, however, when Pasteur developed a vaccine for rabies. It dramatically saved the life of a child bitten by a mad dog, and from all parts of the world those who had been bitten by rabid animals were brought to Paris. Governments, communities, and newspapers joined in raising the funds to send them. On March 1, 1886, Pasteur reported to the Academy of Sciences that out of 350 treated, only one had died.

The awed academy voted unanimously to establish an institute for anti-rabitic vaccination and research. An international subscription was opened and soon filled. The funds came readily.

On November 14, 1888, the institute of which Pasteur had always dreamed was dedicated; it was named in his honor.

"Alas, mine is the poignant melancholy of entering it as a man 'vanquished by time,'" said Pasteur in his address.

An apartment had been provided for Pasteur in the institute, and it gave him easy and convenient access to his laboratories. But his health was failing, and work became increasingly difficult. On Pasteur's seventieth birthday, December 27, 1892, a resplendent celebration was held at the Sorbonne. Citations were presented to him from the world's leading scientific societies, and Dr. Joseph Lister, who had employed Pasteur's principles to revolutionize surgery with antisepsis, spoke. "Pasteur has lifted the veil that for centuries has hidden the infectious diseases," he said.

As Pasteur rose to embrace and thank the famed English physician the applause was thunderous. Pasteur was too deeply moved to deliver his own address. His son read his words for him. Pasteur addressed himself to the young, calling upon them to devote themselves to the progress and welfare of mankind: "You must have the right to say, on approaching the great goal: 'I have done all I could do.'"

The heartfelt words were the last Pasteur was to present at a public gathering. Another stroke in 1894 further incapacitated him, and death came on September 28, 1895.

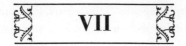

VII

FISCHER AND BUCHNER:
ESSENCES OF LIFE

O<small>F ALL THE STUDENTS</small> who flocked to the laboratory of the famed Adolf von Baeyer at the University of Strasbourg, none was surer or more brilliant than tall, bright-eyed Emil Fischer. From the first it was evident that he had come to exactly the right place for him.

Fischer had known when he was in his teens where his interests lay. His father had attempted to get him into the family lumber business, and at seventeen Emil was apprenticed for two years to his brother-in-law. It proved only a slight detour and delay. The business could not have interested Emil Fischer less, and he spent most of his time in a back room carrying on experiments in physics and chemistry.

The young Rhinelander—he was born on October 9, 1852, at Euskirchen near Cologne—was fascinated by laboratories. He also closely followed the great debate that was preoccupying and exciting Europe: does life originate spontaneously or do living things spring only from their own parents? He knew too about the dyes and drugs coming from the new German chemical factories. Although Fischer could only sense that rich opportunities lay ahead, chemistry in fact stood at the opening of one of its brightest eras.

If Fischer was "too stupid" for the lumber business, his father was not reluctant to see him go to the university to study chemistry. The senior Fischer was impressed by the profits being made in the rapidly expanding chemical industry.

In 1871 Fischer enrolled at the University of Bonn to study chemistry with Friedrich Kekule, the discoverer of the struc-

ture of benzene. The following year, in the German tradition
of moving from university to university, Fischer went to the
new University of Strasbourg. It had been established at the
close of the Franco-Prussian war and Baeyer, already famed
as the discoverer of indigo, was head of its department of
chemistry. Fischer was eager to study under this master of
chemistry, and remained with him until he received his doctorate.

The following year, in 1873, when the great Liebig died,
Baeyer was accorded the high honor of being invited to take
his place at the University of Munich. He invited Fischer to
accompany him, and Fischer happily accepted.

As Baeyer's assistant, Fischer was not loaded with teaching
duties; his time was kept free for research. Baeyer then was
deep in further research on dyes. Fischer not only aided him in
this work, but did some additional work in the dye field with
his cousin Otto Fischer. But Fischer was his own man. He did
not let the general research direction of the laboratory draw
him entirely away from the work he most wanted to do.

In 1875, when he was still only twenty-two, Fischer discovered a substance that was to prove one of the most useful of
chemical tools, phenylhydrazine. It was the key that would
unlock the structure of the sugars, and the sugars in their turn
would open the way into that hidden universe that underlay
and shaped and controlled the visible being of men, animals,
and plants. Phenylhydrazine was justly called the Rosetta
Stone of chemistry.

At the time Fischer began his work, it was known that living
things are largely aggregations of carbon compounds and that
the carbon compounds are divided into fats, proteins, and carbohydrates. The sugars make up the largest part of the carbohydrates. But the structure of the important sugars and of
the still more important proteins was unknown. Both undoubtedly were composed of simpler elements, but what these
substances were and what position they occupied no one could

say. The most essential parts of the human and animal body were still enigmas.

The sugars had not remained an unsolved problem for lack of study. Innumerable scientists had worked with them, only to be repelled by their formidable complexity. Lavoisier had succeeded only in showing that sugars are "burned" in the human body and that they yield energy in the process. Pasteur in his turn had not gone beyond the demonstration that they could be broken down into carbon dioxide and alcohol—if a living cell was present. But science had been unable to progress much further; it halted at this borderline where chemistry and biology met and merged.

One of the obstacles was the difficulty of working with the sugars. In their pure form they were easy to crystallize, as anyone might note by glancing at the sugar in the bowl on the breakfast table. But when combined with other materials, as they always were in the sugars of animal and plant bodies, they tended to remain in a syrupy form. No method that science could devise could coax them out of this union. Then Fischer discovered phenylhydrazine. By combining with sugar, it broke the sugar's tight association with other materials. Once this was accomplished, the sugar could be separated from the phenylhydrazine and isolated. For the first time it became possible to obtain and study the various kinds of sugar which supplied energy to animals and plants.

It was clear at once that this was a discovery of importance. Yet few could foresee to what wide understandings it would lead. Looking back many years later, Martin Onslow Forster, the English biochemist, said that when he considered Fischer's discovery of phenylhydrazine he felt as though he were observing the modest source of a mighty river.

Between the development of the tool and the separation of the sugars lay an enormous amount of work. But Fischer was in a position to do it, and he was undaunted by the prospect. In 1885, when only thirty-three, he was appointed full profes-

sor of chemistry at the University of Würzburg. The university
not only broke most of its precedents in naming so young a
man; it also provided him with a fine new laboratory built to
his specifications.

Fischer spent countless hours there. Bending over his test
tubes day after day and breathing the fumes that arose from
them, he began to suffer from what was called chronic poisoning. The ill effects often made him touchy and irritable, but he
let no personal discomfort interfere with his work or his enthusiasm for it.

One after another he separated the sugars: glucose, or grape
sugar; fructose, or fruit sugar; maltose, or malt sugar; and many
of the others. The sugars were made up of a chain of six carbon
atoms with six oxygen and twelve hydrogen atoms attached to
them like so many pendants on a necklace. If the hydrogen
and oxygen were attached at certain points, Fischer saw, he
had glucose. If the pattern was different, if they were attached
in different ways at different points, he had another of the
sugars.

Fischer saw that the sugars are formed by a linking together
of the materials of which they are composed. Perhaps this was
the way the plant manufactured glucose, and the human body
too. The plant takes carbon dioxide and moisture from the air
and in the presence of chlorophyll converts them into glucose.
And we change the sugars we eat, whether cane or honey or
milk sugar, into simpler sugars and then into glucose, for only
glucose is found in the blood.

But how did this linking come about? How were sugars
made? The latter question was the critical one, for separating
the sugars and working out their structure were only a part of
the problem. The chemist has not mastered his subject until
he can put the parts together again in their original form. Synthesis is the final test, the ultimate goal.

Baeyer, a highly interested observer of his former student's
work, suggested on the basis of some work of his own that the

plant might first make formaldehyde and then, by putting some of the molecules together, a molecule of sugar. Under certain circumstances, it had been proved, formaldehyde could yield a sugar-like substance. Baeyer's intuition proved correct. Acting upon it, Fischer transformed the sugar-like substance into a form of sugar, and then changed the sugar into glucose.

The first stage in the chemical process that enables a plant to live had been duplicated in the laboratory. It was a triumph that would have been impossible even a few years before.

Having learned how sugars are put together, Fischer made many of them. A study of the sugar structure indicated that there should be sixteen different sugars if the carbon, hydrogen, and oxygen of sugar were arranged in all possible ways. Fischer succeeded in the amazing feat of synthesizing twelve of the possible sixteen.

Some of the sugars that Fischer made seemed identical with the natural ones. Only one flaw betrayed the fact that they fell short of that perfection. When Fischer put samples in a polarimeter, they did not rotate the light to either the right or the left; they were not asymmetric, as Pasteur had maintained all natural things are, and as all natural sugars were known to be. Fischer knew what had to be done. Using Pasteur's method of separating the right- and left-oriented crystals of his sugar, Fischer succeeded in producing sugars wholly identical with the natural ones. And confirmation was given to Pasteur's theory.

Chemists in his own country and throughout the world watched these achievements with an admiration bordering on awe. In 1892 Fischer was invited to become professor of chemistry at the University of Berlin, the highest honor that could be offered to him in his own country. Ten years later, in 1902, he received the second Nobel Prize to be given. It recognized his work on sugar as one of the great triumphs of chemistry.

The work on sugar would have been enough for one lifetime and certainly could have completely filled any man's initial career. Fischer, though, had managed to carry on another original series of studies at the same time, and would go on to even greater accomplishments.

Having seen the value of one touchstone, phenylhydrazine, Fischer glimpsed the exciting possibility of another. It was the familiar uric acid, the same uric acid whose urea Wohler had synthesized. Urea had proved that the products of the human body were not mystic creations, and another of the qualities of the uric-acid group, the readiness with which it combined, promised to lead into other new places, and new places of importance.

In plants one of the principal uric-acid products was caffeine, the ordinary caffeine of coffee. Among its corresponding products in the human and animal cell were three whose names sound like ingredients of a witch's brew—xanthine, theobromine, and guanine. These were among the products formed by the breaking down of proteins, the all-important proteins, the unapproachable proteins that were almost the equivalent of life itself. But before that infinitely promising door could be opened even a bit, the uric-acid group had to be studied thoroughly.

Fischer obtained most of the animal uric-acid products with which he worked from guano, the excrement of sea birds. Addressing one scientific audience about his research, he told them he might apply to his raw material a remark once made by the Emperor Vespasian about tax money that came to him from unclean sources. The Emperor had remarked: *"Non olet"* ("It does not smell").

Fischer ferreted out the constitution and structure of the uric-acid group. This enabled him to trace uric acid to one parent group that he named the purines. The purines were made up of five carbon, four hydrogen, and four nitrogen atoms. In 1898 Fischer succeeded in making a purine in his laboratory. With the basic structure in hand, he and his collaborators in the end worked out more than 130 related substances.

In addition to their significance in the life of plants and men, the purines were highly useful to the drug industry. From one of them the German chemical factories made the sleep-inducing drug veronal.

Fischer once exhibited a small amount of veronal to a large audience. One tenth of it, he remarked, would be enough to send the entire audience into a peaceful slumber. With the touch that made him a favorite as a speaker, Fischer went on: "Should the mere demonstration of this soporific, coupled with this lecture of mine, take effect on any susceptible persons present, there is no better remedy than the cup of tea which we are to enjoy later, for tea and coffee contain a chemical substance which stimulates the heart and nervous system."

As Fischer worked further with the sugars, he found that the surest way to determine when he had successfully synthesized any particular sugar was to submit it to the yeasts that attacked and broke down the comparable natural sugar. If the yeast took to his synthetic product and decomposed it into alcohol and carbon dioxide, he knew that success was his. The yeasts could pick and choose their own sugars as unerringly as a mother her own child.

Fischer could not escape being drawn into a study of these "agents of change," the directors of the constant process of upbuilding and breaking down which he saw occurring.

Berzelius and Liebig had insisted that such agents were catalysts. But what did this mean? About the only answer the chemists had been able to give was that when very small amounts of catalysts were present, very large changes occurred. Liebig thought it might be due to some vibratory effect. Pasteur, as Fischer well knew, had insisted that the sugars could be broken down and transformed only in the presence of the living cell, or possibly of some substance produced by it.

After long dispute some of the extracts from the saliva and stomach which could bring about changes in proteins and carbohydrates were designated as enzymes. Presumably they were non-living substances of a chemical nature. The yeasts and similar ferments were placed in another vital category, as the "true ferments."

Fischer was impressed by how selective the yeasts and enzymes were among both the natural and the synthetic sugars. He added some yeast to a container of maltose, or malt sugar. It was soon fermenting. But emulsin, one of the stomach enzymes, produced no effect. Exactly the opposite was true of lactose, or milk sugar: it responded to emulsin and not to yeast. Fischer tried the various yeasts and sugars in a polarimeter. Then he saw that the yeasts would attack only the sugars that had the same orientation as their own, whether it was left or right. In short, the yeast and sugar had to have the same basic architecture, the same configuration. It came to Fischer that the two fitted together like a lock and key, and thus his brilliant and exact lock-and-key analogy was born.

Fischer inevitably asked the next question. Would there be the same lock-and-key fit of enzyme and organic matter? He began studies with animal materials.

In the meanwhile, a scientific accident—which, like many others, was only partly a matter of chance—altered the whole approach to the problem of the lively, particular enzymes and ferments.

During the autumn holidays of 1896 Eduard Buchner, the head of the analytical section of the department of chemistry at the University of Kiel, went to visit his brother Hans, director of the Hygienic Institute at Munich. The institute was engaged in animal and agricultural research, and Eduard suggested to his brother that yeast might yield a preparation that could be of therapeutic value. Hans welcomed the idea, and Eduard went to work.

He had no regrets about using his holiday for more work on yeast—his interest in yeast and fermentation ran deep. Soon after he obtained his doctorate at Munich and became a teaching assistant, he decided that he would try to extract the fermentative principle of yeast. The director of the laboratory did everything to discourage him. The masters of chemistry had tried this very thing and had failed. The great Pasteur himself had ground, frozen, and pulverized yeast in an attempt to discover whether there was a chemical principle that could be separated from the cell, as Liebig and some of his other opponents maintained. He had got nowhere. Forty years of effort since that time had met with no greater success. Buchner was vigorously advised not to waste his time. The young graduate stubbornly refused to be turned away—and he knew how to persist. Since his father's death when he was eleven he had made his own way. And he had decided that fermentation was a field for study. He had become interested in it when he worked in a preserving factory between two of his years at college.

At Kiel, Buchner began to grind up some yeast cells with sand. When he had mashed them into a plastic mass he wrapped his material in a cloth and subjected it to heavy pressure. About 330 cubic centimeters of juice were squeezed out.

Buchner again ground the residue with sand and again put it under heavy pressure. He obtained another 150 cubic centimeters of juice. He filtered the juice a number of times until it finally emerged as a clear, slightly opalescent, yellow liquid with a pleasant yeasty odor. He thought that it might be very good for some of the animals with which Hans was working. But Hans was not ready to use it immediately, and to preserve it Eduard decided to add some sugar.

Less than fifteen minutes later he happened to glance at his yellow juice. Bubbles were rising in it. It was fermenting! Buchner bent over the bubbly mixture with surprised disbelief. The grinding, the pressure, and the filtering surely could have left no whole yeast cells. And yet, in the absence of cells, fermentation was occurring! Buchner knew the significance of what he was seeing, and he faced the stirring fact that he had accomplished what the masters of chemistry had failed in. Forty years of effort to extract the principle of yeast were being crowned with success. And Pasteur had been wrong, or at least partly wrong, in maintaining that true fermentation can occur only in the presence of a living cell. At the moment it looked as though the dispute that had torn Europe for decades was to be settled in favor of the non-vitalistic side.

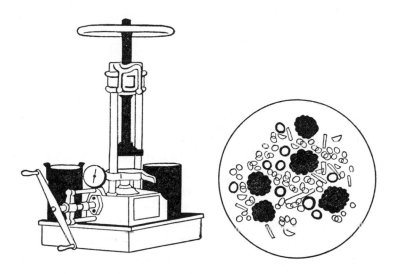

*Settlement of an old controversy. Buchner ground up yeast cells (*CIRCLE*) and put them under heavy pressure. Despite the destruction of the whole cell, the yeast juice fermented. The claim that fermentation could occur only in the presence of a whole living cell was undermined.*

Because he recognized all the far-reaching implications of the bubbling, Buchner hastened to check it in every possible way. The yeasty juice held true. It fermented grape, fruit, and malt sugar with equal vigor. But when he tried it with milk sugar (lactose), nothing happened. The lactose was no more affected by the yeast juice than by living cells of brewer's yeast.

Buchner had to make certain, though, that the fermentation was not being produced by a few whole cells that might somehow have slipped through the destructive grinding and squeezing. He refiltered his juice with filters that would certainly have trapped any whole cells. The new filtrate did not ferment a sugar solution quite as rapidly as the first juice, but it converted it into alcohol just as surely. The juice even retained its fermentative potency after two weeks in an icebox.

In his paper reporting his historic discovery, Buchner summarized the conclusions that he believed it made possible: "(1) the complicated apparatus of the yeast cell is not required for fermentation; and (2) the bearer of the fermenting action of the press juice is probably a dissolved substance, and doubtless a protein. It will be called zymase [yeast enzyme]."

Buchner was still not certain whether his new zymase should be considered another of the "unorganized" (non-living) enzymes or something different. There seemed to be a difference in kind between the fermenting action of yeast or zymase and the action of the stomach enzymes. The decomposition of sugar into alcohol and carbon dioxide appeared more complex, and still it had been accomplished only with yeast materials.

"It can hardly be doubted," said Buchner, "that zymase belongs to the true proteins and stands closer to the living protoplasm of the yeast cell than does invertin [a non-living enzyme].

But much that had been debatable and obscure was now clear. An issue had largely been resolved by new data. It was something in the yeast cell, rather than the cell proper, which produced fermentation, though the fermentation material came from a living cell.

In the end the further distinction that troubled Buchner, the distinction between zymase and the other enzymes, was found not to matter. All were enzymes, agents of change and action. But Buchner's work meant that other enzymes could more easily be sought out and studied. A new era was opened.

In 1903 Buchner was awarded the Nobel Prize for his discovery "that alcoholic fermentation of sugar is not dependent on the activity of bran cells but is brought about by an enzyme contained therein, the so-called zymase."

Buchner's discovery gave new impetus to the work Fischer was doing with enzymes. Zymase, the new yeast enzyme, behaved in exactly the same way as the others. It would act only with certain sugars. Fischer's lock-and-key analogy was again supported. In the yeast cell Fischer found another enzyme, sucrase, which would act only on sucrose, cane sugar. And it was the same with the enzymes in animal tissues.

As he continued his work with the animal materials, Fischer realized that the enzymes, in breaking down proteins, were offering a means to investigate these prime materials of living things.

More than half a century earlier Gerardus Johannes Mulder, a Dutch chemist, had pointed to the supreme importance of the proteins. "There is present in plants and animals," he said, "a substance which is . . . without doubt the most important of all the known substances in living matter, and without it, life would be impossible on our planet. This material has been named Protein."

"Protein" came from the Greek *proteios:* "of the first rank." Berzelius had suggested the name to Mulder.

It was wholly appropriate. The human body is made up of about sixty-four per cent water, fifteen per cent proteins, fifteen per cent fatty materials, five per cent inorganic substances, and about one per cent carbohydrates, but among these materials the proteins were regarded as foremost. They were known to make up much of the muscular tissue, the bones and cartilage, and the skin, and time was to prove that the enzymes which direct the enormous complex of actions that constitute life also were proteins.

At first Mulder and Liebig thought that the proteins were a

single substance, a solid though varied building block. But
soon they learned that the proteins were themselves made up
of simpler units, called amino acids. One of them had been
identified before Fischer began his work.

Fischer took some of the fine shimmering filaments of natural
silk—a protein—and, to break them down, put them on to boil
in a mixture of water and sulphuric acid. For twenty hours he
continued this constant boiling. He then neutralized and filtered and evaporated the soggy residue that had formed. Some
of the amino acids were thus obtained in crystalline form. In
other experiments, he mixed other proteins with some of the
enzymes, such as the pepsin of the stomach or the trypsin of
the pancreas, and again was able to obtain the basic amino
acids.

The new laboratory that had been built for Fischer when he
went to Berlin was at last finished after a delay of seven years.
Fischer's renown, coupled with its facilities, drew students
from all around the world. Assisted by what was almost an
army of students, Fischer succeeded in separating and isolating nineteen of the twenty universal amino acids that, in varying proportions, made up all proteins.

Fischer was not satisfied to stop with the phenomenal feat of
isolation. The amino acids were only the links in the chains of
the proteins, and putting the chains together would be the final
test.

"If one wishes to attain clear results in this difficult field, one
must first discover a method which will permit the experimenter to join the various amino acids to one another step by
step and with well-defined intermediary products," said
Fischer.

One amino link had somehow to be joined to another, and a
third to the first two, and then a fourth, and so on. And a two-
some would constitute one product, a threesome another, and a
foursome still another. The most complicated and largest of
Nature's living materials could not be synthesized in one grand
swoop.

If such chains were to be formed, if the amino acids were to be joined, the secret of how they were coupled had first to be discovered. The separate bits would no more fly together in the laboratory than would a handful of beads.

As he delved into this problem, Fischer discovered that there is a molecule of water at either end of each amino acid. He also saw that when two amino acids were joined, the intervening bits of water disappeared. Somehow, it appeared, the water

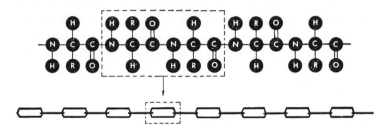

A chain. Proteins are chains of repeating groups (outlined in broken line). The groups are made up of amino acids, each of which contributes identical units to the backbone, plus distinguishing radical side units (designated R). Fischer put together such a chain.

molecules were sheared away and the two links then came firmly together; the chain was lengthened by another segment.

Fischer put the discovery to immediate use. He succeeded in shearing off the water molecules from two amino acids, which then fused together. Using the same method, he added another link to the end of his tiny new chain. And he kept daringly on, like a juggler adding another and still another and then another to his precariously built-up stack of blocks.

Fischer continued the breath-taking operation until he had linked eighteen amino acids. In comparison to the chains that Nature puts together almost instantaneously in living bodies, Fischer's was a very modest one. The principal protein of egg white, to cite one example, is formed from about four hundred amino-acid links. But for man to have joined eighteen links where not even two had been put together before was a triumph of understanding and performance. One of the innermost and most vital of Nature's secrets had been mastered.

And the triumph was complete. Fischer could see at once that his phenomenal eighteen-link chain resembled one of the simpler natural proteins. Did he dare to hope that it was one? One test, he knew, would be determinative: the reaction of enzymes to the newborn chain.

Fearfully Fischer mixed his prodigious chain with trypsin, an enzyme from the pancreas which acts only on proteins. His anxious wait was not long. The trypsin began to act. It attacked and broke down Fischer's eighteen-link creation, which he had named octadecapeptide, as effectively as though it were a natural protein. The key fitted the lock, and then Fischer knew finally that he had achieved something unprecedented: the making of one of the most complex and essential of all natural substances. His new protein did not exactly duplicate any known protein, but Fischer knew even then that there were thousands of kinds of protein in a single human body—today science would say at least one hundred thousand. The new protein was one with all the others; to all intents and purposes, it was a protein and not simply an imitation or an approximation.

Fischer had little expectation that men or animals would soon be eating his octadecapeptide instead of meat or milk. "The starting material cost two hundred and fifty dollars," he said, "so it has not yet made its appearance on the dining table."

Fischer had received the Nobel Prize for his work on sugar. There was no prize adequate for his greater work on proteins, although all the world's honors in chemistry were bestowed on him, including England's Faraday Medal in 1907.

The German chemist went to England for the ceremony of presentation. Sir Henry Roscoe, introducing Fischer to a distinguished audience, spoke of his synthesis of sugars and then of "how much greater will the world's expression of gratitude be when we learn that success has attended the apparently almost insoluble problem of the synthesis of proteins."

Fischer was also a prophet honored at home. When the Rockefeller Institute was established to permit scientists to devote full time to research, Fischer feared that the scientists of his own country, who had to teach as well as devote themselves to the laboratory, might be outdistanced. He urged his government to establish a research institution where a similar opportunity for pure research would be offered. His recommendation was adopted, and on January 11, 1911, the Kaiser Wilhelm Research Institute was opened, with Fischer delivering the principal address.

Leading German chemical factories had long pleaded with Fischer to become a director and take charge of their research. With very little hesitation, Fischer refused. He would not be drawn from the research to which he had devoted his life, and he was convinced that he could contribute most to German chemistry by furnishing it with a stream of superbly trained young chemists. Though Fischer would not accept a formal position in industry, he nevertheless maintained extremely close advisory ties with the factories. He was the authority, the final arbiter of German chemistry. It was his methods the industry used for the production of caffeine, theobromine, and many others of their most important chemicals. His veronal was one of the valuable drugs.

When the First World War began, Fischer soon saw that the shutting off of the supply of Chilean nitrates would cripple German ammunition production, and he so warned the War Ministry. This advice was not what the war leaders wanted to hear, and it was rejected with a rebuke. Events soon proved Fischer right, and the warlords appealed to him to get them out of their difficulties. Fischer made a detailed report on how to obtain a supply of ammonia from the coke ovens, and his advice guided the development of a synthetic nitric-acid industry that rapidly grew into a huge undertaking. Historians have since maintained that Germany could not have continued in the war after 1915 if it had not been for the synthetic nitrates.

A shortage of camphor produced another war crisis. Fischer solved it by showing his country the way to develop a satisfactory substitute. He also took the lead in producing benzene and toluene from natural gas, and heavy oil from napthalene.

Fischer seemed to be a magician, capable of synthesizing in a test tube almost anything the hard-pressed German war machine and economy had to have. Miracles were expected of him.

But the most critical shortage of them all was developing— food. The supply of meats and fats all but disappeared. Once again a commission was organized with Fischer at its head.

Fischer worked feverishly in the laboratory, trying to turn starch into a digestible fodder for horses and cattle. He even tried to make acceptable foods from leaves, rushes, and wood, but this was more than his chemical genius could accomplish. The health and energy of the people declined, and as this toll made itself felt, disease increased and production fell.

In a solemn memorandum addressed to the military and civil governments in 1918, Fischer again sounded an unwelcome warning. He told the German leaders that science could not devise a substitute for the physiological necessities, for the essential nutriments the human body requires. A nutritional pattern built in the long course of human evolution could not be abruptly changed. Fischer warned too that psychological breakdown would follow upon a lack of nourishment. Heroism and patriotism alone, he sadly said, could not sustain a population. Again the German government ignored a warning of disaster and went on with the war.

The days that followed were dark, for Fischer as well as for his country. His two younger sons died in the war. The laboratories had been stripped of their younger men and even those in the middle ranks were going.

Buchner was one of them. He entered the army as a captain of artillery. After several years of service he returned to the University of Würzburg, for research and the training of chemists were suffering badly. But when the United States entered the war, Buchner returned to the front. While with his troops, transporting munitions on the Rumanian front, he was struck by a shell fragment. He died two days later at the age of fifty-eight.

With his world collapsing around him, Fischer channeled all his time and efforts into his laboratory. He was co-ordinating his work on the purines and carbohydrates when death came in 1918.

The divisions and scars of World War I lasted long after peace came. But Fischer's contributions to science and the understanding of life surmounted even such deep rifts. On October 28, 1920, Martin Onslow Forster delivered a Fischer memorial address before the British Royal Society:

"Reflecting on the essence of life in its chemical aspects, regarding the act of living as a complex alternation of digestion, assimilation, and oxidation, the mind begins to arrange in one beautiful fabric the colored strands from which is woven Fischer's contribution to the knowledge of centuries. He not only regularized the most fruitful of laboratory methods for studying life processes, but he assembled more richly and in greater variety than any other chemist, the materials on which these processes depended. Carbohydrates, glucosides, depsides, purines, and polypeptides have during the years of his activity been brought to our delighted vision and ranged in perspective by his control of enzymes. As interpreted by him, we recognize amino acids as the basis of our being."

VIII

ROUX AND DRIESCH: HALVES AND WHOLES

*When I look at a dividing cell I feel
as an astronomer might do if he be-
held the formation of a double star:
that an original act of creation is taking place before me.*

WILLIAM BATESON

THE EGG is a nearly spherical object, simple and elegant of line. It could not bear less resemblance to the complex, leggy, heady, articulated beings from which it comes, or to the beings like them to which it will give rise. How this single cell and the single cell that fertilizes it can divide and redivide and multiply until their bulk is increased astronomically staggers the imagination. Even more marvelous is the organization of this multitude of cells. With what appears to be inevitability they arrange themselves into tissues and organs, and the tissues and organs into moving, functioning, intelligent beings. What is more, this feat of organization is accomplished with a co-ordination of timing and sequence which is nearly unfailing. No work of man even approaches this miracle of development, a miracle that springs from the roundish little egg. To para-phrase: never did so much come from so little.

As young Wilhelm Roux (1850–1924) studied medicine at Jena, he became fascinated by this miracle of development. The making of the heart, the skin, the brain, the whole com-plex individual from one cell no bigger than the point of a pin did indeed seem beyond physical law. Yet, if urea could be compounded in the laboratory as Wohler had done, if fermen-tation was a chemical action as Buchner had shown, and if even proteins were chemical compounds, Roux felt that this wonderful ordering of development must also be a matter of physical and chemical action. The nineteenth century could not explain the processes or even define all of them; biochemistry had not advanced that far. Nevertheless, if the processes were not mystical, Roux believed that it should be possible to study them experimentally.

For his doctorate he did a thesis on the haemo-dynamic factors that control the formation of the blood vessels. At about the same time he became impressed with the theories of the noted German zoologist August Weismann. It was Weismann who had all but destroyed the Lamarckian theory that acquired characteristics are inheritable. He did it by the simple expedient of cutting off the tails of five generations of mice and demonstrating that the tails of the fifth generation were just as long as those of the first. The only variations that are heritable, Weismann argued, are those which have their origin in the germ cell. Weismann pictured the nucleus of the fertilized egg cell as a mosaic in which the "primordia"—the beginnings—of each organ lie "side by side, separate from each other like the stones of a mosaic, and develop independently although in perfect harmony with one another into the finished organism." According to this proposal, one cell would receive the "primordia" for the head; others, the units for the feet, the skin, and all the other parts of the animal.

Roux determined that he would seek proof of this plausible theory. But how? If the nucleus was a mosaic and the mosaic was divided into segments, each segment would bear only a part of the original whole. If one of the segments was destroyed, Roux reasoned, the larva should lack the organs that would normally develop from that segment.

To test this idea, Roux decided to use the soft, slimy eggs of frogs. As he watched, a small indentation appeared on one of the eggs, and the egg split into two. Roux took a hot needle and killed one of the two parts. The surviving half—blastomere—like all frog eggs, divided and redivided. When the process was completed, Roux saw to his amazement that he had half a tadpole. It was as indubitably a half as though he had taken a razor and sliced a normal embryo in two. The halfness showed up particularly well in the anterior, or head, of the embryo.

Roux was elated. Here was remarkable experimental proof of the Weismann theory that the egg contained some kind of structure which divided and distributed the factors that would later give rise to each of the organs of the animal. What better proof could there be than the half-embryo? When half the egg material was destroyed, the part of the embryo that it would have produced was lost. Half was removed, and half the tadpole did not develop. Roux hastened to publish his remarkable results. His paper came out in 1888.

Three years later another young German biologist decided to repeat Roux's experiment. Hans Driesch (1867–1941) was in Naples at the time, working at the Zoological Station there. After completing his studies in the German universities he had gone on a tour of the Far East and, returning to Europe, had stopped in Italy.

Driesch was only twenty-four, but he was thoroughly trained. He had studied with the top German authorities at Hamburg, Freiburg, Munich, and Jena and had carried on his studies in the Far East. Along the way he had become interested in the astounding process by which a single cell develops into intricate living things. Driesch was inclined to think, with Roux and Weismann, that the incredible development would be possible only if constructive materials in the egg cell were distributed to the cells into which the egg divides.

Instead of repeating Roux's experiment exactly, Driesch decided upon a variation of it. He would use the eggs of the sea urchin rather than those of the frog. For one thing, they were plentiful around Naples.

The eggs were only about a tenth of a millimeter in diameter, but large enough to be seen by the naked eye. Against a dark background one of them looked like a tiny white point. And they were easy to work with—the sperm entered the egg in open water.

Driesch also knew that the sea-urchin eggs could withstand rough treatment. Others had demonstrated that they could be broken apart, and that the fragments which survived would go on segmenting. "I took advantage of these facts for my purposes," Driesch explained.

As soon as the sperm—about one four-hundred-thousandth of the volume of the egg—entered, a membrane formed around the fertilized egg. And then began the wonderful process in which the egg, without ever pulling apart, divides itself into smaller and smaller segments. In this way the "large" egg cell is reduced to "normal" cell size and the cells are made ready for the production of new living matter or growth.[1] They also become maneuverable.

Driesch studied this cleavage miracle closely, as many had done before him. To understand it was essential for the work he wanted to do—to explore further by experiment into what Driesch call the "great problem of becoming."

As Roux had seen too, a little indentation first appeared in the round egg cell. Soon the egg was split into two halves. Then came another cleavage down through the egg, at right angles to the first. The egg had been quartered.

This division was only a beginning, but the next cleavage came in a different way. If the cell were thought of as a globe, it could be said that it was cut through on an equatorial plane. Now there were eight segments.

Driesch pondered over the strange variation that appeared in the cleavage process at this point. There was another cut

---

[1] Growth is the production of new living matter over and above that which was contained in the fertilized egg. In contrast to the first cleavage or segmentation of the egg, it comes about either as a result of the capture of food by a free living larva, or by utilization of a store of food material provided for an embryo, either in the egg cell or by means of a placenta.

through, both in the top and bottom segments. But at the bottom, in the equivalent of the southern hemisphere if the egg were still thought of as a globe, the division was not an even one. The lower row of segments was quite small. And the cells into which they divided at the next cleavage also were small. Thus, a number of small cells were congregated at what would be the south pole of the globe. They were called micromeres.

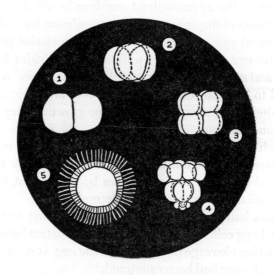

A sea-urchin egg divides. It splits into halves, into quarters, and into smaller segments, until when segmentation ends, there are exactly 808. A hollow ball has been formed, cilia sprout, and the egg is ready for growth.

The continuing divisions left the cells at the opposite end, the north pole, somewhat larger than the middle cells.

By the time there had been ten divisions each egg was split into exactly 808 segments. Had each of the cleavages been even, 1,024 cells would have been produced. However, the little cells at the bottom divided a bit more slowly, and thus the cleavage of the sea-urchin egg always ended with the sphere split into 808 parts rather than into the larger number.[2]

The segments had gradually been arranging themselves into rings, and, as the last cleavages were tangential, the 808 segments formed a hollow sphere. Its surface was made up of plump, roundish little segments looking something like the drupelets of the raspberry or blackberry.

At this point the segmentation of the egg was complete. The big cell had been divided into cells of normal size. All cleavage could end.

With the egg's first stage of life completed, the hollow ball of cells sprouted cilia or little waving hairs. After the larva broke out of its membrane it used them as paddles to swim nimbly about in the salty sea water.

The nubbly little ball held still more surprises in store; only Act One had been performed. At the south-pole end, where the micromeres were concentrated, a crater appeared and about fifty of the cells tumbled inward over its edges. For a while they lay in a tangled heap just inside the sphere's wall. Shortly, though, Driesch saw them begin to move around, and soon they had sorted themselves out into a ring around the "pole." And then the ring changed into a triangular structure, or, more accurately, into an approximation of the capital letter A. In the two angles where the crossbar joins the two downstrokes, new cells began to cluster. They were the first beginnings of the sea urchin's skeleton. The "ball" was acquiring a right and a left side. It had had an upper and a lower end before; now it was taking on that asymmetry that, as Pasteur had seen, always characterizes living things. When one watched living things take form, it was not surprising that they should

[2] If you would like to see the mathematics worked out:

1. $1 \times 2 = 2$	6. $2 \times 32 = 64$
2. $2 \times 2 = 4$	7. $2 \times 64 = 128$
3. $2 \times 4 = 8$	8. $2 \times 128 = 256$
4. $2 \times 8 = 16$	9. $2 \times 256 = 512$
5. $2 \times 16 = 32$	10. $2 \times 512 = 1,024$

have rightness and leftness; it was a fundamental of the way in which they were made.

Act Two brought another odd occurrence. At the "south pole," where the cells had fallen in, a tube began to grow. It grew longer and longer until after a few hours it reached the opposite "pole" of the larva. It was the beginning of the intestine.

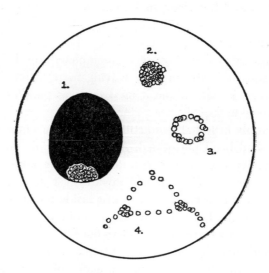

A sea urchin takes form. (1) A crater forms and about fifty cells tumble into the hollow interior. (2) At first the cells lie there in a tumbled heap. (3) They form a ring. (4) They arrange themselves into an "A" and the sea urchin's skeleton begins to round into shape.

While the tube was pushing through the interior as certainly as engineers driving a tunnel through a mountain, some of the cells from the crossbar cluster began to wander through the hollow interior, which by this time was filled, not with sea water, but with a gelatinous-like substance. Somehow in their wanderings the cells stopped in certain places, where they built up the typical skeleton of the sea urchin.

Driesch was concerned, however, with the earliest stages; the secret of development had to be sought here. In repeating Roux's experiment he decided to make use of the sea urchin's hardihood. Instead of using a hot needle to kill one of the halves produced in the first cleavage, he selected a number of eggs in the two-section stage, put them in a test tube, and shook them violently. In some cases the motion split the two halves apart; in some, it killed one half without damaging the other.

In either case, Driesch wanted to see what would happen to a surviving half. As Driesch watched, the surviving half began to divide, just as it would have done if it had still been linked to a sister half. The half split down and through in the normal manner. At what would have been the sixteen-cell stage, the half was made up of only eight segments: two micromeres, two large cells, and four of medium size. If a normal egg had been cut in two upon reaching the sixteen-cell stage, the half with which Driesch was working would have been exactly duplicated. It was all working out precisely as Roux had found; so far there was no divergence from the Roux results. It was getting late, however, and Driesch decided to go home.

The development of the roundish, grapefruit-shaped sea urchin proceeds rather rapidly. Generally the cleavage of the cell into its 808 divisions and its roundness are accomplished in about fifteen hours.

Knowing this, Driesch went back to his laboratory late that evening to see how his half was faring. At that time it was made up of about 202 segments, and he noticed that the edges of the semi-hemisphere were bending together a little, almost as though they were about to curl themselves into a sphere.

The next morning Driesch hurried to his laboratory again. The edges of the half had come together and a whole round organism was swimming around in his dish. It differed in only one important way from a normal sea-urchin larva: it was about half the usual size. It was a diminutive!

Driesch had been so convinced by Roux's results and had so little expected any such development that he decided it must be simply some kind of curling-together. He surmised that the next morning he would find only a half again, and he rather anticipated that the intestine might come out on one side of the little organism, perhaps as a half-tube.

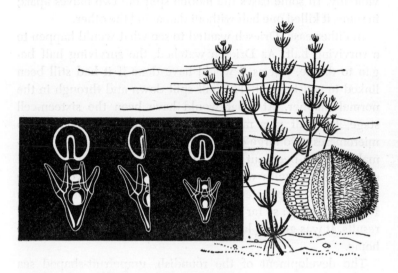

Wholes from halves. Driesch destroyed half a sea-urchin egg. Instead of the half-embryo he expected, a whole but diminutive animal developed. Thus, the egg was not a mosaic of traits. RIGHT: *A sea urchin with half of the spines removed.*

"But things turned out as they were bound to, and not as I expected," said Driesch.

The next morning there was no half-organism in his dish, but a small, whole, normal one. A whole had sprung from a fragment.

Driesch was profoundly impressed. His final results differed diametrically from Roux's.

An organism that had been cut in half had become a whole

again by a process of rearranging its material and without anything that resembled regeneration in the sense of budding from a wound. Driesch's mind leaped to the implications of the amazing change-about that he had witnessed.

If one half of the egg were capable of forming a whole organism, it was impossible to believe that the nuclear germ plasm had been divided in two. If the half had received only half the nuclear material, it would have been in no position to produce a whole; it would have lacked half the "primordia" or cues.

The round grainy little organism swimming around in the dish was enough, Driesch realized, to overthrow the contention of Roux and Weismann that the development of all the different parts of living things could be explained by a differential splitting up of the nucleus and a delegation of specific parts—such as a head-producing part—to certain cells.

Driesch foresaw another result. If the form of living things was not determined by a mechanical splitting up of determinative materials, there must be something else to explain why everything moved into its place and developed into the complex structures of living things. Another force would have to be at work, and Driesch thought that it would be an immaterial one. He recognized, however, that any such conclusion would need more and careful support if it were to get any consideration at all.

The young German biologist eagerly continued with the experiment that had been so fruitful. He let one of the sea-urchin eggs divide into quarters and then destroyed three of them. From one quarter came a tiny but whole organism. Driesch also found that if only one of the first four quarters was cut away, the complete organism showed no effect at all. As full and perfect a sea-urchin larva developed as if there had been no loss. Each segment must have received a full complement of machinery, rather than a partial one.

Driesch had gained a clear understanding of the essentiality or non-essentiality of each of the first four quarters. He did not know enough about the actual process of segmentation. The way to learn about it, he saw, was to interfere with the process again and see what happened.

He first raised the temperature of the sea water in which the sea-urchin eggs floated. In another experiment he diluted it. These fundamental changes in environment immediately altered the cleavage stages. Sometimes the micromeres did not appear at the sixteen-cell stage, as they normally would have done. Sometimes they appeared as early as the eight-cell phase. But whether the micromeres appeared early or late, the larva developed normally. So, Driesch concluded, it was not necessary for cleavage to occur in exactly a set order; the cell and its parts were quite versatile.

Driesch asked another question about the sea-urchin eggs. What would happen if their spatial pattern was disarranged?

Driesch decided to try pressing some of the eggs between two plates of glass. As he very gently increased the pressure of his hands on the glass, the eggs spread out into flat rounds, much as a ball of putty would flatten out under the same kind of pressure. But the pressure and the deformation did not kill the eggs. Cleavage went on, although only at right angles to the direction of the pressure.

At this moment Driesch lifted the glass off his little pancake eggs. Almost at once they began to divide in the other plane.

The experiment was a very satisfactory one. By pressing the eggs at different stages of cleavage, Driesch could obtain whatever kind of cleavage he wanted to study.

When he kept the eggs under pressure until the eight-cell stage was complete, the eight cells were lined up one beside the other, instead of in the usual rings of four cells, one above the other. But the eggs soon made up for this interference. As soon as he lifted off the sheet of glass, the next cell division occurred at right angles, and where there had been only a pancake of cells there were then two plates of eight cells each, one above the other. The egg rapidly rounded into form. It was the same if he kept the pressure on until the sixteen-cell stage was reached. In that case he had sixteen cells in a flat plate, but at the next free division two plates of sixteen cells one above the other were produced. The egg seemingly was not dependent on any one way of achieving results.

The egg also had astounding resistance. After all the pressing, the spatial changes, and the interference with the timing of their development, the eggs, in most cases, developed into lively, normal larvae. Instead of chaos there was order.

Driesch obtained comparable results working with the eggs of the frog, the annelids, and the ciona.

Having explored the effects of cleavage, the scientist decided to see what would happen if two eggs were fused. Very delicately Driesch pressed together two eggs that had completed their cleavage and were made up of 808 segments. They fused, and from them he succeeded in raising one giant organism.

In the first experiments Driesch had obtained several larvae from a material that ordinarily would have produced one. In the new fusing experiment one was produced instead of two. Both cases, Driesch maintained, contradicted the Roux-and-Weismann theory that differentiation could be explained by an unequal splitting of the nuclear material, by a sending out of heart material to one cell, liver to another, and skin machinery to a third. He considered the theory demolished, and time was to prove him right. Division during cleavage is qualitatively equal; each cell receives the same material; each cell gets a full set of blueprints. But a new problem was raised. If each segment possesses the factors to produce both a head and a tail, why is it that in normal development certain cells do produce a head and not a tail?

Differentiation still had to be explained. Why did some cells in the very beginning of cleavage move to the right and some to the left? How did all the different organs arise?

"There must be somewhere in the egg itself a certain factor which is responsible for at least general orientation and symmetry," Driesch argued.

Perhaps, he thought, such a factor had its seat in the protoplasm, the material surrounding the nucleus, if not in the nucleus itself. Again theory had to be tested.

Driesch had become acquainted with the American geneticist T. H. Morgan, and the two agreed to work together in trying to find out how the egg influences the organization of the structures that come from it. For their experiments they chose the eggs of the ctenophore, a sea animal somewhat resembling the jellyfish. Other workers had demonstrated that isolated ctenophore segments behaved like similar segments of the frog's egg; they formed half-organisms too.

By a delicate operation Morgan and Driesch cut away a bit of the protoplasm of the egg just before it began to cleave, and they succeeded in doing it without damaging the nucleus in any way. They hovered anxiously over the eggs until larvae developed from them. Then, to their immense gratification, they found that in every case where a cut was performed on the side of the egg, a similar defect appeared in the larva.

Although the nucleus had not been touched, damage to the protoplasm had effected a change in the development of the egg. The importance of the protoplasm had been proved, Driesch announced.

Additional proof that they were on the right track soon came in. Morgan, with the assistance of other workers, pressed a frog egg in the two-cell stage between sheets of glass and in such a way that the two segments were separated. He then turned them over. From both segments he succeeded in rearing a small whole tadpole. Morgan later repeated Roux's experiment exactly, killing one of the first two segments with a hot needle. If he did not touch the surviving segment again, a half-embryo developed; if he turned it over, a whole embryo resulted.

"There cannot be any doubt that in both of these cases it is

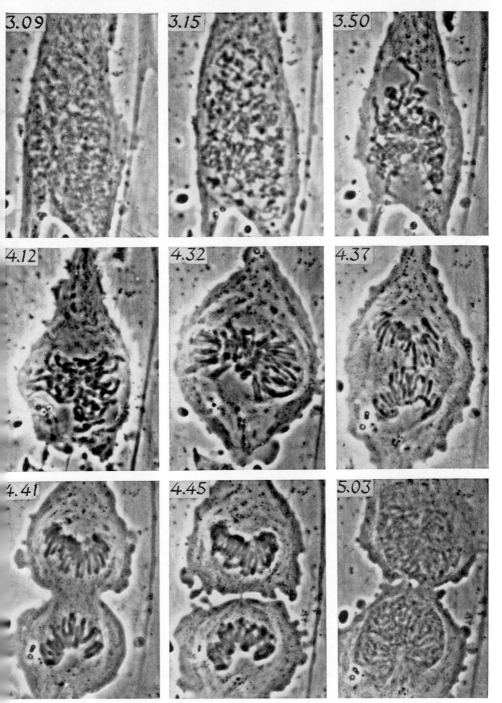

A cell divides in less than two hours. Stages in the division of a "spindle" cell of amblystoma heart in tissue culture are shown, with clock readings in the upper left corner.

PLATE I

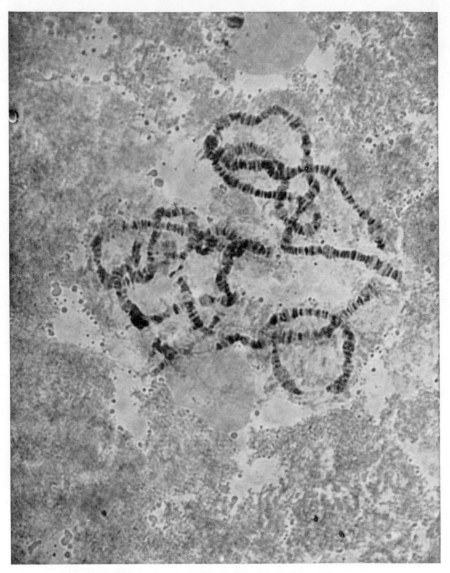

Giant chromosomes of a fruit fly enlarged 500 diameters.

PLATE II

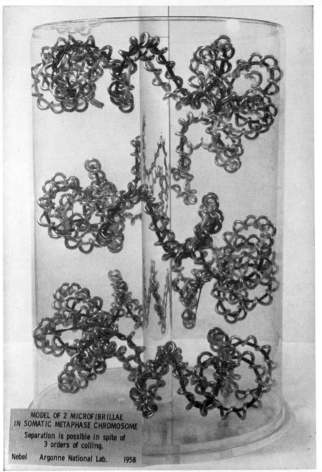

MODEL OF 2 MICROFIBRILLAE
IN SOMATIC METAPHASE CHROMOSOME
Separation is possible in spite of
3 orders of coiling.

Nebel   Argonne National Lab.   1958

The coiled coils of the chromosome. ABOVE: *Model of a section of a chromosome. The dark thread running through the coils is DNA.* BELOW: *Both the double-coiled structure of the chromosome and the coiling of the halves is shown in this fine electron micrograph by J. Herbert Taylor of Columbia University. This partially unwound chromosome comes from an Easter lily. Magnification about 1900 diameters.*

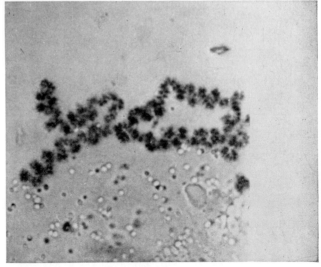

PLATE III

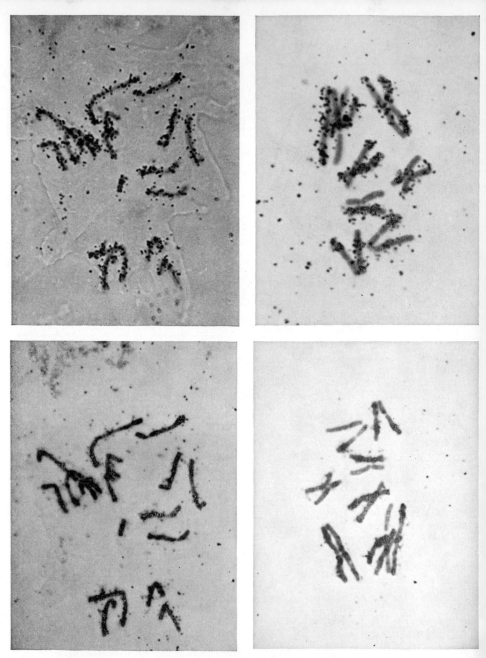

Duplication of chromosomes visible in radioactive solution. ABOVE LEFT: *Chromosomes of a cell of Bellevalia, a plant of the lily family. They have duplicated once in radioactive solution, which has tagged both members of each pair.* ABOVE RIGHT: *Chromosomes that have duplicated once in radioactive solution and once after the cells were removed. Only one member of each pair is tagged, except where the segments have crossed over.* BELOW LEFT: *Same as above left, in an earlier stage of development.* BELOW RIGHT: *Same as above right, earlier stage.*

PLATE IV

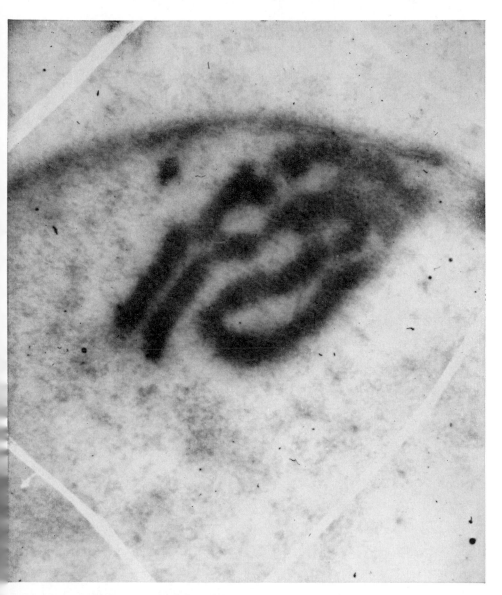

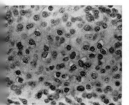 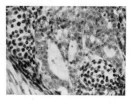

ABOVE: *A human chromosome magnified 36,000 times.* BELOW: *Cells specializing as cartilage or kidney tissue.*

PLATE V

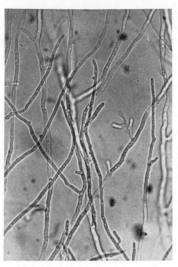

Normal branching filaments.

Bubble mutations on branched filaments.

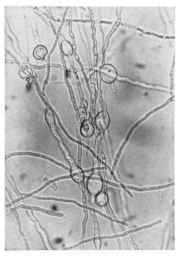

Normal fruiting body.

The coralloid mutation of normal fruiting body.

Mutation in molds: Schizophyllum, a common wood-rotting mushroom.

PLATE VI

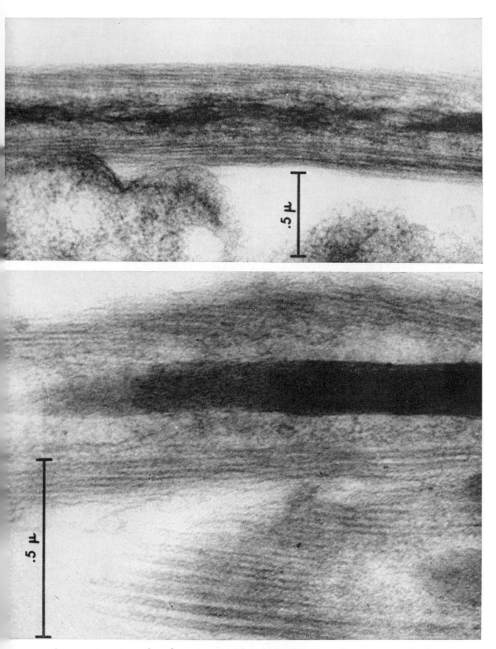

A rare view into the chromosome. The dark streak in the center of both electron micrographs is made up in part of coiled DNA.

PLATE VII

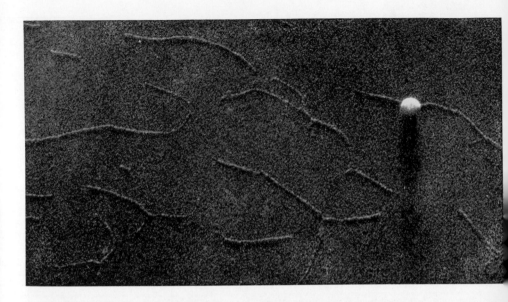

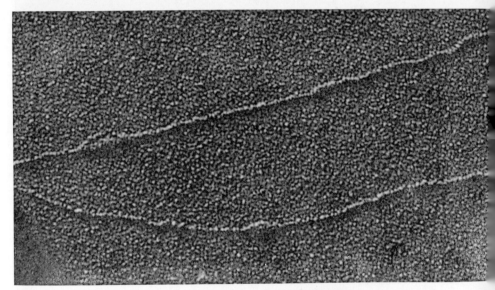

ABOVE: *Coils of DNA from salmon sperm, magnified 91,000 times (the white ball in this electron micrograph was used for measurements).* BELOW: *The veritable stuff of life: the long-coiled thread of DNA. An electron micrograph of DNA from calf thymus enlarged 146,000 times.*

PLATE VIII

the possibility of a rearrangement of protoplasm, offered by the turning over, which allows the isolated blastomeres [segments] to develop as a whole," said Driesch.

It was all a matter of how early localization occurred. As Driesch put it, "There exists in every egg an earliest stage in which all parts of its protoplasm are equal as to their prospectivity and in which there are no potential diversities or restrictions of any kind." If you went far enough back, all parts could become all things. Specialization came later and at various times.

The ingenious and pioneering experimental work of the biologists was beginning to explain a few of the mysteries of development. And yet to Driesch, who had been led into philosophy as he studied these deep mysteries, the explanations seemed only to be superficial, to explain nothing at all. The physical processes that separated and distributed the organ-forming substances of the egg and all of the processes of development seemed to him only means to an end, not the ultimate explanation.

"We must be cautious in admitting that any organic feature has been explained, even in the most general way by the action of physical forces," he warned. "What seems at first to be the result of mechanical pressures may afterwards be found to be an active process of growth.

"All of these processes are only the means of the organism, and can never do more than furnish the general type of events. They do not constitute life—they are *used* by life; let it remain an open question for the present how the phenomenon of 'life' is to be regarded."

It is the form of the whole that matters, Driesch maintained. He was able to show that in the miniature larvae that he raised from isolated egg segments, the size of the cells remained normal. Only their number was reduced.

This was interpreted by Driesch as showing that the cell is a sort of material used by the organism, just as a workman can construct very different buildings from stones of a given size. But, Driesch warned, there had to be the workman, the concept, the master plan.

At the same time that he ruled out physical and chemical forces as the answer to the whole of development, Driesch conceded that the environment played a part in shaping the form and organization of living things.

Like any adult organism, the egg cell required a certain amount of heat and oxygen and, if it grew in the sea, a certain salinity. Experimental work demonstrated that there was a maximum and minimum of each which could be tolerated. Exactly the right amount of salt in sea water promoted the development of the sea urchin; too much or too little disturbed it.

In one experiment the calcium was removed from the sea water to test the effect on sea-urchin eggs. In the calcium-deficient water, cleavage went on quite well, but after each cleavage the cells separated and went drifting off. At the end of the ten divisions the 808 cells were at the bottom of the dish, swimming about individually in chaos instead of in a round compact, functioning organism.

Environment certainly had an effect on development. To Driesch, however, it was no more the answer or the cause than were the internal physical and chemical processes of development. "There must be something else which is the sufficient reason of individual form production," he insisted. "Life, at least morphogenesis, is not a specialized arrangement of inorganic events; biology therefore is not applied physics and chemistry. Life is something apart, and biology is an independent science."

Driesch was breaking completely with the "mechanistic" tradition of Wohler, Fischer, and Roux. If the "physical facts" are insufficient to explain any phenomenon, he held, it was justifiable and necessary to introduce another explanation.

Driesch thus turned back to the ancient explanation of the inexplicable: vitalism. He went back to Aristotle, even borrowing his word, *entelechy*—"a something that bears the end in itself." Driesch explained, however, that he would use the old Greek word only as a mold to be filled with new contents.

"All attempts to conceive the organism as a mere aggregate of cells have proved to be wrong," said Driesch. "It is the *whole* that uses the cells."

It is life itself, a non-material force, Driesch insisted, that produces order and form.

The German biologist thus gave new vigor to an ancient debate, mechanism versus vitalism. After seeming to be settled, the old quarrel was opened again. In the meantime most biologists went on studying and seeking the mechanisms.

Driesch moved in the other direction. At the University of Cologne and later as professor of philosophy at the University of Leipzig he turned increasingly to the mystical, and ultimately became deeply interested in parapsychology. Instinct and action, he maintained, could never be explained mechanically. And, firm in the conviction that there are explanations which go beyond the senses and beyond the mechanics of physics and chemistry, he died at Leipzig in 1941.

IX

DE VRIES AND MENDEL: HEREDITY AND UNITS

THE GREAT MASS of yellow flowers in the corner of a fallow Dutch field glowed like gold in the warm light of the early evening.

Hugo De Vries (1848–1935), professor of botany at the University of Amsterdam, noticed them as he passed nearby. He saw that the brilliant flowers, Oenothera lamarckiana, must have escaped from the adjoining park. This struck De Vries as a promising circumstance; it was, in fact, a situation of the very kind he was looking for. Perhaps these tall plants with their crowns of yellow blossoms might vary somewhat from the primroses from which they had come.

The Dutch botanist was a reverent admirer of the work of Charles Darwin and an advocate of the theory of evolution. But he was troubled about one major difficulty in the theory which had persisted even into the 1880's. It seemed to De Vries that there could be no question about Darwin's basic theory that "descent with modification is the main law of nature in the organic world," and yet how did the modification come about? Could natural selection acting only on the infinitude of small variations that occur in all individuals account for the wide differences between species and for the diversity of the living world?

As a botanist, De Vries knew that breeders could go only so far in working with individual variations. There was a limit to how pink a rose, how tall a plant, how hardy a bulb they could develop by crossing two varieties. They could never obtain anything new until some new and different character appeared in Nature to give them the material with which to work. Darwin himself, though not all of his followers, had emphasized the importance of the wholly new—the sport, as he called it— that sometimes appears. If the problem were to be understood, De Vries thought, Nature should be studied in the act of changing. He decided to seek for evidence of large natural changes. They would most likely be found, he was sure, in some place where plants were multiplying rapidly in a new setting. That was why, aside from their beauty, De Vries's attention was caught by the rampant primroses.

The botanist began to examine the plants closely. He soon saw that the tall, densely leaved stems with their yellow-petaled flowers exhibited a high degree of variability, particularly in the shape of their leaves, their mode of branching, and their size. Also, some were annuals and some biennials.

"Here was a wonderful opportunity of getting an insight into the phenomenon of variation as exhibited by a plant that was multiplying rapidly," said De Vries.

Thus began one of the most thorough flower studies ever made. De Vries took a house near the primrose field, and in the second summer of intensive examination of the plants was rewarded by finding ten specimens of a new type. They were growing all by themselves in a corner of the field, well removed from the mass of the plants. The petals were small and more oval than the heart-shaped petals of the lamarckianas. The leaves also were smaller and, De Vries thought, "produced a much prettier foliage." Without any transition they had suddenly come into being! A new species had been created by mutation—the word De Vries used in preference to Darwin's "sport." De Vries happily named his new species Oenothera laevifolia.

During the next twenty years De Vries observed and raised 53,509 primrose plants, and among them found eight new species.[1] The new forms in every case appeared full-blown, with-

[1]. Some of the changes that De Vries considered new species were later found to be only modifications.

out gradation, without step-by-step change. And, once established, a new form maintained itself intact. All the while the
other plants went on year after year repeating themselves with
only the usual small variations.

"If our gigas [giant] and rubrinervis [red-veined] were
growing in equal numbers with the lamarckiana in the native
field, would it be possible to decide which of them was the
progenitor?" asked De Vries.

As he completed his prodigious experiment, De Vries
could formulate some of the laws of mutability which underlay
the spectacle of the yellow flowers. He saw that each character
—each differently formed leaf, each varied petal, each height
—varied by itself. A new red-veined leaf could appear without
any change occurring in most other parts of the plant. One
character, or at most a small group of characters, mutated at one
time. There was never an over-all change in all parts of the
plant.

"Attributes of organisms consist of distinct, separate, and independent units," said De Vries. "These units can be associated in groups, and we find in allied species the same units
and groups of units."

A mutation, then, was a change in a hereditary unit that was
later to be called a gene. The idea was a radical one that ran
counter to the prevailing and traditional concepts of an over-
all becoming, an over-all molding to a new environment.
De Vries searched the literature for other evidence of an independent unit of heredity.

In a work on hybridization by a German scientist, W. O.
Focke, he found a reference to some hybridization experiments by an Austrian monk, Gregor Mendel. Focke noted:
"Mendel believed he had found constant numerical ratios
among the types produced by hybridization."

Numerical ratios. That interested De Vries, and he tracked
down the reference. In a publication issued in 1866 by the
Brünn Society for the Study of Natural History he found a

monograph by Gregor Johann Mendel, of the Augustinian monastery at Brünn.

The author of the monograph was born on July 22, 1822, into a long-settled peasant family living in the tiny village of Heinzendorf in what was then Austrian Silesia and is now Czechoslovakia. As a boy he aided his father in the grafting of trees and in cultivating the garden that was a part of "peasant holding no. fifty-eight." He received additional training in horticulture and beekeeping at the village school. Johann did so well in this work and in his academic studies that his teachers urged that he be sent on to the high school at Troppau. Mendel never lost his love of growing things as he struggled to make his way at Troppau and later at the Philosophical Institute at Olmütz. Gradually this early interest turned into a wider interest in science, although little science was included in the institute's course.

Mendel finished his two years at Olmütz with a fine record, but in a state of physical exhaustion. His parents had tried valiantly to help their promising son through school, even turning over to him the dowry of one of his sisters. They simply did not have the funds to take care of even the extremely modest cost of his education. Through most of his years at school Mendel was on "half-rations" so meager that he was constantly hungry and scarcely had the energy for his studies and the tutoring that he was always forced to do. As he finished the two-year institute course, he knew that he could no longer go on. The university was out of the question. In desperation, Mendel appealed to one of his teachers for advice.

Many years later in a third-person autobiographical note he wrote: "It had become impossible for him to continue such strenuous exertions. It was incumbent on him to enter a profession in which he would be spared perpetual anxiety about a means of livelihood."

The teacher understood. He suggested that Mendel enter the Augustinian monastery at Brünn. It was noted for the

learning of its monks, and there Mendel would have an opportunity, free of the pressure of earning a living, to go on with
the studies that he loved. His teacher would be happy to rec-
ommend him. Mendel gratefully accepted. A letter went to the
monastery calling attention to Mendel's "most exceptional" reports at the institute and to his "very solid character." And so it
came about that on October 9, 1843, Mendel was admitted to
the monastery as a novice. He assumed the name of Gregor.

From the beginning, the life there was a happy unfolding for
the long-strained young man. Mendel tells the story in his
autobiography: "Now that he had been relieved of anxiety
about the physical basis of existence, which is detrimental to
study, the respectful undersigned acquired fresh courage and
energy, so that it was with pleasure and love that he undertook
the course of classical studies prescribed for the years of pro-
bation."

In his free time he occupied himself with the small botanical and mineralogical collections available to the monastery. His fondness for natural science grew with every fresh
opportunity for making himself acquainted with it. "Although
he had no oral guidance in this undertaking, and perhaps there
is no other department of knowledge in which the self-taught
student has such difficulties to face and moves so slowly toward his goal, he has ever since been so much addicted to the
study of nature that he would shrink from no exertions that
might help him, by further diligence on his own part and by
the advice of men who had had practical experience, to fill the
gaps in his information," Mendel wrote.

On Mendel's twenty-fifth birthday, July 22, 1847, he was
ordained a sub-deacon and two days later a priest. A short
though earnest trial revealed that the duties of a parish priest
would weigh unbearably upon him. He could not witness suffering without becoming ill himself. The abbot of the monastery
recognized that Mendel's worth lay elsewhere and wisely assigned him to teaching. The young monk was appointed a "sup-

ply" teacher in the high school at Znaim in southern Moravia. As he did not have a teacher's certificate, he could not be given a full appointment. Mendel could not have been happier with this turn in his life, and he at once took to teaching, as he had to life in the monastery, "with pleasure and love."

Mendel was so excellent a teacher that the head of the school confidently urged him to try for a teacher's certificate. Mendel wrote the necessary essay and presented himself in Vienna for the oral examinations in the natural history and physics that he wanted to teach. He failed to pass the examination, partly, it seemed, because he lacked certain formal knowledge of his subjects. In part his failure may have been due to the conviction of the friendly chief examiner that the unusual young teacher should be given an opportunity for "higher scientific training" at the University of Vienna.

The abbot of the monastery agreed, and Mendel went to the university for four terms. At the end, he returned to teach in the Brünn "Modern School."

Mendel was a friend as well as an instructor to his pupils. They remembered him for years afterward—the kindly, patient, heavy-set monk in the frock coat, tall hat, and high boots considered proper for an Augustinian serving as a schoolmaster.

They also remembered their visits to the monastery garden. Smiling at them through his gold-rimmed spectacles, Mendel would show them all the wonders of the beautiful gardens, the pineapples growing in the forcing-house, the bees, and the many pea plants climbing on staves and strings in the long narrow garden just outside the monastery walls. Mendel used plain words to explain to his pupils how one kind of pea was being crossed with another, and if the reference to sex produced a titter, Mendel quickly checked it: "Don't be stupid, these are natural things." He did not tell them, though, that he was the experimenter.

Soon after entering the monastery Mendel began trying to develop new colors in flowers. He also took up the breeding of gray and white mice. Although the latter experiments were dropped after a while, probably at a hint of ecclesiastical disapproval, they were a certain indication that the work with flowers was not a fancy but the first approach of a serious scientist to a fundamental problem.

Mendel's own account of how he happened to begin his studies is a simple one. As he tried to produce new colors in his flowers, he acquired considerable experience in artificial fertilization. His interest was aroused by the surprising and unaccountable results that he sometimes obtained. Whenever he crossed certain species, the same hybrid forms cropped up with striking regularity. But when he crossed one of his hybrids with another, some very different characters sometimes appeared among their progeny.

These phenomena sent Mendel to the literature. He searched all the books available in the monastery and elsewhere in Brünn. A number of scientists were working with the problem of hybrids, but no one had discovered any law governing their formation—if, indeed, anyone could conceive of a law capable of explaining the infinitude of forms in the multitude of plants. Inheritance in all its profusion seemed beyond any nailing down.

Mendel nevertheless had seen certain forms appearing with regularity. Others too had noted this phenomenon. They had not, as far as Mendel could find, counted the forms and classified them. Nor had anyone arranged hybrids according to their generations or worked out their statistical relationships. Mendel, in his remote Austrian town, did not realize that even his concept of counting and figuring the mathematical relationships of hybrid plants was original and entirely his own.

To study heredity properly, Mendel saw, a large number of generations would have to be bred. He also recognized that many plants would have to be included in each generation. A few might produce a misleading picture. "It indeed required some courage to undertake such far-reaching labors," Mendel wrote later in the introduction to one of his monographs. "It appears, however, to be the only way in which we can finally reach the solution of a problem which is of great importance in the evolution of organic forms."

The year was 1854. Many people were asking how the great number of species could have arisen, and yet Charles Darwin would not publish *The Origin of Species* for another five years. It seems unlikely that the Austrian monk was planning a direct study of the great problem of evolution. His interest was concentrated on heredity and how traits could be handed on from parent to offspring. Nevertheless, as his words show, Mendel was well aware of the evolutionary significance of the work he was about to launch.

Mendel planned the big experiment with care and foresight. His first requirement was a plant with varied characters, each of which bred true to form. If a plant produced green peas, he had to be sure that it would go on producing green peas if crossed with another green-pea plant. Mendel also had to have a plant that could be protected from foreign pollen during its flowering period. If even one bee carried in some pollen other than that he would dust on, the whole experiment would be upset. Equally important, the characters had to be easily observable and countable. It was a huge task Mendel was laying out for himself.

The patient monk did not hurry. He tried out enough plants to see that the common pea would best meet his specifications for an experimental plant. His next job was to make sure of his material.

Mendel obtained thirty-four more or less distinct varieties of peas from seedsmen and planted them in his monastery garden. With the exception of one whose seeds quite evidently had been mistakenly mixed, each variety yielded offspring exactly like itself. He repeated the plantings during a second year. The results were the same.

His seeds, then, were reliable; he had his raw material. From the thirty-four varieties Mendel selected twenty-two, and from these, seeds with seven sharply contrasting pairs of characters. As he wanted to make no fine-line decisions about whether or not a part of a plant had changed, he selected the following clear-cut differences with which to work:

1. The form of the ripe seeds—round or wrinkled;
2. The color of the peas (the seed)—yellow or intense green;
3. The color of the transparent seed cover or skin—white or grayish;
4. The form of the ripe pods—inflated or constricted between the peas;
5. The color of the unripe pods—green or yellow;
6. The position of the flowers—distributed along the stem or bunched at the top: in other words, axial or terminal;
7. The length of the stem—tall (six or seven feet) or dwarf (three-fourths to one and a half feet).

Each kind of seed went into its own jar—to await the spring of 1856.

Mendel was at last ready to launch his experiment proper. In one section of his long narrow garden he planted round seeds, and in the next section, wrinkled ones. In other sections went the yellow and the green, and, in their own places, all of the others. Keeping the characters that he wanted to compare next to one another would simplify the work that lay ahead.

The peas did well in the warm, gentle Austrian spring and soon were ready to blossom. Mendel then had to work rapidly, for timing mattered. He opened some of the pretty flower buds of his wrinkled plants, removed the keel from each, and pinched off the stamen to prevent the peas from fertilizing themselves in the normal manner. Then he tied a little paper or calico bag around each one to protect the exposed stigma.

As soon as the pollen had ripened in the adjoining round peas, Mendel collected a bit on a fine camel's-hair brush and, removing the bags on the wrinkled peas, dusted it on their stigmas. The little bags then were tied on again to keep away the bees and other pollen-carrying insects. To make certain that his experiments were not affected by which plant served as the seed parent, Mendel also reversed his fertilization procedure. Some of the pollen from the wrinkled peas was deposited on the prepared stigmas of the round.

The same meticulous process was repeated in each of the other special plots. Altogether Mendel made 287 cross-fertilizations on seventy plants. It was a good growing summer and the peas flourished in what the monks called Mendel's "pea plantation."

Mendel was in the garden early and late, watching over the maturing plants. His first indication of what was happening would come when the pods formed in the "unripe pod color" section of his garden. As the pods appeared and filled out and grew longer, Mendel saw with elation that all of them were green. Whether they grew in the "yellow" half of the plot and came from parents that had produced yellow pods or in the "green" half and sprang from parents with green pods, all of them hung green on the vines. Yellow and green parents alike had produced green offspring. Mendel searched his plants. He could not find a single yellow among the unripe pods.

Confirmation of this striking result came as the summer drew to a close and the pods dried on the vines. Mendel had to let the pods in the "ripe pod form" section dry thoroughly, for only then were the shape of the pods and the color of the peas they contained completely "set." As the pods turned dry and brownish, there could be no doubt. All of them were inflated. It was as though the "constriction" of half of the parents had never existed.

All of this foretold the outcome of his other experiments, and yet Mendel did not dare to be sure. He tremblingly prepared to open the first pod in the "seed color" section. Would the peas so snugly contained in it, invisible until the moment of opening, show only one color? Here was the final, the critical test. In an instant's glance he saw that there was no question. The peas so nicely ranged against the sere brown of the pod were an unmistakable bright orangey yellow. Mendel harvested his other pods and opened them one by one. Each was filled with yellow peas alone. Not a pea was green or displayed even a trace of its half-green ancestry. If the peas had been pure gold, they could not have looked better to the happy monk.

It was the same when Mendel opened the peas from his "seed form" plot. All of them were round. This time it was the wrinkling of half of the parents which had disappeared.

During the winter, as he studied his jars of peas and the way all had completely taken on the character of one parent, it was evident that one characteristic in each pair had been entirely "dominant" over the other. Mendel decided to designate the hereditary trait that prevailed as a "dominant." Later he named the other factor, the one lost to sight, a "recessive."

Only the first step had been completed in the big experiment. The next, the crossing of hybrid with hybrid, had to await another spring. As the sun grew warm and the spring rains fell, Mendel planted his hybrid seeds. Each carefully marked group went into its own plot, but this time his procedure would be different. He would not operate on the buds. He would permit the peas to fertilize themselves in the natural way, and thus would obtain a cross of two identical hybrids.

The plantation was again filled with pea vines, and Mendel waited as patiently as he could for the pods and peas to form and dry.

As the young pods grew, Mendel saw a few yellows appearing among the greens. He counted both colors and entered the figures in his notebooks. When the pods dried in the "pod form" plot, some were crinkled around the peas they contained; they were, in the terms he was using, constricted.

The others were inflated. Again Mendel counted both types, and again he reserved judgment.

At last the day came when the pods could be gathered. Mendel opened the first pod from the "seed color" beds and looked upon a remarkable sight. In the pod with four bright yellow peas was one of green. It seemed to glow against the yellow and the honey tones of the pods. The green was no accident. Most of the pods contained both green and yellow peas. The green of the grandparents was reappearing, and it was as sharp, as clear, as unequivocal as though it had never been associated with the yellow through one entire generation. Mendel no longer had to question. The green had not been lost. Somehow this heritage from the grandparents had persisted and had come forth again.

Mendel began his tally, the tally that he was relying on to explain the relationships to which the yellow and green peas testified. From his 258 plants he obtained 8,023 peas. Exactly 6,022 were yellow and 2,001 green. It was immediately evident, when the score was kept in this way, that three fourths were yellow and one fourth green. The ratio was 3 to 1, the same ratio he had seen in the color of the unripe pods and in the form of the ripe ones.

Mendel went on to his computation on seed form. The 253 hybrid plants in the "seed form" experiment produced 7,324 peas, of which 5,474 were round and 1,850 wrinkled. Therefore the ratio was 3.01 to 1, or virtually the same 3 to 1.

The same significant ratio turned up in all the other crossings of hybrid with hybrid: 3.15 to 1 on the color of the seed coat, 2.95 to 1 on the form of the pod, and within this range for all the others. The average for the entire group was 3 to 1. Here was no chance combination of numbers, but a regularly occurring phenomenon, a revelation of the long-hidden workings of heredity.

Mendel continued his plantings through six or seven generations in all cases. As he did so, he learned that the 3-to-1 ratio, which was based on the appearance of the peas, was actually a 1:2:1 ratio when the true nature of the peas was revealed by later plantings.

Mendel planted the wrinkled peas from the first hybrids in a place of their own. They yielded only wrinkled peas and continued to produce only wrinkled as long as he planted them and permitted them to fertilize themselves. They were pure recessives.

But the round peas from the hybrid parents produced both round and wrinkled seeds. One fourth were true rounds and, as long as they were planted, would yield only round peas. Two fourths were round in appearance, but were actually hybrids and would produce round and wrinkled peas in a steady 3-to-1 ratio. The wrinkled peas from the union were again pure wrinkled and never would yield anything but their own kind.

"It can be seen," said Mendel, "how rash it may be to draw from the external resemblances conclusions as to their internal nature."

Appearance meant little or nothing. It was not surprising that human beings had eternally been bewildered when they tried to understand heredity. The surface differences of off-spring were legion in themselves, and yet below the surface lay still other differences and possibilities for variation.

With the clarity and simplicity of genius, Mendel labeled the "dominant" in the union with a capital A, and the recessive with a small a. A constant dominant thus would be formed by the coming together of two A's, and it would be described as AA; a hybrid by either Aa or aA; and a recessive by aa.

With this understanding, it was possible for him to chart this coming together and separation and the clear-cut results that it produced. Mendel drew, and the world has since followed, his chart of heredity.

In initiating his work Mendel had kept his attention fixed on a single pair of characters. He inevitably had to ask whether the same laws of development would apply if several diverse characters were united. Suppose the parents differed in two characteristics.

Mendel crossed peas with round yellow seeds with those bearing wrinkled greens. As roundness and yellowness were dominant, he expected that all of the peas from the union would be round and yellow. And so they turned out to be.

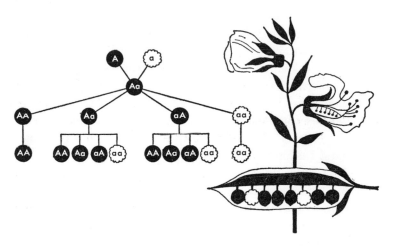

The crossing of round and wrinkled peas reveals the laws of heredity. All of the first generation were round. But when two round hybrids were crossed, the wrinkling of one of the grandparents reappeared, in the ratio of one to three. Another generation reveals the true nature of the hybrids.

The next year Mendel let the round yellow hybrids fertilize themselves. When the peas were ripe, some of the monks and others interested in science gathered around for the opening of the first pods. Tension mounted as Mendel cracked open the dry pods. And then even the uninitiated were startled. In the one pod lay four different kinds of peas: round and yellow, wrinkled and yellow, round and green, and wrinkled and green.

It was almost overwhelming to see Nature, supposedly unpredictable Nature, responding with such precision to an experimental test.

Mendel eagerly counted the 556 peas borne by the fifteen
double-hybrid plants he had grown. He had 315 round and
yellow peas, 101 wrinkled and yellow, 108 round and green,
and 32 wrinkled and green. When two pairs of characteristics
were crossed, the ratio was no longer 3 to 1; it was 9:3:3:1.

Charles Darwin also had experimented with peas and had
noticed that the hybrid divided 3 to 1, but Darwin was no
mathematician and did not pursue this revealing indication of
order in heredity. Mendel, on the other hand, was an excellent
mathematician. The new experiment confirmed what he had
already glimpsed in his first experiments. He was simply obtaining every combination that could be formed by the separate
factors present. If A and a were combined, only one combination could be formed: Aa. If Aa and Aa came together, four
combinations could be made: AA, Aa, aA, aa. And this was
exactly what had happened.

And if two series were united—$A + 2\ Aa + a$ and $B + 2$
$Bb + b$, sixteen different groupings could be produced. And as
the dominants would determine the appearance of each group,
the result would be 9 AB, 3 Ab, 3 aB, and 1 ab—exactly what
he had found in the pods. The results were as precise in the
peas Mendel harvested as in his equations.

Mendel now felt virtually certain of the principle that lay
behind all the different forms of nature. He felt, though, that
his tests should be carried at least one step further, for these
were strange and unheard-of laws that he was working out.
Mendel decided to study three differing traits.

This was the most difficult of all his experiments. Round
yellow peas with grayish seed coats were crossed with pollen
from plants bearing wrinkled, green, white-skinned peas. It
took "time and trouble," Mendel noted, but the twenty-seven
groupings that his calculations showed should result did come

from the union. He obtained all the combinations that could be made by putting together three series, $A + 2\ Aa + a$, $B + 2\ Bb + b$, and $C + 2\ Cc + c$. Again Mendel could see how it went. With one pair of hybrids, three kinds of offspring; with two, nine; with three, twenty-seven. The combinations piled up, three times three times three, in cubic ratio.

Mendel had no way to look into the egg and pollen cells to search for the hereditary factors whose existence he inferred from his experiments. His results, however, were explainable in no other way. Just as Mendel had grasped the secrets of the combinations of these factors, so did he reason out the biological basis that had to underlie them. He formulated three laws of inheritance:

1. All living things are a complex of a large number of independent heritable units.

2. When each parent contributes the same kind of factor and the two come together in the offspring, a constant character is produced. But if one parent contributes one kind of factor, say A, and the other another, say a, a hybrid results. When the hybrid forms reproductive cells, the two differentiating elements "liberate themselves" again and thus are free to form new combinations in the next union.

3. The factors are unaffected by their long association in the individual. They emerge from the union as distinct as when they entered it.

In a letter to a fellow scientist Mendel enlarged upon this radical idea: "The course of development consists simply in this: that in each successive generation the two primal characters issue distinct and unadulterated out of the hybridized pair, there being nothing whatever to show that either of them had inherited or taken over anything from the others."

This was Mendel's ultimately famous law of the purity of the gametes, or reproductive cells. Mendel himself modestly regarded it only as a hypothesis, and felt that he must subject it to additional tests.

If the hereditary factors separated and re-combined as his work indicated, there were two ways to prove it. He would fertilize the hybrid *AaBb*, a plant having round yellow seeds, with pollen from the parent plant *AB*, which also had round yellow seeds. As far as the eye could see, both were exactly alike. Actually the hybrid would have four factor pairs—*AB*, *Ab*, *aB*, *ab*—and the parent plant only *AB*. Mendel figured out all the combinations that could result if these pairs were combined. There were four: *AAb*, *AaB*, *AaBb*, and *AB*. And as each pair would contain a dominant, all should have round yellow seeds.

Mendel made his proposed cross-fertilization. As the young plants matured, he again watched anxiously, knowing once more exactly what results he should obtain if his theory was correct. At last the pods were ripe and dry. They contained ninety-eight peas, and every single pea was round and yellow.

Mendel's second test was a "back cross with the recessive parent." The hybrid again had the egg cells *AB*, *Ab*, *aB*, *ab*, and the green wrinkled parent, *ab*. In his notebook Mendel noted the combinations that should result: *AaBb* (round and yellow), *Aab* (round and green), *aBb* (wrinkled and yellow), and *ab* (wrinkled green), and all of them should appear in equal numbers.

His plants in due time produced 31 round yellow peas, 28 round and green, 27 wrinkled and yellow, and 26 wrinkled and green. If enough plants had been raised, the slight variations in numbers would have disappeared. The peas developed exactly as Mendel's theory had forecast and in the ratio he had predicted—1:1:1:1. "In all the experiments," said Mendel, "there appeared all the forms which the proposed theory demands."

The most severe tests had been applied. His theory had been proved with a certainty that exceeded all expectations, and Mendel could admit to himself that he had discovered some of the true laws of heredity.

At last the time had come to report on his eight years of unremitting work. During the fall and early winter of 1864 Mendel checked and rechecked his findings. In his fine copperplate script he wrote the paper that eventually would explain to the world the all-important phenomenon of heredity.

The Brünn Society for the Study of Natural Science was holding its February 1865 meeting at the Modern School, the school in which Mendel taught. The night was cold and snowy, but most of the forty members came to hear Mendel report on the work he had so long been carrying on at the monastery. Curiosity about it was keen.

As Mendel read, this curiosity gave way to incomprehension. The several botanists in the society were as much confused by the report on invariable hereditary ratios in peas as were the other members—a chemist, an astronomer, a geologist, and an authority on cryptograms. Mendel spoke for the hour allotted to him, and then announced that at the next meeting he would explain why the peculiar and regular segregation of characteristics occurred.

The next month, as Mendel presented his algebraic equations, attention wavered. The combination of mathematics and botany which Mendel was expounding was unheard of. And the idea that lay behind it, that heredity was a giant shuffling and reshuffling of separate and invisible hereditary factors, stood in such diametrical contrast to all that had been taught that it probably could not be grasped. No one rose to ask a question. The minutes recorded no discussion.

A number of the members spoke to Mendel afterward about his experimental work. "I encountered various views," Mendel told his friends. "No one undertook a repetition of the experiment."

The editor of the *Proceedings* of the society extended the usual invitation to Mendel to prepare his paper for publication in the society's journal. "I agreed to do so," said Mendel, "after I had once more looked through my notes relating to the various years of the experiment without being able to discover any sort of mistake."

Mendel's monograph—*Versuche uber Pflanzenhybriden*—appeared in 1866. According to the society's custom, copies of the *Proceedings* in which it was included were sent to Vienna, Berlin, Rome, St. Petersburg, and Uppsala. But the brief paper that could have altered all ideas of heredity, and at a time when Darwin was still at work on the role of heredity in evolution, attracted no attention.[2] It sat all but unread on library shelves.

Mendel was deeply disappointed. He understood the large significance of the work he had done and the bearing it could have on the discussions of evolution which were then preoccupying Europe. Mendel decided to make one more attempt to place his work before a man qualified to appreciate it and bring it to the attention of the scholarly world.

On New Year's Eve, 1866, he wrote a long and carefully composed letter to Karl von Nägeli of Munich, one of the outstanding botanists and scientific men of Europe.

"Your well-known services in the detection and classification of plant hybrids growing in the wild state make it my agreeable duty to bring to your kindly knowledge the descriptions of a few experiments concerning the artificial fertilization of plants," Mendel began.

He enclosed a copy of his monograph and suggested that if Nägeli should be interested in checking the experiment or pursuing the subject further, he would be very happy to furnish him with the seeds. He also indicated that he was thinking about carrying on some experiments with the variable hawkweed plant, which Nägeli and other botanists had intensively studied.

"I hope," Mendel wrote, "that you will not refuse me your

[2] *The Origin of Species* had been published in 1859, only seven years earlier, and Darwin was at work on his book on *Variations in Animals and Plants under Domestication.*

esteemed participation when, in any instance, I need advice."

Several months passed before Nägeli replied. Then the tone of his letter was definitely condescending. His only comment on Mendel's work was that, "far from being finished," it was just beginning. Nevertheless, he asked for some of the seeds Mendel had offered and suggested that Mendel would do well to proceed with the study of his plant, the hawkweed or Hieracium.

Mendel had raised more than 10,000 hybrid plants and had recorded his observations on 12,980 specimens, but he took no offense at Nägeli's comment that he was only beginning, or at the botanist's obliviousness to the importance of his results. Delighted that the great man had deigned to write to him, Mendel at once sent him 140 envelopes of his seeds. This gift launched a correspondence that continued for nearly eight years.

Through Nägeli's influence Mendel shifted more of his work to the hawkweed, a plant difficult and unsuitable for his purposes. Nägeli sent him a few specimens from the Alps, but Mendel had to collect most of his material in the nearby mountains. By this time he had grown quite stout and the rugged field trips were taxing. Work on the minute dandelion-like plant also was demanding. It was almost impossible to remove the anthers from the blossoms without having pollen fall upon the stigma or injuring the pistil so that it withered away. To see, as he slit the buds with a fine needle, Mendel had to use an "illuminating device," a mirror and lens. The sun shining upon it badly strained his eyes, and for some months he had to discontinue his work.

Mendel succeeded in raising only six hybrids from the widely varied hawkweeds, and the six were puzzling. Some of them resembled the mother plant and some were in between the two parents. Only the color of the flower followed the rules Mendel had discovered in the pea. Nothing was known at the time about apogamy, a process in which the seed is formed

without fertilization, but this was the unusual phenomenon
into which Mendel had stumbled or, rather, been led. In effect, the hybrids that resembled the seed plant were nothing
more than shoots.

As he worked with both Pisum and Hieracium, Mendel had
not neglected to ask the essential question: would the same
laws appear in other plants? Behind this question lurked the
larger query: was it possible that these were universal laws?
Mendel modestly refrained from stating this latter question,
but in corners of his garden he experimented with beans, corn,
and flowers, most particularly snapdragon, stock, violet, and
four o'clock.

The hybrids of the four o'clock and of maize behaved exactly like those of peas, and so did the beans in their height
and the shape of their seed pods.

Upsetting results began to appear only when Mendel crossed
a bean having white flowers and white seeds with a purple-
flowered plant that had red seeds splashed and flecked with
violet. In the first generation all the hybrids bore reddish
flowers, and yet the red was much less intense than that of
the red parent. When these hybrids flowered, however, Mendel was confronted not with the white and purple-red flowers
of the grandparents, but with a dazzling burst of color. One
out of the thirty-one blossoms was a pure white; the others
ranged from a pale violet to the deepest red. The color of the
seed coats ran equally riot.

It was a disturbing result. Mendel anxiously asked if he
could have been wrong in his earlier conclusions. He could
not believe that possible, for he had worked too carefully and
cross-checked too thoroughly. There had to be another explanation. As he sought for one, Mendel recalled the extraordinary variety in the color of all "ornamental flowers." Color in
flowers was known to be highly variable, and some observers
argued that this rich and seemingly unpredictable palette of

colors was a perfect illustration of how devoid of rules heredity was. To Mendel such a conclusion seemed unthinkable.

Others held that the profusion of color was produced when the stability of species was upset or disturbed by cultivation. And yet what was there in the simple transference into garden soil which could effect such a thorough and persistent revolution in the plant?

"Changes of type must take place if the condition of life be altered and the species possesses the capacity of fitting itself to its new environment," Mendel reasoned. "It is willingly granted that by cultivation the organization of new varieties is favored, and that by man's labor many varieties are acquired, which under natural conditions would be lost; but nothing justifies the assumption that the tendency to the formation of varieties is so extraordinarily increased that the species loses all stability and the offspring diverge into an endless series of extremely variable forms."

If change of environment produced hereditary changes in the plant, Mendel was quick to see that a lack of change should produce plants that were constant. This was not the case at all. In fact, it was under the stable conditions of the garden that plants were most variable. Almost the only exceptions to this rule were the peas and other legumes whose organs of fertilization were protected by a keel. And even the legumes had given rise to numerous varieties in a cultural period that Mendel thought must extend backward for at least a thousand years.

Rejecting the traditional explanations, Mendel concluded that there must be another explanation of variability. "Various experiments force us to the conclusion that our cultivated plants with few exceptions are members of various hybrid series, whose further development in conformity with law is changed and hindered by frequent crossings inter se."

Mendel was venturing with a sure step into some of the

fundamental problems of evolution and heredity. From his own acute observation and perhaps from reading Darwin he saw that plants had to adapt to their environment to survive, and yet he was not beguiled by Lamarck's theory that direct inheritable changes could be produced by environment—in the case Mendel was considering, by a garden setting.

If the color of flowers was not determined by a single hereditary factor but by two factors, A_1 and A_2, the spectrum of color could easily be explained. If this were the situation and two characters were crossed, nine colors would be produced in sixteen combinations, $9:3:3:1$, and only one of the blossoms would be white.

"It would be well worth while," he told the Brünn society, "to follow up the development of color in hybrids by similar experiments, since it is probable that in this way we might learn the significance of the extraordinary variety in the coloring of our ornamental plants."

This was exactly what Mendel was doing. He had not missed the significance of the way cultivated plants were usually grown—in masses and close together. There was every opportunity for reciprocal fertilization, and it was where this mingling of pollen occurred that one found the great and beautiful vareity of colors that existed in gardens. To make certain that he was reasoning correctly, Mendel grew a white-flowered Dianthus caryophyllus that had been derived from a white-flowered variety in the hothouse. No other pollen could reach it, and it produced only white flowers. The same was true of a red-flowered variety. When it was protected from cross-fertilization, it yielded only red flowers.

"Whoever studies the coloration that results in ornamental plants from similar fertilization can hardly escape the conviction that here also the development follows a definite law which possibly finds its expression in the combination of several independent color characters."

In actuality he had correctly interpreted the in-betweenness of color in the bean plants and, far beyond this, the in-betweenness of a great number of traits in all plants and living things, including man. Although he knew nothing of how hereditary units were ranged in the cell or of the biochemical processes that underlay the phenomena he saw, Mendel had worked out the principles of heredity.

Mendel himself did not realize how far he had gone. Despite his ability to explain both in-betweenness and the clear-cut results he had obtained with peas, he was troubled by the difference in pattern and by the erratic failure of the hawk-weed to follow all of the rules. Mendel did not think that he had discovered the universal law of heredity. He believed—mistakenly—that he had fallen short of this ultimate objective.

Despite these discouragements, Mendel's interest had not flagged, and he would have continued his experiments if that had been possible.

On April 1, 1868, when he was forty-six, Mendel was elected abbot of the monastery. He sadly left the pupils and the teaching that he loved so well. In accepting the duty and the honor that had been conferred on him, he had high hopes, however, that he might be able to increase his research. The full gardens of the monastery would be open to him; his plants would no longer have to be crowded into the little strip beneath the walls.

Mendel soon discovered that this hope was illusory. The abbot of the important monastery was called on for in-numerable civic duties in addition to those of administration. He was expected to serve on the administrative council of the Moravian mortgage bank. He must become a member of the agricultural committee. He was called upon to preside at meetings.

By the end of his first year in office, Mendel realized that he would not be able to go much further with his research. When he presented his Hieracium paper to the Brünn Society on June 9, 1869, he apologized for the "slight results." "The

conviction that the prosecution of the proposed experiments
will demand a whole series of years and the uncertainty
whether it will be granted to me to bring the same to a conclusion have determined me to make the present communica-
tion," he said.

The demands upon Mendel's time only increased. As he
anticipated, he was unable to go on with his hybridization
work, although he improved and extended the gardens of the
monastery. Many of the fruit trees bore the little lead seals,
initialed GM, that he attached to all his grafts.

In such spare time as he had, Mendel also continued his
studies of bees. He had always kept bees in hives to which he
attached slates showing when the queen had been installed,
out of which crossing she had come, and the date of the
nuptial flight and the slaughter of the drones. After he became
abbot he had a special fertilization cage built to limit fertilization to one kind of drone.

Mendel also continued the observations he had long made
for the Central Institute of Meteorology. A tornado struck
Brünn in 1870. Mendel characteristically made precise scientific observations of the pieces of tile that went flying through
his room: "Since there are double windows and the projec-
tiles went through both strata, the relative position of the
opening in the outer and inner panes shows their trajectory.
But, according to the before-mentioned law of circular storms,
the missiles ought to have come from the NNE, NE, and
ENE." In his report Mendel even indulged himself in a little
fun with the townspeople who attributed the freaks of the
storm to the doings of the devil.

After 1874 his small margin of time for scientific work was
reduced still further. The German Liberal Party passed a law
taxing the monasteries for the support of the other activities
of the Catholic Church. Mendel regarded the tax as an in-
vasion of the ancient rights of the monastery, rights he had
sworn to protect. He refused to pay.

Friendly officials tried in every way to persuade him to comply, even hinting that if a token payment were made, most of the tax could be forgotten. Mendel would have none of such evasion. A principle was at stake, and he would not yield. All conciliation having failed, the state was left with no choice except to sequester the property of the monastery. Mendel fought all the harder, and the struggle went on for fourteen years. Under the strain of it, the abbot's health began to suffer.

Mendel's weight had increased over the years, and finally dropsy developed. After an illness of many months Mendel died at the monastery on January 6, 1884.

The town of Brünn turned out for the funeral services for the prelate. Grief was deep at the loss of a priest so gentle and yet so unrelenting in his fight for what he believed to be the right. To many of his former pupils, his friends and associates his passing also was a keen personal loss. Mendel had touched many lives. But in all the assembly that filled the church there probably was not one person who knew that a great scientist had gone or even suspected that the reputation of the man they were laying to rest would prove imperishable.

Mendel's experiments with peas seemed to have been entirely forgotten except by the few who knew of them personally. No one thought to preserve his papers and records; they were destroyed.

As the years passed and men continued to work at the basic problem of how the characteristics of the parent are passed along to the offspring, others sought some of the answers by studying hybrids. They drew closer to Mendel's work. W. O. Focke, one of the scientists studying heredity, somehow came upon a reference to Mendel's work. He told Hugo Iltis, Mendel's fellow townsman who devoted many years to writing a biography of the monk, that he did not know what had drawn his attention to Mendel's work and led him to look up his

writings. Focke failed to see that Mendel had discovered the
answers that he and other students of heredity were seeking,
but he was sufficiently impressed to list the Mendel monographs in his own book on hybrids.

It was there that De Vries found the reference. Having seen
how new characters can appear without transition and how a
leaf of the golden primrose might vary without any other
change in the plant, De Vries was equipped to understand
Mendel's report on separate hereditary factors and constant
hereditary ratios. Thirty-five years after Mendel had completed his work, his monographs at last were read by a man
who could appreciate their significance. De Vries knew at
once that Mendel had discovered the long-sought secret of
heredity, and that the honor of solving one of the most fundamental of all problems belonged to the obscure Austrian monk.
The Dutch botanist did not hesitate to call full attention to
Mendel, although he had thought until he opened the long-un-
known monographs that the credit for the all-important insight
and discovery was to be his own.

In a paper that he read before the German Botanical Society
on March 24, 1900, De Vries told of the events that had led him
to Mendel.

"My experiments led me to formulate the two following
propositions," he said.

"1. Of the two antagonistic qualities, the hybrid always ex-
hibits one only and that in full development.

"2. During the formation of the pollen cells and ovules the
two antagonistic qualities separate from each other.

"These two propositions were, in their essentials, formulated
long ago by Mendel for a special case. They fell into oblivion,
however, and were misunderstood. According to my own experiments, they are generally valid for true hybrids. . . . This
important monograph [of Mendel's] is so rarely quoted that I
myself did not become acquainted with it until I had con-

cluded most of my experiments and had independently deduced the above propositions."

On April 24, one month after De Vries had reported his discovery of Mendel's work, a German scientist, Karl Correns, went before the same society to tell how he too had come upon Mendel's discovery. He had been experimenting with peas and maize and had found the constant ratios that he thought were his own discovery until he found Mendel's reports.

"In noting the regular succession of phenomena and finding an explanation for them I believed myself, as De Vries obviously believed himself, to be an innovator," said Correns. "Subsequently, however, I found that in Brünn during the sixties the Abbot Gregor Mendel, devoting many years to the most extensive experiments on peas, not only had obtained the same results as De Vries and myself, but had actually given the same explanation, in so far as this was possible in the year 1866. . . . This paper of Mendel's to which Focke refers (though without ever doing full justice to its importance) is among the best works ever written on the subject of hybrids."

A third scientist, the Viennese botanist Erich Tschermak, had come to the same discovery at the same moment.

Tschermak had decided to repeat Darwin's experiments on the hybridization of the pea. In the first generation, all the seeds resembled the dominant parent. In the second generation they split three to one.

On June 24, exactly two months after Correns's report and three months after De Vries's, Tschermak reported to the same society how he too had discovered Mendel: "Correns' recent report shows that his experiments, like mine, confirm the Mendelian doctrine. The simultaneous discovery of Mendel by Correns, De Vries, and myself seems to me particularly gratifying. I too, as late as the second year of my experiment, believed that I had happened upon something entirely new."

The dramatic triple discovery of the work of Mendel by a

Dutch, a German, and an Austrian scientist and their simultaneous confirmation of his brilliant findings caught world-wide
attention. The years of oblivion suddenly were ended. At last
there was recognition of a great scientist, and understanding
that heredity was not a matter of chance or an unfathomable
chaos. One of man's oldest desires, to know how the distinctive-
ness and the very form of living things are passed along from
parents to progeny, was at long last satisfied.

Mendel's brief monographs were reissued, and biology was
thereby revolutionized. A whole new approach to an understanding of living things and to the natural law that underlay
the surface was opened.

The sudden world acclaim of Gregor Mendel came as an
almost inconceivable surprise to the town of Brünn. At first the
local contributions for a statue came in slowly, but gradually
the realization grew of how momentous were the findings
made in the monastery garden more than a third of a century
earlier, and a fine monument was erected. Dedicated in 1911,
it shows Mendel, a kindly solid figure, standing against a background of his pea and bean vines. Its inscription reads simply:
"To the investigator P. Gregor Mendel, 1822–1884."

When 1922 brought the hundredth anniversary of Mendel's
birth, a centenary festival was held in Brünn. World War I had
come to a bitter close only four years before, and normal communications had not been restored between the scientists of
central Europe and the rest of the world. But Mendel belonged
to all. To honor the man who had explained so much of how
men came to be as they are, German, Czech, English, and
French scientists joined in the ceremonies before the Mendel
monument in Brünn. The animosities of a world war were laid
aside to commemorate the universal discoveries of Gregor
Mendel.

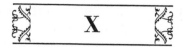

MORGAN:
THE LINE-UP OF HEREDITY

Bottles upon bottles of fruit flies filled the Columbia University laboratories of Thomas Hunt Morgan.

It was 1910 and Morgan had been engaged for about a year in what was to be the great work of his life—the study of heredity with Drosophila melanogaster, the little fruit flies that buzz so persistently around overripe fruit. The time was right for it.

Morgan had been born at Lexington, Kentucky, on September 25, 1866, and named for General John Hunt Morgan of Morgan's Raiders.[1] Like many other born scientists, he began to collect fossils, birds' eggs, and birds before he was ten. At the early age of sixteen he entered the University of Kentucky, and after graduating in 1886 he went on to Johns Hopkins, where he received his Ph.D. in 1890. Morgan had been an exceptional student all along the way, and a fellowship permitted him to carry on his studies in Europe. At Naples he met Driesch. The German biologist, then in the midst of his famous discoveries about the division of the cell, fired the young American with his own enthusiasm for experimental zoology.

Soon after Morgan's return to this country and his appointment as professor at Bryn Mawr, he began a series of studies of the frog's egg. The Roux experiments had shown the puzzling fact that when half a frog's egg was cut away, only half an embryo was produced, though a similar halving of the egg of the sea urchin produced a whole miniature embryo. Morgan wanted to resolve the contradiction. He killed one of the blastomeres—the first segmentation half—of a frog's egg and, instead

[1] J. P. Morgan, the financier, also was a member of the family.

of leaving the egg right side up, turned it upside down. With this treatment it developed into a small but perfect embryo. The brilliant experiment finally put an end to the idea that the egg was a mosaic or collection of hereditary pieces. If a perfect whole could be developed from any half, all of the determinative elements had to be present in each segment of the egg.

This and other work marked Morgan as a gifted scientist. In 1904 he was appointed to the faculty of Columbia University as professor of experimental biology.

With his interests and background, Morgan had eagerly followed the rediscovery of the Mendelian laws four years earlier, in 1900, and the rush of experiment it prompted. Morgan was skeptical, though, about some of the Mendelian findings. It seemed impossible to him that two hereditary units would not be affected by their association in one individual.

Mendel had emphasized that no matter how often he crossed green with yellow, the two colors emerged in the next generation as sharp and distinctive as though they had never been together. This, Morgan thought, could not possibly apply to all heredity. Mendel himself had found that crossing red and white flowers produced pink and a range of shades.

"Once crossed," Morgan argued in 1905, "always contaminated." He also endorsed an attack by the scientist Oscar Riddle on the Mendelian law of the purity of the gametes. Riddle scoffed at the idea of "hypothetical particles . . . packed with unthinkable precision, order, and potentiality . . . into chromosomes."

The whole matter needed study and investigation, and Morgan wanted to get into it. As he discussed the possibilities, a friend, F. E. Lutz, called his attention to Drosophila as experimental material. The common little flies grew from egg to maturity in twelve days and showed clearly marked characteristics. They would be a great improvement over Mendel's peas. Morgan decided upon an experiment.

Drosophila soon proved even better than Lutz had said. The

flies bred rapidly in the great numbers that Morgan knew would be necessary if valid findings were to be made. And they could be readily studied and tallied.

Morgan had been running one "pedigree culture" for about a year when among the flies there suddenly appeared one with white eyes. The eyes of the fly normally are red. Morgan realized at once that the odd, white-eyed fly would give him exactly the marked material, the tag, that he needed.

He bred the lone white-eyed fly to one of the red-eyed females. In very short order he had 1,237 red-eyed offspring. They were hybrids, exhibiting only the dominant red eye color in accordance with Mendel's laws. The test would come when the hybrids were mated.

Again Morgan did have long to wait. The red-eyed hybrids produced 2,459 red-eyed females, 1,011 red-eyed males, and 782 white-eyed males. There was not a single white-eyed female among them. This was no quirk of heredity—not with 782 white-eyed males and not even one white-eyed female. It was another revelation of heredity's working.

Somehow in certain cases heredity was linked to sex. Somehow white eyes had been transmitted to the grandsons only. A facet of the laws of heredity was being revealed as strikingly as when Mendel broke open his first hybrid pea pod and saw one bright-green pea nestling among three yellows.

Morgan at once began to seek for an explanation of his remarkable results. As he did so, he was led into full agreement with Mendel and into territory Mendel had not entered.

Mendel had seen that the roundness, the wrinkling, the yellowness and greenness, and other characters that he studied must have their bases in some kind of physical unit that could be passed along from parent to offspring. He did not attempt to face up to the question of where this unit could be found in the living cell. It was, however, a question that could not long be avoided. Where were the units, and how could the coming together and separating, the assortment and reassortment indicated by the appearance of the peas and other living things take place? Where was the mechanism?

It would, in fact, have been impossible for Mendel to grapple with the big question of mechanism. In the 1850's and 1860's not enough was known of the inner structure of the cell to permit even a start.

By 1910, when Morgan was confronted by the strange linkage of white eyes and sex in Drosophila and by the Mendelian ratios, the situation was entirely different. During the half-century in between, scientists had found that the nucleus of every cell contains a number of tiny threadlike structures. The twisting threads took dye very readily and, when they had been colored, could easily be seen under the microscope. Because of their staining propensities they were called chromosomes (*chromo* for color, *somes* for bodies—thus, "colored bodies").

Every single cell in a living body, it was learned, contains the number of chromosomes characteristic of its species—the human, forty-six; Drosophila, eight; the mouse, twenty; Mendel's garden peas, fourteen.

Close observation also revealed that the chromosomes move about in the nucleus, going through a process of division and a series of maneuvers startling and awe-inspiring in its order, complexity, and rapidity. The maneuvers could be seen as distinctly as those of troops on a parade ground.

Before they began, the cell appeared to be in a resting period. The chromosomal material seemed to be broken into bits and dotted all through the nucleus. As the resting period came to an end, the bits came together in a long curling strand. Soon it split in two longitudinally, and two long strands lay side by side. The double thread then thickened and pulled apart into separate pairs of chromosomes—much as though two lengths of string had been snipped into pieces of varied lengths. The two chromosomes of each pair sometimes still lay parallel, but sometimes they loosely twisted about each other.

By this time the wall of the nucleus had broken and the

chromosomes began to move toward the nuclear center or equator. With the microscope—and later with a movie camera —it was easy to watch them arranging themselves there in an orderly array.

Soon afterward one member of each pair of chromosomes was dragged—almost, it seemed, by the scruff of the neck—to the two poles of the nucleus. A wall then grew between the two polar clusters. Shortly—in human beings the time is about eighty minutes—there were two cells where before there had been only one.

The precise dance of division had endowed each new cell with an exact duplicate of the chromosomes of the cell from which it came. Each cell was guaranteed the same genetic constitution as nearly all the other cells of the body. And as this division was repeated millions upon millions of times, the human being, or any other living thing, grew from a single cell into a full-size adult. The same process constantly replaced older worn-out cells with new ones.

This ordered, shuttling process of cell division varied only in one case: the formation of the germ cells, the egg and the sperm. When an egg or a sperm was to be produced—in contrast to a body cell—the chromosomes did not split longitudinally. They broke only into the separate chromosome lengths, and two lengths came together to form a pair. When the pairs collected at the cell's equator and then pulled apart, each cell received only half the full complement of chromosomes.

The way thus was prepared for the new individual. With each egg and sperm contributing half the full quota, the new individual created by the union of the germ cells acquired the full and proper number of chromosomes for his species. And half his hereditary equipment came from the mother and half from the father. Life could be carried on in its eternal pattern.

By 1900, when Mendel's work was discovered, this remarkable process and mechanism of cell reproduction was understood in its essentials at least.

Only two years later W. S. Sutton put two and two together. He suggested that the chromosomes might be the bearers of Mendel's hereditary traits. In their coming together and separating, the chromosomes supplied almost exactly the kind of mechanism required to produce Mendel's results. Mendel had demonstrated that when tall green peas were crossed with dwarf yellow the offspring might include tall-yellow and dwarf-green as well as tall-green and dwarf-yellow. Tallness did not necessarily go with green seeds, or shortness with yellow. In the same way, said Sutton, the movement of one pair of chromosomes is probably independent of the movement of other pairs. Here was the mechanism the Mendelian theory needed. The two matched.

A few years later William Bateson and R. C. Punnett crossed a sweet pea having a purple flower and a long pollen grain with one having a red flower and a round pollen grain. But instead of getting the free assortment of characters which Mendel had obtained with his tall-green and yellow-dwarf peas, Bateson and Punnett found that the red flower and round grain tended to stay together. Other investigators came upon the same puzzling tendency: certain traits stayed together more frequently in the wider hereditary shuffle than they did in Mendel's peas. Some traits seemed, in fact, to be coupled.

Then Morgan found the relation of whiteness and maleness in Drosophila. It seemed to be similar in nature to the "coupling" of "long" and "purple" in sweet peas. It looked as though certain traits were linked. Perhaps such traits all were situated in the same chromosome. If they were in the same chromosome, they would remain together as the chromosome went through its divisions.

"It was obvious from the beginning," Morgan argued, "that there was one essential requirement for the chromosome view, namely, that all the factors carried by the same chromosome should tend to remain together."

"Therefore since the number of inheritable characters may be large in comparison with the number of pairs of chromosomes, we would expect actually to find not only the independent behavior of pairs, but also cases in which characters are linked together in groups in their inheritance."

Drosophila had four pairs of chromosomes, and if Morgan was right, it should be possible to map the factors carried by each. The theory was subject to proof. It would, however, take a huge experiment.

Morgan always succeeded in surrounding himself with able students and collaborators. With their aid he began breeding the little flies in prodigious numbers. The assortment of milk bottles in which the flies were kept filled every available square inch of the "fly room." The eight desks of the "fly squad" could barely be crowded in.[2]

Each of the thousands upon thousands of flies had to be studied with a hand lens. But the laborious scrutiny and the scale of the experiment paid off; other mutations, the raw material needed for the work, appeared. Among the mutants was a fly with black body color and the tiny remnants of wings described as "vestigial."

Morgan crossed one of the blacks with a wild-type fly that is gray and has long wings. All of their offspring, as expected, were of the wild type. But when one of the hybrid sons was mated to a black-vestigial female, the offspring were of two kinds only: half were black-vestigial and half the wild type. The two mutant characteristics that went in together came out together, and their normal opposites—allelomorphs, the scientists call them—also came out together. Not a single fly in this

[2] In the summer the fly squad moved en masse to Woods Hole, Massachusetts. The bottles of flies—each marked with scraps of paper torn from the envelopes that had enclosed Morgan's mail—were shipped in barrels. The other animals of the laboratory—a fine assortment of chickens, pigeons, mice, and rats—were carried by hand on the Fall River Line.

generation was black with long wings or gray with vestigial wings. The Mendelian assortment did not quite work; the predicted four types had not appeared.

What did the unusual result indicate? Charted, it was easy to see. Morgan assumed that the genes for black (b) and vestigial (v) were carried by the same chromosome, and the normal genes for wing and color (BV) by the other chromosome of the pair in the wild fly. In the first filial generation the flies would be $BbVv$. The presence of the dominant genes for both color and wings would make the flies gray and long-winged in appearance. However, two types of germ cells would be produced by this generation, bv and BV. If such a fly were crossed with a black-vestigial (bv), the offspring receiving the bv germ cell from the father and the bv from the mother would be black-vestigial. Those getting the BV from the father and the bv from the mother would be the wild type. Only the two kinds of offspring would be produced—exactly as they had been in the experiment.

In a relatively short time the Morgan laboratory studied the inheritance of more than a hundred characters. There was no doubt that characters in Drosophila were inherited not only in linked pairs, but also in linked groups.

One large group of characters always went along with either the male or female. It was quite clear that they were carried by one of the Drosophila sex chromosomes. Two other large groups of characters also remained together. One of the groups was made up of "brown," "chubby," "flipper," "fringed," "narrow," "telescope," and more than fifty others. Thus, when a fly was brown, it was also chubby and had all the other linked traits.

And then a characteristic appeared which did not go with the sex group or either of the other two. A year later still another characteristic cropped up which was linked to the last one, but was inherited independently of all the others. Every other trait singled out after this belonged to one or another of the four groups.

The four carefully charted groups indicated four chromosomes as certainly as did the sight of the four chromosomes under the microscope. Any remaining doubts dissolved. The site of the hereditary units whose existence Mendel had de-

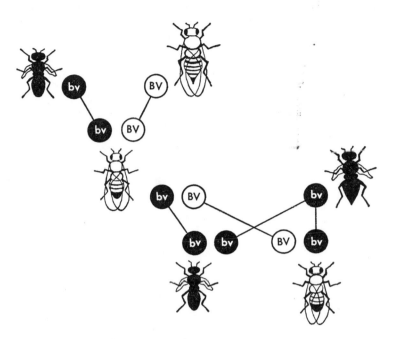

Linkage. The traits "black" and "short wings" were inherited together, as were the color "gray" and "long wings." Not a single black fly with long wings or gray with vestigial wings was produced in this mating. The reason: the hereditary material for the two linked traits was carried by the same chromosome. The two went together.

duced had been found. Morgan's work and the investigations of others all pointed to the same locus—the chromosome.

Understanding of the mystery of life had advanced again. The search for the explanation and cause of the form, the diversity, and the functioning of life had moved from the organs to the tissues, to the cell, and now to the twisting little chromosome threads within the cell. As the search went deeper, it came to the smaller and smaller, and yet each time it penetrated below the previously known appearance of things, order was found and explanation of much that had been obscure. At the same time, another cause always lay deeper still. The search did not reach its end.

One of Drosophila's pairs of chromosomes was small; it seemed to consist of little more than two dots. The other three

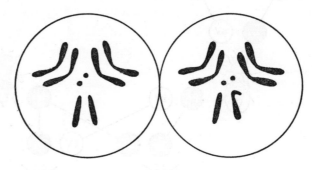

The chromosomes of the fruit fly. Here is the hereditary material of Drosophila. LEFT: *the female.* RIGHT: *the male.*

pairs were many times larger. One of the large pairs had something of the bent shape of a boomerang. Another large pair, in the female, was made up of two more or less straight threads; when diagrammed, they resembled two broad strokes with a stub-pointed pen. But in the male, the microscope showed, the two members of the pair differed. One of the chromosomes resembled the straight threads of the female pair; the other had a hooked end.

As the relative size of the chromosomes was determined, another most enlightening fact stood forth. Their sizes corresponded to the sizes of the four groups of hereditary characters Morgan had discovered. Morgan had two large groups of characters that stayed together, a very small group, and a fourth sizable group linked to the sex of the flies. Here was added confirmation that the hereditary units were grouped in the chromosomes.

The difference in the sex chromosomes had to be investigated. The three straight sex chromosomes, the two in the female and the one in the male, were soon named the X chromosomes. The male chromosome with the hooked end was called the Y.

Peering through his microscope and working on "the problem of the three chromosomes," Morgan could trace the maneuvers of the two pairs, the four individual sex chromosomes. As he did so, he and others working along the same lines solved one of the most ancient of human mysteries.

When egg cells were formed in the female Drosophila, each received one of the X chromosomes. In the male, half of the sperm came to have the male's X, and half had his Y chromosome. The remainder of the process was not difficult to figure out. If the Y-endowed sperm fertilized an egg, an XY individual, a male, resulted.

If, on the other hand, the egg with its X chromosome was fertilized by the X sperm, an XX individual, a female, was produced.

For the first time the inheritance of sex could be understood. The eternal riddle of why an approximately even number of males and females are born into the world was at last solved, and it was all a matter of a simple Mendelian assortment of hereditary units. Given the three like and the one unlike chromosomes, there was only one way in which it could work out, if sufficient numbers were taken into consideration. The mechanism was simple and certain.

"The old view that sex is determined by external conditions is entirely disproved," said Morgan. "We have discovered an internal mechanism by means of which the equality of the sexes is attained. We see the results are automatically reached, even if we cannot entirely understand the details of the process."

This work with the sex chromosomes explained the production of the red-eyed flies and the white-eyed male in Morgan's earlier work. He could now work out the whole course of genetic events that had produced the odd white-eyed male and

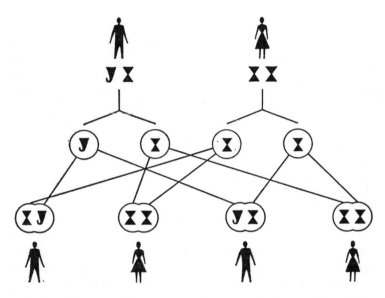

Solution of an ancient mystery—the approximate equality of the sexes. With the male bearing an XY chromosome and the female XX, it is inevitable that approximately equal numbers of males and females will be produced.

the other, red-eyed flies. Each egg of a red-eyed mother would have an X chromosome bearing the factor for red eyes (R). Half the chromosomes of the white-eyed male would carry an X chromosome with the factor for white eyes. The other half would have a Y chromosome, a chromosome without any genes for eye color.

Any egg (*XR*) fertilized by the father's *Xw* would produce a red-eyed female—female because of the *XX*, and red-eyed because the red would be dominant in the *Rw* pair. Any egg (*XR*) uniting with the *Y* chromosome would result in a male' with red eyes (*XYR*). Thus, the first generation of a cross of a red-eyed female and a white-eyed male would, as Morgan's earlier experiments had shown, be made up of red-eyed males and red-eyed females.

But the hybrid red-eyed female would in her turn produce two kinds of eggs, *XR* and *Xw*. The hybrid male also would produce two kinds of sperm, *XR* and the empty *Y*. A crossing of the two would yield two red-eyed females (*XRXR* and *XRXw*), a red-eyed male (*XRY*), and a white-eyed male (*XwY*). This was the only possible outcome. No white-eyed females could come from such a union. Any time that an *X* chromosome with its *R* met another *X* chromosome, it also would be bearing an *R*, and the inevitable result would be a red-eyed female.

The red factor was quite certainly placed in the *X* chromosome, but its presence there could be confirmed by additional experiments. Morgan made them all. Short of some disarrangement, the transmission of *XR* together worked out as certainly as though two were being multiplied by two. It was exactly the pattern of inheritance of color-blindness in the human. Heredity was a very satisfying problem with which to work; predictions could be exactly confirmed with living material.

Occasionally, however, Morgan found instances in which whole blocks of genes from one chromosome had shifted to the corresponding chromosome of the pair. Certain changed groupings of characteristics indicated what had happened almost as clearly as though he had seen it taking place.

To study this problem Morgan again crossed a black fly having vestigial wings with a wild type, gray with long wings. The offspring of course were of the wild type. Morgan then repeated another experiment. He again mated the hybrid male with a black-vestigial female. His aim this time was to establish the genetic make-up of the male beyond all question, and as both "black" and "vestigial" were recessive characters, they would not obscure the male's genetic make-up. The experiment underwrote the fact that the genes for "gray" and "long wings" were linked, for out of it came only the two original types of flies, wild and black-vestigial.

With this groundwork laid, Morgan was ready to go on. He mated the hybrid female—in appearance gray and long-winged—with a black-vestigial male. As the flies hatched, excitement swept the laboratory. Everyone hurried in to see. This time there were four kinds of flies. A careful count showed that 41.5 per cent were gray-long, and 41.5 per cent black-vestigial, but 8.5 per cent were black-long and 8.5 per cent gray-vestigial. Something had happened. "Gray" and "long wings" were no longer always in the same chromosome. In a few cases "gray" was now with the "vestigial-wing" factor. In a few other cases, 8.5 per cent, "long wings" and "black" had got together.

Morgan could interpret what had occurred, and many later experiments were to substantiate his analysis. When two chromosomes come together just prior to the formation of the germ cells, they often twist around each other. The twisting has been seen in innumerable microscopic photographs. If, in this twining, the chromosomes break, sections of the two may be interchanged. In that case, when the chromosomes again part, as they do in the normal process of cell division, each carries away a new section.

Morgan jotted down a pattern to illustrate. If one chromosome originally bore genes *ABCDEFGHIJKL* and the other bore the corresponding genes *abcdefghijkl*, they would line up in the following way:

ABCDEFGHIJKL
abcdefghijkl

If, in twisting together, sections were interchanged, the chromosomes on parting might well have the following make-up:

ABCDEFghijkl

abcdefGHIJKL

A diagram of the twisting made the mechanism evident.

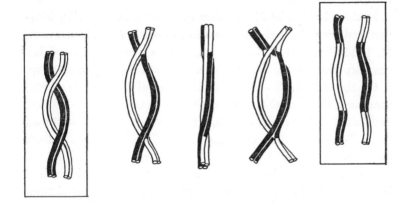

Crossing over of the chromosomes. As these bearers of heredity twist together and exchange their parts, living things with new assortments of characteristics are born.

The appearance of the long-black and gray-vestigial flies could be explained. Each chromosome had exchanged a part with its mate. Morgan named the process "crossing-over." Here was a mechanism, a partly visible mechanism, to account for the interchanges that he saw in the flies in the bottle. It was the only possible explanation when both genes lay in the same chromosome, as previous experiments and results had shown that they did. Another part of the hidden working of Nature was being revealed. Morgan pushed on to explore the opening offered by crossing-over.

Instances of double crossing-over began to turn up. As the
chromosomes twisted about each other, sometimes breaks occurred toward both ends and two sections or parts were interchanged.

All of this pointed unmistakably to one conclusion: the genes
are arranged in linear order in the chromosome. Ultimately
Morgan and many other workers in the field were able, by
studying crossing-over, to map the positions of certain genes in
the chromosomes.

In their book *The Mechanism of Mendelian Heredity* Morgan and his principal associates in the work, A. H. Sturtevant,
H. J. Muller, and C. B. Bridges, used a map of Drosophila's
chromosomes as the frontispiece. It was a most unusual map.

On the straight lines representing one of Drosophila's chromosomes, the scientists marked the places of "yellow," "white,"
"echinus," "crossveinless," "cut," "tan," "vermilion," "miniature,"
"sable," "garnet," "forked," "bar," "cleft," and "bobbed"—their
colorful and descriptive names for the genes.

It was also a curiously made map. Not one gene locus had
been determined by direct measurement; each place had been
fixed by studying certain evidences—say, garnet eyes—by cal-
culating what they must represent, and then by proving the
calculation by breeding new generations of the buzzing little
fruit flies. In one sense, the map resembled the maps of unseen
ocean bottoms made by bouncing unseen sound waves against
the elevations and depressions of the ocean floor.

And yet the map was accurate. Using it, the scientists could
predict how much crossing-over there would be and what traits
would appear in the offspring of any cross, and then see the
flies born with the predicted kind of wings or eyes or color. It
was almost uncanny.

"Given the distance between any two factors on the map, the
per cent of crossing over between them can always be calculated from the distance," said the scientists in their book. "This
shows that the amount of crossing over is an expression of their

position in a *linear series*. This striking fact . . . is a strong argument that the factors are actually arranged in line in the chromosomes."

Photographs showing the chromosomes as strings made up of what seemed to be a series of disks or flattish beads merely confirmed the linearity of the hereditary material already established by Morgan's calculations, his tabulation of eye color, wing shape, and other characteristics of thousands of swarming laboratory flies.

For seventeen years the Morgan fly squad bred fruit flies. "There can have been few times and places in scientific laboratories with such an atomosphere of excitement and such a record of sustained enthusiasm," Sturtevant wrote many years later. The spirit was in large part traceable to the enthusiasm, the open-mindedness, and the sense of humor of "The Boss," as the squad called Morgan, their bearded, energetic, but never dictatorial chief.

The results were well worth the effort, they all knew. The world's doubts about the Mendelian laws were wiped away as thoroughly as Morgan's early skepticism. "Be skeptical as we will," said Morgan, "the facts will impress themselves on anyone who takes the pains to think them over."

The facts piled up by Morgan and his resourceful, brilliant associates not only supported the Mendelian laws and explained the approximately equal numbers of males and females in the world, but also established that the mechanisms of the body were exactly those required for the working out of the Mendelian laws of inheritance.

These were basic matters that had been explained. Interest ran high, and many honors came to the man whose work with fruit flies was showing men that their very identities were shaped by the orderly maneuvering of bits of matter in the nucleus of the cell. Happenstance and mystery once more lost ground, and the modern chromosome theory of heredity was established.

In 1924 Morgan received the Darwin Medal, and in 1933 the crowning honor of them all—the Nobel Prize for his "discoveries relating to the hereditary functions of the chromosomes."

In 1928 Morgan became professor of biology at the California Institute of Technology and the head of its Kerckhoff Laboratories. He remained in the West, working constantly in the laboratories, until his death on December 4, 1945.

Part Two

UP FROM THE BASE OF LIFE

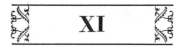

XI

MULLER:
MUTATIONS AND THE NEW

ALL RESEARCH ROADS converged on the chromosome and the hereditary material of which it was made. Unquestionably the little strings of matter were the bearers of heredity. They were the only physical substance of the parent handed down to the offspring, the veritable link that had been passed along from generation to generation since the beginning of life. In every cell of every living thing lay a part of the past.

But what was this material and what were the units—the genes—which Morgan's work indicated were strung out along its length? How could an all but invisible bit of matter carry all the specifications for making living things what they are? Somehow this minute fleck of matter had to be studied.

The problem was how. How could the hereditary material itself, as distinct from its behavior, be measured and analyzed? At the time there was no way to separate a "gene" as such, or to photograph its depths or structure. Almost the only way *in* was to try to study the changes that occurred at points in the chromosome, in the genes. Here was one clue as to what might be going on inside. Mutations might tell something about the nature and the organization of the invisible hereditary units.

The difficulty was that mutations were exceedingly rare. Morgan had worked for a year and bred millions of flies before the fly with the white eyes turned up in his cultures. Perhaps not once in a million replications did a gene change, and then perhaps more generations were necessary for the change to become visible in the form of a white eye or an altered wing or some other differing characteristic. If science could find a way to produce more frequent mutations, it would have a most useful probe of the gene and chromosome. Many workers jumped into the search, one of them Morgan's former student and associate H. J. Muller.

Muller was born in New York, December 21, 1890. He took his undergraduate and graduate work at Columbia University and, after a year away on a teaching fellowship, returned to Columbia in 1912 as a member of the faculty. One of the major members of the Morgan "fly squad," he had a part in discovering the linear order of the chromosomes and in other notable findings on the mechanisms of heredity. Not until 1920 was he permanently drawn away from Columbia. In that year he went to the University of Texas as an associate professor of zoology. At Texas and later at the University of Indiana he continued his research into the hidden depths of heredity.

What causes genes to change? Muller constantly asked himself. The very rarity of mutations suggested that their occurrence had little relation to the ordinary variables of the environment, such as heat, cold and accident.

This was not surprising, for the genes were extremely well protected. Inside the body, inside the cell, inside the nucleus, they were protected by the nuclear membrane, the cytoplasm, the cell wall, and the remainder of the body. They could scarcely have been better wrapped or more invulnerable to the normal changes in environment, or even to bad jolts, or to infections that might shrivel the flesh.

All of this had long since been made abundantly clear by ordinary experience and experiment. Children were born in the usual pattern regardless of what had happened to the parents, and Weismann had cut off the tails of five generations of mice only to find the tails of the sixth generation as long as those of the first.

But the gene is essentially a chemical complex, and chemical reactions are speeded by heat. Muller decided to make a systematic trial of what high temperature might do to the genes and chromosomes. He worked for nearly eight years, and found that a rise in temperature does cause a slight increase in mutation frequency. Heat seemed to hasten mutations in flies to about the same degree that it steps up chemical reactions. Heat, then, did not seem to be the cause of mutations, and the slight increase in frequency did not supply the mutations needed for study.

But if the normal range of external variations did not affect the gene, possibly extremes might. Muller, Morgan, and a host of other scientists tried every device of maltreatment they could think of to "crack" the gene. "In the course of this work," said Muller, "animals and plants have been drugged, poisoned, intoxicated, illuminated, kept in darkness, half smothered, painted inside and out, whirled round and round, shaken violently, vaccinated, mutilated, educated, and treated with everything except affection from generation to generation."

None of the violence produced the slightest result. The maltreated flies or plants or animals gave birth to others just like themselves, or showing only the usual variations. Their heredity was unchanged.

And yet mutations happened all the while. Among twenty million flies that the Drosophila workers studied, four hundred mutations were found. Something had caused them. If gross forces produced no effect, what subtle force could be at work, what force that could operate independently of even the most drastic changes in the physiological state of the organism? Muller decided to go back over his work and reconsider it in the light of this question.

As he checked back, Muller came upon a report he had written in 1920. It emphasized that when a mutation occurred in one locus (or point in the chromosome) in Drosophila, the other genes were unaffected. No mutation occurred among the thousands of genes in the same chromosome, or even in the twin gene in the other chromosome of the pair.

Muller stopped and pondered. Here were two genes of

identical chemical composition, lying in the same cell and not much more than a thousandth of a millimeter apart, and yet some force caused one to change profoundly and altered the other not at all.

And it was the same in all other plant and animal cells, the evidence indicated. This was pin-pointing the pin point. What force could strike at such a minute point and at no other?

As so frequently happens, the asking of the right question opened the way to the answer.

"The conclusion seemed to me to become increasingly probable," said Muller, "not that mutations were causeless or expressions of 'the natural cussedness of things,' or of the devil . . . but that they were not ordinarily due directly to gross or molar causes, but must be regarded as the results of ultramicroscopic accidents—events too far removed in fineness to be readily susceptible of any exact control on our part.

"In other words an appeal was made to the newly found world of the little, which the old-line biologist and philosopher do not always take sufficiently into consideration."

The world of the little! One part of it would fit the gene situation exactly. No matter how well guarded and protected the gene might be, it could not escape natural radiation or the interplay of the ultra-magnetic forces that are the base of all matter.

"The outstanding ultramicroscopic agent that could strike willy-nilly through living things, causing drastic atomic changes here and passing everything by unaltered there, not a ten thousandth of a millimeter away, is pre-eminently the X ray, or the X ray and its accomplice, the speeding electron," Muller thought.

There was nothing in the protoplasm to stop X rays or the shorter-length gamma and cosmic rays. Generally the rays would pass right through a cell. Occasionally, though, there might be a collision and an electron would be knocked out of the atom that stood in the way. The atom would be altered and the molecule in which it lay would be chemically changed. Other atoms also might be affected. The hurtling electron, moving with bullet effect, might tear through hundreds of atoms lying in its path. The changes in their structure would, in turn, cause them to undergo new chemical unions or disunions.

"If a gene is a molecule, with properties depending on its chemical composition, it can be shot and altered by electrons resulting from the absorption of X rays or rays of shorter length," Muller continued, developing his argument.

But X rays had been tried before in the effort to reach and alter the gene, and the results had been indecisive.

Muller nevertheless was so convinced by his logic that he decided upon a new and thorough-going test. His first problem was to find a dosage strong enough to produce a mutation—if his theory was correct—and yet not strong enough to kill or sterilize the flies. He began a series of experiments in the fall of 1926.

From his previous work Muller had stocks of made-to-order flies. He knew exactly what combinations of genes they had in their cells, and that if certain crosses were made, certain conspicuous effects would show up. He also knew that if certain expected combinations failed to appear, it would indicate that a mutation had given rise to a lethal gene, one that killed the fruit flies bearing it before they could hatch. By observing what traits appeared or failed to appear, Muller could trace any mutations to their chromosome positions. Muller thus was set to find our whether X rays could be one of the long-sought causes of mutation.

Muller and his assistants put hundreds of fruit flies in gelatin capsules and placed them under an X-ray machine. A press of a button and the rays shot through the flies. The dosage, it turned out, was strong enough to produce partial sterility, but the flies were not noticeably disturbed. They hovered over their banana mash as usual.

The X-rayed flies were then bred to untreated mates. At the same time hundreds of other untreated flies from the same stock were crossed with similar mates. They would serve as controls. In the two groups the matings ran into the thousands. Muller wanted to settle the matter beyond any doubt.

The scientist did not have long to wait. In ten days thousands of mature new flies were buzzing vigorously around in the bottles, and the startled scientist was looking upon such an array of mutations as had never been seen before.

There were mutations and mutations and mutations. The nearly overwhelmed scientist counted flies with bulging eyes, flies with flat eyes and dented ones, flies with purple, yellow, or brown eyes, and even flies with no eyes at all. There were flies with curly hair, with ruffled and parted hair, with fine and coarse hair, and some were bald. There were flies without antennae, flies with broad wings and down-turned wings, with outstretched wings, with truncated wings, and with almost no wings at all. There were big flies, little flies, active flies, and sluggish flies. Some were long-lived, some short-lived. Some preferred to stay on the ground, others avoided the light, and some had a mixture of sexual characteristics.

"They were a motley throng," said Muller. "To the toiling pilgrim after plodding through the long and weary deserts of changelessness, here indeed was the promised land. The results in these experiments were startling and unequivocal. The roots of life—the genes—had indeed been struck and they had yielded."

The mutants, of course, were not concentrated in any one group of flies. They were spread through thousands of cultures and were found by "raking through" hosts of flies.

"But what a difference from the normal frequency of mutation!" Muller exclaimed.

When the heaviest X-ray treatment was used, about one seventh of the flies displayed demonstrable mutations. Muller anxiously checked the mutations that had occurred in his untreated control group. This would be the test. Then he saw that the X rays had increased the frequency of mutation 150 times, or 15,000 per cent. A result could scarcely have been more decisive.

But the experimenters knew that other questions would have to be considered. Were the X-ray mutations of the same nature

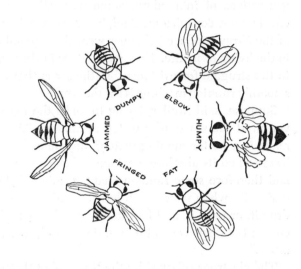

A motley throng. Fat flies, dumpy flies, flies with curly wings or no wings, and scores of other mutations were produced when the parent generation was subjected to X rays. The "roots of life" had truly been struck.

as those occurring spontaneously? Here was another triumph. Many of the mutations were exactly the same as those which had cropped up many times in work with Drosophila. Muller recognized the familiar white eyes, the well-known vestigial wings. Even the position of the mutated gene was the same in the chromosome.

Some of the mutations, it was true, were of a kind not seen before. No one had previously reported encountering splotched wings. But this posed no difficulty; new and previously unseen mutations continued to be found in the untreated flies too.

In every way, the X-ray mutations conformed to the behavior and character of the mutations that had been studied in the past.

Most of them were recessive. For this reason some of them did not make their appearance until after one, two, or three generations of inbreeding. Some were slight in their visible effects, some conspicuous. And, like the natural mutations, most of the X-ray-produced changes were detrimental to the animal in the living of its life. They were "steps in the wrong direction in the struggle for existence," in the sense that any upset in a smoothly running machine is for the worse.

Suppose, said Muller, trying to make the matter clear, that you prod the works of a watch at random. "Are you likely to make it a better-running watch? But unless the organization has reached its absolute maximum of efficiency, *some* changes, and therefore some random changes, might help. And so occasionally when your watch has stopped you may knock it, or drop it, or prod it, and find that by the lucky replacement of a cog, or the displacement of a grain of sand, it starts up merrily again."

The electrons released by the X rays shot through the cell in such a way that they were as likely to hit one gene as another. Thus, they were random disturbances and as likely as the prodding of a watch to be detrimental. Exactly as did natural radiation, they upset the established order.

Many of the X-ray-produced mutations, like some of the natural ones, played such havoc that they were lethal. They so disturbed the organism that the fly was killed before it hatched, unless there was a normal gene from the other parent to dominate the lethal one and save the fly's life. In the latter case the recessive lethal was passed along to the offspring. If in any later generation it came together with another recessive gene, it worked its destruction then.

Muller bred generation after generation of his X-rayed, mutated flies. Some were carried through seventy-five generations, the equivalent of some twenty-five human centuries. After seventy-five generations the white eyes produced by the first X rays were as white as when they had originally appeared. The X-ray mutations, like the natural ones, were permanent. They obeyed the same Mendelian laws as did the naturally changed genes, and the mutated flies were true new varieties.

By all the indications, artificial radiation was similar in its effects to natural radiation. And yet was it entirely so? Could it ever produce changes that were beneficial, or was it wholly destructive? Muller used the words "beneficial" and "destructive" with caution. In the long run, who could say what might be beneficial? If the environment changed completely—say, if a new ice age should come—a change detrimental in the climate of today might save the species. Muller put the question in a more limited sense. Could a mutation occur in either direction? If the development of legs on the forehead was "destructive," would another mutation eliminating them be "constructive"?

In an attempt to clear up the point, Muller, with the assistance of his wife, began a series of tests with bristled flies. Straight bristles are dominant over the recessive forked ones. X-ray treatment caused some "straights" to mutate to forked, and some "forkeds" to change to straight. If the one change was a loss, the other was a gain.

"Doubtless, as in the case of most chemical reactions," Muller cautioned, "most mutations are changes involving substitutions and rearrangements rather than mere losses and gains."

Sometimes when Muller beamed his X rays on the flies in the little gelatin capsules, the chromosomes were broken. An end might be snapped off, and it might later attach itself to a broken piece from any one of the other chromosomes.[1] The microscope

[1] Muller later demonstrated that broken chromosomes could join only with other broken pieces of chromosome. The broken surfaces are, in effect, sticky, and this holds them together.

showed this clearly. Radiation, in fact, produced havoc among the chromosomes. Muller also proved the point by breeding the altered-chromosome flies. Whole new groupings of traits appeared. The finding not only proved that X rays produce change in chromosomes, but also demonstrated that the "mechanical theory" of crossing-over was a correct one.

No one could think that the mutations induced by radiation were a phenomenon peculiar to flies. It was clear that radiation must be the cause of many mutations; Muller had discovered a universal cause. For the first time since Mendel had worked out the principles of heredity in 1865, the cause of variability—a central problem of evolution—could be in part understood. Muller modestly said none of this; he announced simply that X rays produce mutations.

The far-reaching significance of the work was immediately recognized. Others hurried to repeat and test it.

While Muller was engaged in his experiments, L. J. Stadler of the University of Missouri had independently decided to see whether X rays would produce mutations in corn and barley. He wheeled a portable X-ray machine out into the sun-baked cornfields and turned the rays upon the young corn. The seed of the X-rayed corn was planted, and when it matured, Stadler was greeted with a burst of mutations.

R. W. and A. R. Whiting X-rayed wasps. Other investigators turned X rays on Jimson weed. Fly or wasp, corn or Jimson weed, strange and numerous changes appeared. The invisible rays wreaked their effects wherever they struck.

"With these widely separated bits of the living world sampled and with all responding positively, it is a reckless critic who still would cast doubt as to the probable generality of the phenomenon," Muller was at last willing to say.

The drastic effect of the X rays at once suggested that other forms of radiation, particularly radium and cosmic rays, might produce similar changes in the genes. Both radium and cosmic rays are of short wave lengths, high frequency, and great energy. It seemed highly probable that they too would knock out electrons at random.

Frank Blair Hanson, at Washington University in St. Louis, put some fruit flies in two-and-a-half-inch vials, and exposed them to radium for nine hours. About thirteen per cent of the flies developed lethal mutations. The number of mutations seemed to depend upon the number of electrons released.

"This being true," said Hanson, "and there being no evidence of a minimal or threshold dosage, we are forced to conclude that the minute amounts of natural radiation present everywhere in Nature, most of it of terrestrial origin . . . , must be producing some mutations in the living things on earth. These mutations must be very scattered and very infrequent in proportion to the total non-mutated population, because the amount of natural short-wave radiation is very small in any given case, but considering the extent of the earth and the multiplicity of living things, the total number of mutations so produced per year must be very considerable."

Here were scientific findings of prime importance. For the first time men could comprehend how the new comes into the world—the new character, the change that in the shaping of natural selection has enabled living things to fill most of the niches of the earth, the air, and the water around them, and to survive when the climate turned markedly wetter or drier or hotter or colder. Mutation was a major force in evolution.

Nevertheless, interest in the discovery did not extend far beyond scientific circles. The country was preoccupied with other matters—the stock market crash of 1929 and the years of depression which followed. No one knew that before long the explosion of an atomic bomb and atomic testing would fill the atmosphere with new radiation. Muller had no idea that he and other scientists would have to abandon their traditional scientific reticence and walk onto the political stage to warn the world that excessive radiation from man-made explosions could have the same effects upon the human genetic material as the laboratory X rays did on fruit flies. Who could have foreseen that the truths revealed by beaming X rays at fruit flies would become the overriding political issue of the future?

By 1946, however, the full significance of the Muller discoveries was clear. Muller received the Nobel Prize for his "discovery of the production of mutations by means of X-ray irradiation."

A new danger terrorized the world, but on the other hand a way had been opened to study the slender threads of matter which control the destinies of humans and all other living things.

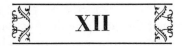

XII

BEADLE AND TATUM:
OF MOLDS AND MEN

Two young scientists, one from Paris and the other from Wahoo, Nebraska, were deep in a long discussion. In the laboratories at the California Institute of Technology, where both were engaged in research, and at lunch or dinner they returned again and again to the same problem: the frustrating lack of knowledge about the manner in which the hereditary materials act upon development.

Mendel and Morgan had shown very clearly how hereditary traits, our likenesses and differences, are transmitted from parent to offspring. The hereditary factors had been tracked to the chromosome, and Muller had proved that the hardy, heavily protected chromosomes and their genes could be altered by the chance hit of radiation.

But all of this only raised the new question of how this hereditary material exercises its control. How could this infinitesimal bit of matter order the structure, the shape, the physical behavior of life? How could so small a structure determine so unerringly whether two small cells are to be man or tadpole or mold?

The more the two young scientists debated the problem, the more they were convinced that the hereditary units must exert their effect through chemical action. At least this was a possibility that could be investigated. The two, Boris Ephrussi and George Wells Beadle, decided to see what they could find out about the chemical action of the gene.

At the time—1933—Ephrussi held a research fellowship at Caltech. The next year Beadle obtained a leave to work in

Paris with Ephrussi at the Institut de Biologie Physico-Chimique.

To seek evidence of the gene's mode of action, the two scientists began transplanting embryonic materials from one animal to another. The biological authorities at the Sorbonne who were consulted about the plan did not encourage them. In fact, they told them that their prospects of achieving anything "were terrible"—Beadle's words. Nevertheless, Ephrussi and Beadle refused to be dissuaded.

And then one day they discovered that a transplant had succeeded and they had produced a fly with three eyes. The two happy scientists spent the day at a sidewalk café celebrating the remarkable feat. But at once they began to worry. How could the large number of chemical actions that must enter into the formation of an eye, or even the color of an eye, be traced to a gene?

Before the work could go much further, Beadle returned to the California Institute of Technology. Ephrussi joined him there for a year of follow-up work. In 1937 Beadle became professor of genetics at Leland Stanford University.

Beadle had been born on October 22, 1903, on a farm near the picturesquely named Nebraska town of Wahoo. He might have followed his father into farming if a high-school teacher had not aroused his interest in science. To prepare for a career in science, Beadle entered the University of Nebraska's College of Agriculture at Lincoln. There he was introduced to genetics and knew that it would be his field. After completing his graduate work at Cornell and Caltech he joined that mecca of all young geneticists, the new laboratory that Thomas Hunt Morgan had established at the California Institute of Technology. It was then that Beadle met Ephrussi and the two discovered their common dissatisfaction with the gaps in genetic knowledge.

At Stanford, Beadle continued the work he had begun with Ephrussi, and interested Edward L. Tatum in joining him in it. Tatum, a chemist trained at the University of Wisconsin, had recently come to Stanford as a research associate in biology.

"It was a slow, discouraging job, trying to identify chemical disturbances underlying inherited abnormalities," Beadle later recalled.

Beadle and Tatum felt that a new approach was needed. It occurred to them that it might be better to reverse the procedure and look for mutations that might influence known chemical reactions.

"The idea was simple," said Beadle, sketching its main points: select an organism, such as a fungus that has simple nutritional requirements; induce mutations that observably alter those requirements.

"We hoped," said Beadle, "to discover how genes function by making one of them defective."

It was a long way around that Beadle was proposing, but it seemed the only way to study a stronghold too small to be seen or grasped, or cut apart or manipulated by even the most sensitive of techniques. Beadle used an analogy to explain his proposed approach:

Suppose you wanted to know how an automobile factory worked and yet were absolutely barred from going into it. To see the workers streaming in and the finished cars rolling out would tell very little about how automobiles were made or what each worker did. The problem of understanding automobile manufacture would be a most difficult one. Suppose, though, that one worker could be handicapped in some way. Suppose that his arms could be tied behind him. If the cars then began coming out without radiator grills, it would be fairly easy to deduce that the radiator grill was one separate unit in the car and that it was the defective worker's normal job to attach it. By handicapping other workers in turn, a great deal could be learned about how the hidden factory functioned and automobiles were made.

Casting about for the simple organism needed for the proposed study, Beadle and Tatum were impressed by Neurospora, the red mold that appears on bread in a warm climate.

For one thing, the mold had been well studied; its genetics were known from the work of Bernard O. Dodge and Carl Lindegren. If two of the lacily branching twigs of Neurospora were brought together, one of type *A* and the other of type *a*, they would fuse sexually and form a fertile cell *Aa*. But if there

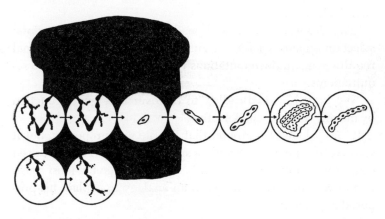

Neurospora, the red mold that grows on bread, can reproduce either sexually, or asexually by simple cell division. TOP ROW: *Sexual reproduction. Type A and Type a fuse to form a fertile cell and then a fruiting body.* LOWER ROW: *A branch grows by simple cell division.*

was no union of the two types, Neurspora also could reproduce non-sexually—that is, by simple cell division, as many plants do. In the later case, the new branches would be exact genetic duplicates of the branches from which they came—*A* branches would produce only *A* offspring and *a* branches only *a*'s. Neurospora increased at a phenomenal rate. A branch could multiply a millionfold in a few days, and a truckload of the red mold could be produced if it was needed.

The bread mold also was remarkably easy to feed and succor. It thrived in a test tube on a bit of agar jelly containing a mixture of mineral salts, sugar, and a single vitamin, biotin.[1] From these simple ingredients Neurospora could produce all the other vitamins and amino acids required by molds for life and lush growth—and by men, for the nutritional requirements of men, molds, and all living things are essentially the same. The mold, however, had the advantage of being able to manufacture all its sustenance with the exception of biotin, whereas men must depend upon their food—and thus on other living things—for their vitamins.[2]

Neurospora thus was chosen.

This could be no small experiment. It had to begin as an enormous fishing expedition. The scientists were convinced that mutants demonstrating the effect of gene on enzyme must exist. But could they find them? "We had only one worry," said Beadle. "It was that their frequency might be so low that we would get discouraged and give up before finding one."

To offset the repeated discouragement that might come with testing a few spores at a time, they decided to isolate at least a thousand spores before testing them for mutants. They also decided that they would take only one spore from each fruiting body.

The experimenters began by exposing several hundred of the asexual *a* spores of Neurspora to X rays. Muller's work had shown that this would produce mutations. What mutations and how many would have to be determined later.

The immediate task was to cross the treated *a* spores with

[1] Biotin had only recently been discovered, and supplies in the quantities that the experimenters would require had become available only a short time before. The experiment could not have been made a year earlier.

[2] By definition, a vitamin is a substance we need in very small quantities and must have for life, but cannot manufacture for ourselves in our own bodies and thus must obtain elsewhere.

the untreated *A*'s. The cross worked well, and in short order a profusion of molds, heavily laden with Neurospora's fruiting bodies, grew in the test tubes.

One by one, Beadle and Tatum placed the fruit masses under the microscope. With tweezers they gently pressed the spongy fruit. Out came the spore sacs, long pods plump with the eight spores each of them contained, and looking like well-filled miniature pea or bean pods.

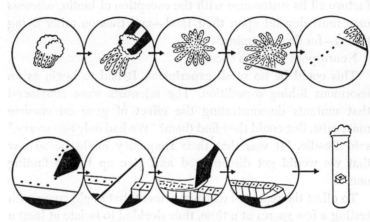

A mold culture is prepared. Spores are pressed from one of Neurospora's fruiting bodies, and separated on squares of agar jelly.

Working very carefully with a needle, Beadle pressed out the spores from each sac. He was careful to keep the eight in the order they had occupied in the pod. Four of the spores were type *A*, the type of one parent, and four were *a*, the type of the irradiated other parent.

As each of the shiny black specks was only about one thousandth of an inch long, they were visible only under the microscope. Nevertheless, Beadle and his co-workers maneuvered each one onto the edge of a sheet of agar jelly. When they were in place, the scientists cut the jelly into squares. A spore decorated the top of each square like a single grain of caviar on a bit of toast. The squares and their spores were popped into test tubes, and the tubes were closed with wads of cotton.

Were there mutants among them? Beadle and Tatum still had no way to tell, for Neurospora, unlike the fruit fly, had no red eyes to change to white. A chemical change affecting nutrition would offer no surface evidence. Two or more generations would have to be grown before the scientists could know whether a mutation had occurred.

Meanwhile, they must preserve all their material and thus make certain that they had a stock for future experiments. Therefore, all the spores were placed on a rich culture. It supplied not only all the nutrients the red mold normally required, but also an assortment of amino acids and vitamins that might be needed if a mutation had rendered some one, or some few, of the spores unable to manufacture the usual nutrients. This plan was based only on a hypothesis. Nevertheless, it proved to be justified.

In a few hours, hardy little clumps of red mold grew in the more than one thousand test tubes. The laboratory was gay with color. The experimenters then let the mold multiply asexually.

Only after all these preliminaries were they reaching the critical part of the experiment. Now they transferred a bit of each mold into another tube. This time the tubes were supplied only with the usual simple mold diet. Had any of the molds mutated so that they could no longer live on the customary food? Had some of them developed deficiencies? This was the anxious question.

The mold grew luxuriantly in test tube after test tube. In only two tubes in that whole array was there no growth. The 299th spore was showing no sign of life. Nor was the 1,090th growing. Beadle and Tatum stared excitedly at the lack of growth, at the emptiness and dullness of the two tubes. Here nothingness was a triumph, if it represented a genuine mutation and not an accident.

Other spores from the same stock also refused to grow on the usual medium, and the experimenters knew that they had succeeded in finding the mutation they sought. But what vitamin did the mutated spores lack? What vitamin could they no longer manufacture for themselves?

A systematic set of experiments had to be made to find out. Beadle and Tatum put the usual Neurospora food in ten test tubes and added a different vitamin to each one. The scientists then went back to their supply of the mutated mold, took little snips, and added them to the ten tubes. All they could do then was to wait for a trace of red—evidence that the mold was growing. Soon they saw the red of the mold beginning to appear in the tube to which they had added vitamin B-6. The little tendrils spread upward into a healthy, multiplying lot of red bread mold. The mutant Neurospora had found the one ingredient it could no longer make for itself, and it grew exuberantly. The mutant spores in the other tubes found no B-6, and they showed no sign of life. Without B-6 they were doomed.

For Beadle and Tatum, it had been a long and tedious groping in the dark for something, they could not foretell exactly what, that might or might not be there. But the little plant thriving on the usual diet plus B-6 told them that success was near.

"So far," said Beadle, "everything had been according to theory." Everything indicated that one gene—one part of the Neurospora chromosome—had changed, and that this was one of the genes which normally would have enabled the mold to manufacture its own B-6. But Beadle and Tatum did not yet "know" that the change in Neurospora's manufacturing abilities was thus produced. A scientist does not take such a point for granted.

"Genes are defined as units of inheritance," said Beadle. "In order to tell whether the new strain differs from the old one in one gene, we had to determine in an experiment if it differed in one unit of inheritance."

Once more Beadle and Tatum returned to the mutant mold. They crossed one of its spores with the normal, wild type *A* Neurospora. A fertilized cell was formed and soon grew into a strong plant. The spores from its sacs had to be separated as before.

If a gene was affected, four of the spores should grow well on the normal diet, and four should languish.

Beadle and Tatum put the eight spores in tubes with the usual food and a supply of B-6. Again they had to make sure that the defective strain would not be lost. All eight molds did well, and multiplied asexually. One spore from each tube then was transferred to a tube without added B-6. The spores were offered only the usual unsupplemented food.

This was the final test. The case rested upon what would happen in the eight tubes. The scientists again waited anxiously for the first sign—the first showing of red—that would tell them whether they had penetrated another of the secrets of the gene or had spent months of work in vain.

Four of the tubes burst forth with a fine new red growth of Neurospora. Four showed no sign of life. Would growth still appear? The scientists had to be certain that the four which were genetically defective would remain dead. The four did. Many other tests confirmed the finding.

The mutated gene had been passed along in regular order to the offspring; it was inheritable. With the 299th spore, Beadle and Tatum had succeeded.

There could no longer be any serious doubt that a mutation could alter the chemistry, and hence the whole functioning, of an organism. Neurospora's inheritance of the new inability to make B-6 underwrote the fact that the change was in the gene and the chromosome. The gene, then, did determine the chemical behavior of molds; the genes acted chemically.

Undoubtedly the system was the same in men and all living things. The change in Neurospora suggested that far back in man's ancestry, mutations might have destroyed our ability to fashion vitamins. We had found it possible thereafter to pick up the required nutriments in our food. Indeed, if we had not, there would have been no humans alive today to deduce what had happened. The race could not have survived.

The findings also supported earlier suggestions that diabetes

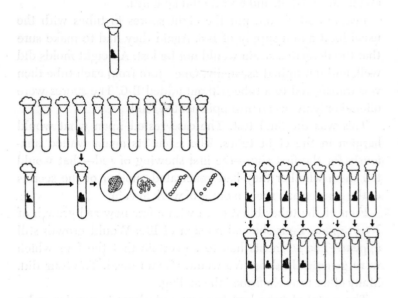

Discovery of a mutation and of how heredity exerts its effects. X-rayed Sex A spores are placed in tubes with various food substances. Only the spore that finds Vitamin B-6 grows. A mutation has rendered it unable to produce this necessary nutrient for itself.

The mutated spore is crossed with a normal one.

To assure a working stock of the offspring, all are supplied with B-6. All grow.

Branches are placed in tubes lacking B-6. Four grow, four do not. Four have inherited the mutated deficiency of one parent. A change in the hereditary material alters the chemistry and functioning of the organism.

might represent a genetic inability to make insulin, and hemophilia, the loss of a gene to control the clotting of blood.

Beadle's and Tatum's big experiment indicated in addition that a change in one gene—one section of a chromosome—modified one reaction.[3]

At the same time, the investigators had developed an invaluable tool for the study of the still inaccessible gene. Before they reported their first results in 1941 a number of other defective molds had been found, each of them requiring some extra outside vitamin or suffering from some other gene-controlled handicap. The 1,090th spore, for example, could not live without supplemental vitamin B-1. Sterling Emerson, a member of the research group, even discovered another mutation which caused Neurospora to accept a sulfanilamide compound that prior to the change had acted as a poison.

Within a few years more than eighty thousand spores of red bread mold were grown in the Beadle-Tatum laboratory. An overwhelming majority of the molds, even after irradiation, developed normally. But among the eighty thousand were about four hundred mutants, some of which were very odd molds indeed.

But still the question had to be asked: how did the gene accomplish its control, how did its alteration change the ability of Neurospora to make B-6, or whatever the compound might be?

"It is believed," said Beadle, "that in these cases the genes act as a pattern from which enzymes are copied and that the enzymes set the pattern and shape the special products on which life depends."

The work with Neurospora developed another clue to the gene's action. In irradiating the mold, Beadle and Tatum

---

[3] The effects of the one altered reaction might, nevertheless, be multitudinous. In the human race the lack of one vitamin, say B-1, produces an inflammation of the nerves, muscular disability, rigidity of the limbs, widespread edema, a gradual withering away, and finally death.

"knocked out" a gene that had to do with a substance named indole. Its results were not to be seen directly, but molds unable to make their own indole were also unable to make the highly essential tryptophane, one of the building blocks of protein.

The scientists went to work to try to determine what was happening. They found that if the mutant mold was supplied with indole from the outside, all went smoothly and the chemical production line could move again.

And then another mutant turned up which also affected indole. It permitted Neurospora to begin the manufacture of indole, but halted the process before it was finished. In that case, if the same analogy may be used, the production line started to move but was halted. The material that was to be used in making indole was brought to the assembly point but could not be employed, and there was a backing up. Tatum, by some very fine analysis, determined that the material that was backing up was anthranilic acid. Thus a whole chain of chemical events affected by a gene was worked out—anthranilic acid to indole, to tryptophane, to protein. The pieces would not fit together and move if one of the links was missing or altered.

A report had come in showing that rats fed on diets rich in tryptophane did not need the vitamin niacin. This suggested to Tatum that possibly niacin, in the teeming factory of the cell, is made from tryptophane. Some studies with the strain of mold which could not make indole, and hence tryptophane, soon proved the point. The mold did derive its niacin from tryptophane.

All of this had a direct bearing on the lives of men. For many years the dietary disease pellagra had been attributed to a number of causes: poor quality in dietary protein, a toxic factor in Indian corn (as many pellagra victims had lived on cornbread, fat bacon, and molasses), or lack of a vitamin. Then in 1937 C. A. Elvehjem of the University of Wisconsin discovered that the vitamin niacin could bring about spectacular cures of black tongue, a disease in dogs similar to pellagra in man. Niacin was quickly supplied to human sufferers from pellagra and a rapid cure followed. With pellagra so dramatically cured by a vitamin, the earlier discussions of other causes of the disease were forgotten.

Neurspora suggested a deeper cause. Perhaps the reason sufferers from pellagra lacked niacin and had to be given big doses of it was that they could not manufacture their own, and perhaps the reason they could not was that the proteins they ate did not supply enough tryptophane to make this possible.

"The corn-toxin theory also has a reasonable base," said Beadle, "there appear to be chemical substances in the grain that interfere with the body's use of tryptophane and niacin in such a way as to increase the requirements of those two materials."

The lowly bread mold was not only showing more about the working of the gene, it also was going to the root of some of the troubles of men. The basic reactions in men and molds once again were shown to be the same.

A change in a gene produced a direct change in the way molds and men produced materials essential to their lives; a change in a gene also affected the paths that had to be un-deviatingly followed in the grand process. The gene determined not only how the living edifice was built, but also how it ran.

Science was getting closer to the great riddle of how we happen to be what we are.

Closer, yes, but it was still far away from the ultimate answer.

In 1941 Morgan retired as head of the department of biology of the California Institute of Technology. For five years the institute sought carefully for a worthy successor. In 1946 it found him in Beadle.

When Beadle went to Pasadena, Caltech's division of chemistry was headed by Linus Pauling, a chemist whose studies of the forces that cause atoms to join into molecules had led him into the formation of hemoglobin, the red matter of the blood cells. He was a biologically minded chemist and Beadle a chemically minded biologist.

The two quickly joined forces and outlined a fifteen-year program of research on the fundamental problems of biology and medicine. The Rockefeller Foundation made continuing grants of about $100,000 a year, and other funds poured in for a major attempt to go still further in deciphering the nature of living matter.

"We are seeking to uncover the principles that govern the fundamental processes of life," Beadle explained.

The organization of science was changing. The unified effort to develop the atomic bomb had demonstrated what could be done by a team effort. As the explosion of the bomb brought World War II to an end, there was a demand for unified efforts to solve some of the other problems of mankind. The California project was one step in this direction.

As one of the heads of the biological enterprise, Beadle had less time for his own work. He drew a gifted group of scientists to Pasadena to take part in this new concentrated study. There they had great freedom to work in an atmosphere that *Time* in a "cover story" about Beadle described as one of "amiability spiced by high intellectual excitement."

Beadle and his colleague Pauling also gave part of their time to laying before the country the dangers of excess radiation. The explosion at Hiroshima had ended the illusion that the scientist could remain quietly behind the walls of his laboratory, ignoring the consequences of his findings. A new era in the relation of science to society was dawning, and the California scientists typified it.

Beadle and his wife, a newspaperwoman, live just across

the street from the laboratory in a house long occupied by the Morgans. The gardens are bright with flowers, many of them genetic experiments. Wandering about are the Beadles' Siamese cats. The geneticist explains that their rich cream-and-sable coloring results from a mutated gene that permits dark pigments to form only in the places of low body temperature, the ears, the tail, the paws.

With the Morgan, Muller, and Beadle-and-Tatum findings, research made a long advance. The new understandings that followed only underwrote the importance of the principles worked out in the studies of the red bread mold. In 1958 Beadle and Tatum—the latter then at the Rockefeller Institute—were awarded the Nobel Prize "for their discovery that genes act by regulating specific chemical processes."

Professor Torbjoern Caspersson, a member of the award panel and himself a distinguished geneticist, added: "Their discovery offered the first chance to understand the mode of action of the genes and is one of the foundations of modern genetics."

Some four centuries ago Paracelsus observed: "The human body is a conglomeration of chymical matters." The work of Beadle and Tatum at last demonstrated that the conglomeration was given form and order by the material of the chromosomes. The master control had been found.

XIII

THE VERITABLE STUFF OF LIFE

THROUGH MOST of the years while the three M's—Mendel, Morgan, and Muller—were discovering the amazing hereditary feats of the chromosomes, bottles of a gummy white powder sat on the shelves of many laboratories.

It was in fact the veritable stuff of those chromosomes. It might have been labeled, if anyone had recognized its full significance and had been endowed with the uninhibited imagination of a medievalist rather than the steely restraint of a scientist, the elixir of life, the quintessence of life. In actuality it bore the label "Nucleic Acid," and the bottles gathered dust.

Mendel had barely finished his work and taken on the duties of the Abbot of Brünn when the white powder was discovered—in 1869.

A young Swiss biochemist, Friedrich Miescher, was completing his studies in the Strasbourg laboratories of one of the leading scientists of the day, Felix Hoppe-Seyler. Miescher was assigned to make some chemical analyses of the cell, and he was having difficulty in breaking down its stubborn entity. It occurred to him that pepsin, the stomach enzyme that digests the proteins we eat, might act upon the proteins in the cell.

Miescher mixed a solution and dropped in some pus cells. His idea worked beautifully. The pepsin quickly broke down the cells and disintegrated their proteins. Nevertheless, quite a bit of material was left. Miescher, who even as a student made a practice of examining all the materials with which he was working, decided to have a look at it. He put a bit of the cellular residue under his microscope. A surprising sight met his eye. While the cells as wholes had disintegrated, the nucleus of each remained and was intact. Although a little shrunken, it had survived the tearing apart of the cell.

Miescher was excited and curious. He made a chemical analysis of the nuclear stuff. And then another surprise awaited him. The nuclei differed in chemical composition from all other reported cellular materials. Miescher decided to call this unique material "nuclein."

Hoppe-Seyler at first could scarcely believe that his student could be right. A check of Miescher's careful work, however, disclosed that he was. What was more, Miescher's finding seemed to hold for other nuclei too. Hoppe-Seyler himself succeeded in obtaining a similar "nuclein" from yeast cells.

Miescher in the meanwhile returned to his home at Basel. It was a fortunate place for him to live and work. In the 1870's the salmon still swam up the Rhine as far as the falls above Basel, and salmon sperm made an unsurpassed material for the study of the nucleus of the cell. The salmon nucleus was exceptionally large; in fact, it made up more than half the dry weight of the sperm cell.

Each spring Miescher joined the fishermen at the foot of the falls. As he cast his nets into the river churning with the fish, he obtained a supply of fish sperm ample to meet his experimental needs for the rest of the year.

With this excellent material, Miescher made progress in his work. He was soon able to do an improved job of separating the nucleus from the remainder of the cell—that is, from the cytoplasm. Miescher also improved his methods of removing the protein from the nucleus, though he still had to use strong acids for the separation. Nevertheless, he obtained a good supply of pure nuclein.

Miescher was thus able to push on with his analyses of this unusual material. It was made up, he found, of carbon, oxygen, hydrogen, nitrogen, and phosphorus, the elements of most living things. Others, following Miescher's lead, pointed out that in solution nuclein was an acid and should properly be called nucleic acid. Miescher agreed to this amendment in title.

Always hoping to carry his great series of experiments further, Miescher published little of his work. Only after his death in 1895 did his friends assemble his notes in a book honoring his memory and testifying to his achievements. It still has not been translated into English.

In one sense, nuclein or nucleic acid was the heart of the heart of the cell, and even at a time when the role of the nucleus was little understood, its importance was obvious. Albrecht Kossel at the University of Heidelberg and P. A. Levene at the Rockefeller Institute in New York continued the investigation of Miescher's interesting white powder. What was it? How were its atoms put together? These old and persistent questions had to be asked about any new material, and answers had to be found.

The two large laboratories at Heidelberg and New York— Miescher had worked alone—learned that nuclein was a very large molecule indeed. Compared to any ordinary molecule of, say, table salt, or even to many protein molecules, it was a whale among minnows. They also discovered that it had a very long thread-like structure. When they broke down the thread, it dissolved not into its constituent elements, but into sub-units, each sizable and complex in its own right. The sub-units in their turn were composed of five-carbon sugars— five sugar molecules—to which were attached four different kinds of nitrogen-containing assemblies. The units—sometimes there were as many as three thousand of them—were held together with phosphoric-acid bonds.

This complex material was given the formidable name of (d)eoxyribo(n)ucleic (a)cid. Thereafter it was to be known as DNA.

The giant molecule had been dissected into what might be called its sinews and bones, and that seemed to take care of the problem. There was not much more to be done with it at the time. So the gummy white powder made up of the huge molecules, made up of the complex sub-units and sub-assemblies, went into the bottle and onto the shelf. And there it sat, receiving relatively little attention.

Some years later the German biochemist Robert Feulgen happened to treat some DNA with the acid fuchsin. He was startled to see it turn a brilliant purple—fuchsia. Nevertheless, the color reaction seemed so incidental to him that he did not even try it on a living cell. When he did—in 1924—an even more startling and welcome experience awaited him. The chromosomes of the cell to which he applied the acid suddenly stood forth in bright glowing color; they could be seen as sharply as a lighted sign in the night. Each chromosome was presented in its full form in the rich, unmistakable color. It was the clear, decisive kind of test of which the biochemist dreams.

From this time on, biochemists had only to apply fuchsin to find whether nucleic acid was present in a cell. If it was, it jumped forth in purple. They used the test on all kinds of cells, and by this tracking with a purple-red color discovered that nucleic acid is found only in the chromosomes of cells. They of course tested the remainder of the cell also, but, no matter how much fuchsin acid was spotted on the cytoplasm around the nucleus, no sign of purple appeared there. The cytoplasm was Feulgen-negative. In this way it was learned that DNA is concentrated in the nucleus and in the nucleus alone—unless it is in transit from one cell to another.

All of this was interesting to know; it added to the store of knowledge to be able to spot DNA in the chromosomes of the nucleus and there exclusively. But the information created no great ferment in an era when attention was concentrated not on science, but on the booming stock market and other excitements.

Except for this small flare-up of interest, the bottles of nuclein continued to sit on the shelves and gather dust.

This obscurity did not begin to lighten until 1931. In that year the German biologist Joachim Hämmerling undertook some experiments with a little single-celled, mushroom-shaped plant called Acetabularia. There are many varieties of the small green plant, each with its own distinctively shaped "cap." What interested Hämmerling was Acetabularia's ability to grow a new cap if its original one was cut off.

The German scientist decided to see what would happen if he transplanted a nucleus from the stem of one variety to the stem of another and then cut off the little plant's head. The operation was performed. As Hämmerling anxiously watched, Acetabularia, true to its nature, grew a new "cap," but the new one was not its own "head"; it was the cap of the variety from which the nucleus had been taken. The transplanted nucleus had directed what kind of head the plant should have. With a new nucleus in place, the traditional pattern of growth was completely upset and a new one substituted. It could only mean that the nucleus and the nucleus alone determined what the plant was to be—for nothing else had been changed.

For the first time it thus became clear and certain that it was not the whole cell that called the turn and form of life; it was the nucleus. One small part of the cell was the determiner of a plant's fate, and perhaps of man's as well.

The work of Morgan and Muller had indicated very strongly that the seat of heredity was even more restricted. Their famed experiments with heredity and mutation pointed not to the whole nucleus as the critical center, but to the chromosomes within the nucleus and to the "factors" within the chromosomes called the genes. Beadle's experiments with the red bread mold, Neurospora, then dramatically wiped out any lingering doubts about the prime importance of the chromosomes. The chromosomes and their hereditary material exerted complete and sweeping control over the chemical processes of the cell and thus over all that living things are.

As the war-torn 1940's began, the whole situation thus was changed. The chromosomes were marked as the key to heredity. If the answer to the form and functioning of life was ever to be found, it undoubtedly would have to be sought in the little bent chromosome strings and in the gummy powder of which they were made. The world was deep in war, and scientific effort was centered on the atom. Nevertheless, the bottles of DNA were at last taken down from the laboratory shelves, and the stuff that Miescher had extracted from pus and salmon sperm cells moved from obscurity into the center of world-wide attention.

But much, much more had to be learned about the chromosomes and DNA. Dozens of urgent questions had to be answered.

As Miescher had early recognized, the DNA was combined in the chromosome with protein and other materials. Many scientists, knowing well the essential role of protein in all the other life processes, were convinced that the protein in the chromosome rather than the little-known DNA would prove to be the base, the pattern, the key. Or—who could say?—it might even turn out to be some other nuclear material present only in a trace amount. Science had tracked the quarry to the nucleus and the chromosome, but the end was still not in sight. A whole new search had to begin.

Among the laboratories that entered the new delving into the innermost recesses of living material was that of the Rockefeller Institute. To determine whether the basic substance was DNA or protein or perhaps some unknown element, a better separation of the nuclear materials would first have to be made. The hydrochloric and sulphuric acids that Miescher had used to divide the nuclear materials were harsh and had destroyed most of the delicate cell structures. A gentle, non-destructive separation rather than a violent assault was needed.

No salmon swam up the Hudson or the East River to supply the two Rockefeller experimenters, A. E. Mirsky and A. W. Pollister, with choice salmon sperm, but they obtained plentiful stores of carp sperm from the city's markets. In an attempt to break down the nucleus gently, the scientists put the carp sperm in a salt solution. The method worked splendidly.

The cytoplasm was washed away without any apparent change in the nucleus and without any marked change in the main outlines of the cell. After more separations Mirsky and Pollister obtained a viscous, colorless solution.

Under the microscope the scientists could see that the solution was a mass of delicate threads. Mirsky stirred them with a small rod; it was the kind of thing a biochemist does almost automatically. With a start, he saw that the fibers were collecting on his rod. He gave it a few twirls, and the fibers matted on it so tightly that he could lift them intact out of the solution.

"Our first success in preparation of chromatin threads came while we were working with a material from which the threads can be isolated with such ease that we had the good fortune to obtain them entirely by chance," said Mirsky.

Mirsky and Pollister put the remainder of their material through two additional processings. Each time they collected the fibers by winding them around stir rods.

The little threads they were collecting proved to be almost pure chromosomes; for the first time chromosomes were being extracted intact from nuclei, and the scientists were obtaining the natural threads instead of a powder. It was, said Mirsky with notable understatement, "a simple and rapid" way to separate chromatin.

Using these methods (which in a non-technical summary sound far simpler than the complex, delicate operations they were), the Rockefeller Institute group prepared chromatin threads from many animal tissues, including the brain, kidney, pancreas, spleen, liver, and thymus. And they also separated them from plant tissues.

"It would appear likely," said Mirsky, "that nucleohistones [DNA and the particular kind of protein associated with it] are universal cell constituents, because in addition to their isolation from many different animal tissues it has been possible to prepare them from plant tissues, wheat germ, and bacteria.

"Their physico-chemical properties are all strikingly similar. . . . All contain a high percentage of DNA and all contain exceedingly basic proteins."

But the great protein-DNA question had not been settled, for both leading candidates had been found in virtually all kinds of tissues.

Mirsky saw where a clue might lie. Were both DNA and the proteins present in constant amounts? Distribution might afford an indication of their respective functions.

The Rockefeller Institute group and a group in Strasbourg headed by the late André Boivin undertook to measure the quantity of DNA in the nuclei of the various kinds of cell. Mirsky in one experiment, in which he used the blood of a rooster, counted the number of red cells in a given volume of cells. The DNA in that volume was then measured and divided by the number of cells. That gave him the DNA quota per cell. He also worked out a way to make the DNA count in an individual cell. Both methods gave the same result. The nucleus of a rooster cell contained 2.3 hundred-millionths of a milligram of DNA. And, significantly, all the other body cells of the rooster contained the same amount.

Although every normal body cell of any one species might bear the same amount of DNA, the scientists learned that the amount varied for each species. Each species had its own characteristic count of DNA—the frog 15 hundred-millionths of a milligram to a cell, the green turtle 5.3 hundred-millionths.

The emerging rule, that the body cells of each species carry a constant amount of DNA, varied only in a few cases that underwrote its accuracy. The sperm cells, the scientists found, contained exactly half as much DNA as other cells. When sperm and egg united, the correct DNA amount for the species was re-established. It began to look as though DNA behaved as a hereditary material.

There also are cases in which the nuclei of some cells have double or quadruple sets of chromosomes. If the investigators were reasoning correctly, such cells should contain twice or four times as much DNA as cells with the ordinary set of chromosomes. Mirsky hurried to check. They did.

Nuclear protein, however, was not so evenly distributed. Some cells had large amounts of it, some small.

"All of this shows that DNA is closely associated with the hereditary factors of chromosomes and most likely forms part of the stuff of which the hereditary factors are made," said Mirsky. "The chromosomes, of course, contain other substances besides DNA [e.g., various proteins], but none of these other known constituents is distributed in nuclei in the same regular way."

Distribution therefore indicated that DNA, and not protein, was the bearer of heredity. The hereditary factor would have to be distributed as DNA was. And yet no one had been able to demonstrate incontestably and directly that the prime role belonged to DNA.

As frequently happens in science, the crowning bit of evidence developed unexpectedly. In 1928 Fred Griffith, an English bacteriologist, was engaged in studies of pneumococci, the bacteria that cause pneumonia. His hope was to find some means of controlling the disease.

Griffith injected one strain of pneumococcus known as Type I into thirty-six successive generations of mice. In the long passage through the bodies of the animals, the virulent Type I strain changed—it lost the gummy capsule that surrounded it and at the same time became weakened and harmless. Many vaccines are made in precisely this way. Injected in their weakened or attenuated form, they still stimulate the production of antibodies and thus protect an animal or human from the virulent form of the disease.

In the course of his work, Griffith one day injected a mouse with some of his attenuated Type I strain. At the same time he gave the little laboratory animal a shot of heat-killed pneumococci of Type III. The latter was a highly virulent, capsule-enclosed strain, but it had been killed by treating it with heat. This was another standard method of preparing a vaccine.

Thus, the mouse received what should have been two innocuous shots, one dead and one so weakened that it was not supposed to be virulent.

In a short time Griffith was amazed to see that the mouse had "pneumonia"; it was extremely sick. The animal was sacrificed and its blood cells were examined. Griffith saw that the heart blood cells were swarming with virulent pneumococci, Type III bacteria, all fully enclosed in the particular gummy capsules of Type III.

Griffith's first thought was that there had been a slip-up in the killing of the Type III germs. Perhaps the bacteria had not been dead, as he had thought. He quickly injected some of the same batch of heat-treated bacteria into a large number of mice. Not a one of them developed the disease; in not an instance did the bacteria multiply. The bacteria, then, had been killed.

Only one conclusion could be drawn. The living, naked, and supposedly harmless Type I bacteria had multiplied and somehow changed into encapsulated, virulent Type III! It was the kind of impossibility which tells a scientist he is face to face with a new fact. The nearly unbelievable transformation that Griffith saw in the dead mouse could only mean that the heat-killed, encapsulated bacteria had transmitted their hereditary constitution to the Type I germs. The new heredity then must have taken control. It had not only produced capsules on the Type I bacteria, but capsules characteristic of Type III.

When the newly created Type III's were injected into other mice, the bacteria bred true. The former Type I bacteria had, in every sense, become Type III. A genuine hereditary change had taken place. Somehow hereditary material had been transmitted from Type III to Type I. Somehow it had retained all its effectiveness when the cell in which it lived was dead.

This bacterial instance of one breed seemingly changing into another aroused great interest. Scientists could scarcely have been more astonished if a cat had given birth to a dog. Martin H. Dawson and R. H. Sia of the Rockefeller Institute then succeeded in producing the same transformation in a test tube. They added heat-killed cells and living but weakened cells to a nutrient solution. Again the "dead" cells imposed their constitution on the living.

And this was not a phenomenon confined to penumococci. G. P. Berry and H. M. Dedrick inoculated rabbits with a mixture of active fibroma virus and a heat-inactivated myxoma virus. Again a harmless virus was transformed, and again a hereditary factor was proved transmissible regardless of its environment.

As the cell was "dead," it looked very much as though some substance other than the cell as a whole must transmit heredity. The search was narrowing. And yet until the 1940's, when all the signs began to point toward one special part of the chromosome, the full implications could not be drawn. Only then could the question be asked: what is the active principle? What is the substance that can induce a complete transformation in the life and heredity of another organism?

The effort to find the elusive principle, to isolate it, to understand it was gathering new momentum. Another group at the Rockefeller Institute, including O. T. Avery, Maclyn McCarty, and Colin Macleod, set out to discover it in the Type

III pneumonia cell. One by one they tested and eliminated possible suspects. The gummy capsule was removed from the cell. Without it the naked cell was still able to hand on its ability to form more capsules of its own kind. Thus the capsule was ruled out. The investigative team next delicately took away the protein that made up a substantial portion of the cell. Its removal made no difference. The fraction of the cell left after the protein was gone still caused Type I to change into Type III.

The potent remainder was none other than DNA. Pure DNA. The merest trace of the nucleic acid could persuade Type I pneumococci to forgo their own heritage and synthesize capsules not of their own type, but those of Type III.

If any doubt remained that DNA was the do-er, the scientists ended it by removing the DNA from a group of Type III cells. When this was done and III was mixed with I, there was no change whatsoever in Type I. With the instigator gone, nothing happened, and Type I remained true to its own form and tradition.

"Transmission of hereditary characteristics in pneumococci by means of DNA provides a beautiful example of one of the principles of heredity," said Mirsky. "What is transmitted in us from one generation to the next is not a characteristic eye pigment or blood type or other hereditary trait. Rather, it is a set of factors in chromosomes which are able to influence the activities of the cells so that certain eye pigments and certain substances responsible for blood types are produced."

A bacterium that causes pneumonia had indicated to a surprised scientific world that DNA, and DNA alone, is the carrier of heredity. The proof had come from an odd quarter.

Further proof was soon to come from another unlikely source—a tiny virus, only seven millionths of an inch long, which invades and attacks bacteria.

In 1949 Thomas H. Anderson of the University of Pennsylvania and Roger M. Herriott of Johns Hopkins University made a curious discovery about the virus or bacteriophage called T2. It was inactivated if water was rapidly added to a salt solution in which it was suspended. In an attempt to find out what had happened, the scientists put some of the inactivated phage under a microscope. It was, they saw, only an empty shell, a "ghost." It had lost its contents.

Several years later Alfred Day Hershey and Martha Chase,

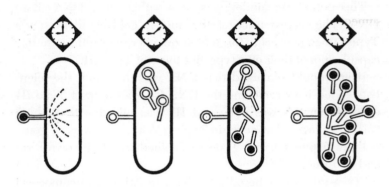

The super-speedy virus. A virus shoots its DNA into a cell at 9 a.m. Some twenty-four minutes later the virus has taken over the cell, manufactured about 200 replicas of itself, and is breaking out of the cell.

working at the Cold Spring Harbor genetics laboratory of the Carnegie Institution, took up the interesting problem of the virus ghost. They began to re-study it with labeled, radioactive materials.

By 1952 they had the astounding story in all its essentials. The bacteriophage particle thrust its pointed tail into the wall of a bacterium and shot its contents into the interior of that cell. The emptied coat remained outside, like an emptied syringe. Twenty-four minutes later the bacterium burst open, and out came two hundred new viruses, each an exact copy of the invader.

The injected material had taken control of the cell and used the cell's contents to produce new viruses of its own kind. The scientists, however, had to establish beyond reasonable doubt whether or not it was DNA that had been injected into the cell and had taken command. A number of experiments were made.

In one of them Hershey and Chase killed the bacteria with heat. The phage was not in the least deterred. It injected a cell exactly as though the cell had been alive, entered, and assumed control. Taking another group of bacteria, the scientists introduced DNAase, the enzyme that breaks down DNA, almost immediately after the phages had shot their contents into the bacterial cells. The enzyme acted upon the material in the cell exactly as it did upon "naked" DNA outside the cell. Thus the material injected into the cell was marked as DNA by the enzyme that acts only on DNA.

Photographs showed the empty phage coats sticking to the outsides of the bacterial cells like arrows in a target. Hershey thought that it should be possible to shear them off and test them. He put some of the "ghost"-studded cells into a Waring Blendor—the machine used in the kitchen for making milk-shakes—and recovered more than eighty per cent of the original coat of the virus. The coat consisted largely of protein, and its removal made no difference to the multiplication of the virus inside the cell. That continued exactly as though the protein "coat" sticking on the outside of the cell had not been stripped away.

At first, however, Hershey and Chase were cautious. They reported only that the protein coat of the virus T2 had no function in the growth of phage, and that DNA did have a function.

Confirmation came rapidly. Lloyd M. Kozloff of the University of Chicago even found the "muscle" and the remainder of the mechanism used by the phage to squirt its DNA into the cell.

Thus, it was virtually certain. In some way that had still to be defined, an almost inconceivably small amount of the white gummy powder that Miescher had discovered was the carrier of most, if not all, of the information and plan that account for the complexity of the countless billions of living creatures.

But the full story of nucleic acid was not told. Not long after Miescher isolated DNA, another unique form—ribonucleic acid —was found in the nucleus of the yeast cell. Like DNA, it was composed of sugar (though a different sugar), phosphorus, and four other groups of material. Three of the latter—adenine, guanine, and cytosine—were the same as in DNA; the fourth, however, was uracil. The uracil took the place occupied by thymine in DNA.

The (r)ibo(n)ucleic (a)cid—RNA—seemed to occur only in plant cells, and for many years it had been considered only a plant nucleic acid. DNA, it was thought, was confined to animal cells. This false distinction was upset in 1924 when Feulgen began to apply his fuschia color test to all kinds of cells. The bright purple-red testifying to the unmistakable presence of DNA appeared in wheat and other plant cells, and RNA was found in animal cells. Both nucleic acids then appeared to be constituents of all cells, plant and animal.

To say, however, that both nucleic acids were found in the cell or even in the nucleus of the cell was only vaguely to locate them in the great subcontinent of living matter. Their specific territories had to be marked out, and this required some fine exploring.

Martin Behrens, a pupil of Feulgen's, was one of the first to work on this exploration. Behrens separated the nucleus from the remainder of the cell. He used a grinding and freezing process that did relatively little damage to the cell structures and gave him pure nuclei and pure cytoplasm.

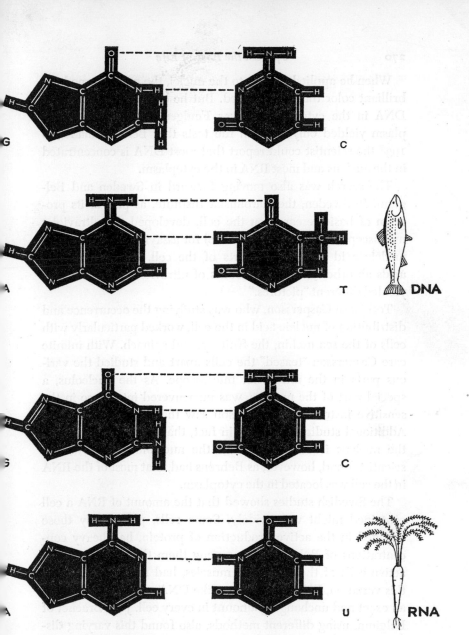

DNA *and* RNA *bases.* TOP: G *and* C, *and* A *and* T *make up the four units of* DNA. BOTTOM: RNA *varies only in one base. It is composed of* G *and* C, *and* A *and* U. *Here are the master controls of life.*

When he applied fuchsia to the nuclei, the nuclei turned the brilliant color that he expected. But he could find no trace of DNA in the cytoplasm; it was Feulgen-negative. The cytoplasm yielded only RNA in the tests that Behrens made. In 1938 the scientist could report that most DNA is concentrated in the nucleus and most RNA in the cytoplasm.

The search was also moving forward in Sweden and Belgium. In Sweden, the Karolinska Institute, as part of its program of basic research on the cell, developed the ultraviolet microscope into a quantitative tool for assaying the amounts of nucleic acid in different parts of the cell. The two nucleic acids absorbed differing amounts of ultraviolet light and thus yielded different "pictures."

Torbjoern Caspersson, who was studying the occurrence and distribution of nucleic acid in the cell, worked particularly with cells of the sea urchin, the fruit fly, and spinach. With infinite care Caspersson "teased" the cells apart and studied the various parts in the ultraviolet microscope. As the nucleolus, a special part of the nucleus, was maneuvered into place in the sensitive instrument, Caspersson saw that it contained RNA. Additional studies indicated, in fact, that most of the RNA in the nucleus is concentrated in the nucleolus. The Swedish scientist found, however, as Behrens had, that most of the RNA in the cell was located in the cytoplasm.

The Swedish studies showed that the amount of RNA a cell contained might vary widely. Some cells, particularly those engaged in the active production of protein, had heavy concentrations of RNA. Others, among them the physiologically active cells of the heart and muscles, had relatively little. In this variation, RNA was most unlike DNA, which is present in an exact and unchanging amount in every cell. Jean Brachet of Belgium, using different methods, also found this varying distribution of the "second" nucleic acid.

The Swedish group went even further in its tracking of the nucleic acids. Holger Hydén discovered that the RNA in the cytoplasm was often clustered around the nuclear membrane. Could it be moving from the nucleus into the surrounding cytoplasm? The question was for the future, but the location of both RNA and DNA in the cell was being fixed. The territories of both were being defined.

XIV

CRICK AND WATSON: DNA, A HELIX

"I believe that the elucidation of the structure of nucleic acid is the most important scientific problem we face today. It is vastly more important than any of the problems associated with the structure of the atom, for in nucleic acid we are dealing with life itself."

WENDELL STANLEY, 1957

AND SO IT WAS DNA. The limitless diversity of life, its orderliness, its form and continuity were controlled and conveyed by the amazing substance called DNA, or in a few cases by the other nucleic acid, RNA. Without the organization of DNA, there would be no living world as we know it.

But how could a bit of matter, a bit measured in hundred-millionths of a milligram, bear within itself all the instructions needed for the construction of a human being or a fruit fly or a lettuce leaf?

For the building of a modern skyscraper, a structure that in size outruns the ordinary building as the huge DNA molecule does most molecules, hundreds of sheets of drawings, each crowded with details and plans, must be prepared. Even this great mass of plans would be as nothing if human beings had to prepare working drawings for the construction of another human being or even a mosquito.

Height, sex, color, all the gross structural features would have to be worked out, and so would all the interior arrangements, the form and placement of the organs and tissues and of the 1,000,000,000,000,000 cells, and all the apparatus for the production of new cells and new beings. It is difficult even to imagine the plans that would be required for the building of a complex living creature.

And yet, all the evidence showed, DNA did the whole over-whelming job. Somehow all the plans and specifications were encompassed in an invisible speck of matter deep in the nucleus of the cell. It seemed a fantasy of fantasies, an im-possible, nearly inconceivable feat of engineering and design. Yet it was a reality, a reality re-created and repeated billions of times each day.

How? How could so much be concentrated in so little? How was it possible for DNA to store and transmit the master plan of life? What was its structure that it could perform such prodigies?

The question, as the 1950's began, was almost as baffling and overpowering to scientists as to anyone else. But the time had come when it could be faced. The accumulation of knowledge about heredity and the new findings about the chemical and physical nature of DNA for the first time made an approach possible.

Work began in laboratories all over the world. Some even believed that the stage was being set for "the grand finale."

In the great laboratory headed by Linus Pauling at the California Institute of Technology, Pauling and Robert B. Corey pondered the DNA question.

They knew that DNA is a long thread. X-ray-diffraction pictures suggested that the threads might be coiled. Exten-sive studies and calculations indicated to the two scientists that DNA might consist of three chains intertwined.

They set down their ideas in January 1953 and sent a de-tailed report for publication in the *Proceedings* of the National Academy of Sciences. It was published in the following month.

On January 2, Pauling and Corey also sent a brief note on their proposal to the English scientific journal *Nature:* "We have formulated a structure for the nucleic acids which is compatible with the main features of the X-ray diagrams and the general principles of molecular structure and which accounts satisfactorily for some of the chemical properties of the substances."

The Californians were aware that the same engrossing question—the great how of DNA—was being studied by F. H. C. Crick and a young American, James Dewey Watson, at the Cavendish Laboratory of the University of Cambridge. They sent Crick a copy of their full report.

Crick and Watson were indeed in the middle of the same investigation. They too were trying to discover the structure of the fabulous DNA.

Crick was unusually well prepared to work with what was in part a problem of physics and mechanics. He was originally trained as a physicist. During World War II he had worked for the British Admiralty on the design of sea mines. At the end of the war, however, Crick had reached a decision: he wanted to work with living materials, to go into molecular biology. He obtained a Medical Research Council studentship and entered Strangeways Laboratory at Cambridge. While he worked on the "cytoplasm of chick fibroplasts," he said, "I read everything I could get my hands on."

With his training completed, he joined the Molecular Biological unit at Cambridge and went to work on nucleic acids and viruses. He pondered the problem of how DNA accomplished its miracles of control and reproduction. This led him straight to the problem of its structure, for DNA was a unit without superfluities. Its secret, Crick was convinced, must lie in the way it is made. As a man familiar with scientific problems of structure, it seemed to Crick that a fruitful approach to understanding what DNA was like in space would be to build a model of it.

Watson had come to Cambridge as a research fellow and had two years to devote to work in the laboratories there. He was enthusiastic about the idea, and the two joined forces.

"We were convinced," said Crick, "that we could get somewhere near the DNA structure by building models."

In effect, the two scientists were taking on the construction of a three-dimensional jigsaw puzzle with a number of rotatable joints. There was very little to guide them except the way in which the pieces had to fit together; there was, after all, no picture on the box lid.

The pieces that must be fitted into the structure were, however, well defined. Chemical studies had supplied their shapes and measurements. First there were the sugar molecules—each five-sided. They were joined to one another by a kinky phosphate molecule.

And then there were four other important pieces, each with its own distinctive shape. One was called adenine, one guanine, one cytosine, and one thymine—or, more conveniently A, G, C, and T. All four were known as bases.[1]

Thus, there were six kinds of pieces in all. And there were generally the same six, whether the DNA came from a liver cell, a blood cell, from a human, a calf, or a root tip of grass.[2]

A few other essential facts were known. The sugar and phosphate pieces formed long, regular chains, repeating the same sugar-phosphate sequence over and over again, exactly like any chain made of a succession of alternating large and small links. As a result, the chains were about a thousand times longer than they were wide.

Watson and Crick also knew, as they began work, that the four "bases," A, T, C, and G, were attached at right angles to the sugars. As to their order, there was little information.

On the other hand, much had been learned about how all atoms, including those of DNA, fit together. Studies of the atom had shown how atoms are joined, the angles of joining, and inter-atomic distances. By putting the six DNA pieces

---

[1] The term "base" was used in its chemical sense—a compound capable of combining with a proton or hydrogen ion.
[2] There are minor exceptions to this.

together as physical and chemical laws indicated they must go, Watson and Crick hoped to build a structure that would at least approximate the true structure of DNA. It would be shaped primarily by the fitting together of the parts, as a branch of a tree might be simulated by someone who put together its separate sections without knowing how the finished branch should look.

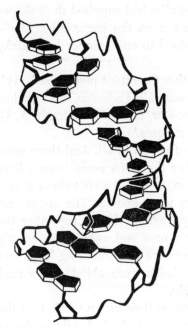

DNA in wire. Long and short bases—the "steps"— and side chains all fitted together in a helix.

Formidable difficulties clearly could beset such a course, all the more so because some of the pieces might rotate in any direction. Even though one part was linked to another correctly, should it turn to the right or to the left? On which side of the chain should the bases be placed and how should the chain itself turn?

With a good supply of wire and thin little pieces of metal

cut in the form of "bases," Watson and Crick started to put together the sugars and phosphates. They soon ran into trouble. The phosphate pieces tended to be either too far apart for the sugars to fill the gap between them or so close that the sugars could be made to fit only by grossly violating the rules governing such contacts.

Several false starts nevertheless provided heartening lessons and welcome reassurance. Errors were soon revealed. Anything other than the fundamentally correct construction would lead to one kind of jam or another. Only the right way would work. The problem was to find it.

Watson and Crick began again. They saw that they would have to work with all the pieces at once, and as they had no way of determining what base would fit into which place, they used an "idealized" structure. The pieces then began fitting together. The experimenters found themselves with half of a chain ladder. The sugar and phosphates formed one long chain; the bases attached to it like half-rungs.

A second chain was assembled. If it was turned upside down and brought close to the other and the two were twisted together, the bases, with their hydrogen atoms acting as joiners, came smartly together.

Watson and Crick had a helix—a spiral staircase!

Technically, a helix is wound around a cylinder, whereas a true spiral starts at a point and winds upward in increasingly wide convolutions, like a top. Despite the distinction, helical staircases—an excellent illustration of the helical principle—are commonly called spiral staircases. Thus, the experimenters found in their hands a miniature, gracefully spiraling staircase. The sugar-phosphate chains formed the frame of the staircase; the bases formed the steps or treads.

As far as they had gone, the pieces fitted together amazingly well. The puzzle was falling into place, and the two Cambridge scientists felt that they were making headway.

While Watson and Crick were fitting together their little

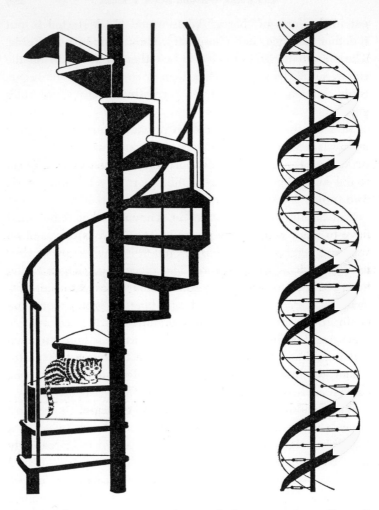

Two spiral staircases. LEFT: *One made by man.* RIGHT: *Nature's own—DNA. One is large and one is infinitesimally small, but both are built on the same principle.*

wire model of the DNA molecule, M. F. H. Wilkins, the late Rosalind Franklin, and a group of associates at King's College, London, were trying to solve the mystery of DNA and its unknown master structure by the use of X rays.

No ordinary microscope, not even the powerful electron microscope, can penetrate deep enough to disclose the arrangement of the atoms inside a molecule. X rays, though, with their short wave length, can "resolve" deep and exceedingly small structures. The rays do not produce a picture in the usual sense of the word, but as they are deflected by the material under study, they reveal a repeated or periodic part of a structure. The photographs resemble rings of shadow, darkened here and there by small dense lines. By measuring the lines, the scientist can, with what he calls luck, work out the form of many hidden structures.

The King's College group extracted DNA from various materials and drew it out into long fibers. Judging by DNA's behavior and its ability to produce such a rich assortment of traits and structures in living things, the London scientists anticipated that it would have an extremely complex structure.

The X-ray pictures revealed exactly the opposite.

"The basic molecular configuration has great simplicity," Wilkins reported, his surprise and wonder clearly coming through his words.

The "simple" structure that he found was a helix. DNA in its natural state was a simple twist, a coil.

The X rays could not show the sequence of the "bases," but they could reveal how frequently the "spiral staircase" turned. For every ten phosphate groups it seemed to make a complete turn. The X rays also showed that the chains were almost fully extended. "Hence," said Wilkins, "when the nucleate fibers are stretched, the helix is evidently extended in length like a spiral spring in tension."

Equally surprising to the King's College group was their discovery that all DNA, regardless of whether it came from animal, fish, or plant, had an identical X-ray pattern. Each DNA thread was a spiral staircase. Thus, in outline they all looked the same, and there was no general difference in form to account for the almost limitless differences of the two kingdoms and their countless species and individuals.

But how could a structure appear so regular when it produced such diversity, and when some of its major parts differed, as chemical analysis showed that they did? It was confounding.

Wilkins and Crick of course knew of each other's work. It was nevertheless a welcome moment when each informed the other that he had a helix. A model based on the laws of stereochemistry, and X-ray studies had independently shown the same basic structure for DNA.

The two groups decided upon a joint announcement. In a one-page note in *Nature* of April 25, 1953—it was sandwiched in between an article on wind currents in the sea and Letters to the Editor—Watson and Crick wrote: "We wish to suggest a structure . . . for the salt of DNA." The London group, after briefly presenting its data, pointed out that its findings were "in reasonable agreement with the model described by Watson and Crick."

The X-ray pictures helped quickly to solve one moot point. Although the model had indicated that there were only two chains in the DNA structure, Pauling and Corey had postulated three. A careful study of the X-ray densities went far to confirm the fact that under all normal circumstances there are only two.

The Cambridge research team also was able to work further on the problem that had puzzled Wilkins when he saw the similarity of structure of all DNA and yet knew that the hereditary material had somehow to produce almost boundlessly different effects. That took them to the bases—the steps in the staircase. They were different.

Working with their model, Watson and Crick had found that

they could not put the bases—the treads—into it in any way
that they might choose. A special fit was required.

Each of the steps had to be made up from two pieces—the
bases projecting from both chains. The problem was that some
of the "half-steps" were long and some short. If two "longs"
joined, the step they formed would be far too large to fit the
space between the two chains; if two "shorts" came together,

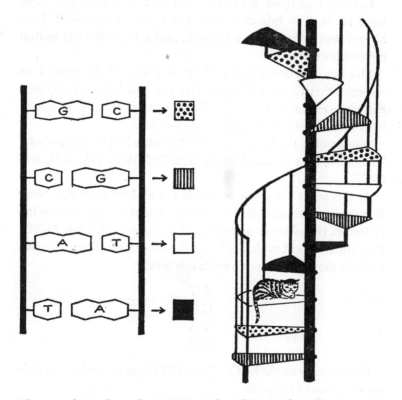

*The four basic "steps" of DNA and of life. A short base on one
chain always joins with a large on the other. The result: four different kinds of steps, all of the same width. Here is literally the
base of life. The varying order of the four in the DNA helix ultimately accounts for all the variety of the living world.* RIGHT: *The
plan visualized in a man-made staircase.*

the step would be too small to fill the gap. But Nature had not produced disjointed structure.

With brilliant insight, Watson and Crick saw what the plan was. A "short" base on either chain always joined with a "long" unit on the other. Joining a long and a short made a step exactly equal in length to all the others, and the resulting staircase was a strong, balanced one—in fact, an excellent helix.

Chemical analysis indicated that this was how the steps were made. The inference here too was that a small T base always was joined with a large A, and a large G base united only with a small C.

The combination of A with T and C with G proved so essential that Crick, with a puckish sense of humor, suggested that some enthusiastic biochemist might wish to name his newly born twin daughters Adenine and Thymine.

The small or the large base might be attached to either chain. Therefore, four kinds of "steps" resulted: A-T, T-A, C-G, and G-C.

At this point the scientists made the all-important discovery that the four steps might follow one another in any order in the staircase. If the bases along one of the side chains ran ACTG, the four would fit with TGAC on the other side chain. The two sections then would match up in this order:

A-T
C-G
T-A
G-C

Or the order might be CGAT, or GATC, or any other possible combination of the four.

It is perhaps easier to visualize the sequence if it is thought of in terms of color. If the four kinds of steps were white, black, blue, and red, the order of the color would not at all affect the structure of the staircase. Imagine a staircase with a long flight of black, red, white, and blue steps.

Could this one point of difference in the DNA molecule—the

varied order of four different kinds of "steps"—account for all
the differences in living things? Such a simple foundation for
the almost infinite variety of life seemed almost inconceivable.
But was it?

In a single long, slender strand of DNA there might be about
ten thousand "steps." In the forty-six chromosomes of the human body the number of "steps" might mount to about one
hundred million. In addition, the one hundred million "steps"
would be subject to alteration by mutation, and that would
make possible still more new combinations. (If this seems
nearly incredible, think of the number of words that can be
made from the twenty-six letters of the alphabet, or the variety
of hands that can be dealt from a deck with only four suits of
cards.)

The simplest calculation indicated that DNA could do it.
The varying arrangement of the four kinds of "steps" in its
spiral staircase could produce all the intricacies of the human
body, the uniqueness of the two billion people of this globe—
no two of whom are alike, with the exception of identical twins
—and the myriad variety of the rest of the living world.

"Such an arrangement," said Crick, referring with classical
underemphasis to the "steps" in his model, "can carry an
enormous amount of information."

The coiling thread of DNA was so small that it could be
photographed only by the most powerful of electron microscopes and at magnifications of five hundred thousand times or
more, but it was sufficient for the task assigned to it: the shaping of life.

A genetic material, however, has a second vital function to
fulfill. In addition to controlling the specific development of the
rest of the cell, it must duplicate itself, or, as the scientists prefer
to say, replicate.

"The exciting thing about a model of this type," said Crick,
"is that it immediately suggests how DNA might produce an
exact copy of itself."

Watson and Crick suggested that as a first step in replication the DNA helix might unwind and the chains separate. The hydrogen bonds that join the two pieces of the "steps" are easily broken.

Suppose then, said Crick, that circulating in the cell were a host of DNA precursor units—the kind of units out of which the thread is built. If an A unit with a sugar and phosphate attached should brush up against a T base on the opened chain, it might attach itself. On the other hand, if a drifting C or G unit touched the A base it would not fit and thus would move on until it came to a base to which it could attach. Gradually a new chain complementary to each of the old chains would be formed, and the new chains would have the same alignments as the original chains. All the bases would be arranged in a distinctive order, the distinctive order of the species. The two new chains would then have only to twist together to form a new DNA spiral staircase.

The proposal of a DNA structure that would at the same time enable DNA to control the formation of the individual and to fulfill the consummate requirements of a genetic material occasioned profound excitement throughout the scientific world. Suddenly a host of facts could be explained or were potentially explainable. Where before had been only impenetrability and confusion, now there was light.

But could this simple, elegant proposal for solving the most basic of life's mysteries be the correct one? The little model in the Cambridge laboratories was only a contraption of wire and metal. It had to be proved. Its proposals had to be subjected to every possible test.

Scientists shot straight for the heart of the matter—the major test of replication. How could the DNA coils wind and unwind? If the long fragile threads were twisted as the X rays and calculations showed, a single DNA spiral molecule might make about two thousand turns. If this unit were part of a larger unit, as there is a possibility that it may be, the turns could increase into the millions.

The problem was a formidable one. Crick suggested that the synthesis of a new chain might begin as soon as the original chains started to unwind. In that way only a short stretch, an end, would be in the single-chain stage at any one time. Only a relatively few units would be added at any one stage. And the formation of the new chain would unwind the old. It was a point to be argued and worked out, for solving the problem of

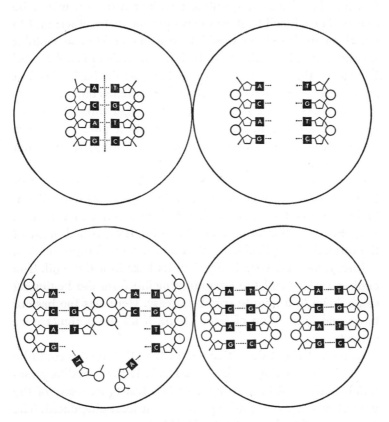

New DNA. *Possible replication mechanism. The two chains of* DNA *pull apart. Each part picks up new complementary parts, and a new chain is formed.*

structure did not at the same time solve the whole biological problem.

Wilkins later proposed that the unwinding might not be difficult if the hydrogen bonds holding the steps together broke and re-formed in a "process like melting and solidifying."

And would the exact precursor units needed for the assemblage of a new chain always be on hand when they were needed? Some scientists thought not. One with a stinging wit mocked the idea at a scientific meeting: a demon would be needed in each cell to steer the proper pieces together; and to get them to the chain would take a higher kind of cellular intelligence quite unlikely "to be found outside of Cambridge." His attack, though, was directed not against the basic idea, but against an explanation of how it might be carried out.

Differences would persist, for no one had directly seen or measured a DNA helix. The Crick-Watson model therefore was still regarded as a model, a proposal, a suggestion, rather than a proved structure.

On the other hand, the evidence that DNA is made up of two complementary chains and varied bases was overwhelmingly supported by X-ray, chemical, and physical evidence. With the exception of certain difficulties, it explained many of the formerly inexplicable mysteries of form and reproduction.

Life, it seemed very likely, had its base in a tiny coil. The endless variety and the continuity of life from the beginning came down to a minute spiral staircase. Here was the base of bases and foundation of foundations, if all the portents were correct.

One great if not definitive test of the DNA theory could be made. This was the synthesis of DNA. If the hereditary material itself could be put together in a test tube, many of the gravest problems might be solved, or at least elucidated. The search turned to the synthesis of DNA.

XV

OCHOA AND KORNBERG:
THE SYNTHESIS OF DNA AND RNA

THE RACE WAS ON and the goal within sight.

The determinative stuff of life had been traced from the organs to the tissues, to the cells, to the nucleus, to the chromosomes, to DNA and RNA. The chemistry of both had been solved and their probable structure worked out. This brought the next great goal nearer: the synthesis of these master materials of life.

Only when DNA and RNA could be broken down into their constituent parts and put together again would science know with reasonable certainty that it had the ultimate building blocks—the units used by Nature for the construction of the whole living world. And only then could science approach the problem of the organization of life, and the failure of organization—cancer, aging, and other medical problems—without guesswork about the basis upon which they rest.

In one sense, however, these were largely unspoken goals.

Severo Ochoa and his aides, Marianne Grunberg-Manago and Priscilla Ortiz, were working on another part of the problem of DNA and RNA.

Ochoa, the head of the department of biochemistry of New York University, was studying the mechanics of phosphate incorporation into ATP (adenosine triphosphate), the important compound that supplies energy for most of the functions of the cell.

As long ago as 1888, Miescher had written to a friend: "I cannot help regarding the chemical dynamics of phosphoric acid toward water, bases, and proteins as one of the most promising keyholes through which it should be possible to peep into the interior."

Nothing had since altered the wisdom of the observation. Ochoa's approach, however, was a different one and strictly of

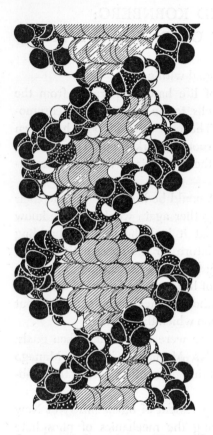

A molecular model of DNA.

the twentieth century. He used that unique product of the post-war era, a radioactive labeled material—in this case, radioactive phosphate—for peeping into what Miescher had referred to as "the interior." By its emissions, the radioactive phosphate could be traced into any "interior" it might enter.

The New York group prepared extracts of Azotobacter vinelandii, a nitrogen-fixing bacterium of the soil. When they incubated the extract with the radioactive phosphate and ATP, the labeled phosphate was rapidly incorporated into the ATP.

But the ATP used in the experiment also contained a bit of another material, ADP—(a)denosine (d)i(p)hosphate. The latter consisted of adenine, the A base of RNA and DNA; a sugar molecule; and the phosphate. As a group, it was called a nucleotide. Experiment revealed that it was the incidental ADP, and not the ATP, which incorporated the labeled material. With this lead, the research group found that the three other nucleotides of RNA—G, U, and C—also could incorporate labeled phosphate. Thus, the four "steps" of RNA could be marked almost as clearly as though they were made luminescent.

Continued studies showed that another exciting development occurred simultaneously. With an enzyme serving as what the layman might call an arranger, the four little pieces of RNA were assembled into new, large, thread-like molecules. The little threads were made up of the same kind of units as RNA, and their presence in the test tube meant that for the first time in the history of biochemistry a "polynucleotide"—a chain of nucleotides—had been achieved outside the living cell. Again, an investigation directed to one goal—the study of ATP—had led to quite another.

Ochoa was born in Luarca, Spain, in 1905 and took his medical degree from the University of Madrid. He graduated with honors and joined the faculty. But these were not times in which a man could quietly devote his life to medicine and research. Spain soon was torn by civil war, and Ochoa fled to Germany. He later went on to Great Britain and in 1941 came to the United States as an instructor and research assistant at Washington University in St. Louis. In 1942 he moved to New York University, where in 1954 he was named chairman of the department of biochemistry.

The tiny polynucleotide threads held forth a large promise.

Perhaps it would be possible to synthesize RNA. But if this beckoning goal were to be achieved, it was clear that the enzyme which figured in the ordering of the units would have to be obtained in as pure a form as possible.

Ochoa and his staff began to grow Azotobacter on a large scale. The bacteria had to be cultured for fifteen hours and the tiny enzyme fraction separated from the relatively great mass of the organism. The Azotobacter cells were centrifuged, ground in a mortar, extracted, re-extracted, centrifuged further, and treated in many other painstaking steps to isolate the enzyme. Through this intricate processing, Ochoa succeeded in obtaining the enzyme in a relatively pure state.

The scientists were ready then for another crucial experiment. The purified enzyme was incubated with ADP. This time a chain was formed which was made up entirely of adenine-containing nucleotides. Using the analogy of color again, the new structure could be compared to a spiral staircase with steps all of one color—say, blue.

Nothing similar existed in Nature, and the remarkable new chain was quickly named—or perhaps it might be said, nick-named—Poly A. Its uniqueness was far from a disappointment, for it showed that the researchers were on the right track. In addition, the new coil would be useful for research.

Ochoa and his associates similarly mixed the purified enzyme with diphosphates containing C and U. These also proved to be building blocks, and Poly C and Poly U came into existence. The laboratory did not succeed as readily in preparing a satisfactory Poly G.

The chains that the New York scientists had produced could be stretched into long fibers, much as natural RNA can be. When this was done and X-ray-diffraction studies were made by Alexander Rich of the National Institutes of Health in Washington, it was found that the synthetic fibers produced patterns very similar to those of RNA.

Another experiment had also become possible. The New

York University group mixed some of the new Poly A and Poly U fibers in an aqueous solution. While they watched, the solution thickened; there was a rapid and notable increase in viscosity.

What had happened? X-ray-diffraction tests revealed that Poly A and Poly U had wrapped around each other and formed a double-stranded spiral. The A and U bases had indeed come together, as Watson and Crick had postulated. And their X-ray pattern was nearly indistinguishable from that of RNA.

A further experiment of extreme importance still lay ahead. It would determine whether scientific history had been made and another frontier passed.

Ochoa prepared a solution of all the four diphosphates of A, G, U, and C. The Azotobacter enzyme was added, and history truly was made. The four units were assembled into the matched chains and helix of a natural RNA.

Nothing like the material in Ochoa's test tube had ever before been produced except in the living cell. It was another of those rare moments in which science succeeds in duplicating a process and result that has been Nature's exclusively since the beginning of life. Not since Wohler had made urea from simple chemicals and Buchner had prepared a yeast extract that could ferment sugar in the absence of the living cell—not since those stirring days had there been anything comparable.

Ochoa and the New York workers sensed what they had, but all possible tests had to be applied, and were. The results were striking. In X-ray diffraction the pattern of the new AGUC was identical with that of natural RNA. Its molecular weight was in the same range. Other tests were passed with the same exactitude.

Though Poly AGUC undoubtedly was a nucleic acid, it might not specifically duplicate any existing RNA, any more than nylon does silk. The order of the RNA bases varies from species to species. An English scientist, R. M. S. Smellie, who was working in Ochoa's laboratory, found nevertheless that when

Poly AGUC was prepared from equal amounts of the four diphosphate precursor units, it had the same base composition as natural RNA isolated from Azotobacter. It looked as though a duplicate of natural Azotobacter RNA might have been made.

"The present information on size, structure, X-ray diffraction, and behavior toward different enzymes indicates," said Ochoa, "that synthetic RNA is closely related to RNA. Indeed, AGUC appears to be indistinguishable from RNA."

But could synthetic RNA fulfill the ultimate requirement of a true genetic material? Could it reproduce itself and hand its distinctive pattern on to its progeny? In one sense this was asking if it could take on the qualities of life. The scientists preferred to put the question in other terms: could synthetic RNA show biological activity? Could it impose its pattern on a virus in the manner of natural RNA? It is a question still unanswered.

While the Ochoa laboratory was working toward the synthesizing of RNA, another search that would have appeared even more incredible only a few years earlier was under way in the Middle West. This was a search for the secret of DNA, that base of bases and first of firsts.

The story had begun a few years before. In 1946 a young Brooklyn-born scientist, Dr. Arthur Kornberg, joined the Ochoa laboratory for a year of graduate work. Kornberg had been graduated from the City College of New York in 1937 at the exceptional age of nineteen. For the research he wanted to do, he needed a degree in medicine, so he had entered the University of Rochester. Soon after taking his degree, he joined the United States Public Health Service and did research at its National Institutes of Health at Bethesda, Maryland.

As he probed into the intricacies of the cell, Kornberg wearied of the frustrations. "I got tired of feeding things into one end of an animal experiment and watching something come out the other, without understanding what goes on in the middle," he explained.

The outstanding man working with the things which "went on in the middle"—primarily with the enzymes in general charge there—was Ochoa at New York University. In 1946–7 Kornberg went to study with him for a year. "Kornberg possessed an extremely brilliant and rapid mind," Ochoa later recalled. "I can say that he was my best student."

Kornberg went to Washington University in St. Louis as a professor of microbiology at the School of Medicine. By that time his interest in enzymes had deepened. While Ochoa worked with the enzymes that might play a part in the fashioning of RNA, Kornberg studied the enzymes that might put together the separate building blocks or units of DNA.

A logical point of beginning was the enzymes that assembled the simplest units in the DNA molecule. If they could be found, the way would be opened to the next step in the formation of DNA and then the next. Kornberg had no expectation that the pathway to DNA would be a simple one. He had long since found, he once explained, that "simplicity is not necessarily a virtue" in working with life processes.

Kornberg began searching in Escherichia coli, a common bacterium of the intestinal tract which reproduces itself every twenty minutes. He was looking for an enzyme that would enter into the production of DNA. To obtain a workable amount of the enzyme, Kornberg started with a few grams, but before long was working up hundred-pound quantities. At first he broke the bacteria down by bombarding them with high-frequency sound.[1] In this way he obtained an extract that was cell-free. By the most exacting kind of chemical work he then succeeded in purifying the enzyme extract some thirty-fold. It still was not pure, but it was approaching a usable stage.

At about this time, a hint that it might be worth while to try the enzyme on thymidine developed from the work of a colleague at the Washington University School of Medicine,

---

[1] High-frequency sound waves can break down many physical and biological objects and are frequently used in research.

Dr. Morris Friedkin. In 1954 Friedkin found that if thymidine—the T base and sugar on the DNA spiral staircase—was
labeled with radioactive carbon 14 and mixed in a test tube
with chick-embryo tissue, the labeled thymidine was picked up
and incorporated in the tissue's DNA. Here was direct evidence
of thymidine's entrance into DNA.

Kornberg lost no time in acting upon the lead. He incubated
some radioactive thymidine, which Friedkin supplied, with the
enzyme fractions he had extracted from E. coli. It was a significant experiment, and it worked. The thymidine was incorporated into a DNA fraction, and a substance was produced
which had some of the properties of DNA.

Almost at that moment Ochoa announced the synthesis of
RNA with an Azotobacter enzyme. If there had been any doubt
about the promise of the course Kornberg was following—
the use of enzymes—it was promptly ended. Events now
moved even more swiftly.

In a "preliminary note" in *Biochimica and Biophysica Acta*
in 1956 Kornberg reported "the conversion of C-14 thymidine
via a sequence of enzyme steps to a product with the properties of DNA." He added: "We have now extended these studies
to include adenine, guanine, and cytosine, and with partially
purified enzymes from E. coli we have further studied the
nature of the polymerization reaction."

The whole scientific world knew that Kornberg was drawing
close to the great goal, the synthesis of DNA. News from St.
Louis was awaited with the keenest of anticipation.

The St. Louis research team bent with renewed effort to the
still formidable task ahead. It was clear that the enzyme from
E. coli would have to be further purified. With the hardest of
work they succeeded in purifying it a thousandfold as compared to the original cell-free extracts.

Originally the enzyme had been extracted as a nucleo-pro-
tein. To purify the enzyme still further, it was necessary to
strip away the DNA. When this was done, the blueprint was

removed. There was nothing left to give form to a new DNA, for the protein could not supply the directions that could come only from the DNA. Obviously when the time arrived to try the synthesis experiment, some DNA would have to be added.

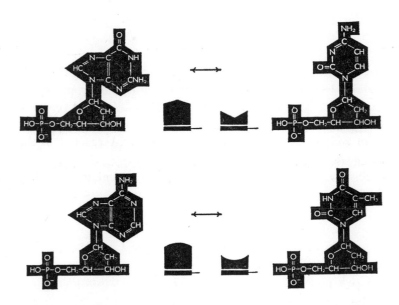

The four building blocks of DNA. TOP: G (deoxyguanylic acid) *and* C (deoxycytidylic acid). G *and* C *always go together.* BELOW: A (deoxyadenylic acid) *and* T (deoxythymidylic acid) *form another pair.*

The work on purification also suggested that all four nucleotides, A, C, T, and G, would have to be present if DNA were to be produced.

At last all was ready. The four units, a bit of DNA, and the purified enzyme were mixed together. It was a fateful moment. In the test tube there formed a product that appeared to be DNA.

It was DNA! The potent material that shapes our destiny had been synthesized. An impossibility, or what would have seemed an impossibility only a few years earlier, had been achieved.

The tests underwrote the nearly incredible indications. The synthetic DNA contained the four nucleotides—the four steps in the DNA staircase—in typical linkage. It exceeded the DNA added by twenty times.

When carbon-14 was incorporated and the synthetic DNA was broken down by the enzymes that attack DNA, the units obtained "were shown by a variety of chemical and enzymatical analyses to be identical with those obtained from native DNA."

In sedimentation tests, too, the new DNA reacted in the same way as the natural product.

Discoveries scarcely dreamed of were coming at such a rapid rate that a gathering of scientists was needed. The new developments had to be considered and discussed. Johns Hopkins University, with support from the Atomic Energy Commission, called a "Symposium on the Chemical Basis of Heredity" at Johns Hopkins in 1956.

Crick presented his model, and Ochoa and Kornberg their work.

"The discovery of the polynucleotide phosphorylase [the RNA enzyme] has raised more questions than it has answered," said Ochoa. "While there is little doubt that the enzyme can bring about the synthesis of polynucleic acids like RNA, and may even be responsible for the synthesis of RNA in the cell, a number of other questions have been only partially answered, or have as yet not been answered at all."

In plant viruses, RNA is the carrier of genetic information. It plays the role that DNA takes in the viruses that attack bacteria and in plant and animal cells. Thus, there had to be different kinds of RNA—somehow the RNA had to differ in order to produce different viruses. "Now that we know in a general way how RNA is made, we may ask how a specific RNA is made," said Ochoa.

The discussion of the problems still to be settled only emphasized the distance the scientists had come.

This was also the case when Kornberg spoke. DNA had been synthesized, he told his fellow scientists, and he summarized for them his latest findings. Each week brought more certainty. But, Kornberg went on, "we must learn more. . . . The overriding question remains. How is biologically specific DNA formed?"

The material in the test tubes was deoxyribonucleic acid. It was not the specific DNA that would produce a John Jones or a rabbit or a stalk of asparagus. Whether the synthetic DNA could produce an image of itself, replicate itself, and create more DNA in its own pattern was not known. But even that fundamental problem could now be approached. "The enzymatic synthesis of a bacterial transforming factor, once regarded beyond experimental reach, has now become an immediate objective," said Kornberg.

Bentley Glass of Johns Hopkins, a co-chairman of the conference, was in complete agreement: "With this achievement there now lies before us the dazzling prospect of synthesizing such units of heredity as a bacterial transforming factor, or a 'gene,' or TMV [tobacco-mosaic virus]. But to do this we must first learn a way to control the sequence of nucleotides in a polynucleotide chain. That will be the next great step in the artificial synthesis of genetic material."

The world's leading authorities on the cell were present, many of them presenting papers on other phases of the rapidly growing exploration. All were aware that doors which had always been closed had now been opened. The future might well yield almost any results in a science that could synthesize RNA and DNA, the most complex and difficult of all molecules.

In summarizing the work of the conference, Glass cast aside

the usual scientific reserve. "The reports of Ochoa on the successful synthesis of RNA and of Kornberg on that of DNA aroused the highest enthusiasm among the participants in the symposium," he said.

"Clearly these advances bring within reach not only the artificial synthesis of hereditary material, but open up breathtaking vistas down which one may glimpse the controlled syn-

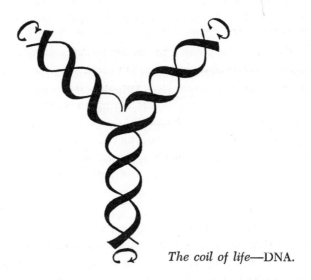

The coil of life—DNA.

thesis of proteins and a full understanding of the mechanisms of genetic and enzymatic control over metabolism and growth.

"A major 'break-through' has undoubtedly been achieved, perhaps the greatest in biochemistry since Eduard Buchner established the nature of enzymes."

The next few years brought additional recognition of these achievements. In 1959 the Karolinska Institute, which acts for the Nobel Prize committee in the field of physiology and medicine, recommended that the 1959 prize be given jointly to Ochoa and Kornberg. The two American biochemists, the New York professor and his onetime student, were given the highest honor the scientific world affords for their "discoveries of the mechanisms in the biological synthesis of ribonucleic acid and deoxyribonucleic acid."

The institute expressed its particular pleasure that it was honoring "two of the best biochemists of the present time in their most active age." Ochoa was fifty-four and Kornberg forty-one.

The institute added: "The two scientists did not solve the question: What is the origin of life? But they clarified many of the problems of regeneration and continuity of life."

As the first announcement of the prizes came over the wire, the phone began ringing in Ochoa's laboratory. Soon the room was filled with reporters and microphones, and someone brought in champagne, which was served in paper cups from the water cooler.

How did Ochoa feel about the honor? He answered gravely: "I think it is a very great honor. I do not believe that a scientist seeks or needs compensation—he gets compensation from his work—but if there be other compensation this would be it."

Earlier in the year Kornberg had gone to Stanford University to head the department of biochemistry. On a trip east to speak at the National Institutes of Health, he had stopped for a visit with Ochoa. The two are warm friends. Neither then knew that within a few days they would be sharing $42,409, the amount of the 1959 Nobel Prize for medicine and physiology. As soon as Ochoa received the first informal notice about the prize, he phoned Kornberg in California. The two decided that much of the pleasure would come in sharing the same award.

Because of the time differential, the formal notification of the award reached California early in the morning. A reporter phoned Kornberg at five a.m. But Kornberg had already been awakened by the family's elkhound puppy. A memorable day began early.

Since the time of Lavoisier science had always had to look deeper and ever deeper for the cause of all the manifestations of the living world. Each success had only opened new questions: what lay beneath, what produced the newly found surface? The effective cause always was still beyond reach. With the synthesis of DNA and RNA, science had reached the source, the foundation of it all. It is true that the nuclear materials are composed of atoms, but in Nature the atoms are used in groups, and the groups, the units that determine what all the rest is to be, are the nucleic acids, DNA and RNA. They are therefore the base of bases.

From this point on, the great problem would no longer be to trace all that men are back to the physical and chemical beginnings. That now had been done. The direction could change. Science could work upward. It could make a new approach to the innumerable unsolved problems of how bits of DNA and RNA evolve into the complexities of men, plants, and microorganisms.

XVI

DNA'S INGENIOUS MECHANISMS

BY PUTTING TOGETHER a few bits and pieces from the living cell, science had succeeded in closely imitating Nature's own way of making the key stuff of life, DNA and RNA.

For the first time the bits and pieces had been identified. Never before had anyone been able to say: this *is* the hereditary material, this *is* the stuff of which it is made, this probably is the way in which it is put together. It was one of the greatest achievements of science.

But how did the hereditary materials contrive their effects? How did the DNA fit into and control the chromosomes? How did DNA and RNA pass along their distinctive patterns? Though DNA and RNA had been made in the test tube, the test-tube products did not make new copies of themselves; that ultimate step had not been accomplished. All of these problems were related; they were a part of the formidable and nearly unexplored task of translating chemical and physical findings into the actual living structures that man can see with a microscope and, in the end, with the unaided eye.

Since the rediscovery of Mendel's work in 1900 it had been clear that the chromosomes were the structures that controlled heredity. They carried on and reshuffled the materials that accounted for all likenesses and differences.

But if the Crick-Watson model for DNA was correct, how did the DNA fit into the chromosomes and control them? As usual, there was no easy way to seek the answer to this difficult question. Science could try to work up from DNA to the chromosomes, and from the chromosomes down to DNA. Perhaps between the two approaches an understanding could be reached.

The microscopes showed indisputably that just before the cell divides, the two thick strands that make up the chromosomes pull apart. One goes to each daughter cell. And then for a while they strangely disappear. The thick threads that stood out in the old cell as clearly as furniture in a house cannot be found in the new, even with the most powerful of microscopes. It is one of the most successful and mystifying of vanishing acts.

When the chromosomes again become visible, shortly before the cell is to divide again, each strand—called a chromatid—is linked with a new partner. Somehow it has made a replica of itself, and once again there are two strands to go to new daughter cells.

Science long had puzzled about what happened during the period of invisibility. There seemed to be two possibilities. Perhaps the strand that had come from the parent cell acted as template or mold for assembling another chromatid just like itself. Or perhaps it broke down into small pieces that then assembled into new chains.

If the process of heredity was to be understood and related to the replication of DNA, science would have to try to find out what occurred during the blackout. By the 1950's there was a new prospect for success in such an undertaking. New radioactive materials were available which could be used to label the chromosomes. A labeled chromosome could be followed by its radioactive emissions, even though its structure was entirely invisible to the human or microscopic eye.

Friedkin and Kornberg had demonstrated that when thymidine, one of the four bases or "steps" in the DNA spiral staircase, is mixed into a medium in which cells are growing, it is "taken up" by the chromosomes and their DNA. None of it is used in any other part of the cell. Thus, it seemed likely that if thymidine were labeled with a radioactive tracer, it

Robley C. Williams places a specimen in an electron microscope at the Virus Laboratory of the University of California.

PLATE IX

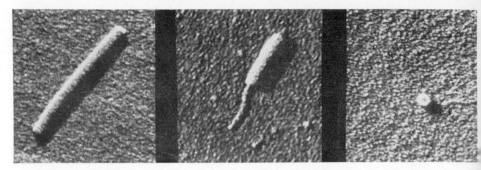

Unusual serial photos in a magnification of 150,000 times. LEFT: *The intact tobacco-mosaic virus rod.* CENTER: *The virus with its protein tubing partly removed and its nucleic-acid core protruding from both ends.* RIGHT: *A short cross-section of the protein tube, showing a central hole.*

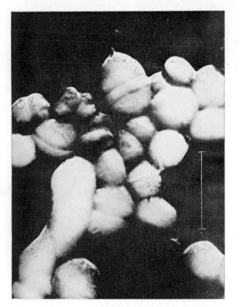
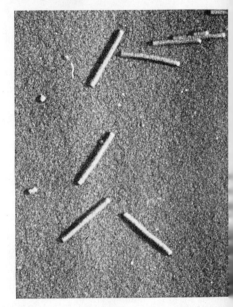

The electron microscope, with magnifications up to 200,000 times natural size, brought virus particles well within visual range. Yet virologists could see precious little until Robley C. Williams metal-plated infinitely small objects. LEFT: *The grotesque shapes of chromium-shadowed* Staphylococcus aureus, *the bacterium causing boils.* RIGHT: *Uranium-plated tobacco-mosaic virus, previously a vague bit of straw under the electron microscope.*

PLATE X

A giant, walk-in model of the human cell, twenty-four feet in diameter and twelve feet high, prepared by the Upjohn Company, on exhibit in the Chicago Museum of Science and Industry. Its designer, Will Burtin, stands inside.

PLATE XI

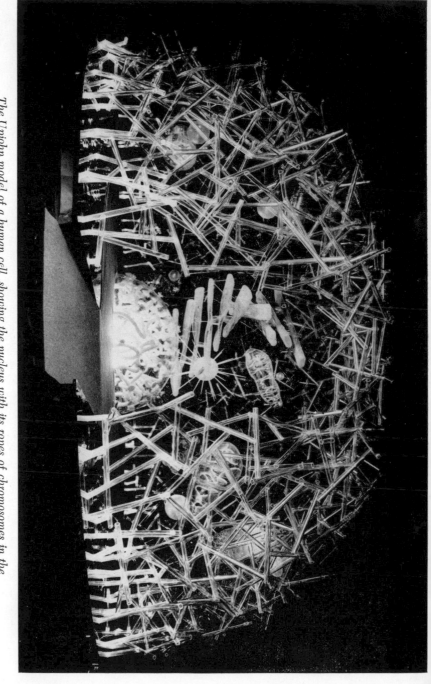

The Upjohn model of a human cell, showing the nucleus with its ropes of chromosomes in the center. The flattened white sacs rising from the nucleus probably carry chemicals from one part to another. The spiked sphere touching them is the centrosome, crucial in cell division. Above the centrosome and also to its right are blimp-shaped mitochondria which turn food into energy.

PLATE XII

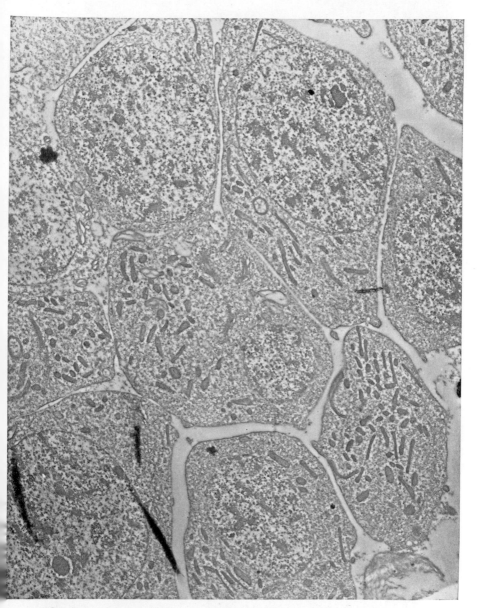

The dark elongated bodies of the mitochondria, the power plants of the cell, can be seen in this cell photograph. Here the chromatin has not come together in the chromosomes, visible as thick, speckled areas.

PLATE XIII

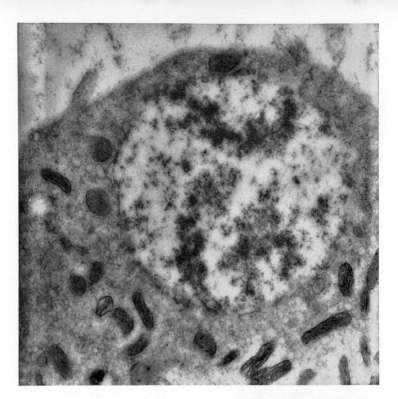

Power plants of the cell—mitochondria—cluster around a cell nucleus.
Below: A cluster of mitochondria. The
dark granules scattered about them
are probably RNA. Magnification
about 17,000 diameters.

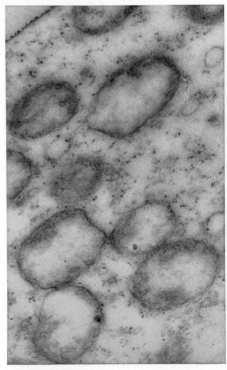

PLATE XIV

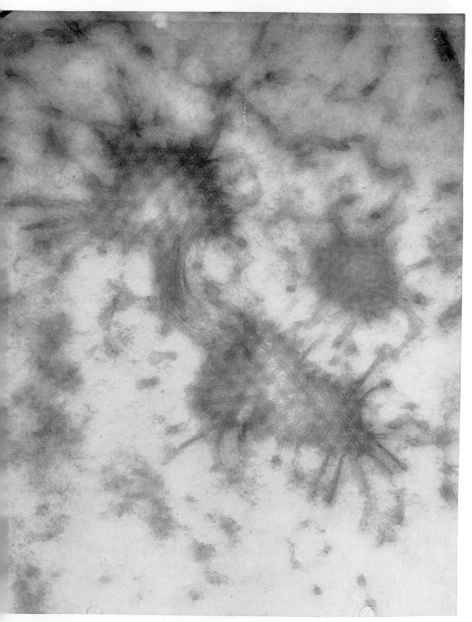

Network in the cell. The beautifully meshed structure is part of the endo-plasmic reticulum. The material, from a sperm cell of the grasshopper, is magnified 42,200 times.

PLATE XV

ABOVE: *Striated muscle. Overlapping of fibers creates bold, striped effect. Each diagonal ribbon is a thin section of a muscle fiber.* CENTER: *Extremely thin section of muscle. Half close the eyes to see full effect.* BELOW: *Cross-bridges connect thick and thin muscle filaments, enlarged 325,000 diameters. Note two thin filaments between each thick pair, and the bridges which probably move them back and forth in a sliding movement.*

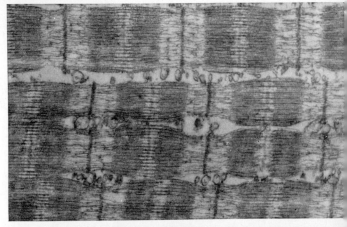

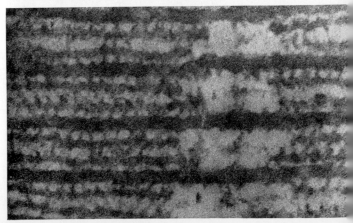

PLATE XVI

could be followed into the chromosome and, as a part of the chromosome, through all of the chromosomal peregrinations.

J. Herbert Taylor, professor of cell biology at Columbia University, with Walter L. Hughes and Philip S. Woods of the Brookhaven National Laboratory, labeled some thymidine with radioactive hydrogen (called tritium). They then mixed some of the labeled material into the medium in which they were growing bean roots. Eight hours later they also treated the roots with a drug that prevents the cells from dividing further, although it permits the chromosomes to go on multiplying.

When the labeled thymidine had been absorbed, Taylor squashed a few of the bean cells on a piece of glass and covered them with a sheet of photographic film. The rays emitted by the radioactive thymidine would darken the film and thus reveal where the thymidine was concentrated.

In the new cells, no chromosomes could be seen with the microscope. But as Taylor bent over the film, he saw the area above the round nucleus become specked with little black dots. It was almost as though it were peppered with the spots. The thymidine therefore was distributed all through the nucleus. Perhaps the original chromatid had broken down into pieces, although this was not certain.

But the verdict was not in. Taylor squashed some other bean cells when the process of cell growth had gone a little further. By this time the chromosomes were visible; they had taken form. Their characteristic form was outlined in black dots on the film.

At this stage, before the chromosomes could undergo their next division, Taylor removed the bean roots from the labeled medium and put them in a non-radioactive solution. Thus, the cells drew the material for the formation of new chains from unlabeled material.

When each chromosome had assembled a new partner, Taylor again squashed some of the cells and covered them with

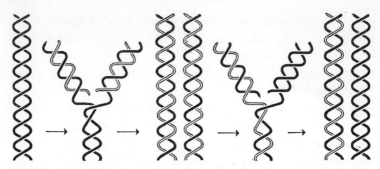

DNA *molecules. Each consists of two chains. To duplicate, they unwind and assemble a new partner. If the new chain is drawn from radioactive material, one of the chains in the new helix will be labeled (shown in outline). If, at the next division, the new chain comes from non-labeled material, only one of the descendant helixes will contain a labeled chain.*

film. This time one half of each chromosome produced a speckled image on the film; the other half was unmarked, except where segments had twisted together and crossed over. One half was old, one half was new.

"What might this mean?" asked Taylor. "The simplest and most likely answer was that a chromatid itself consists of two parts, each of which remains intact and acts as a template."

Clearly, the radioactive speckled chromatid had been passed along intact from parent to daughter cell, as it might have been if the chromatid were a DNA double helix whose two chains had untwisted and assembled new chains from the materials in the cell.

"Our picture of the chromatid as a two-part structure fits very well with what we know about the DNA molecule and with the Crick-Watson theory," said Taylor. "DNA too is a double structure, consisting of two complementary helical chains wound around each other. And some of our recent experiments indicate that the two strands of a chromatid are complementary structures."

Was it possible that a chromatid was simply a chain of

DNA? It was a tempting idea, Taylor acknowledged. A little calculation, however, showed that the solution could not be that easy.

If all the DNA in a chromatid formed a single chain, the chain would be more than a yard long and would have to make more than three hundred million turns. That it could untwist, as it would have to do for the assembling of a new chain, appeared an impossibility. In addition, Taylor knew, a chromatid has the wrong proportions for a single DNA chain. Just before division a chromosome is about one hundred times thicker than a linear DNA chain would be and only one ten-thousandth as long. In other words, the chromatids were much too short and too thick to be single chains of DNA.

High-power microscopes suggested an explanation. They disclosed that the chromatid is truly a strand wound into a helix, but that it is so tightly wound that it twists into a series of secondary kinks, "like a coiled telephone cord." The kinks were easily visible.

Nevertheless, the problem of how DNA makes itself into a chromatid and a chromosome still was not answered. Taylor decided to try to devise a model.

It was, of course, an established fact that the chromosomes contain protein. Taylor therefore postulated a long protein backbone from which DNA coils would branch off like ribs. The model suggested a centipede with its legs branching off from the long, narrow body, and it soon became known as the centipede model. Taylor visualized the backbone as a two-layered one whose layers could pull apart. In such a structure the DNA coils would be attached to one layer only. If this was the case and the layers separated, the DNA spirals could unwind for the assembling of new chains. Each would then be in a position to assemble a new chain, and a new chromatid could be built duplicating the old.

There was, however, one major difficulty with the early Taylor model. The genetic material is arranged in linear order, as the maps of the geneticists have repeatedly demonstrated. If the DNA spirals waved loosely about, attached to the backbone only on one side, the linear order would be at least partly disarranged.

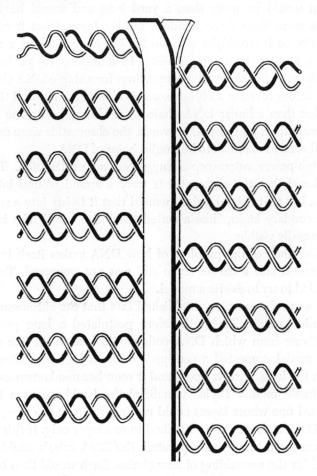

"Centipede" model of a chromatid, one of the halves of a chromosome. One chain of each DNA molecule is anchored to the front layer of the protein "backbone," and one to the back. If the backbone pulled apart, the DNA molecules would unwind. Each could then build a new partner.

At this point Ernst Freese of Harvard University suggested that there might be two spines instead of one and that the DNA chains might stretch between them, like the rungs of a ladder. Then the DNA would be held in its proper order.

If the two spines came together, a long tube would be

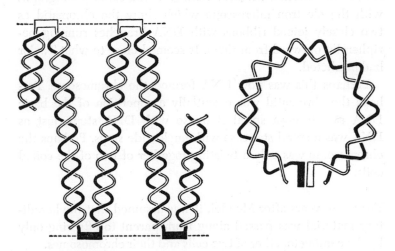

Another suggested model of a chromatid. One end of the DNA chain is attached to one column, and the other to the opposite. If the two backbones curled together, a tube would be formed. It would resemble the thick chromosomes shown in photographs.

formed, and the tube, like the phone cord, might curl up into a tight helix. It might closely resemble the thick chromosomes seen in innumerable cell photographs.

The arrangement can be shown by a little demonstration. Imagine that your fingers are the proposed DNA coils and your palms the protein backbones. Hold the hands thumbs up and parallel, and bring the fingertips together. You at once have a ladder (similar to the DNA's own structure). Then bring the bases of the palms together. You have a nicely formed tube.

If such a model was stretched, the two halves would pull apart. Each would be in a position to collect new units complementary to itself and form a new chain.

After Taylor made his proposal, Montrose J. Moses of the Rockefeller Institute for Medical Research and Don W. Fawcett of the Cornell Medical College made some photographs with the electron microscope which show the chromatid as two closely joined ribbons with DNA branches running peripherally outward from them. It seemed close to what Taylor had predicted.

Perhaps this was how DNA formed the chromosome. Perhaps the chromatid was essentially a repetition of the basic DNA structure—a spiral staircase with DNA steps, just as DNA was a spiral staircase with nucleotide steps. Perhaps the chromosome was only a twisting together of two of the coiled coils.

For many years after Mendel, it was assumed that the hereditary material was passed along from parent to offspring only by the coming together of two cells and their chromosomes.

The strange behavior of the pneumococci in Griffith's work awakened the scientific world to the possible existence of other means of transmitting heredity. If a Type III bacterium could somehow transfer its hereditary material—DNA—to a Type I bacterium and transform it into a Type III, undoubtedly heredity worked in ways that had not previously been suspected.

The work with the viruses that attack bacteria had revealed another of the hidden processes of transmission. The tiny T2 bacteriophage shot its DNA into the bacterium it attacked, and used the substance of the bacterium to produce two hundred replicas of itself.

And then it was learned that in certain cases RNA can play the same role as DNA in transmitting the master pattern of life.

The trail that led to RNA had its beginning in 1935 when Wendell Stanley, in one of the classic experiments of science, discovered that the tobacco-mosaic virus could be crystallized. The little virus that could multiply and spread like wildfire on the leaves of a tobacco plant could be crystallized, just as an inanimate substance could be. The experiment raised the whole question of where life begins, but it also led to new understandings of heredity and its transmission.

Stanley thought at first that the little crystal that could so dramatically come alive on tobacco leaves was entirely a protein. It was two years later that the English chemists Frederick C. Bawden and Norman W. Pirie found that the crystal contained six per cent of RNA. It was only ninety-four per cent protein.

Stanley went on to become the head of the virus-research laboratory at the University of California at Berkeley. In 1952 he invited Heinz Fraenkel-Conrat, a German-born scientist then working for the Department of Agriculture in California, to join the staff. Fraenkel-Conrat was engaged in basic protein research as part of the department's effort to find new uses for agricultural surpluses.

At the University of California virus laboratory, situated in the hills overlooking the campus and the city of San Francisco, Fraenkel-Conrat undertook work on the tobacco-mosaic virus, commonly known as TMV. In 1955 he decided to try a gentler way of separating the virus protein from its RNA (the virus had no DNA). He wanted later to try to put the two parts together again in such a way that the reconstructed virus would "have some life in it."

The scientist treated one group of TMV rods with a household detergent. That removed their protein coats very effectively. He subjected another group of rods to a treatment designed to remove the twisted cables of RNA from their cores. It was delicate, elaborate work requiring all the finesse of a highly skilled biochemist.

Robley Williams, the electron-microscope expert of the laboratory staff, looked at both materials with his powerful instrument. In one test tube Fraenkel-Conrat had some thin, naked strands of RNA. In the other were invisibly small protein molecules that tended to form hollow cylinders. Fraenkel-Conrat planned to test both on the tobacco plants that were grown on the roof of the laboratory.

The scientist brushed some of the hollow cylinders onto healthy leaves. On other leaves he put bits of the naked RNA strands.

He knew that a good lively TMV virus could in forty-eight to seventy-two hours cover the leaves with darkish-green spots. But when Fraenkel-Conrat went up to the roof to check, the leaves were as smooth and green as ever; no splotches were to be seen. The leaves had been unaffected by either solution. It looked as though the two were impotent.

Nothing had come of the experiment, but Fraenkel-Conrat had prepared extra supplies of both materials. Although he had few expectations of any unusual results, he mixed the two together. In a few minutes one of his associates noticed an opalescent sheen on the solution. Such a sheen appears when particles are forming.

Fraenkel-Conrat and Williams examined the mixed material under the electron microscope. This time they saw perfectly formed TMV rods. The naked strands were inside the protein cylinders, although the cylinders were not their own. The RNA helixes, in effect, had moved into houses newly built from isolated materials.

The scientist again went up to the roof garden and applied some of the reconstituted rods to new, healthy tobacco leaves. This was on a Friday. Fraenkel-Conrat is generally in the laboratory during part of Saturday and Sunday, but on Monday when he made his check of the garden to see what had happened, the tobacco leaves were covered with splotches. The spots were not quite so numerous as those produced by natural

TMV, but there was no question about the liveliness of the infection created by the artificially made rods.

A living thing had been taken apart and put together, and yet it was alive and growing.

Fraenkel Conrat and the laboratory did not immediately report the amazing thing which had happened. Much more work had to be done. It was, the scientist explained, a matter of 'repeat, repeat, controls, repeat, controls. . . ." When the finding was thoroughly verified and the report appeared several months later in the *Proceedings of the National Academy of Science*, the headlines burst forth. "Life Created in the Test Tube," some proclaimed. "Man-Made Virus," others read.

Fraenkel-Conrat and the California laboratory shuddered. The headlines went beyond what had happened. The scientist was even more distressed when further work revealed that the RNA alone could produce the dark infectious spots on the tobacco leaves. Great amounts of the RNA were required to produce the disease, but it was unmistakable. Seemingly, the delicate, extremely fine strands of RNA—to call them hair-like would be a gross exaggeration—had been damaged when Fraenkel-Conrat tried them alone in his first test of the separated materials. When greater care was used in separating the fragile RNA core and greater amounts were applied to the tobacco leaves, it took hold and multiplied.

"Our conclusion," Fraenkel-Conrat told a scientific meeting, "is that infectivity is a property of nucleic acid per se."

Having emphatically made his point, the scientist added: "We can now gracefully retreat from a position we never held or expressed. Life was not here created in a test tube, since the nucleic acid alone shows 'signs of life' similar to those of the original virus."

In its true proportions, the finding was of sufficient importance. A simultaneous finding in Germany helped to establish the point.

Some fifteen years earlier Gerhard Schramm of the Max

Planck Institute for Virus Research at Tübingen, Germany,
had become fascinated by the idea of breaking the virus apart
and reconstituting it from its parts. "We found," he reported
later, "that we could separate the protein from the nucleic acid
and that from this protein we could again prepare virus rods."

At the time no one suspected that the bit of nucleic acid removed from the rods was of any importance. When the re-
formed rods, lacking RNA, failed to infect tobacco leaves, the
experimenters were deeply disappointed. "Naturally this was
because there was no nucleic acid in the rods," Schramm said
later. In the forties, however, the experiment did not seem to
offer further possibilities, and Schramm went on to other work.

In 1953 and 1954 the world was suddenly awakened to the
master role of DNA. Listening to Fraenkel-Conrat's report at
the International Congress of Biochemistry at Brussels in 1955,
Schramm could understand why the re-formed rods had been
so innocuous. He and Von Alfred Gierer then delicately took
the virus apart by a complex process involving phenol. This
time they found that RNA alone could infect tobacco leaves.
They had an active virus that attacked tobacco leaves. Their
method of separating RNA and protein had been entirely different from that of Fraenkel-Conrat at Berkeley, but the results were the same.

When there was no DNA present, as in the virus, RNA performed the role of DNA. RNA carried the master plan, the
hereditary information.

Fraenkel-Conrat further established the point in an experiment with rib grass. A strain of TMV which attacked rib-grass
had two amino acids in its protein "overcoat" which were ab-
sent from other TMV. Fraenkel-Conrat separated the little
cord of RNA from the protein of the special strain. He mixed it
with the protein of ordinary TMV, and then reversed the experiment, mixing the RNA of the common TMV with the protein of the special strain. True to the indications of the earlier
work, the hybrids always bore all the characteristics of the

strain that furnished the RNA. RNA could scarcely have been more certainly singled out as another master control.

Thus, in the virus, heredity could be passed along by RNA.

The transmission of heredity was proving unexpectedly varied. The discovery of still another way in which the pattern of life can be passed along from one generation to the next came about almost by accident.

In 1951 Joshua Lederberg, twenty-seven-year-old geneticist of the University of Wisconsin, and Norton D. Zinder, a twenty-three-year-old graduate student, were following up on an interesting finding made earlier by Lederberg and Tatum at Yale University. In 1946 Tatum and Lederberg had discovered that bacteria which normally multiply by straight cell division will, under certain other conditions, mate. By crossing two strains of Escherichia coli, a common bacterium of the intestinal tract, they had produced offspring with some of the characteristics of both parents. It seemed unlikely that only these two strains among all bacteria could mate, and so Lederberg and Zinder decided to see if they could find other instances of mating.

For their first experiment the new team chose two strains of a bacterium called Salmonella typhimurium, which produces a disease in mice resembling food poisoning in man. One of the strains of Salmonella was unable to produce one of the amino acids needed for its survival—say, A. The other lacked the ability to manufacture another essential acid, which may be called B. However, each could synthesize the amino acid the other could not make.

If the two mated, some of the offspring should inherit from one parent the ability to synthesize A, and from the other the ability to make B. The doubly endowed offspring should be able to live on a medium that would have proved fatal to either of their handicapped parents, the experimenters reasoned. If such offspring were produced, large colonies of them should appear on the medium in a few hours, and the scientists would have an unmistakable demonstration that mating had occurred. It was thus that the scientists planned their experiment, and so it worked out.

However, to make certain that mating had occurred, Lederberg and Zinder decided to mate two strains that differed in more than one trait—the equivalent of Mendel's crossing of round yellow peas with wrinkled green. They expected that some of the bacteria produced would be more like one parent and some more like the other. But, as Robert Burns observed many years earlier, the schemes of mice and men gang aft a-gley. The offspring all resembled one parent.

What was even more puzzling, one of the strains always acted as the donor and the other as a recipient. The strange imbalance could not have occurred if a simple mating had taken place. What could have caused the odd results? the two scientists asked. A mutation, perhaps? They had to rule out that possibility, for in case of mutation one strain would not always have served as the donor.

About the only possibility that Lederberg and Zinder could think of was that they had stumbled into an unusual case of "transformation," another instance of the nucleic acid from one strain taking control in the nucleus of another. And yet no one had ever reported such a case in Salmonella. Their only recourse, therefore, was to try to dig deeper—to try to work out the baffling results by experiment.

To test the transformation idea, Lederberg and Zinder made a special U-shaped tube, with a filter dividing the two arms of the U. The filter barrier would halt the direct meeting and mating of the two strains.

In one arm of the U they grew one strain of bacteria and in the other, a second. To permit the exchange of secretions from the two, they alternated suction and pressure so that the liquid —but not the bacteria—ran back and forth through the filter.

The two strains were then transferred to another medium. They grew well. Some of the offspring from one arm of the U displayed the traits of the strain in the other arm. Evidently DNA from one had got through to the other. The case for transformation seemed to be proved.

But Lederberg and Zinder were extremely careful workers who did not take the obvious for granted. They decided to try a more conventional transformation experiment also. The

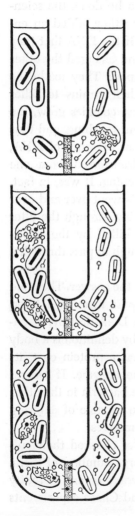

A new genetic mechanism is found. TOP: *On the right side of the U tube is one strain of a bacterium, and on the left side, another. The right strain harbors a latent virus. After breaking up some of the cells, the virus passes through the filter at the bottom of the tube.*
CENTER: *The virus multiplies rapidly in the left strain. Some viruses pick up pieces of the genetic material of the left strain and carry it back through the filter.*
BOTTOM: *The viruses invade the bacteria and incorporate the left-strain genetic material in the genetic make-up of the right strain.*

recipient strain was treated with DNA extracted from the other strain. This time the offspring displayed no new traits; in fact, they showed no effects at all. The experimenters were surprised but not unprepared for this result. Salmonella seemingly could not be altered by transformation, and something else must have effected the change in their tube experiment.

Baffled, but certain about what had to be done, the scientists went back to the U tube. This time they added an enzyme to destroy any free-moving DNA. If the DNA that they assumed had moved through the filter and changed the other strain were taken out, what would happen? They made the experiment. Once again they shifted their strains to other media and let them multiply. As the new colonies grew, the same changes appeared as before. Without touching, and thus without mating, and without the apparent presence of DNA, hereditary traits had somehow been transferred from one strain to another. The mystery was deepening. It was, in fact, as baffling as any whodunit. The scientists went over and over what had happened. Whatever was getting through the filter and affecting the other strain was not killed by the DNA-destroying enzyme. And it was small enough to pass through a filter.

The words themselves began to suggest the answer. They had a familiar ring—something that could pass through a filter, something that was not affected by the DNA-destroying enzyme. That sounded like a virus. A virus by definition is a body that can pass a filter. And because it has a protein coat, its DNA core could not be touched by the enzyme. If viruses passed through the filter and reached the bacteria in the other arm of the U tube, they would be quite capable of entering the bacteria and producing replicas of themselves.

Hot on the trail, Lederberg and Zinder checked their cultures for viruses. And there they were, large numbers of them.

And yet how could viruses act as carriers of any heredity other than their own? In the Hershey and Chase experiments

the invading T2 bacteriophage had imposed its own hereditary pattern on the bacterium. In this case it looked as though
the virus had served only as a carrier. To suggest that a virus
might pick up the DNA of one bacterial strain and carry it to
another bacterium was unheard of. The implications were

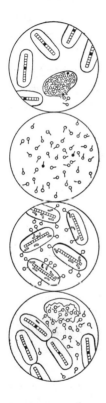

Transduction. TOP TO BOTTOM: *A virus
takes over a cell and picks up some of its
genetic material. The viruses move on.
They infect other cells. Some then produce
more viruses, and some "hand over" to the
invaded cell the genetic material they have
picked up. Occasionally a bacterial gene is
taken in but not incorporated in the chromosome of the invaded cell.*

frightening. If this were true, the viruses that cause many
human diseases might carry genetic material from one cell to
another. It was enough to give the investigators pause, and
yet no other explanation appeared possible.

And so it proved to be. It turned out that the virus involved
was a latent one that did not quickly cause the disruption of

the bacterial cell it invaded in the first arm of the U tube. But when it later caused the break-up of the donor cell, it emerged carrying a particle of the Salmonella DNA in its genetic core—in its DNA. The virus, with the piece of bacterial DNA in its constitution, easily passed through the filter in the U tube used in the Lederberg-Zinder experiment and invaded a bacterium in the other arm of the tube. There, because it was a latent virus, it again did not cause an immediate disruption of the bacterial cell—the cell did not break up within the next twenty-four minutes. Instead the DNA particle that the virus had carried in from the donor bacterium took its place in the chromosomes of the recipient cell and altered the character of the bacterium's offspring.

"It was pure chance that one of the strains chosen for our studies contained a latent virus and that another was susceptible to this virus," said Zinder. "We had not expected to encounter a new genetic mechanism and, considering the many factors that had to be in harmony, the discovery was extremely fortuitous."

In the early experiments the piece of DNA picked up by the virus and carried to a new cell appeared to be very small. Lederberg and Zinder thought that it might correspond to a single gene—a single locus on the DNA coil. Later, however, in collaboration with Dr. Bruce Stocker of London, they found that the transporting virus might transfer two traits at a time. Evidently it also could pick up and transport larger bits of DNA.

"We have succeeded in transducing [the term used for the virus transfer system] almost every trait that we can reliably detect by experiment, including drug resistance, motility factors, and antigenic factors," Zinder later reported.

The discovery of a new genetic mechanism was a matter of first importance. In 1958 Lederberg shared a Nobel Prize with Beadle and Tatum. The high honor was given specifically for his "discoveries concerning genetic recombination and organization of the genetic material of bacteria." Lederberg, then only thirty-three, was one of the youngest Nobelists in history.

Thus another genetic mechanism was added to the growing list of ways in which DNA passes the hereditary material from one organism to another. Transduction joined sexual fertilization, cell division, virus injection, and transformation as tools

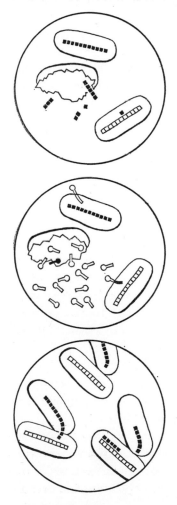

Three methods of transferring genetic material from one bacterial cell to another. TOP: *Transformation—when the cell is broken, a small bit of genetic material makes its way into another cell.* CENTER: *Transduction—viruses pick up DNA from one cell and carry it to another.* BOTTOM: *Mating—two cells come together in direct contact, and DNA is transferred.*

of DNA. And if no DNA were present, RNA could pass along the pattern of life.

Nature was displaying an undreamed-of versatility in transmitting and organizing the precious, thoroughly protected stuff of life. DNA was not only a truly remarkable substance in itself; its manner of expressing its dictates—and they are dictates—was at the same time ingenious, direct, subtle, and certain.

XVII

PAULING AND SANGER:
THE PROTEINS—ANOTHER COIL

"When we understand enzymes—
their structure, the mechanism of
their synthesis, the mechanism of
their action—we shall understand life
. . . except for those aspects of life
that involve mental processes and I
have no doubt that enzymes are im-
portant for these too."

LINUS PAULING

IT WAS IN 1838 that Gerardus Johannes Mulder happened upon the substance in plant and animal cells that seemed to him "the most important of all known substances." Without it, he saw, there would be no life as we define it, and he named it protein—"primary, holding first place."

The choice of name proved wise and accurate. The new century only emphasized the first importance of the material Mulder had found. By the 1950's more than a hundred thousand kinds of protein had been identified in the human body. Proteins, it was clear, are the stuff of the muscles, the bones, the cartilage, the skin, the blood, and the other organs. The enzymes, most of the hormones, and the antibodies that defend us against viruses are proteins—and the viruses themselves are largely protein. "The most significant thing about proteins," said Crick, "is that they do almost anything. . . ."

At first Mulder, and Fischer, the famed German chemist who also became involved in the study of these remarkable materials, thought that the proteins were solid units, the ultimate building blocks of Nature. It was soon discovered, however, that the proteins were made up of amino acids. Fischer succeeded in linking together eighteen of them and creating an artificial protein or partial protein. After that, progress was slow, for the huge proteins—a molecular weight of 25,000 is typical—defied analysis.

In the meanwhile, attention shifted to another group of materials which appeared to be of almost equal import. They were discovered about the middle of the eighteenth century by Réné de Réaumur. Réaumur was hard put to defend his contention that the foods we eat were not broken up in the stomach by what amounted to a band of little demons. Suddenly an idea came to him. He placed a piece of meat in a perforated metal tube, attached a string, and offered it to his falcon. The bird gulped the tube, string and all. After a short time Réaumur pulled up the tube. The meat had largely disappeared; only a bit of stringy substance remained. Réaumur still did not know what had dissolved the meat, but he was certain that it had been disposed of by some natural process and material. The year was 1752.

Somewhat later Spallanzani, the Italian abbot, repeated the experiment with himself as the subject. Spallanzani swallowed meat in a little wire cage and hauled it up at various intervals. By 1780 he was able to announce that meat is decomposed by substances in the juices of the stomach.

There the matter rested, except for continuing argument. That flourished. William Hunter, famous English physician, finally was driven to protest at a medical meeting: "Some physiologists will have it that the stomach is a mill, others, that it is a fermenting vat, others again, that it is a stew pan; but in my view of the matter, it is neither a mill, a fermentation vat, nor a stew pan; but a stomach, gentlemen, a stomach."

In the late 1830's and the 1840's, as Schwann worked to convince the world that all living things are composed of cells, he found that a very special substance in the stomach effectively does the work of mill, vat, and stewpan.[1] He called it pepsin, and it was identified as an enzyme—belonging to a group of substances active in "zyme," the Greek word for yeast or leaven.

It was entirely by accident that at about the same time a brilliant American physician was directly observing this same remarkable enzyme substance at its highly efficient work. In 1822 a French Canadian voyageur who had come into the rough fur-trading post at Fort Mackinac on the Great Lakes became involved in a fracas and received the full blast of a gun directly in the abdomen. The explosion ripped away the wall of the stomach. Dr. William Beaumont, a young surgeon of the U.S. Army Medical Corps, who was in charge of the post hospital, rushed to his aid. Dr. Beaumont did what he could, but that was not much. The young man, Alexis St. Martin, nevertheless survived the first day, and Beaumont saw a chance to save his life.

Although the doctor performed a number of operations, the wound healed only around the edges. As he labored over his patient, Dr. Beaumont found himself looking directly into the stomach's cavity. He could almost see the processes of digestion at work. Beaumont realized that he was perhaps the first medical man in history to be presented with such a sight, and he launched a long series of the most careful studies and observations.

When the authorities at the fort tired of caring for St. Martin and wanted to ship him back to Lower Canada, Beaumont took him into his own home. He also took St. Martin with him when he was transferred to another post and eventually to St. Louis.

When St. Martin ate, Beaumont saw that juices oozed into the stomach and dissolved the food. The doctor removed some of the juices and tried them on food outside the stomach. They were equally effective.

[1] See Chapter IV.

By this time St. Martin had realized his value as a scientific subject, and he was becoming increasingly difficult. To Beaumont's great distress, he ran away, interrupting an unparalleled experiment. Four years later, however, St. Martin came back with a wife and two children. In return for supporting the entire family, Beaumont was permitted to continue his studies.

Beaumont tried to enlist the interest of medical schools, but when it was not forthcoming he continued alone, measuring, observing, testing the reaction of the powerful enzymatic stomach juices to hunger, thirst, and taste.

Over a period of years other enzymes, all of which were potent activators, were found in many other substances. It was then that the bitter dispute as to their nature sprang up between Pasteur and Liebig. Only in 1897 was it seemingly settled by Buchner's discovery that the liquid from yeast could ferment sugar even though no living yeast cell was present. Enzymes, then, could act without the presence of the living cell, though many of them ordinarily acted only in the cell.

This still did not explain what the powerful enzymes were or how they can convert the food we eat into new tissues, energy, and reserve materials, and do it with great rapidity at normal bodily temperatures and pressures. Such reactions outside the cell could be accomplished only with high heat, strong acids, and heavy pressures.

At the time when enzymes were discovered, Berzelius had pointed out that they are catalysts—they can initiate and accelerate chemical reactions without themselves being altered or used up in the process. The explanation, however, helped little. If the amazing action of enzymes was to be understood, science would have to discover what they were and why they worked as they did. The search began.

All around the world, laboratories delved into the maze of the enzymes. But the most ingenious chemists could not isolate them pure and free of all other materials. They always were joined with proteins, and the belief grew that enzymes might themselves be proteins.

Another school, led by the German authority Richard Willstätter, insisted that the proteins in the enzyme solutions were impurities, and that the enzymes were something else again, "substances unknown to chemists."

In the 1920's when James Batcheller Sumner of Cornell University decided to try to isolate an enzyme from jack beans, his friends and associates urged him not to run into "that wall." Sumner knew what he wanted to do, and refused to be dissuaded.

He planted a plentiful lot of beans. When they were ripe, he ground them up in an old-fashioned coffee mill and began the long and arduous task of getting out the enzyme. The first step was easy. He filtered the solid part of the beans out of the thin brownish soup that had been produced when he added water to the ground beans. He then added a little urea to the husks. If the enzyme was present, he knew, it would quickly break the urea down into amnonia and carbon dioxide. Nothing happened. He next added a little urea to the liquid he had filtered off, and this time there was fast action. The enzyme was in the liquid.

Sumner painstakingly removed one material after another from the solution. Finally he was down to a residue from which he could not extract any additional extraneous matter. His only alternative was to shift his approach and hunt for something that might dissolve the enzyme and precipitate it without affecting the other remaining materials. A professor with whom Sumner had studied at Harvard suggested that he try acetone.

The final step, Sumner insisted, was "absurdly simple." He mixed acetone with his residue and allowed it to filter overnight. The next morning he placed a drop under the microscope. Floating about in the liquid were some tiny octahedral (eight-sided) crystals. Sumner knew instantly that he was looking upon a pure enzyme—a sight that no one had previously seen, for organic substances do not crystallize until they are pure or virtually so.

Tests still had to be made. Sumner centrifuged out the crystals, concentrated them, and tried them on the urea. They were highly active and tore it apart. There could no longer be any doubt. That afternoon Sumner phoned his wife: "I have crystallized the first enzyme."

And that enzyme was a protein! Every test that Sumner could apply proved it conclusively, and Sumner, as was his privilege, named the new enzyme protein "urease" (by this time it had been agreed that all enzymes would bear the name of the material they act upon plus the suffix "ase"). Like many other proteins, it was a huge molecule, with a molecular weight of 483,000.

Sumner's announcement that an enzyme had been separated and that it had proved to be a protein was not at once greeted as a triumph. Willstätter, the arbiter of enzyme chemistry, derisively attacked the finding. He insisted that the protein Sumner had obtained was merely the carrier of the enzyme. Because of his stand, most of the scientific world viewed Sumner's claim with caution.

Willstätter did not temper his opposition even when he came to Cornell as a guest lecturer. On Sumner's home ground he poured forth his scorn and disagreement. Sumner did not retreat before the onslaught. He quietly enlisted the assistance of a friend who knew German well and prepared an article explaining and supporting his crystallization of the protein urease for the German publication *Naturwissenschaften*.

Still the German attack continued. Another scientist visiting at Cornell lectured on what he called Sumner's errors. Again Sumner stood firm. He requested permission to present a lecture before the same class, and not only carried the students with him, but convinced the critical visitor that the enzyme was indeed a protein.

Was it possible that all enzymes were proteins? Spurred by Sumner's achievement, others went to work to try to settle the critical issue. Unfortunately, the process used to separate urease could not be applied in detail to the separation of other enzymes. Most of the others had their own requirements. Not until four years later, in 1930, did John H. Northrop of the Rockefeller Institute for Medical Research succeed in purifying pepsin, the digestive enzyme Schwann and Beaumont had identified almost a century earlier.

Pepsin too proved to be a protein, as have fifty or more enzymes purified since. By 1947 virtually all doubts were gone, and the 1947 Nobel Prize for chemistry was presented jointly to Sumner for the isolation of the first enzyme and to Northrop for the separation of pepsin.

The ranks of the proteins were being increased from other directions also.

From ancient times men had known that if an immature bird or animal were castrated, certain sexual characteristics —in birds, the comb and the characteristic call—would fail to develop. Many centuries later—in 1849—A. A. Berthold showed that such sexual changes were produced by the sexual glands, and a few years later Claude Bernard proved that certain organs could secrete powerful substances directly into the blood stream. In 1905 the word "hormone" (from the Greek *hormon*, "arousing, exciting") was proposed for these internal secretions that acted as "chemical messengers," exerting their effects at a distance from their source.

By the 1930's many hormones were being identified. Some scientists maintained that each organ secretes them. Among them were hormones to regulate the flow of the food elements between the organs of storage, processing, and utilization, and hormones to adjust the rate and kind of energy production. They were essentials.

When science succeeded in purifying these powerful and vital substances, most of them proved to be proteins.

For many years, too, science believed that proteins might also be the carriers of heredity. They had many of the qualifications for this role, though evidence was lacking.

Thus, everywhere that science probed, the proteins appeared to be truly foremost; they seemed to be almost synonymous with life itself. If life was to be understood and progress was to be made against cancer and other diseases linked with basic life processes, knowledge of the proteins was absolutely necessary.

Fischer had shown that proteins are made up of chains of amino acids. Some of the chains were grouped together in long fibers, as in the muscles; others were globular in form, as in blood and the white of egg. But no one could say what these structures were, or how the amino acids were ranged together to form the protein chains. The awful complexity of the huge protein molecules defied all efforts.

The light microscope could not penetrate to their structure, and X rays helped only slightly. X-ray-diffraction photographs could indicate the direction in which the structures of the protein molecule scattered the rays, but the hundreds of thousands of atoms in proteins produced pictures showing such a galaxy of shadows and points that interpreting the data proved as overwhelming as attempting to untangle the proteins themselves.

Progress thus was slow and disheartening. Rebelling against the frustration, Linus Pauling and his colleague Robert B. Corey at the California Institute of Technology decided in 1937 to undertake a new approach to the baffling problem of the proteins. Pauling and the laboratory he headed would start by trying to learn as much as possible about the basic atomic structure of the amino acids of which the proteins were made. In short, he would start at the beginning.

Pauling had recently become the director of the Caltech laboratory and was eager to study the fundamental organization of living matter. His interest was an inevitable outgrowth of the work he had been doing on molecular structure.

In 1922 when Pauling first arrived at the Pasadena school to do graduate work—he had been born at Portland, Oregon, on February 28, 1901, and had recently been graduated from the Oregon State Agricultural College—the emphasis in the department of chemistry was on physical chemistry. Pauling was caught up in the enthusiasm. In his first three years at Caltech the tall eager young man with the upstanding shock of curly hair became so fascinated by the physical aspects of chemistry that he considered specializing in atomic physics.

A Guggenheim Fellowship took him to Munich to study for a year with Arnold Sommerfeld, then to Copenhagen and Zurich for another year of work with Niels Bohr and Erwin Schrödinger. In this stimulating climate Pauling's interests centered on the forces that bind atoms into molecules. The outcome was a book that became famous, *The Nature of the Chemical Bond*. With the new understandings it provided, science could predict how substances might be put together and could design them to order. Its insights contributed substantially to the development of the great synthetic drug, fiber, and plastic industries.

"I was a physical chemist with this dominating interest in the forces which cause atoms to join into molecules and to react with one another," Pauling once explained to George Gray of *Scientific American*.

The forces, of course, were electrical. Pauling had begun his studies with what he called the "simpler" molecular structures, those of the metals and inorganic compounds. One day, however, he tested an organic molecule, hemoglobin, the protein that gives blood its red color.

As he worked, Pauling discovered that in arterial blood this large protein molecule is repelled by a magnet; in venous blood it is attracted. From this point on, Pauling was inescapa-

bly interested in the science of life. He went on to study the
chemical bond between hemoglobin and the oxygen it picks
up in the lungs, and, beyond such specific problems, the principles that control the basic processes of life. And the proteins.
he saw, held the key to them.

Pauling started his great planned protein experiment with
a study of the distances between atoms in the protein molecule and of the angle of the chemical bonds. It required the
most rigorous exactitude. Four post-doctoral assistants spent a
year each working out the structure of one crystal, the amino
acid called threonine.

Several later studies went a little more rapidly, and then
the Pauling group saw that a pattern was emerging. The distances and angles were almost the same for a number of simple molecules related to proteins. So remarkably close were
they, the researchers found they could predict what the dimensions of the strands making up the proteins would prove
to be.

Another point of similarity turned up. The six atoms of the
amide group—one of the protein groups—all lay within an
extremely short distance of a common plane; they were turned
the same way. And the group—gratifyingly, as far as the scientists were concerned—was a rigid part of the chain. With
the rigid units as markers, Pauling saw that the chain twisted.

All the help that could be obtained was badly needed, for
the chain might twist in many ways. Gradually, though, Pauling worked out the distance between a nitrogen atom and an
oxygen atom, and thus learned the length of the hydrogen
bond connecting the two. Pauling knew then how some of the
main units should turn and how far apart they should be.

It began to look as though all the main units in the chain
might be alike, differing only in their side attachments.

When Pauling put these pieces of information together and
considered what kind of structure could fit the specifications,
he found there was only one: a helix—a spiral staircase.

"When asymmetric objects in space are joined together in such a way that each has the same geometrical relationship to its neighbors, a helix is formed," Pauling explained.

And this was true whether the resulting structure was an unseen molecule, a staircase, a cord, or, for that matter, a little girl's curl.

Pressing ahead with this exciting find, Pauling and his group worked out the number of turns in the helix, and the rise from

A helix. The three-dimensional configuration of the protein chain showed scientists that it twisted into a helix or spiral.

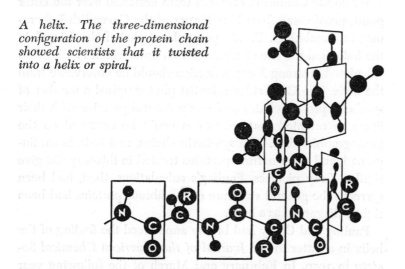

one base or step to another. The long-hidden structure of protein was finally being revealed. Was it possible that this helix represented the structure of hair, horn, muscle, and the other proteins in the same classification? The experimenters hopefully put the question. They could not give an affirmative answer, for the X-ray diagrams of the natural materials and the new helix did not quite match.

At this point help came unexpectedly. A group of English scientists, C. H. Bamford, W. E. Hanby, and F. Happey, made some X-ray photographs of synthetic protein strands in which all the amino acids were chemically identical. Pauling saw with excitement that their pictures were identical with the X-ray patterns that would be produced if a bundle of his helixes were brought together. A test was soon made. A helix with eighteen amino acids in five turns corresponded particularly well with the English photographs. In addition, the Pauling photographs were similar to those produced by horsehair.

While the California research team hesitated over the latter point, proof came from Max Perutz of the Cavendish Laboratory at Cambridge. Perutz pointed out that if the "steps" in the helix had the rise of 1.5 Angstrom units which Pauling had calculated, a strong X-ray reflection should be observable from the helix. The Cambridge scientist photographed a number of synthetic protein chains and many natural proteins with their fibers so oriented that reflections could be captured on the photographic plate. The synthetic chains, and hair, horn, fingernail, and other natural proteins treated in this way did give similar X-ray pictures. Pauling's calculations, then, had been correct. The general structure of the fibrous proteins had been rightly diagnosed as a helix.

Pauling and Corey had briefly announced the finding of the helix in a letter to the *Journal of the American Chemical Society* in 1950. In February and March of the following year they were ready for a series of momentous reports in the *Proceedings of the National Academy of Sciences.*

On February 28 they reported: "We have now used this information to construct two reasonable hydrogen-bonded helical configurations for the polypeptide chain. We think that it is likely that these configurations constitute an important part of the structure of both fibrous and globular proteins as well as synthetic polypeptides."

On March 31 the tremendous scope of the findings was made clear. Pauling announced specifically:

That hair, muscle, horn, nail, and quill are helixes;

That collagen—the protein of the tendons, bone, tusk, skin, cornea of the eye, intestinal tissue and probably the reticular (network) structure of cells—is a helix;

That synthetic proteins are helixes;

That feathers fall into the same coiled pattern;

That it is not unlikely that the globular proteins, including the hemoglobin of the blood, are helixes.

In short, Pauling was saying, the most basic materials of life are helical coils, spiral staircases.

An oddity in the first X-ray photographs of both horsehair and the synthetic proteins had attracted the attention of all the scientists working with the pictures. It was a strong reflection that appeared just above and below the central image. At about the same time both Pauling in California and Crick at Cambridge suggested that such reflections might be produced

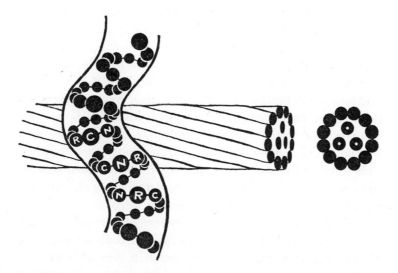

Coiled coils. Horsehair and many natural materials are made up of coiled coils—helixes coiled into cables, something like this section of a commercial cable.

if several helixes were twisted about one another. Crick called them "coiled coils." And so it proved to be.

Protein strands were twisted into cables, and cables into what might be called hawsers!

Although X-ray photographs could not entirely settle the structure of horsehair and similar fibrous proteins, it looked as though horsehair were made up of six alpha helixes coiled tightly into cables, and as though six of the cables were then twisted to form a thick rope—a rope that on the surface was a single horsehair.

The pervasiveness of the helix, the beautiful simplicity of its structure, its inevitability if there is to be a repetition of a certain kind, suggested that the helix might be found in other parts of Nature. "It tempted us to look for helixes in larger structures," said Pauling.

Workers in the University of California at Berkeley placed under the electron microscope one of the whip-like lashes with which certain bacteria make their way about. X-ray-diffraction studies had indicated that the appendage, called a flagellum, probably was made up of helixes.

Suddenly the whole structure stood forth. The flagellum was elegantly made of three "ropes" twisted about one another. Measurements indicated that each rope was composed of seven cables, each made of seven alpha helixes.

Again the insignia of Nature was the coil.

"The time has now arrived," said Pauling, "when it is possible to track the structure of living organisms down through successively smaller orders of size, without a gap, from the whole animal through the cell to the atoms."

Pauling had tracked down the general shape and organization of the proteins, and for this he had been awarded the Nobel Prize in 1954. But still no one had been able to work out the sequence of the amino acids in the long, coiling protein chains. That was the next major work ahead.

. . .

In England, at Cambridge, young Frederick Sanger was already at work on this all but impossible undertaking. Disregarding impossibilities, he had decided in 1944 to tackle the problem of sequence. Perhaps Sanger's courage stemmed from his youth: he was twenty-six and had obtained his doctorate at Cambridge only the year before. World War II was ending, and it was possible to look forward to research unrestricted by wartime necessities.

For the epic experiment on which he was embarking, Sanger chose the insulin molecule. It was one of the few proteins available in a purified form. A molecule of insulin from beef cattle contained "only" 777 atoms—other protein molecules ran into the thousands and even the hundreds of thousands. Science also had discovered that the insulin molecule is made up of 254 carbon atoms, 377 hydrogens, 75 oxygens, 65 nitrogens, and 6 sulphurs. This imposing array was organized into seventeen kinds of amino acid. Beyond this the jungle was all thickness and entanglement. No one could even speculate on what the sequence of the seventeen amino acids might be or on how they might be arranged in the insulin chain.

And yet the sequence was all-important. A change in the order in which the amino acids were arranged in the protein chain would produce a different kind of protein.

Sanger began by breaking the insulin molecule into pieces. A complete dissolution would have been of no help, for that would have destroyed the very sequence Sanger wanted to study. By randomly breaking the protein molecule, Sanger hoped that he could find a few recognizable pieces that might fit together and show him how the chain was built.

E. O. P. Thompson, who worked with Sanger, compared the procedure to "dropping billions of plates on the floor" and trying to put them back together again. The difference was that Sanger's pieces were invisible; they could not be seen even with the most powerful microscope.

Sanger combed through his invisible debris, his stupendous pile of jigsaw pieces. He had one device to help him. The end of a chain could be dyed a bright yellow, and thus could be nicely labeled.

Sanger treated the fragments with the yellow dye. Among them, two picked up the bright color. This showed the scientist that he had two ends of chains. It followed that insulin was made up of two chains.

Then, turning to other methods that enabled him to work with as little as a thousandth of a gram of material, Sanger separated the amino acids in the insulin molecule. In this way he found that there were fifty-one of them. Clearly, some of the seventeen kinds of amino acid in insulin occurred a number of times.

Among the fifty-one, Sanger found three units of cystine, an amino acid that differs from all the others in having a connective device at either end. It was, so to speak, a two-handled unit. This indicated to the scientist that it would serve as a cross link connecting the two chains. His idea proved correct. When Sanger treated the material to break up the cystine, he found that he had two chains. He had succeeded in separating the two parts of the insulin molecule.

Going back to the yellow dye again, Sanger singled out the amino acids with which the two chains began. The amino acid called glycine was in the number-one place on one chain, and phenylalanine in the lead position on the other. The general outlines of the picture thus were beginning to fill in. At the same time the years were passing.

Sanger again went back to chain-breaking. He colored the ends of a number of glycine chains and then broke them into pieces. Among the fragments he came upon one glycine to which an isoleucine unit was attached. The debris of another glycine chain yielded a bit made up of glycine-isoleucine-valine-glutamic acid-glutamic acid.

Sanger recognized that he undoubtedly had the first five units of the glycine chain and in their proper order. He must have repeated it happily—glycine-isoleucine-valine-glutamic acid-glutamic acid.

In the same way, Sanger found the first four units on the other chain—phenylalanine-valine-aspartic acid-glutamic acid. He had only forty-two more places to go.

Tirelessly Sanger and a colleague, Hans Tuppy, concentrated on the phenylalanine chain. They once more broke it into bits, identified the bits one by one, and then tried to fit them into order.

At last they succeeded in piecing together five sections of the chain. The sections, however, refused to join. Sanger realized that several links must be missing, and that he would have to find them.

Sanger suspected that the missing links had been destroyed in the breaking of the chain, and that he would have to work out a gentler method of taking it apart in order to preserve them. It was a setback, but Sanger and Tuppy went to work again. They developed the gentler method required and with it obtained longer fragments, different from those which had come from their earlier, more drastic system. In some of the pieces some bonds remained intact. Here were the missing links.

With all of the sections and links in their hands, the scientists spent another solid year in forging their complete chain. Finally the phenylalanine chain was entirely assembled. It had thirty links—thirty amino acids—and the prodigious job was done on one chain.

It took another year to put together the shorter glycine chain of twenty-one amino acids. Although not so long as the phenylalanine chain, it was more difficult, for it offered fewer clues. There were fewer distinctive pieces. As Thompson (who was then assisting Sanger) said, two of the amino acids, glutamic acid and cystine, cropped up in so many fragments that it was bewildering and baffling. But at last the scientists seemed to be within sight of their goal. Only a few seemingly lesser problems remained to be solved.

Appearances, however, were deceptive, and nothing was ever to be easy in the mammoth Cambridge experiment. The trouble was that glutamic acid and aspartic acid often were converted into a second form when the chain was separated with acid. Either form was a possibility for the chain. To determine which was the correct one took another long series of studies.

Not until the end of 1952 were both chains assembled. At this point only one question remained. How did the two chains fit together to form the insulin molecule? In the perspective of what had gone before, this did not appear an overly difficult problem.

Sanger and Thompson knew, of course, that the bridges which held the two together were made by cystine, and they knew that there were three cystine units, and therefore three bridges. Where exactly did they cross? With tireless patience the scientists again broke down some of the chains to look for the "bridge ends" that would place the bridges. And they found none! There seemed to be no pattern of connections, for the connecting bits went every way, in a chaotic helter-skelter. It was an appalling development, enough to cause a lesser team to despair. Sanger and Thompson only dug in once more. They suspected again that the disorder was wrought by the breaking down of the chain, and investigation proved this to be true. The acids used to separate the links had also opened the cystine bonds and created the chaos they found.

Again they went back to their test tubes, and again they found a new way of breaking down the chain. By using both enzymes and acids, they separated the chains in such a way that fragments were obtained with intact bridge ends. The bridges were fitted into place, and in 1954, after ten years of unflagging work, the insulin molecule was completely assembled.

The line-up of the chain could be charted.

30	Alanine	
29	Lysine	
28	Proline	
27	Threonine	
26	Tyrosine	
25	Phenylalanine	
24	Phenylalanine	
23	Glycine	
22	Arginine	
21	Glutamic acid	Aspartic acid
20	Glycine	Cystine
19	Cystine	Tyrosine
18	Valine	Aspartic acid
17	Leucine	Glutamic acid
16	Tyrosine	Leucine
15	Leucine	Glutamic acid
14	Alanine	Tyrosine
13	Glutamic acid	Leucine
12	Valine	Serine
11	Leucine	Cystine
10	Histidine	Valine
9	Leucine	Serine
8	Glycine	Alanine
7	Cystine ———— Cystine	
6	Leucine	Cystine
5	Histidine	Glutamic acid
4	Glutamic acid	Glutamic acid
3	Aspartic acid	Valine
2	Valine	Isoleucine
1	Phenylalanine	Glycine

For the first time in history the internal structure of a protein was completely known. One of the essential fastnesses of Nature had been penetrated and brought to light. It was a monumental, an incredible accomplishment.

The scientific world applauded wholeheartedly when Sanger received the Nobel Prize for chemistry in 1958. He was then forty.

Citing Sanger for having unlocked the secret of the "most complicated of all substances occurring in Nature," the Swedish academy in presenting the prize to him continued: "Many hormones, all enzymes so far known, viruses, toxins which cause disease and antibodies which give immunity to disease are all proteins. In all tissues of the body, in muscle, nerves, and skin, protein forms an essential functional constituent.

"Sanger's methods and results have opened a road to the determination of their detailed structure and thus one of chemistry's greatest problems has found its solution in principle."

XVIII

FOUR = TWENTY = INFINITY

A YOUNG WOMAN who was very ill came into a large city clinic. The doctors soon diagnosed the illness from which she was suffering as sickle-cell anemia.

She had heard the dread words before, for several other members of her family had died of the disease. She could not know, though, how small was the cause of her illness or that it was one of the most striking of all proofs of DNA's complete, super-precise control and determination of proteins and of life as a whole.

A change in an almost inconceivably small point, a single nucleotide "step" in the DNA spiral staircase of one chromosome, had altered the hemoglobin or red pigment of her blood from round to sickle-shaped. For reasons that medicine has not yet completely fathomed, this change had turned health into illness. Life and death depended upon one "step" in the long DNA helix.

The reach of DNA was long, its consequences infinitely large.

The revolutionary discovery in the 1950's that DNA and RNA, and not the proteins, were the carriers of heredity and the ultimate shapers of human destiny meant that the proteins, in all their vast variety, must either directly or indirectly be formed by the nucleic acids. But how? At first science could only speculate. Even the relationships that scientists were certain must exist were difficult to demonstrate. And yet if the DNA molecule with its distinctive arrangement of "steps" controlled the formation of a particular protein, proof should be discoverable. Vernon M. Ingram and a Cambridge University group decided upon a test.

Suppose, Ingram reasoned, an abnormal protein arose from the mutation of a gene (a word losing caste but newly defined as a section of the DNA helix). By chemical analysis of the deviant form and the normal it should be possible to discover how they differed and then perhaps to track the change to the place in the DNA helix where it occurred.

Exactly such a mutation was available—sickle-cell anemia. One evening in 1945, Linus Pauling of the California Institute of Technology was having dinner in New York with a group of physicians from some of the leading medical schools. One of the doctors fell to discussing sickle-cell anemia, and remarked that the red cells are twisted out of shape in the venous blood of a patient, but resume their normal globular form when the blood passes through the lungs and enters the arteries.

"The idea burst upon me," Pauling later related, "that the molecules of hemoglobin in the red cells might be responsible for the disease—that the disease might be a molecular one involving an abnormal sort of hemoglobin manufactured by the patient because of the possession of abnormal genes in place of normal genes that control the manufacture of normal hemoglobin molecules."

Pauling sensed that the idea was a correct one. "I wish that it were possible for me to describe the feeling of happiness that came along with the idea," he said.

Later work confirmed what might have been called Pauling's hunch or insight. He demonstrated that the disease is a genetic one and that normal and sickle-cell hemoglobin differ in electrical charge.

This was about all the information that was available. If the disease was to be tracked back to its point of origin, Ingram knew, he would first have to discover what part of the hemoglobin molecule was altered. This alone was a large assignment, for, like many other proteins, the red blood cell was an enormous one. It was made up of more than three hundred amino acids of nineteen different kinds. The staggering problem that faced the Cambridge scientist was how the three hundred in sickle cell differed in arrangement from the three hundred in normal hemoglobin.

From various indications Ingram thought that the change must lie in one small section. But which?

Beginning his work, Ingram broke the long coil of sickle-cell hemoglobin into a number of pieces. The trypsin, the digestive enzyme that he used, broke the chain at each point where a lysine or arginine molecule occurred and gave him twenty-eight pieces. Which was the guilty one?

Ingram put a drop of the solution near the edge of a large sheet of moist filter paper and passed an electric current through it in order to separate the twenty-eight pieces. When the sheet had dried, the scientist was ready to "fingerprint" all of the twenty-eight suspects. It was to be a very special kind of scientific fingerprinting.

Ingram held the sheet so that the edge with the spots touched a liquid. As the liquid crept up the paper the twenty-eight spots moved upward too, according to their varied adsorbency. Some came to rest high on the sheet and some lower, but each occupied a slightly different place, like notes in a musical composition. "I call the map a fingerprint of the hemoglobin," said Ingram.

His next step was to prepare a similar map of normal hemoglobin and thus to fingerprint it too.

How did the two sets of fingerprints compare? Ingram noticed one small difference. The spot that he had numbered "four" on the sickle-cell chart was slightly displaced from the point Number Four occupied on the normal chart. It was a bit out of line, and its disarrangement indicated a difference in electrical charge of the very kind that Pauling had discovered. Spot for spot, all the other drops occupied exactly the same position on the two charts.

The finger of suspicion therefore pointed to Number Four. Ingram cut it out of the chart and washed it out of the paper. His next step would be to put it through the same process again. The little spot, however, yielded such an infinitesimal speck of material that he had to fingerprint dozens of other batches to get enough Number Four for the next test. At the end of this tedious process he had the few thousandths of a grain which he required.

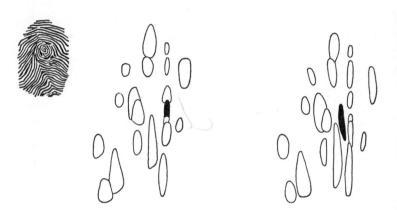

A telltale fingerprint. Fragmentation and fingerprinting show that normal and sickle-cell hemoglobin differ only at one point. The effects are as large as the difference is small.

As the Number Four spot in its turn was analyzed, Ingram saw that both the normal and the sickle-cell Number Four hemoglobin contained the same amino acids—glutamic acid, valine, histidine, leucine, threonine, proline, and lysine.

But again there was one difference. The normal cells had two glutamic-acid units and one of valine; the sickle cells had one of glutamic acid and two of valine.

The difference seemed small, but Ingram knew that it was significant. What might matter even more was the way the units were arranged in the small thread they formed.

By "peeling off" the units one by one, the scientist discovered that in the sixth position in the sickle-cell chain there was a valine unit. In the sixth position in the normal chain there stood a glutamic-acid unit. Otherwise the line-up was exactly the same. Only the player in the sixth position on the Number Four team had changed, but the one change was crucial.

The initial seat of the trouble had been found, and the change in an amino acid which produced sickle-cell anemia had been tracked to its source.

"According to all our evidence," said Ingram, "the sole difference is that in the abnormal molecule a valine is substituted for glutamic acid at one point. A change in one amino acid in nearly three hundred, is certainly a very small change indeed and yet this slight change can be fatal to the unfortunate possessor of the errant hemoglobin."

So striking were the results that John Hunt, another Cambridge scientist, decided to study another abnormal hemoglobin, a rare form known as Hemoglobin C. Seemingly it was produced by a change in amino acids in the same general area. The investigators scarcely dared to think though that both the sickle and C aberrations could occur in the identical section of the hemoglobin chain. "That seemed too pat to be true," said Ingram.

But it was true. The fingerprinting of Hemoglobin C disclosed another change at Spot Four. This time the abnormal spot was not only displaced, but also broken in two. The scientists were soon to learn why.

The sixth-place unit, the one that was replaced by valine in sickle-cell, gave way in Hemoglobin C to another amino acid, lysine. Suddenly it was clear why the Number Four spot was broken. Trypsin, the enzyme used to sever the molecule, acted upon lysine and arginine—a fact that had been used initially in the experiment. Whenever a lysine unit occurred in the chain, it was of course broken.

Two serious disorders thus were traced back to a change in

a single amino acid in a chain of three hundred. But how had this come about? How had the DNA that must have determined their order made the small but devastating change in one point in the protein?

The question actually was how does DNA produce proteins to its own pattern and order, and, beyond that, why does like beget like? The scientists were coming to the heart of their inquiry, and here, to a certain degree, they had to theorize.

Assuming that DNA was organized in a Crick-Watson helix, Ingram and Hunt drew up a chart of the way one section of its bases or "steps" might be arranged:

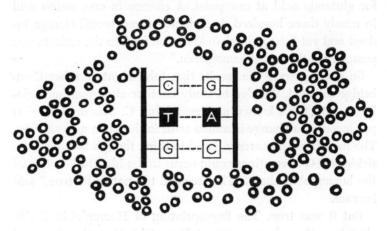

Round, normal blood cells and the DNA line-up that produces them.

If these bases either directly or indirectly assembled a matching amino acid, the result would be glutamic acid, the protein of normal hemoglobin.

If, on the other hand, a mutation changed the T-A "step" to G-C, the DNA blueprint would differ.

Amino acids assembled by such a mold would form valine, exactly the amino acid whose substitution for glutamic acid produces sickle-cell anemia.

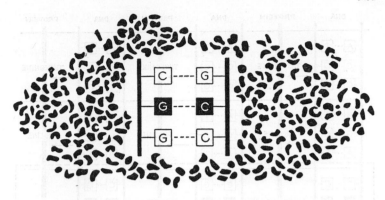

"Sickle-shaped" blood cells and the tiny DNA change that produces them.

A different mutation in the same section, a reversal of T-A to A-T, and the amino acid put together by this mold would be lysine instead of the normal glutamic acid. The result would be the amino-acid line-up of Hemoglobin C.

Thus such mutations in one "step" on the DNA spiral staircase would produce exactly the changes in proteins which research had shown do occur.

The remarkable fineness of the change in DNA and its precise effects on the protein produced in the cell were made even more apparent when they were shown against a somewhat longer section of the chain.

The kind of proof that can be recorded in photographs was not available, but the evidence and the supporting biochemical data were strong—the sequence of bases or "steps" in the DNA helix had determined the sequence of amino acids in a protein. Although the exact mechanism and additional information would have to be sought, Ingram was confident: "The exciting point of these findings is that we are apparently on the right track in our ideas about the mechanism of heredity."

Other evidence, most of it indirect but in agreement with the Ingram finding, was available. Hershey had shown that

348

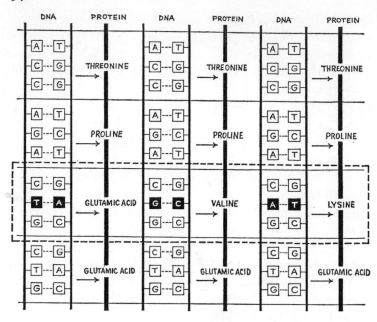

A diagrammatic section of DNA. *A change in one "step" in 300 makes the difference between health and illness.* LEFT: *The line-up of normal* DNA. CENTER: *The line-up with the one small change that produces sickle-shaped blood cells.* RIGHT: *The line-up with another small change that produces another aberration of the blood cells.*

when a bacteriophage infects a bacterial cell, almost all the protein remains outside, and yet that the DNA which enters the cell produces new protein as well as DNA.

In Avery's noted experiment—the one in which DNA brought in from another cell induces Type I bacteria to form Type III capsules—it seemed clear that an enzyme, a protein, was produced and figured in the making of the new capsule.

Rollin D. Hotchkiss and J. Marmur went on to show directly that this is the case. An invading bacterium transformed its host from one unable to use a certain amino acid to one able to use the same nutrient. The investigators found that the transformed organism differed in possessing at least one new enzyme. Here too the DNA had accounted directly for the production of a protein.

These were significant though small evidences of one of the most crucial reactions in life.

Ernest F. Gale of the Department of Biochemistry of Cambridge University set out to find a direct answer to the obvious but still hidden relationship of the nucleic acids and protein.

Gale bombarded bacterial cells—Staphylococcus aureus—with supersonic sound until the cells were disrupted. About half the nucleic acid and a large part of the surrounding cytoplasm spilled out through the broken cell walls. Gale wanted to determine whether the remaining material—material that had now become accessible to experiment—could produce new proteins and enzymes if the necessary raw materials were provided.

The English scientist placed some of the cell fragments in a solution furnished with the eighteen amino acids the bacterium needs for life and growth, and with materials to supply energy. When the solution was properly incubated, it began to produce proteins—and, among them, enzymes. Gale studied three enzymes in particular.

The scientist then removed more of the nucleic acids from the cells. With this, the production of enzymes decreased strikingly and sometimes halted entirely.

Gale carried his experiment further. He reduced the nucleic-acid content of the broken cells—both RNA and DNA—to about fifteen per cent of that of the whole cells. Enzyme production fell off sharply and often stopped.

Could it be started again? Gale added some Staphylococcal RNA to the incubation mixture. The production of two of the enzymes was quickly restored. When he added the four nucleotides—the four bases or steps in the RNA helix—production of the third enzyme started again. The remaining margin of DNA plus the added RNA had been sufficient to start production again, and Gale pointed out that he could give "an immediate affirmative to the question: Is nucleic acid involved in the synthesis of enzymes?"

Gale faced another critical question: what would happen if the DNA in the broken cells was further reduced? He cut it to under ten per cent. Promptly enzyme development (or general protein synthesis) halted. The demonstration was clear-cut. With less than ten per cent of DNA all activity was halted. Activity was dead. With more than ten per cent of DNA and with the addition of other necessary materials, production was resumed. The most critical tests science can apply had been made; an activity had been halted and started again by the addition of measured amounts of materials.

"There is no reasonable doubt that a specific relation exists between DNA and protein," Gale summarized, "but the degree of that specificity and the nature of that relationship await elucidation by direct experiment.

"However, from the experimental results put forward one can deduce that both RNA and DNA are involved in protein synthesis and in the organization of that synthesis to produce specific enzymes.

"Direct experiment has established that DNA is an essential component of the enzyme-forming systems; indirect evidence suggests that DNA determines what enzymes are formed by a cell.

"Direct experiment has established that in the presence of DNA, RNA is essential for actual formation of those enzymes. . . ."

Thus DNA and RNA were experimentally linked to the proteins that give substance to all living things.

The two nucleic acids were linked in the master control of life. But were the proteins directly molded by DNA?

In 1937 Caspersson and Brachet had shown that the synthesis of proteins seems to be very closely connected with

RNA. Whenever the Swedish and Belgian scientists found heavy synthesis of protein going on in the cell, there was RNA. It did not look like simple coincidence.[1]

And then there were the viruses. Tobacco-mosaic virus is made up only of RNA and protein; it has no DNA. And yet when that RNA is shot into the cells of the tobacco leaf, it produces not only replicas of itself but also new protein coats for the new virus, coats modeled to its own pattern and not the pattern of the invaded cell. Clearly RNA had a hand in the production of protein; it was, as one scientist said, "personally concerned" in the turning out of the all-important proteins.

The urgent effort to track the building of living matter had to turn to the DNA-RNA-protein relationship. DNA, with little question, was the master pattern. The evidence pointed to the likelihood that RNA was the negative, the mold from which unlimited copies might be produced. It was an understandable, sensible plan. No architect or manufacturer uses his master plan for actual construction. It must be protected and preserved. Therefore copies—or negatives or prints or molds, as the case may be—are made for production use.

If this was the case, RNA would have to be made in the nucleus by DNA and would have to move out to the surrounding precincts of the cell, where science had found most protein synthesis takes place.

"If the seat of genetic information is [in the nucleus] and the center of its expression is in the cytoplasm, associated with RNA, the picture must include a means of carrying information from nucleus to cytoplasm," said Daniel Mazia of the University of California.

Lester Goldstein and Walter Plaut, two post-doctoral fellows in the Mazia laboratory, set out to check the hypothesis—to discover the trail, if it existed.

The two young experimenters fed an Amoeba porteus with

[1] See Chapter XIII.

material labeled with radioactive carbon—carbon-14. In a
delicate operation they then transplanted the "hot" nucleus to
a "cold" amoeba. The amoeba was undisturbed by getting what
amounted to a new head and heart and went about its business quite normally.

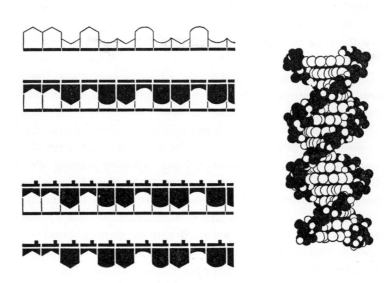

Synthesis of DNA *and* RNA. TOP LINES: *A single, diagrammatic
strand of* DNA *and complementary nucleotides assembled along it.*
BELOW: *By a similar process a strand of* DNA *might assemble one
of* RNA. RIGHT: *The assembled chain as it would look in a molecular model.*

Soon after the operation a few of the amoeba were squashed
under a thin sheet of film. The labeled RNA quickly produced
black spots on the film, and the black spots were concentrated
in the nucleus. It was, indeed, polka-dotted with the radioactive material. Sixty-two hours later other amoebas from the
labeled lot were flattened and placed under the revealing film.
By this time most of the labeled RNA had moved out of the
nucleus into the cytoplasm.

"Clearly," said Mazia, "the RNA label that was originally in the nucleus now appears in the cytoplasm. Subject to certain qualifications, the experiment proves the transfer of RNA from nucleus to cytoplasm."

Here was evidence of the very kind of RNA movement the hypothesis proposed.

Both RNA and protein were thus placed principally in the cytoplasm. The prickly problem then was how one produced the other.

In the late 1930's Albert Claude, who was working on virus-induced tumors at the Rockefeller Institute, found some "small particles" or "small granules" scattered in the cell. He later named them microsomes—"little bodies."

The newly discovered "little bodies" aroused considerable scientific curiosity. Before long it was established that they were largely made up of RNA and protein. More than this, both in the test tube and in Nature—in vitro and in vivo—they had the ability to incorporate amino acids; in other words, they could take up radioactive materials and use them in producing more protein. Did this mean that the microsomes were the site where proteins are produced?

Before much could be settled, there came another unusual report about hitherto unseen depths of the cell. The electron microscope revealed a lace-like network in the cytoplasm, an area that always before had appeared as structureless as a clear drop of jelly. Claude suggested that the network might have some relation to his little granules. But even with the electron microscope, trying to examine the microsomes or the network proved difficult and misleading.

This was the situation until the early 1950's. A succession of improvements in the preparation of material for the electron microscope then produced a "break-through." Exceedingly thin slices of material made it possible to see structures that never before had been visible. The rush to use the new technique was so great, however, that some time passed before the electron-microscopists could get around to the network and the "little bodies."

When they did, the lace-like network—now named the endoplasmic reticulum—turned out to be a system of "tubules and atoll-shaped sacs," all of them connected by more or less continuous canals.

The tubes and sacs were literally studded with little pellets. Sometimes waving arms almost covered with the tiny dark beads extended from the tubules. Great numbers of the beads drifted about freely.

George E. Palade of the laboratories of the Rockefeller Institute for Medical Research and Philip Siekevitz began a study of the newly found system and its parts. Working with beef liver, they identified the "little bodies"—the microsomes—as fragments of the network and the little beads dotting their surface or drifting about as a combination of RNA and protein.

Furthermore, they found the tiny pellets more active than their parent microsomes in the incorporation of amino acids. Also, activity was higher in the attached dark beads than in those floating freely about.

"According to current interpretations," said Palade, "this property [that of incorporating amino acids] indicates that the microsomes contain the sites of protein synthesis."

The general site of protein production, the fountainhead, had seemingly been found.

Additional evidence soon came from other laboratories that had entered the study of the promising pellets.

A group at the California Institute of Technology made up of Howard M. Dintzis, Henry Borsook, and Jerome Vinograd postulated that if the tiny beads and microsomes were the site of RNA synthesis, it should be possible to find out whether they were producing hemoglobin.

With the horrendous procedures of biochemistry, they whirled a sample of rabbit blood in their centrifuges, incubated it, laced it with ice-cold saline solution, centrifuged it again, froze it, and otherwise worked at it to separate the particles and to break them down.

In the little particles thus separated they found growing chains of hemoglobin—hemoglobin in the making, or pre-hemoglobin, as they called it. All of the particles were synthesizing it.

The California group pictured the particles as almost spherical, sponge-like structures with a molecular weight of about 4,000,000.[2] One half of the particle was made of RNA, "which appears to be present as four strands of molecular weight of 500,000." The other half turned out to be largely, though not entirely, "structural protein"—protein forming part of the structure of the particle. In the remainder of the particle they struck the biochemist's equivalent of gold—a small amount of "precursor" protein, or protein-to-be. Here was protein a-borning.

"Taken together with the observed rate of hemoglobin production," reported the scientists, "this amount of precursor protein is compatible with the conclusion that one microsomal particle makes one polypeptide chain of hemoglobin in approximately one minute."

Protein was not only being made in the RNA granules, it was being made in the required amounts—and rapidly.

And so it appeared that DNA, by means still unknown, impressed its unique pattern on RNA, and that RNA moved out into the cytoplasm, where it produced the proteins. The order of procedure had at last been discovered.

The structure of DNA and its encompassing of all the continuity and variety of life in its slender coil was perhaps the greatest of all the mysteries of life, but its general solution did not explain the second cardinal mystery. Nothing that was known could show how the only variable in DNA, the four

---

[2] The weight of any molecule is the sum of the weights of its constituent atoms.

bases or "steps" in the spiral staircase, could produce the twenty amino acids that in their turn formed the hundred thousand and more proteins and the limitless difference of the living world.[3]

Crick, who with Watson had developed the brilliant model of the DNA helix which had opened the whole perspective, had continued his study of how such a DNA could produce the highly specific proteins, the most essential of living materials. The theoretical chemists Leslie Orgel and John Griffith joined him in this study. As they worked, an answer occurred to them which was so clear and so elegant, that it recalled how Mendel had come upon the unfailing mathematical divisions of the hereditary units, those larger expressions of DNA.

It too was a mathematical answer. It was an answer that, given the postulates, could come out in only one way, as does the multiplication of two by two. It pointed to another triumph of numbers and precision in the formerly unpredictable and seemingly chaotic field of life.

Crick kept asking why there were only twenty universal amino acids. Why were no more than twenty amino acids produced by the varying sequences? [4]

"We asked ourselves how many amino acids we could code if we allowed all possible sequences of the four nucleotides of DNA," Crick explained.

To ask was to try. Taking it only as a mathematical problem, the three scientists began to experiment with how many combinations of three they could make out of four factors. The immediate answer was sixty-four—four times four times four. Obviously there were not sixty-four amino acids.

But RNA was not a chance line-up of units. The nucleotides —steps—were arranged in any one species in an unvarying

---

[3] A few other amino acids have been found. However, they occur only in special proteins, and some scientists contend that they arise through an abnormality. Only the twenty are universal.

[4] Each amino acid is made up of three nucleotides, or three of the steps in the DNA and RNA chains.

sequence—except in case of mutation. What kind of sequence was it?

Using the letters A, B, C, and D to represent the four bases of the four common nucleotides, the scientists set down an imaginary sequence:

B C A C D D A B A B D C

If a new chain were to be formed and new triplets were to fit to this imaginary sequence, where and how would they attach themselves? There were three possibilities to consider: the triplets might overlap, they might partially overlap, or they might not overlap at all, in the following way:

```
                        B  C  A  C  D  D  A  B  A  B  D  C
                        B  C  A
OVERLAP                    C  A  C
                             A  C  D
                                C  D  D
PARTIAL                 B  C  A
OVERLAP                      A  C  D
                                   D  D  A
                                      A  B  A
                        B  C  A
                             C  D  D
NO OVERLAP                         A  B  A
                                         B  D  C
```

The Cambridge group was convinced that there was no overlapping.

Another problem had to be faced. In their imaginary line-up of RNA—B C A C D D A B A B D C—which were the triplets? Did the line-up divide into BCA, CDD, ABA, BDC? Or was it -B, CAC, DDA, BAB, DC-? It was not enough that triplets be produced from the four factors—the four steps. The bases in the triplets had to be in precisely the right order—

thus BCA, and not another permutation of those three letters such as ABC or CAB.

Given these restrictions, the scientists asked again how many amino acids could be formed from the four nucleotides.

"We proved," said Crick, "that the upper limit is twenty, and moreover we could write down several codes which did in fact code for twenty things. One such code of twenty triplets written compactly is:

$$
A \quad B \quad {A \atop B} \qquad {A \atop B} \quad C \quad {A \atop {B \atop C}} \qquad {A \atop {B \atop C}} \quad D \quad {A \atop {B \atop {C \atop D}}}"
$$

If the triplets were ABA and ABB and so on, there would be no overlapping and each triplet would be the right one for the RNA into which it would have to fit.

Thus Crick, Griffith, and Orgel suggested an answer which predicted that there should be twenty kinds of amino acids in protein.

"We have deduced the magic number of twenty from the magic number of four," said Crick, using the word "magic" in the special sense of the theoretical atomic physicist. Nevertheless, in its ordinary meaning it conveyed the almost eerie working out and portent of the finding.

When this almost Mendelian solution of the basic replication of life was developed, there was no experimental proof of it. And biochemistry is a science that demands the most rigorous experimental backing. "Most biochemists, in spite of being rather fascinated by the problem, dislike arguments of this kind," Crick said. "It seems unfair to them to construct theories without adequate experimental facts."

Lacking experimental evidence, Crick, Orgel, and Griffith could only say of their illuminating theorem: "It may be complete nonsense, or it may be the heart of the matter. Only time will show."

The immediately pertinent problem was how RNA might

be built to permit such an assembly of the amino acids and
the proteins. At Harvard University, Benjamin Hall and Paul
Doty found evidence indicating that at least some RNA is a
single chain. Could there be little notches or cavities along its
length into which the nucleotides might push for assembly?

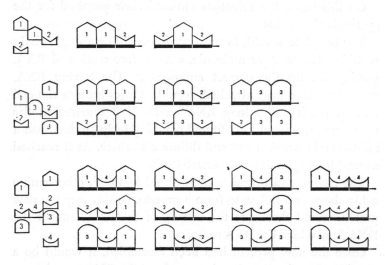

*Four into twenty. One code for the amino acids. Each triplet is a
combination of three of the four nucleotides. If each fits into exactly
the right place on the template RNA without overlapping, only
twenty amino acids—the universal twenty—can be made from the
four nucleotides or "steps" in the living staircase.* LEFT: *A short-
hand notation for the twenty triplets.*

Crick did some thinking about such a possibility, and concluded that it was unlikely. He suggested that the RNA must
consist of a series of sites to which the units for a new protein might be attached—perhaps something like a ship being
tied up to its dock.

If this were the case, how could the "right" triplets for the
assembling of a new chain be brought to the RNA assembly
line? The question was insistently put to the Cambridge scientists.

They suggested in answer that the triplets might be assembled and towed to the RNA template by an adapter molecule and that the adapter might consist of three of the four nucleotides, A, G, U, and C. In effect the Cambridge theorists were proposing sub-assemblies of the triplets.

On this basis, the scientists outlined their proposal for the synthesis of proteins:

The template would, in most cases, consist of a single chain of RNA. The adapter molecule, a small free section of RNA, would pick up the correct amino acid. The towing RNA, with the amino acid attached, would diffuse through the cell until it reached the long RNA chain. If it touched at the wrong point, it would not fit and would quickly (in less than a millisecond) break away and diffuse elsewhere. As it reached a matching triplet, it would attach itself.

The amino acid towed in then would join with other amino acids above and below to form a protein. In this way the new protein would duplicate the line-up of the RNA, and of the DNA from which the RNA came.

Once the new protein had been assembled, it would be a simple matter for it to break away from the RNA template or assembly line. And, once free, the protein could twist into a helix.

Crick warned that this theory would require two kinds of RNA in the cytoplasm: one the "template RNA," and the other a smaller moving piece of RNA. Time would show, Crick had said. He had no way of knowing how soon it would show.

At Harvard University, during the same time that Crick was working on his theory of the protein code, Mahlon B. Hoagland, Paul C. Zamecnik, Mary Louise Stephenson, and Jesse F. Scott were experimenting with amino acids and RNA.

"Quite by accident," said Hoagland, "we discovered that amino acids attach to RNA *before* they are linked together to form proteins.

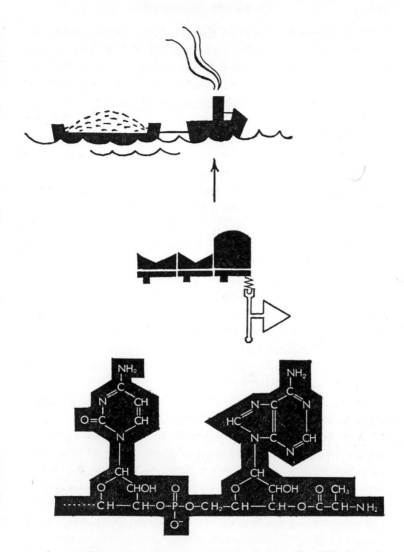

A sub-assembly and towing operation. An "adapter" molecule picks up the "right" amino acid (diagrammed as a triangle) and takes it in tow. The operation suggests a tow-boat in a busy harbor. At bottom is the formula of the last two nucleotides of the transfer RNA with the amino acid alanine attached.

"To our surprise the RNA that binds the amino acid turned out to be not the plentiful template material of the ribosomes [the RNA granules attached to the cytoplasm network] but a small chemical fraction of the soluble part of the cytoplasm."

The Harvard group eagerly followed up this interesting lead. In fact, the amino acids were assembled by the "soluble RNA," Crick's "adapter molecule" and the one that is now named "transfer RNA." Each adapter molecule or transfer RNA was made up of short sub-strings of the nucleotides. As it moved through the cell, it picked up its own amino acid. It then towed the amino acid to the long RNA string in the ribosome—that is, to the master template. "These reactions take place in the soluble fraction of the cell that bathes the ribosomes," said Hoagland.

The Harvard group was able to demonstrate the sub-assembly process in action. Soon after some small pieces of RNA had assembled their amino acids, the Harvard investigators stopped the action and separated the loaded transfer molecules from the other parts of the cell. Thus they obtained pure sub-assemblies, made up of the transfer molecules and their attached amino acids.

At this point the scientists tried a bold imitation of Nature. They incubated the sub-assemblies with a batch of template RNA. Promptly the amino acids disappeared from their conveyors and condensed with other amino acids to form new protein.

Nature's long-hidden process of assembling the amino acids prior to the formation of protein thus was re-enacted in the test tube. It was another of the dramatic experiments of science.

While the Harvard group was at work in this tracing of the course of protein synthesis, they learned that Crick had arrived at the same conclusions on theoretical grounds. "Here was one of those rare and exciting moments when theory and experiment snapped into soul-satisfying harmony," said Hoagland.

Additional evidence that one of the most basic processes of life had been deciphered piled up quickly. Many laboratories were working on "transfer RNA," and they found it in all kinds of cells, from those of bacteria to those of humans.

"We know now," said Hoagland, "that there is a separate transfer molecule for each amino acid."

The molecule was much larger than Crick had anticipated theoretically, but it seemed to perform the function he had proposed.

In the test tube the amino acids had gone from their conveyors to the finished protein state too rapidly for the scientists to "see" what was happening. Nevertheless, the final stage could be deduced.

Hoagland and his associates suggested that when the transfer RNA, towing its newly assembled amino acid, approached the RNA template, one end of the conveyor attached itself to a matching base on the template. If this was the case, the transfer molecule would have to "enter" the RNA granule (ribosome). Harvard experiments demonstrated that the conveyor did just this. As the conveyor hooked onto the template site, Hoagland suggested, the amino acid it was towing might project at right angles to the template.

The effect, as Crick and Hoagland diagrammed it, was one of so many tugs, each with a barge attached, nosed into the docks of their respective companies—say, the ABC Fruit Company, the DEF Oil Corporation, and GHI Sand Company. Thus, a row of barges would extend out into the water. If there was a standing order from some inland-waterway city for fruit, oil, and sand, it would be a simple matter to link up the three barges projecting out from the docks. They could be hooked into a new tow—a chain—and sent on their way. They would already be in the right order.

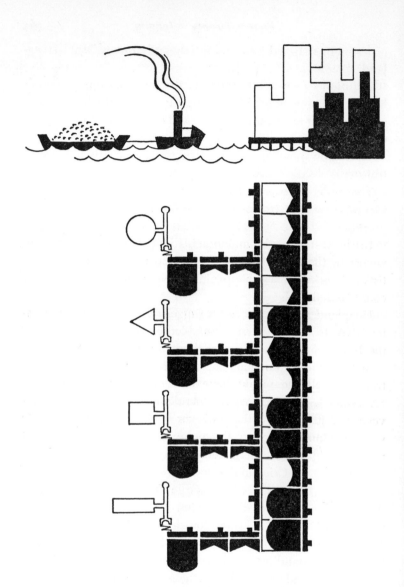

Final assembly line. The towing RNA *finds its proper place on the* RNA *assembly line or template. The triplets are moored at right angles to the "dock," and the amino acids are close enough to snap together and form a protein molecule. So, the model suggests, are proteins made.*

The tugs would then be free to set out again to pick up new loads of the products in which their companies dealt. The fruit tug of course would pick up only fruit, and the other two only sand and oil respectively.

Such a docking plan would produce a precisely ordered chain. A chain made up of fruit, oil, and sand barges would be a distinctive one, and if the barges were amino acids, a distinctive kind of protein. Another chain of gravel, cement, and sulphur barges would be another kind of tow entirely—another kind of protein.

"What distinguishes one protein molecule from another, giving it its marvelous uniqueness, is the number and kind of its amino-acid units and the order in which they are strung together," said Hoagland.

At last science could propose how this order and marvelous uniqueness are attained. It was a matter of four into triplets into twenty, and of an essentially simple sub-assembly and assembly.

And so the building of life was traced from its origin in DNA and RNA into the proteins. It was a clear, efficiently organized operation, but its perfection and significance were sheer magic.

NEW WORLD

A NEW WORLD was discovered in the 1950's.

Until it suddenly came into view with its elaborate structures, its great connective systems, and its complex organization, it had been as hidden from men as the reverse side of the moon.

But no banner lines in newspapers or broadcasts from the scene announced the finding of this world, though it was an eminently important one from the human standpoint, and full of curiosities.

This largely unheralded new world was a miniature one, a submicroscopic one. It was the inner world of the cell, and most particularly of the cytoplasm, the area that surrounds the nucleus.

From the time of Hooke, men had been training their microscopes on the cells that make up all living things.

The nucleus, the controlling center of the cell, was early identified, as was the centrosome—a sun-like body that splits and moves to opposite sides of the cell shortly before the chromosomes pull apart and the cell divides. The light microscopes also revealed some mysterious layered structures and some constantly moving blimp-like bodies, which were named mitochondria.

Then came the development of the electron microscope and the discovery of additional structures within the contained world of the cytoplasm of the cell. Enlargements 300,000 times life size, as compared to the 2,000-fold enlargements of the light microscope, disclosed the lace-like network of the cytoplasm and the beady pellets with which it is covered.[1] But still the cytoplasm of the cell resembled a clear lake in which a relatively few bodies were stationed or moved about. As no one could establish what these casual inclusions did, interest in them was limited.

This was the view of the cell until the break-through of the 1950's in microscope technique coincided with the development of new differential methods of breaking down the cell.

Suddenly then a new, highly organized intracellular world, almost as surprising as that of Leeuwenhoek, burst upon the startled eyes of the scientists.[2]

The clear, translucent lake turned out to be a densely, systematically built area. It was almost as though mists had rolled away and revealed, not a vacant new world, but a full-scale modern metropolis where there had been thought to be relative emptiness.

The supposedly empty or lightly populated cytoplasm was in fact as crowded as a modern city. There were structures everywhere. Some of them were large and semi-autonomous, like a city's skyscrapers, trade marts, and power plants—big aggregations designed to "facilitate, co-ordinate, and control the activity of their component parts." There were areas of specialization: a power center, a manufacturing center, an administrative or executive center—the latter, the nucleus with its DNA.

An elaborate system of canals connected many of the structures, and these thoroughfares teemed with as much activity as the streets of New York or Chicago.

This highly integrated cell-city-world was largely discovered by George E. Palade of the Rockefeller Institute for Medical Research and Fritiof Sjostrand of the Karolinska Institute of Stockholm, Sweden. The scientists not only uncovered this

---

[1] A fly enlarged 350,000 times would be about one and a half miles long.

[2] See Chapter V.

unsuspected metropolis, they photographed it for all to see. Seated at console-like desks and manipulating the controls of their giant electron microscopes much as an organist does his keys, they obtained pictures both of the handsomely patterned cytoplasmic universe and of the interior of some of its organs.[3] The sharply defined organs, the sweeping connections, and the pervasive network all stood forth in these striking photographs.

"What makes the cell complex," said Palade, "is the multitude of its parts and the limited space in which they must operate."

Palade was emphasizing what the new work had shown: the basic parts of the new-found metropolis are simple, mass-produced units turned out by the DNA-RNA-protein machinery. It is their numbers and the resulting congestion that necessitate organization and create complexity.

That there might be organs in the cytoplasm had not surprised science. On the other hand, it had not been anticipated that the parts of the cytoplasm might be integrated into an over-all system, a replica in miniature of the system so well known in the animal body as a whole—the linking of such organs as the heart, liver, and brain, and their functioning as a co-ordinated whole.

That would have been difficult to foresee. Some of the elements of the cytoplasmic system had not been discovered previously, and little was known even about the cell bodies that had been identified. What were their roles? What did they do in the terra incognita of the cytoplasm?

[3] The electron microscope is a highly intricate instrument. Its most immediately noticeable features are an upright seven-foot-long tube of polished steel and the console-type viewing desk. At the top of the tube is a tungsten filament, somewhat similar to the filament in a light bulb. When the tube is pumped to a vacuum, the filament heats and emits a stream of electrons moving at the speed of light. They are guided down to the specimen by magnets that act as lenses. The electrons pass through the specimen, as X rays do through flesh, and an image is produced. The image is enlarged and focused on a viewing screen and photographic plate.

For many years chemists had been breaking down the cell and trying to separate its parts. However, it was almost impossible to obtain a part free of all other material, and until pure parts were available, an investigator could not learn with any certainty what role a fraction might play.

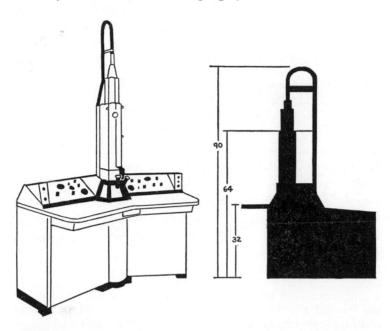

Electron microscope. It revealed long-hidden worlds.

It was sheer coincidence that a centrifuge which could separate the parts neatly, accurately, and without destruction was developed at about the same time as the new thin-slice electron-microscope techniques.

Cytologists—scientists specializing in the study of the cell—minced up bits of animal tissue and stirred them with a pestle until the tissues were broken apart and they had a mixture of the parts of the cell. The mixture was then placed in a centrifuge and whirled at high speeds. First the heavy red blood cells spun off and settled to the bottom of the tube. The remainder of the mixture was transferred to another tube and spun at still higher speeds. At such speeds the blimp-like structures called mitochondria were thrown off. At still higher speeds other parts were singled out. In this way the parts of the cell were separated according to their size and density.

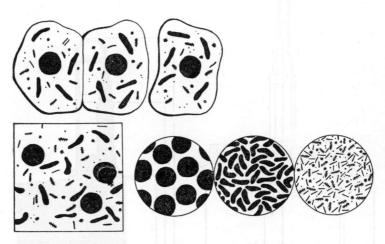

Separation. Intact cells are broken up, and the fragments put into a centrifuge. First the heavier particles, such as the round nuclei are whirled off. Then the blimp-shaped mitochondria. Then, at still higher speeds, the little microsomes or small bodies.

At last science had both pure, undamaged parts and photographs showing how they fitted into the cell. The way was open to determine what the minute bits did in the cell's economy.

Attention at once turned to the numerous and active bodies called mitochondria which appeared in the photographs and in the centrifuge tubes.

Late in the nineteenth century a German scientist, R. Altmann, had come upon some small oblong and spherical bodies in the cytoplasm of the cell. He became convinced that these "elementary granules" were autonomous organs which did much of the work of the cell, and to testify to their importance he named them bioblasts ("germs of life"). To his colleagues, who were unable to find these wondrous bodies, this was pretension. Altmann's bioblasts were ridiculed into oblivion.

There was real surprise when at the opening of this century a new dye, "Janus green," was applied to the cell, and the "bioblasts" Altmann had described stood forth in brilliant color. The little bodies, which often resembled a loaf of French bread, were then given the descriptive name of mitochondria ("granules and filaments"). Their size and diameter also were worked out, although no one could discover what they might do in the live cell. Interest in the little bodies again dwindled.

In the meantime, science was at work on another difficult and seemingly unrelated problem. It was a problem that had been of prime concern since Lavoisier discovered that animals take up oxygen from the air and use it to "consume" the foods they eat. Heat is created in the process, Lavoisier demonstrated, as it is when any substance is "burned." But this left unanswered a multitude of questions about where and how the "combustion" might occur.

Science soon learned that Lavoisier's combustion was a highly complex process—far more than a simple "burning" of foodstuffs. In the early years of the twentieth century the German chemist Franz Knoop suggested that the fatty acids —the products into which the ordinary fats of the foods are broken down—are "burned" by the removal of two carbon atoms at a time in a four-step process of "oxidation." [4]

[4] After our foods are first broken down by chewing, they are further broken down in the gastrointestinal track—the proteins into amino acids, the sugars and starches into pyruvic acid, and the fats into fatty acids. The foodstuffs are then carried by the blood stream to cells in all parts of the body. The cells select whatever materials they require.

At about the same time another German chemist, Otto Warburg, found that an iron-containing catalyst is necessary to "activate" ordinarily inert oxygen and bring it into the combustion process.

A third German scientist, Heinrich Wieland, came forth with proof that the critical step in the whole combustion process is not the oxidation, but the removal of hydrogen from the foodstuffs.

A lively controversy soon was waging over the issue, and not until the 1920's was it settled. In the latter part of the decade David Keilin of the University of Cambridge proved that all three men were partly right. In combustion, hydrogen has to be removed two atoms at a time, but to make this possible oxygen has to be used, and it must first be activated by a catalyst. The true essence of the system, as Keilin demonstrated in a series of illuminating experiments with the wing muscles of bees and moths, is the production and transfer of energy—the transfer of electrons from foodstuffs to oxygen and the liberation of their power for the work of the body.

Exactly how this was accomplished remained unknown. Laboratories all around the world went to work on what proved to be some of the most complicated, tortuous, and labyrinthine experiments in the history of science. They contributed substantially to biochemistry's reputation for being formidable. In the late 1940's, however, Hans A. Krebs, who had left Germany to become a professor of biochemistry at the University of Sheffield in England, worked out exactly what happens—the five steps, known as the citric-acid cycle, in which pyruvic acid, the breakdown product of the sugars and starches, is broken down into Lavoisier's carbon dioxide and water, and energy is steadily released.

During the same years Fritz A. Lipmann, who also had left Germany and was then professor of biochemistry at Harvard University, discovered another substance that played a critical role in the power production of the cell. He named it co-enzyme A, and it was isolated a few years later, in 1951, by Feodor Lynen of Germany.

For their working out of a "critical part of the basic life processes carried on by the cell," Krebs and Lipmann shared a Nobel Prize in 1953.

As the steps in combustion were laboriously and brilliantly established, it became clear that fats, as well as the sugars and starches, were turned into energy in the same way, in the same five-step cycle. Here truly were the processes by which the chemical energy of foods was transformed into the kind of energy that could be used by the animal cell.

"It is plausible," said Krebs, "that nature's mechanisms of converting one form of energy into another—like man-made machines—require energy in specific forms. The transformation of energy would thus proceed in two main steps; the first is the conversion of the chemical energy of a variety of sources into the chemical energy of an energy-rich phosphate bond; the second, the transformation of the phosphate-bond energy into other forms of energy, such as mechanical, osmotic, electrical, or chemical energy.

"In other words, the first stage is a unification of the great diversity of forms of chemical energy in the starting material, and one may look to the tricarboxylic cycle as one of the instruments used in the process of unification. The various foodstuffs yield the same two-carbon units, which are oxidized through a common mechanism."

One of the truly amazing powers of living material was at last being explained. Regardless of the kind of fuel food living creatures might eat—butter or blubber, candy or wild honey, the bread of a commercial bakery or the starch of the South Seas taro root—it is all changed into usable power by the combustion process of the body. It all becomes grist for the mill.

It's a very odd thing—
As odd as can be—
That whatever Miss T eats
Turns into Miss T.

So, perceptively and accurately, observed Walter de la Mare. The remarkable process could build up as well as consume. If there was an excess of fuels, they could equally well be turned into droplets of fat for storage and later use in case of a dearth of fuel. Through this system the human being could survive for as long as thirty days without food. In this respect, the processes that the biochemists elucidated proved far more effective than the gasoline engine, which burns essentially the same material—fatty acids and oils.

This, then, was the enormous complex of actions which occurred in the cell and produced the body's energy. Until the 1950's no one could say conclusively where in the cell these cycles, this manufacturing, this power production took place. The process had been figured out by extracting its products and investigating their workings. The power plant itself and its location still were unfound and unpictured.

Even lacking such essential information, science could approach the important problem of power production in other ways. And this it did.

A Russian scientist, V. A. Belitzer, and a Danish biochemist, Herman Kalckar, proved that the "burning" of foodstuffs is always accompanied by the conversion of (a)denosine (d)-(p)hosphate—ADP, a compound made up of two phosphate groups linked by oxygen atoms—to (a)denosine (t)ri(p)hosphate—ATP, a compound of three phosphate groups linked by atoms of oxygen. ATP, initials destined to become almost as famous and familiar as DNA and RNA, had long since been identified as the fuel produced by the combustion process. It is ATP that enables the muscles to contract, that supplies the energy for the manufacture of the proteins and all the other products of the body, and that otherwise powers all the actions of humans, animals, and microbes.

In 1945 David E. Green of the University of Wisconsin set out to isolate an enzyme that figured in power production. Green worked tirelessly to extract it from the kidney tissues of rabbits. No efforts availed; it was impossible to separate the enzyme from certain other particles in the cell.

"After many grueling months of utterly unsuccessful attempts to separate the dehydrogenase, it dawned upon me that all of these functions, including dehydrogenation, must be welded together in one giant organized unit—a mosaic of many enzymes," said Green.

Most striking was the fact that all of the enzymes needed for the important conversion of foodstuffs into energy were "packaged" in the particle in just the right proportions. "As far as anyone could tell," said Green, "there was no excess baggage. The case for the existence of an organized complex of enzymes —a new kind of unit—seemed overwhelming."

Chemistry had been proceeding on the theory that enzymes act individually or in chain reactions. The proposal of a mosaic kind of operation ran headlong into many accepted tenets.

While this dispute was still unsettled, Van Rensselaer Potter and Walter C. Schneider of the University of Wisconsin and Eugene P. Kennedy and Albert L. Lehninger of the University of Chicago centrifuged out some pure mitochondria—the mysterious little "blimps" of the cytoplasm.

With clear-cut mitchondria they could make the kind of tests required to demonstrate what the oblong little bodies do. The tests were clear-cut too. The long-neglected mitochondria, the seemingly incidental "blimps" shuttling around in the cytoplasm, could perform the whole complex of reactions required to convert foodstuffs into power—the very functions performed by Green's inseparable group of enzymes and the combustion processes described after years of the most laborious work by scores of investigators.

There could no longer be any doubt. The power plant of the cell and the mitochondria were one and the same! The seemingly aimless little bodies moving about in the cytoplasm were some of the body's most essential machinery. The seat of Lavoisier's combustion, of the combustion cycles of the German scientists and the Nobel Prize winners, and of Green's organized enzymes had at last been found. All the pieces of the puzzle fell into place. It was a remarkable convergence, and a new triumph of science.

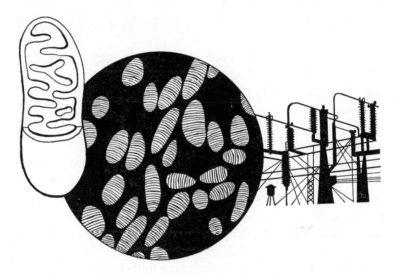

Power plants. CENTER: *Man's own power plants, the mitochondria.* LEFT: *Inside a mitochondrion. Here our energy is produced.* RIGHT: *A man-made power plant.*

"We can regard the mitochondrion as a machine whose function is to generate ATP [the power of the cell] by the oxidation of pyruvic acid," explained Green. "The fuel for the machine is derived from carbohydrates and fats; the furnace is the citric-acid cycle; the main product is ATP, and the by-products are carbon dioxide and water. The same basic mechanism exists in the cells of all organisms that require oxygen—animals, plants, and microbes."

The search for an understanding of how we convert foodstuffs into energy by the use of the oxygen we breathe thus shifted to the mitochondrion. The discovery of the power plant, the identification of its products and of what goes into their processing at each phase, and even the finding of the type of machinery used did not provide a picture or blueprint of the interior of the plant or of its particular machines and their functions. Essentially, science still was looking only at the outside of the plant and at the products that came from it. Much remained unknown.

Fortunately, the new cytological and microscopic techniques made it possible to look into the mitochondrion.

Science saw an outer membrane and, inside, a grid of tubular loops. Thin sections cut through the particle revealed masses of small but extremely dense bits circulating around the tubes—the tubes are called cristae, Latin for "ridges." Inside the loops, as in the center of the letter O, were layer upon layer of a less dense material. In all probability, the latter consisted of the enzymes whose banked occurrence inside the mitochondria had been demonstrated.

"Many experiments demonstrate that the functional units of the mitochondrion have a definite architecture," said Philip Siekevitz, one of the scientists studying the powerhouse of the cell.

Although the full interior was not yet visible and the processes could be only roughly assigned to the machinery in view, experiments also revealed that the outer wall of the "blimps" is semi-permeable, and that most of the energy manufactured within is shot out at once to power other activities of the cell.

In many cases the energy does not have far to go. Many of the cell-generating plants—the mitochondria—are situated very close to the consumers of their power. In muscle cells the mitochondria are clustered in rings around the part of the muscle fiber that actually contracts. In nerve cells they pack around the point at which two cells join, and where the energy of the nerve impulse is transferred. In such insects as the blow fly and the fruit fly, the mitochondria are so thick that they make up about one third of the muscles propelling the wings.

Other mitochondria keep in constant motion in the cytoplasm. The cytoplasm of some cells is literally polka-dotted with the circulating, elongated mitochondrial bodies.

Power production, it was clear, is very efficiently and strategically handled in the cell. As most of the power plants are clustered near the greatest users of power, the mobile mitochondria can easily carry power to all the other parts of the highly organized and densely built city that the cell cytoplasm is proving to be.

The new photographs also definitely located the major manufacturing center of the cell, its protein factories. Some of Palade's illuminating photographs showed that the beady little RNA pellets which may pick up three nucleotides, assemble them into an amino acid, and tow it to the larger RNA assembly line are so numerous and ever present that they suggest the stars in some pictures of the skies. They also showed the granules—the microsomes—in which the RNA assembly line links the newly arrived amino acids into proteins. Palade found strong indications that both pellets and granules—sub-assembly line and full-assembly lines—are fragments of the over-all cytoplasmic network.

"It is evident," said Palade, "that in the case of the endoplasmic reticulum [network] we are dealing with a system of unsuspected complexity that permeates the entire cytoplasm of the cell, and as such can be compared to an intra-cellular vascular system.

"There are no demonstrated functional properties for the entire system, but its layout suggests that it may function as a combination apparatus for separating various substances, facilitating diffusion, importing and exporting matter."

Exactly how this world of the cytoplasm is built by DNA and RNA, those determiners of all cellular order and form, was another matter, a matter for the future. However, there was no doubt that its framework and its building materials were mostly proteins.

"We have come a long way since the cell was considered a bag of loose substances, freely integrating with one another," Siekevitz reflected. "The cell, like the mitochondrion, has a rigorous and compartmented organization. Perhaps this is not surprising. When we build a factory, we do not park its raw materials and machines at random. We arrange matters so that the raw materials are brought near the appropriate machines, and the product of each machine is efficiently passed along to the next. Nature has surely done the same in the living cell."

And so it was in the "city-world" revealed by the microscope and centrifuge. Here were many great structures, some of them as highly organized as the power plants, factories, and skyscrapers of any metropolis, and the whole functioning as closely together, as interdependently, as a city. It was an astonishing world to have appeared in what had once been considered a clear, island-dotted lake. Perhaps time would mark its discovery as one of the great explorations, even in an era that first saw the far side of the moon and aimed its rockets for the stars.

CELLS INTO TISSUES

Each of the 1,000,000,000,000,000 cells in the body of John Jones could potentially produce another John Jones.

At least, each of the billions of Jones cells has a full set of the master plans—the DNA—for Jones, six feet tall, size eleven foot, brown hair, Phi Beta Kappa brain. Each has a full set of the working prints—RNA. Furthermore, each cell has machinery produced by DNA and RNA for turning out the specific building blocks—the proteins—and the power needed for the construction of this one man. Each tiny cell is fully and marvelously equipped.

Of course, each cell does not produce a full human being. Only the first cell normally does that. And probably only the first four cells into which the fertilized egg cell divides could undertake that full task. Many years ago Driesch demonstrated that any one of the first four cells into which the egg of the sea-urchin divides can produce a full, though small, being. In later stages no animal cell, regardless of its potentialities and equipment, has manifested the ability to produce a replica of the organism to which it belongs.

After the first four of the 1,000,000,000,000,000 cells of the adult are formed, a specialization begins. The cells begin to take on different sizes and shapes—nerve cells, liver cells, bone cells, muscle cells, skin cells, brain cells. They coalesce into tissues and organs, and the whole into a distinctive, synchronized human being.

This marvel of an organized multitude growing from one has enthralled the imagination of men from the earliest times. Aristotle argued that the organs, the heart, the brain, the eye are developed successively, "as we read in the poems of Orpheus, where he says that the process by which an animal is formed resembles the plaiting of a net." Epicurus disputed this claim of the successive forming of living matter. Man, he held, must be completely formed in the first cell.

"In the seed are enclosed all the parts of the body of the men that shall be formed," said Seneca. And some of the early microscopists were sure that they saw a miniature man imprinted on the sperm cell.

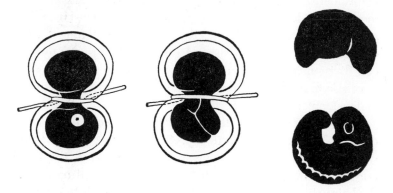

Halves into wholes. In the famous Spemann experiment a sala-mander egg is tied across the "gray crescent" and squeezed into two halves. At first only the half containing the nucleus begins to divide. RIGHT: *The other half also divides and forms a whole embryo. The latter is younger than the embryo from the first half.*

Driesch, one of the first to study the actual miracle of development, was so overwhelmed that he retreated for explanation to a mysterious, vital, non-material force.

But the age-old question could not rest there. While Driesch was still engaged in his work, a young zoologist at the University of Wurzburg, Hans Spemann, began to experiment with the eggs of newts. In their development the eggs of the small lizard-like animals closely followed that of the other verte-brates, including man.

Spemann saw that immediately after fertilization a small gray crescent appeared on the surface of the newt's egg. It seemed to be the first evidence of profound changes going on in the fertilized egg. What would happen to development, Spemann asked, if the egg was constricted in the crescent area just before the first cleavage took place?

The scientist procured a very fine strand of baby hair, made a loop, and slipped it over the middle of the egg. He drew it tight enough to leave only an "isthmus" connecting the two hemispheres into which the egg bulged. Despite this mistreatment, the side of the egg containing the nucleus began to segment. It split into two cells and then into four, before enough nuclear material slipped through the isthmus to start cell division in the second half. Each hemisphere ultimately gave rise to a normal embryo, though the second was younger in development than the first.

The loop constricting the egg had run through the "gray crescent," dividing it vertically. Spemann inevitably asked what would happen if the egg were divided across the "gray crescent" rather than through it. Again he slipped on one of the hair nooses. Both hemispheres divided, but this time with a startling difference. One half produced a normal embryo; the other only a mass of liver, lung, and abdominal cells. Spemann called the shapeless mass *Bauchstück*—"belly piece."

Spemann repeated the experiments, and always with the same results. It was not a matter of nuclear material, for the nuclear material eventually moved through the isthmus and there was division of cells on both sides. The difference apparently lay in the kind of crescent substance the various parts had received. The crescent looked significant.

Spemann began a thorough study of the area. It was in the crescent area that the "crater" first appeared in the hollow ball of cells formed by the segmentation of the egg, and it was here that the cells first tumbled inward, as Roux and Driesch had

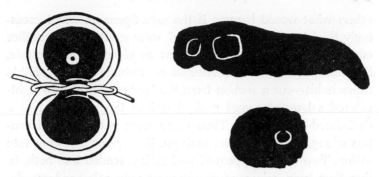

A second classic Spemann experiment. The salamander egg is tied parallel to the "gray crescent." The half with the nucleus develops into a normal embryo. The other half forms a shapeless, unorganized "belly piece."

observed.[1] Spemann watched the cells on the inner lining of what became a big crater change their form and size and gradually coalesce into bones, cartilage, muscle, and blood. The cells in the hollow of the crater altered in other ways and grouped themselves into stomach, liver, intestines, and the other abdominal organs. The cells that remained on the outside of the ball underwent an equally marvelous transformation, turning into skin, nerves, brain, eyes, ears, and the other sensory organs. It seemed to Spemann that the crescent area had set off the whole fateful train of events.

Spemann was a scientist who put every point to the test of experiment. From one embryo he cut a slice of the area destined to become belly; from another, a bit of tissue that would become brain. He then exchanged the two. Both grafts grew, and with results surprising even to the man who designed the experiment. The transplanted flank turned into brain, and the brain graft into belly skin!

The strange success of the experiment suggested still an-

[1] See Chapter VIII.

other: what would happen if the area Spemann was increasingly thinking of as the "inducer" were grafted into another embryo? To make the experiment as clear-cut as possible, Spemann—with the assistance of a graduate student, Hilde Proescholdt—cut a section from the "inducer" area of a light-colored salamander and grafted it into the belly area of a dark–hued salamander. Thus there were two potential centers of organization in one embryo. Both promptly went into action. Two craters appeared, and cells cascaded into both. In due time twin salamanders—Siamese-twin salamanders—developed. The implanted salamander had some dark and some light tissues and organs. Spemann concluded that the transplanted section had transferred its organizing power to its host embryo. It "induced" the surrounding cells to form a second embryo. Spemann named the bit of tissue which induced this extraordinary development "the organizer."

Perhaps, then, the specialization of cells could be explained as an action of a special group of cells. For the formation of an organism as complex as a human being, Spemann assumed that a number of "organizers" would be necessary.

For this remarkable work—"the discovery of the organizer effect in embryonic development"—Spemann received the Nobel Prize in 1935.

But what was this "organizer," this group of cells which seemingly could produce natural order from a random collection of cells? The first idea was that it achieved its effects by setting the cells in motion as they plunged over the lip of the crater. But it was soon learned that the same effects were achieved when there was no motion. The theory was then advanced that the organizer must emit some chemical that could induce other cells to produce special structures.

C. H. Waddington, then at Cambridge, and Johannes Holtfreter, a German scientist who had studied under Spemann, both discovered at about the same time that the "organizer" could induce development even after it had been killed in alcohol. This was an unexpected outcome. A dead bit of tissue had produced the same effect as the live.

At this point of confusion Waddington applied a little synthetic blue dye to the dividing cells of a salamander embryo, and even the dye induced the formation of new nerve tissue. Confusion was compounded. Seemingly, development could be initiated by almost any impulse.

The organizer theory was further upset by a frog-salamander experiment made by Oscar E. Schotté, professor of biology at Amherst College and a former student of Spemann's. Schotté cut a bit of pre-belly-skin tissue from a frog and transferred it to the mouth region of a salamander embryo. As the salamander grew, it developed, not a salamander mouth with teeth and balancers on either side, but a typical tadpole mouth with horny jaws and suckers at either side. The salamander, in short, had a frog mouth. A fantastic composite animal had been produced.

Upon the basis of such living evidence, science had to face the fact that the frog cells were acting on some blueprints of

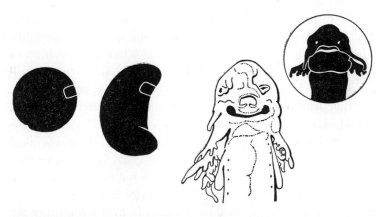

Transplantation. A bit of tissue from the frog pre-embryo is transplanted to the mouth area of a salamander embryo. Result: a salamander with a frog's horny mouth. IN CIRCLE: *Normal salamander mouth.*

their own, rather than on directions from a salamander organizer.

Other evidence pointed in the same direction. In addition, the new work with DNA-RNA and proteins was casting the whole problem into different terms. Spemann did not know when he was operating so delicately on newts and salamanders that each cell carries a complete master plan for the whole individual and for all the specialized proteins needed to produce a newt or salamander or human. Brilliant work had been done and much had been learned about how cells and tissues differentiate, though the basic problem was far from solution. A new approach would have to be made.

A new problem, or an old one in a newly acute form, constantly badgered scientists working with the exquisitely intricate question of how one kind of cell produces many kinds of cells. If a cell could produce, say, a head and foot, why in certain circumstances did it produce a head and not a foot? S. Meryl Rose of the University of Illinois was one of those who went to work on the difficult matter.

"First," said Rose, "we assume that each cell in a developing embryo or regenerating bud has a complete file of blueprints. Then we suppose that a given cell begins to use a given set of blueprints—let us stretch our analogy and say that the cell follows the blueprints filed under A. To put it another way, the blueprints filed under A direct the cell to perform certain chemical reactions.

"Now let us suppose that the products of these chemical reactions enter adjacent cells and prevent them from using their blueprints filed under A. The cells have no choice but to follow another set of blueprints, let us say the blueprints filed under B. Thus they have differentiated from the cell using the blueprints filed under A.

"What is more, the cells using the blueprints filed under B will influence still other cells, causing them to differentiate by acting on the blueprints filed under C. So it would go until all the different parts of an organism were brought into being."

To illustrate the theory, Rose cited the work of Martin Luscher, Swiss zoologist, on termites. Luscher found that unspecialized "nymphs" can develop into the more specialized termite castes—king, queen, and soldiers—if the higher ranks are not filled. They did so when he removed the king and queen. But if there was no vacancy in the specialized ranks, the nymphs did not change. "In the beginning," said Rose, "a termite or a cell has many pathways of differentiation open to it, but as others achieve caste status the open pathways become fewer and fewer."

Another experiment had demonstrated that when the embryo area that develops into the notochord—the equivalent of the backbone of higher animals—is removed, nearby cells flow into the deprived area and ultimately produce a new notochord. "According to this view," said Rose, "a cell adjacent to developing notochord becomes a muscle cell, not because its notochord neighbors say 'Form muscle,' but because they say 'Don't form notochord.'" When the "don't" order was lifted and the way was clear, they formed notochord.

Essentially, Rose was suggesting that the differentiation of cells is controlled by a feed-back system. This is the familiar system under which part of a product produced is fed back into the system to control it. It is in use in countless factories.

Rose planned a series of experiments to find out whether this could be the long-hidden system of the cell. He first cultivated frog eggs in a solution of brain materials. This was drastic treatment, and many did not grow at all. Of those which did develop, most either had no brain or produced a defective one quite late in the process of growth. Eggs cultured with heart solutions had no hearts, and the embryos from eggs raised in diluted blood lacked blood or did not produce it in the normal time. When a solution of organ material was present, a new organ was not produced, even when it was such a prime one as the heart or brain. And the phenomenon proved to be a general one.

It is the rule in plants as well as in animals. As long as there is a growing tip on a stem, other tips do not appear. Rose argued that their development is inhibited. But pinch off the tip, and new tips will grow from other points on the stem. The capacity clearly is there; it merely is not used so long as there is a growing tip at the end of the stem or elsewhere.

"Like normally inhibits potential like," Rose summed up.

Assuming that this was the explanation of why a cell capable of producing any or all of the cells of the body actually produces only one special kind, it still did not explain why particular organs develop in particular places.

Rose, like many of the nation's biologists, goes each summer to the marine biological station at Woods Hole. Each summer the waters there abound in Tubularia, a marine animal with a flower-like head growing upon a stalk. Any piece of the stalk, when cut from the plant, will give rise in about two days to a new head—called a hydranth. But when a stalk was crowned with a daisy-like hydranth, it did not develop new heads—it did not turn into a multi-headed monster.

Rose cut pieces of stalk from red and yellow Tubularias and grafted them together, the rear end of one to the front end of the other. In this unusual situation the front red piece of stalk soon produced one of the usual graceful heads. The rear yellow piece reverted to stalk.

"The rule is that any section of stalk will make that part of the organism which is farthest front, except when the part has already been made," said Rose.

Additional experiments demonstrated that Tubularia is affected only by what is in front of it. It does not "look behind." And so it appeared that development is controlled not only by what has been made, but also by position.

Pursuing this interesting point, Rose grafted the front end of one section of stalk to the front end of another piece of stalk in an experimental version of a head-on collision. The result was that two flower heads formed face to face. Again there was proof that the inhibitory effect is exerted only from front to rear. Rose pointed out that the system of growth in Tubularia is highly polarized.

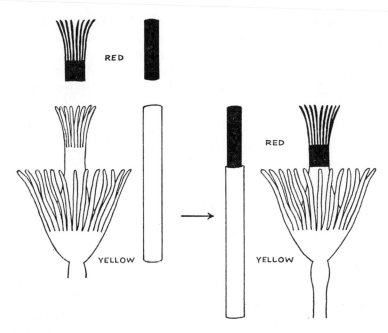

The way ahead. A yellow Tubularia produces its normal double yellow head or hydranth until the tip of a red plant is grafted to it. With this change in signals, the yellow tubularia produces only the parts behind the tip. It no longer makes a tip.

Rose's answer to the pressing question of how cells differentiate—of how muscle and brain and hair cells arise from the one original cell—was a direct one: cells receive a certain kind of architectural information which causes them to use certain blueprints from the whole set of blueprints with which they are equipped.

The Illinois scientist was not speaking in terms of DNA and RNA, but he was coming close to it. His work suggested that the RNA coils busily turning out protein building materials might receive information that would lead them to produce the particular proteins needed—those required for structures not already built.

Again the proposed system, this invisible system of Nature, had a familiar sound. If there is no market for one particular product, an efficient factory shifts to the production of another of its lines. Production is controlled by requirements. The factory does not go on making something for which all requirements have been fulfilled. Possibly RNA did not so do either, and perhaps by turning out proteins for which there was a place, the astoundingly efficient RNA coil might account for the almost miraculous differentiation of living material.

The tubular, the fibrous, the globular proteins and all the other proteins produced by the RNA factories do not long remain single molecules. They soon form tissues and organs, both of which are made up of thousands upon thousands of molecules.

In the great attempt to piece together the story of life, to trace the up-building of the whole complex living world from the minute coils of DNA and RNA, science thus arrived at the point where cells—molecules—unite into tissues. The tissues that Bichat found in all the organs of the human body had been one of the first milestones on the road down to the core, to the base of bases of life.[2]

Until the 1950's, though, the base had not been reached. Science could not begin the formidable step-by-step task of putting Humpty Dumpty together again. Today the work is only getting under way.

As scientists were still unable to proceed upward as Nature must proceed upward in the building of a living animal or plant or micro-organism, the only hope of finding how the

[2] See Chapter III.

tissues are formed was to take them apart and try to put them together again. Until very recently it was a matter of taking the tissues apart. Few were so sanguine as to hope that they could be reassembled.

At the beginning of this century, however, one scientist found a new way to break tissues down into their component cells. Henry V. Wilson of the University of North Carolina was studying the growth and regeneration of sponges. No matter how small the pieces into which he cut a sponge, each could produce a new sponge. Wilson wondered what would happen if the sponge were disassociated into the single cells of which it is made. He hit upon the idea of pressing live sponges through a closely woven cloth. That very effectively broke them down into the single cells he wanted. The division did not deter the sponge. To Wilson's amazement, the single cells began to form little clusters, and in a very short time the little clusters turned into new, fully grown sponges. The experiment, in truth, was a classic one, but most biologists assumed that sponges were a special case. They are more like colonies of cells than a true multi-celled organism. It was largely taken for granted that a more complex, multi-celled organism could not be similarly taken apart and re-grown.

Not until the 1940's did Johannes Holtfreter, who had come to the United States and was teaching at the University of Rochester, demonstrate that the assumption was unfounded. Holtfreter broke down the tissues of young amphibian embryos by treating them with a mild alkali. He stirred the mass of cells he obtained into an indiscriminate mixture. Despite this mixing, the cells began to come together and soon had re-formed the kinds of tissue from which they came. It was almost uncanny.

Science had learned by this time how to grow tissues outside the living body. This offered an opportunity to study human and other animal tissues. To take them apart, however, required finesse, for they were cemented together by "mucoproteins." In 1952 A. A. Moscona, an Israeli working at the University of Cambridge and the University of Chicago, treated some embryonic chick and mouse tissues to remove the calcium in the cement, and placed them in a solution of trypsin, the familiar enzyme of the pancreas. The enzyme completed the dissolution of the cement, and the cells fell apart. "In place of compact, highly organized tissues, there were now scattered, individual, living cells," said Moscona.

The cells from the chick and the mouse behaved very much as had the amphibian cells. At first they moved actively about on the bottom of the culture vessel. All the while they were laying down a delicate film. Within twenty-four hours a few similar cells came together in little clumps. And then came a startling development: the cells within the clusters arranged themselves into definite tissue patterns. Kidney cells formed tubules and soon displayed secretory activity. Liver cells formed globules resembling those of the intact organ and began to accumulate glycogen; heart cells coalesced into "rythmically contracting" tissue. Moscona saw tissue being made.

Paul A. Weiss of the Rockefeller Institute decided to put this remarkable creation of order from randomness to an even more severe test. He mixed together dissociated cells from the skin tissue, the limb-bud cartilage, and the eyeball coating of a chick embryo. Another spectacle was enacted. Clumps formed in which each of the three types of cell coalesced with its own kind.

The limb-bud cells then went on to form bone, the eyeball cells to produce new eyeball coating, and, most astounding of all, the skin tissue began to put out the beginnings of feathers.

"These experiments imply that a random assortment of cells which have never been part of any adult tissue can set up conditions—a field, I call it—which will cause members of the cell group to move and grow in concert, following the pattern of a feather in one case, of an eye in another, and of a bone in still another," said Weiss.

Weiss found the same production of order from chaos at the subcellular level. He made a small cut in the skin of a salamander and watched carefully to see what would happen. At first the wound filled with a mucus-like substance. While new skin formed, tiny fibrils appeared in the cavity. At first they went helter-skelter in every direction, but soon Weiss saw them stacking up in an orderly crisscross. "The underlayer of connective tissue cells produced the fibrils, organizing them out of molecules, while the overlying layer of skin cells organized them into a subcellular construction," Weiss reported.

This extraordinary joining of like with like suggested that certain properties of each cell must serve as cues to others of the same kind. The data, however, were not sufficient to justify so broad a conclusion. An experiment was needed to track the cells and test their attraction for one another.

Moscona designed such an experiment. He mixed dissociated cartilage-forming cells from a mouse and a chick. A fine point was raised. Would the cells coalesce according to animal or organ? Moscona was soon to see. Cartilage cells clumped together. Cartilage cells went with cartilage cells, whether they came from chick or mouse. The separation was according to type and not according to species.

"Intermingled chick and mouse cartilage-forming cells produced a common mosaic cartilage," Moscona said. "Within it cells of both species were equally dispersed and closely bound by a common matrix, in a manner typical for this tissue."

The outcome of the strange experiment opened the possibility of another. What would happen if cells from different organs and different animals were mixed? Moscona prepared and mixed mouse cartilage cells and chick kidney-forming cells. There was no hesitation in the test vessel. The mouse cells grouped together to form cartilage and the chick cells coalesced into kidney tubules. A composite tissue with mouse cartilage lying alongside chick tubules resulted.

Another clue to growth as well as tissue formation came from still another experiment. It had been found that a young kidney-forming rudiment of a mouse embryo would not develop when it was isolated in a tissue culture, but that tubules would form if a little spinal-cord tissue was added. Clifford Grobstein, now of Stanford University, tried a further experiment. He put together dissociated mouse kidney cells with cells

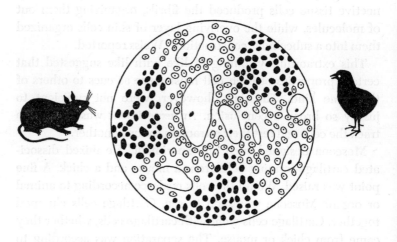

Each to its own type. When dissociated mouse cartilage cells and chick kidney-forming cells are freely intermingled, the darker-staining mouse cells group together to form cartilage, and the chick cells become organized in tubules.

from chick spinal-cord tissue. The cells sorted themselves out, and the chick cells stimulated the mouse kidney cells to form tubules.

These were embryologists and biologists trying to solve the ancient problem of cell differentiation and tissue growth. They were putting their questions to living tissues and to whole cells. The biochemists, all the while, were working with the basic chemical and physical actions that determine the shape and action of living matter.

The data of the biologists were not at first translated into terms of DNA-RNA and protein-power reactions of the cell, and the material of the biochemists was not immediately transposed into terms of cell structure. But the newer experiments and discoveries constantly brought the two closer.

SZENT-GYÖRGYI AND THE HUXLEYS: SLIDING COILS

Our nature is movement. Absolute stillness is death.   Pascal

For centuries men had marveled at motion: the human's walk, the flight of the bird, the run of the animal, and the swift glide of the fish through the density of water; at its strength, the lifting power of an Atlas or the rush of a bull; at its speed, the blink of an eye or the sonic flutter of the hummingbird's wings; and at motion unseen but felt, the beat of the heart or the contraction of a hungry stomach.

All of it, the swift, the powerful, the voluntary, the involuntary, was effected through the muscles.

But how? This most persistent and inescapable of questions pressed hard in a world where a momentary failure of muscle —that of the heart—meant death. How could the muscles, small masses of a pinkish jelly, suddenly grow hard and move a thousand times their own weight and do it several hundred times a second? How could they keep life in motion?

The question carried to the basic principles of life. Clearly, it could not be fully answered without reaching down to the primary organization of living matter, to fundamental architecture and energy production. Until the 1950's there was no possibility of finding the answer by building up from that starting point of life, DNA, and its production and organization of the materials that constitute the muscles.

Few problems in the history of science were more difficult. It was remarkable, therefore, that the discovery of the principle of motion, of the action that enables living things to move and stay alive, came in the decade that also brought the identification of DNA as the beginning and pattern of life, the synthesis of DNA and RNA, the discovery of the coiled structure of proteins and of the protein code, and the finding of the organized world of the cell's cytoplasm.

It was remarkable too that the discovery of how muscle works was made almost simultaneously by two men, and by two men who bear the same famous name, although they are not related.

Early studies of muscle and movement disclosed that the jelly-like muscles are made up of tiny fibers. The little threads are just visible to the naked eye. It could also be seen that the muscles which move the arms and legs and the body generally are "striated"—they are striped in wide and narrow bands as distinctive as the familiar pattern called Roman stripes. In contrast, the muscles of the stomach and other organs are "smooth" or unstriped.

Striped or smooth, all brought the body into motion by contracting, a process in which they grew hard and changed their shape.

By means of the microscope, science found that the visible fibers are composed of bundles of still finer fibers called fibrils. The fibers that could be seen contracted only because the fibrils of which they are made contracted first. It was the old story of research in the mazes of the living body: the effective cause always lay deeper still.

Unquestionably, it lay deeper than the fibrils. At this point, however, science was blocked. The best of microscopes could penetrate no further.

When science is halted in one approach, it tries another. Many laboratories went to work to discover the secrets of muscle by ferreting out the chemical reactions that produce its actions, and by studying its use of the fabulous power sources of the cell, ATP.

Albert Szent-Györgyi, a Hungarian-born scientist who won a Nobel Prize in 1937 for his discovery and separation of Vitamin C, turned to the study of how and why muscle contracts. What is it that contracts, what produces this phenomenon, "one of the most wonderful of the biological kingdom"? Szent-Györgyi asked.

For almost a hundred years muscle had been extracted and made into fibers. But the fibers then were inert; they would no more contract than would an ordinary piece of string.

Szent-Györgyi began by repeating the old experiments. Then he modified the extraction procedures and obtained a thicker, more viscous extract of muscle. Threads were prepared from this material, and the scientist suspended them in a boiled juice he had obtained from muscle. Suddenly there was a violent contraction in the test tube. For the first time muscle was contracting outside a living body. Fine measurements showed that it could have lifted a thousand times its own weight, exactly as natural muscle can.

The concentrated solution had contained many materials. The immediate question that faced Szent-Györgyi was which one of them had caused the fibers to grow hard and contract. Using what he described as a little "scientific cookery," the scientist traced the active agent down to two substances, ATP and potassium ions. They were the instigators of the action. The finding was doubly significant. It proved, Szent-Györgyi pointed out, that ATP makes muscle contract as well as supplying it with the energy for contraction.

"No other substance will serve," said the scientist. "ATP is the cogwheel in the mechanism of contraction, and without it no contraction occurs."

The work showed that the powerful ATP accounts too for the elasticity of muscle. A strip of muscle removed immediately after a rabbit is killed is soft and stretchable. A few hours later, when the ATP has started to decompose, the muscle becomes hard and inelastic. It will break then, as a piece of hardened rubber will. This, the scientist saw, is what happens when rigor mortis sets in. With the supply of ATP exhausted and no new ATP coming in, the muscles "freeze." In rabbit muscles Szent-Györgyi could defer rigor mortis by supplying additional ATP to the separated muscle.

The scientist's next step was to break muscle down into its molecules. Two proteins were obtained: the well-known myosin and another, which was named actin. The two made up most of the solid stuff of muscles; and yet, try as he would, St. Györgyi could not induce either of them to contract separately. It was a startling and upsetting finding. The elemental substances of muscle were not stretchable.

In this strange situation Szent-Györgyi mixed some amounts of the two proteins together in an experiment that has become famous. Together the two did what neither would do separately. They contracted vigorously.

"It is the complex," said Szent-Györgyi, "that has the contractility of muscle. Seeing actomyosin contract for the first time was one of the most exciting experiences of [my] scientific career."

"One of the most mysterious manifestations of life" had been reproduced in the laboratory. The year was 1943.

Somehow the combination of actin, myosin, and ATP produced the motion of the living world. New possibilities opened, and new problems, for the "somehow" had to be solved, and yet could not be solved until it was known how actin and myosin combine in living structures to effect their swift and powerful results.

Many theories were formed. One which was widely held suggested that the actomyosin threads might fold and contract. The proposal seemed plausible.

At about this time the electron microscope began to break through the former barriers to vision. Photographs made by a team at the Massachusetts Institute of Technology, C. A. Hall, Marie A. Jacus, and F. O. Schmitt, revealed what no one had been able to see before. The fibrils were made of still finer threads. Thus, the visible fibers were composed of fibrils that were composed of the newly discovered still finer threads that the scientists named filaments.

The real break-through, however, did not come until the 1950's. H. E. Huxley, a young English scientist who was spending a year at the Massachusetts Institute of Technology, and A. F. Huxley of the University of Cambridge began at that time a direct effort to penetrate to the basic structure of muscle. The new techniques held out the possibility of seeing the inmost structure.

A. F. (Andrew Fielding) Huxley is the grandson of T. H. Huxley, the noted biologist and the great defender of Charles Darwin. He is also a half-brother of Sir Julian and Aldous Huxley. He is both director of studies at Trinity College, Cambridge, and assistant director of research in physiology.

H. E. Huxley, also a graduate of Cambridge, is not related to the other Huxley family. Following the completion of his fellowship work at M.I.T., he returned to Cambridge, and in 1956 joined the staff of University College, London.

H. E. Huxley, working with Jean Hanson, began to prepare muscle for the microscope by treating it with chemicals to preserve its structure. He then "stained" it with a heavy metal —this would improve its visibility in the electron microscope— and placed it in a solution of plastic. The plastic penetrated the entire muscular structure and, when it solidified, turned the muscle into a hard, solid block that could be cut into extremely thin slices. Huxley put one of the thin sections into the electron microscope.

An extraordinary sight flashed into view—the fibers of muscle were arranged in a handsome, patterned, undreamed-of order. Muscle resembled a fine hand-woven piece of fabric. And the fibrils were made up not of one kind of finer thread, but of two. One was twice as thick as the other.

The two kinds of thread formed the warp, the lengthwise

threads of the fabric. All of this was plainly visible, as easily distinguishable as a thick cord and a thin thread would be to the naked eye in a loosely woven piece of upholstery material.

In the psoas muscle from the back of a rabbit, the thicker filaments were about 100 angstroms (an angstrom is one hundred-millionth of a centimeter) in diameter and 1.5 microns in length (a micron is a thousandth of a millimeter). The thinner filaments were about fifty angstroms wide and about two microns long. The two lay alongside—a thick filament and

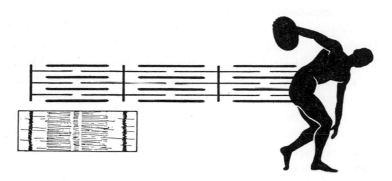

The thick and thin of muscle. The overlapping of the thick and thin filaments accounts for the striped appearance of muscle (box), and ultimately for its power—the discus thrower.

then a thin, a thick and a thin. (Hold the hands parallel with thumbs up and slip the fingers in between one another. Although the fingers are more of a size than the filaments, the general effect can be visualized.)

Lengthwise, along the warp, the arrangement of the filaments was as important as their length. The ends of the thick threads extended beyond the ends of the thin ones. Thus, one sequence was set "in" and one "out," one "in" and one "out." (Slide one index finger alongside the other as far as the first joint. Let the middle finger lie alongside at its full length, or so that it reaches the second joint. Imagine that this in-and-out pattern is repeated.)

As Huxley and Hanson looked at the enlightening microscopic photographs, they saw immediately why muscle looks striated. The dark bands were created where thick and thin filaments lay alongside. The light-toned bands on either side appeared where there were only thin filaments. All of the bands could be explained by the overlapping or lack of overlapping of the thick and thin thread ends. Thus, it developed, striations are a visual effect produced by the position of the muscle threads—in a sense by their weaving.

Using magnifications up to six hundred thousand times, Huxley saw another astonishing part of the muscle structure. The protein fibrils, the photographs indicated, are twisted into coils. Although the coiling could not be finally proved, there were strong indications that Nature was repeating the use of her favorite helix, the spiral staircase of DNA and of the proteins themselves.

Protruding from the myosin filament, at regular intervals of about four hundred angstroms, were "steps" or "bridges," as the scientists named them. The end of the myosin's projecting step or bridge touched the thin actin filaments lying around it. In this way the filaments were linked by a whole series of cross steps or bridges.

The plan revealed was so clear and so brilliantly explanatory of effects that had puzzled science for many decades that Huxley scarcely dared to believe it could be true.

At about the same time, however, principally in 1954, Andrew Fielding Huxley and R. Niedergerke at Cambridge University were studying living muscle fibers in the interference microscope, a special type of light microscope. H. E. Huxley had principally used muscle embedded in plastic.

A. F. Huxley, looking at the living muscle, saw a thick coiled filament and a thin one. He calculated their thickness and length—the thickness of the one was about 100 angstroms and the other about 50; the length of one was 1.5 microns and of the other, 2. A. F. Huxley also studied the bridges and their spacing. They projected from the myosin coils at about every 400 angstroms.

More complete or explicit agreement would have been impossible. Both Huxleys published magnificent pictures showing the structures they had found, and diagrams that could have been used interchangeably.

How did this precisely ordered and integrated fabric work? The question was the equivalent of asking how muscle works, but now there was exciting promise that the answer might be found.

H. E. Huxley and Hanson began by trying to co-ordinate chemistry and the structures they were seeing in the electron microscope. They treated some strips of muscle with the salt solutions that Szent-Györgyi and others had shown can wash away the myosin of muscle. When the treatment was completed, they examined the remaining structure in the microscope. The picture was definite. No thick filaments could be seen. Here was unmistakable proof that the missing thick filaments were myosin.

With this essential point established, actin was removed. When the scientists examined their material, the thin filaments had disappeared. And so the thin filaments were actin. For the first time structure and material had been identified. At last science knew what the fibers of muscle are and of what they are composed.

Studying myosin, Huxley and Hanson found that the length of the filaments did not change as muscle stretched or contracted. Similarly, the actin thread changed only a relatively small amount. The earlier reports of Szent-Györgyi that neither myosin nor actin would stretch or contract came swiftly to mind.

If neither filament changed materially, the stretching and contraction of muscle could not be explained by any folding or shortening of its filaments. Some other system would have to account for the indisputable, powerful action of muscle.

Both Huxley and Hanson and Huxley and Niedergerke came to the same new, simple, and yet startling conclusion.

Muscle contracts and stretches by the movement of the two sets of filaments. "They slide past one another," said A. F. Huxley.

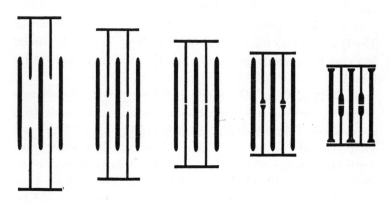

Muscle at work. A muscle stretches, (2) comes to rest, and (3, 4, and 5) increasingly contracts.

The marvelous feats of muscle, then, were a sliding-in and a sliding-out of two kinds of protein filaments. (Again with the hands parallel, slide the fingers together and pull them apart for an approximation of this basic mechanism of motion.)

But what causes the movement? The critical question was immediately raised. Here the photographs supplied only general indications.

As the sliding filaments did not change in length, and each, so to speak, moved back and forth on its own track without touching the filaments alongside it, the search turned to the "bridges." The photographs showed that each did connect two filaments. As in DNA, the interconnections seemed likely to hold the secret.

H. E. Huxley calculated the number of myosin molecules in a given volume of muscle. The figure turned out to be "surprisingly close" to the number of "bridges" in the same volume. "This suggests," said Huxley, "that each bridge is part of a single myosin molecule."

Perhaps the projecting "bridges" oscillated to a limited degree, caught a specific site on an adjoining actin filament, and moved it along.

"They could pull the filament a short distance, say 100 angstroms, and return to their original configuration for another pull," said H. E. Huxley. "One would expect that each time a bridge went through such a cycle, a phosphate group would be split from a single molecule of ATP; this reaction would provide the energy for the cycle."

To enable a rabbit muscle to contract with its characteristic dashing speed, each of the bridges would have to catch, pull, release, catch, pull, and release between fifty and one hundred times a second. Huxley estimated that such high-speed action is compatible with the rate at which myosin catalyzes the removal of phosphate groups from ATP. "When the muscle has relaxed," he said, "we suppose that the removal of the phosphate groups from ATP has stopped and that the myosin bridges can no longer combine with the actin filaments. The muscle can then return to its uncontracted length."

If there were no release and the bridges were permanently anchored at their actin sites, the muscle would be locked and unable to move. It is precisely such a situation that produces rigor mortis. Szent-Györgyi had earlier shown that the cessation of the flow of ATP results in the rigidity of death. The newer research indicated that the mechanism might be the stilling of the bridges.

H. E. Huxley was picturing the myosin bridges and the actin sites that they might catch as essentially a ratchet device or a cog-type operation.

A. F. Huxley suggested a slightly different manner of functioning. "Each of the myosin filaments has side pieces which can slide along the main backbone of the filament," he said. "The slides can combine temporarily with sites on adjacent actin filaments."

To illustrate how slide and actin site might work together, Huxley drew the "slide" with a concave, socket-like tip and the actin site as a round knob. Ball would fit into socket. As the

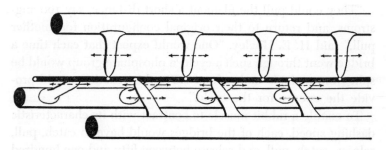

The pull of muscle. In this schematic drawing the cross bridges of three thick filaments are shown pulling one thin filament. The bridges may hook onto an active site, pull it a short way, release it, and hook onto the next active site. The plan suggests a ratchet.

actin was pulled along, the connection would be broken and the slide would be freed to engage another ball site.

The determination of the exact structure would have to await future research. Many additional studies and photographs, however, enabled H. E. Huxley to point out that the projections he called bridges and that A. F. Huxley referred to as slides maintain more or less the same position—at right angles to the filaments, whether the muscles are stretched, at rest, or contracted.

"The only difference between the muscles at different lengths is that the two sets of filaments overlap to different extents," H. E. Huxley summed up. "This must mean that as the filaments slide past each other during contraction, the bridges between them remain attached for a short distance only, and that they must then detach from the secondary filament and reattach at a point a little farther along."

Many additional problems remained to be solved. Some disagreed with the proposals about the movement of the muscles, and emphasized that other explanations of the indisputable photographic evidence might be suggested. But the photographic evidence continued to accumulate.

The final details of the system might vary from the first proposals, but the swift, the powerful, the incessant movement of all living things appeared to be a sliding back and forth of coiled filaments and a connecting and disconnecting of their cross-link bridges.

Another important piece in the over-all structure of life had been put together.

XXII

THE COIL OF THE FUTURE

*Nature herself is to be addressed; the
paths she shows us are to be boldly
trodden; for thus . . . shall we penetrate into the heart of her mystery.*
WILLIAM HARVEY

IN THE STUDY of that nearest and most basic matter of them
all—life itself in all its manifestations—Nature herself has
been assiduously addressed during the past two hundred years.
The paths she showed were carefully and sometimes boldly
trodden. As Harvey predicted, this course has enabled us to
penetrate deep into the heart of life's mystery.

This book has traced the great depth of that penetration—
from surface appearance and actions to the organs that keep us
alive, to the tissues of which the organs are made, to the cells
that compose the tissues, to the focal nucleus, to the chromosomes, the little threads within the nucleus which are the
bearers and distributors of heredity.

And then came the wholly unexpected discovery that the
familiar nucleic acids, DNA and RNA, were the master materials of the chromosomes and of life. Nearly all tests that so
far have been devised show that the two tiny spirals of matter
determine the form and structure of all life, its functioning, its
color, its variety, and its continuity.

Thus, in less than two hundred years from the time when
Lavoisier first demonstrated that man was not a mystic thing
apart but a creature governed by the same physical laws as the
rest of the universe, the base of life was reached. Here was
life's starting point. All that the individual was to become and

his relation to all that had gone before him lay in the infinitely tiny coil of DNA or RNA.

In the early years of the twentieth century an able scientist had ridiculed the idea of particles "packed with unthinkable precision, order and potentiality . . . in the chromosomes." It was unimaginable, but it was so.

Miniaturization had not come into its new use then or even later when DNA was identified. Men made most of their tools and machines larger than life. Often these mechanical implements for the output of power and motion were massive. Their size and the scale of the earth and space made largeness understandable. Against this background it was nearly inconceivable that bits of matter weighing a half-billionth of a gram could function with power, precision, and remarkable certainty. Only with the coming of the electronic age and the exploration of outer space did men move toward miniaturization, the pattern of Nature. The size of DNA may seem more conceivable to the future than to the present.

Nature's superb miniaturization, the use of almost immeasurably small units to create the boundless diversity of life and the packing of them into the coil of DNA, made the study of life as difficult a task as science has undertaken. It was, nevertheless, accomplished, and now many new paths are opening.

Some of them, if boldly trod, may alter the early—the present—concepts of DNA. There are always disagreements, and always new insights.

Other paths lead toward understandings that formerly seemed almost unattainable. Even now science is trying to decipher the "code" of DNA, the order of the four steps in its spiraling staircase which dictate the biological make-up of each of the billions of men, animals, plants, and micro-organisms on this earth. Although the problem imposes great difficulties, there is every likelihood that science soon will be able to analyze the order of DNA as Sanger analyzed that of the amino acids of the insulin molecule.

And for the first time it is possible to work upward, as Nature does, from the simple to the complex. In the past, science had to study life primarily by taking it apart, by working from the finished product to the preceding one. Now it is possible to ask how DNA makes the chromosome, how it shapes enzymes, proteins, and other building blocks to its ends. It is also possible now to inquire how the proteins, enzymes, and other building units come together to form the muscles, the skin, the blood, the brain, and all the other parts of living things.

With an understanding of how cells and body structures are shaped, science can look forward to dealing effectively and knowledgeably with the failures and the breakdowns in the elaborate life process. Cancer is one such failure. Aging is another. Mental illness may be still another. When cause is known, treatment does not have to be so largely by trial and error.

Beyond even such splendid possibilities lie still other prospects. If man understood the organization of DNA and how it achieves its effects, could he not manipulate the process to overcome some of the present "inborn errors in heredity"— the sickle-cell anemias and other inborn defects? Could he not even alter the organization of DNA to increase his own intelligence? Or to assure himself of longer life? Or to improve his physique for whatever the future may hold?

If such control is achieved even in part, the possibility looms that man may be able to regulate his own heritage much as he now regulates many of the elements of his environment. In that event his future evolution would be the outcome not of the blind interaction of heredity and man-made environment, but of his own determination. It is an outlook ineffably dangerous and ineffably promising. So far our understanding of this mortal coil speaks well for the future. It is unmarred by misuse, and stands as one of the summit achievements of man and of DNA.

NOTE ON BOOKS AND MATERIALS

COUNTLESS PAPERS and many books tell the story of the long and continuing search for an understanding of life. With a few notable exceptions, they are highly technical. In few other sciences has so little been written for the layman, who is, in the last analysis, the subject of it all.

In this note I shall indicate only a few major papers or books that deal formally with the work I have described, and whatever non-technical discussions may be available. The latter are likely to be found in the excellently written and excellently illustrated pages of the magazine *Scientific American*. By going to the references given here, anyone in quest of more information may find copious additional references.

Excerpts from the writings of the scientists who have made great discoveries in the life sciences are brought together in several outstanding anthologies. Two that are particularly useful—they give biographical and background material—are *Source Book in the History of the Sciences,* by Harry M. Leicester and Herbert S. Klickstein (New York: McGraw-Hill Book Company; 1952), and *Moments of Discovery,* by George Schwartz and Philip W. Bishop (New York: Basic Books; 1958).

For a brief and authoritative summary of the history of the life sciences, one that carries the story up to contemporary events, see the presidential address given by Sewall Wright at the Tenth International Congress of Genetics, Montreal, Canada, August 20, 1958. It was published in *Science*, Vol. 130, No. 3381, p. 959 (October 16, 1959).

Among the few books for the layman which deal with the growth and development of the life sciences are *Science and the Nature of Life,* by William S. Beck (New York: Harcourt, Brace and Company; 1957), and *Man, the Chemical Machine,* by Ernest Borek (New York: Columbia University Press; 1952). George Gamow touches upon some of the big problems of life in an entertaining and delightful little fable, *Mr. Tompkins Learns the Facts of Life* (Cambridge: At the University Press; 1953).

Well-known books that tell of the lives and work of some of the earlier figures in the life sciences are *Crucibles: The Story of Chemistry,* by Bernard Jaffe (New York: Simon and Schuster; 1951); *Microbe Hunters,* by Paul de Kruif (New York: Harcourt, Brace and Company; 1926); and *Virus Hunters,* by Greer Williams (New York: Alfred A. Knopf; 1959). Biographical material about contemporary scientists may be found in standard works of reference.

Chapter by chapter, the following materials were among those consulted in the writing of this book and may be used as starting points for further reading.

II

There are a number of excellent biographies of Lavoisier. The classic is *Lavoisier,* by Edouard Grimaux (Paris: Ancienne Librairie Germer, Balliere et Cie.; 1896). More recent ones include *Antoine Lavoisier,* by Douglas McKie (New York: Henry Schuman; 1953); *Lavoisier,* by Maurice Daumas (Paris: Presse Universitaire; 1955); and *Torch and Crucible: The Life and Death of Antoine Lavoisier,* by Sidney J. French (Princeton: Princeton University Press; 1941). Lavoisier reports his own work in a number of well-written and meticulously illustrated papers and books. Among them are *Opuscules physiques et chymiques* (English translation, *Essays Physical and Chemical,* by Thomas Henry, London, 1776); *Traité élémentaire de Chimie* (Paris, 1789) (English translation, *Elements of Chemistry,* by Robert Kerr, New York, 1806); *Oeuvres de Lavoisier, publiées par les soins de son Excellence le Ministre de l'Instruction Publique et des Cultes* (Paris, 6 vols.; Vol. 1 [1864] contains the *Opuscules and Traité*); and *Mémoire sur la Chaleur,* by Lavoisier and Pierre Simon de La Place (Paris: Gauthier-Villars et Cie.; 1920). Other *mémoires* are to be found in the *Mémoires de l'Académie des Sciences* (Paris, 1765–83). A brief, authoritative discussion of some of the work of Lavoisier appears in *The Overthrow of the Phlogiston Theory: The Chemical Revolution of 1775–1789,* one of the Harvard Case Histories in Experimental Science, edited by James Bryant Conant (Cambridge: Harvard University Press; 1952).

III

An account of Bichat's brief life is given in *Medical Portrait Gallery: Biographical Memoirs of the Most Celebrated Physicians and Surgeons,* by Thomas Joseph Pettigrew (London: Fisher, Son & Co.; 1888). Bichat's *Treatise on Membranes,* in a translation by F. Gold, was published in Boston by Cummings and Hilliard in 1813. His *General Anatomy Applied to the Physiology and Practice of Medicine* appears in a translation by Constant Coffyn (London: S. Highley; 1824). On the hundredth anniversary of Bichat's death a new biography was published: *Xavier Bichat: Sa Vie, son Oeuvre, son Influence sur les Sciences Biologiques,* by Pierre Emile Launois (Paris: C Naud, Editeur; 1902).

IV

An English translation of Wohler's paper reporting the discovery of urea appears in *A Source Book in the History of the Sciences* and in *Moments of Discovery.* An account of the contemporary reception of Wohler's synthesis of urea is given by W. H. Warren in *Journal of Chemical Éducation,* Vol. 5, No. 12 (December 1928). For the centenary celebration of Wohler's work see *Journal of Biochemistry,* Vol. 22, p. 1341 (1928).

A biography of Liebig by W. A. Shenstone—*Justus von Liebig: His Life and Work, 1803–1873* (New York: The Macmillan Company; 1895)

—deals almost as completely with Wohler. The life work of Liebig is discussed by August Wilhelm Homan in the Faraday Lecture for 1875 (London: The Macmillan Company; 1876). Liebig's complete work in chemistry was published in English by T. B. Peterson, Philadelphia, in 1852.

V

Hooke's theory of the cell is delightfully set forth and illustrated in his famous *Micrographia* (London: Jo. Martyn and James Allestry, Printers to the Royal Society; 1665).

Leeuwenhoek's matchless letters to the Royal Society are collected in *Select Works of Antony van Leeuwenhoek*, translated by Samuel Hoole (London: Whittingham and Arliss; 1816). Two other excellent books on Leeuwenhoek are *Antony van Leeuwenhoek and His "Little Animals,"* by Clifford Dobell (Amsterdam: N. V. Swets & Zeitlinger; 1932; 2nd edition, New York, 1958), and *Measuring the Invisible World*, by A. Schierbeek (London: Life of Science Library, Abelard-Schuman; 1959). De Kruif's chapter on Leeuwenhoek in *Microbe Hunters* is famous.

Brown's discovery of the nucleus of the cell is reported in his article "On the Organs and Mode of Fecundation in Orchidae and Aslepiadae," *Transactions of the Linnean Society of London*, Vol. 17, p. 685 (1833).

Dutrochet: *Recherches anatomiques et physiologiques sur la Structure intime des Animaux et des Végétaux et sur leur Motilité* (Paris: Chez J. S. Bailliere, Librairie; 1824).

Schwann's *Microscopical Researches in the Accordance in the Structure and Growth of Animals and Plants* and Schleiden's *Contributions to Phytogenesis* are brought together in an English translation by Henry Smith (London: Sydenham Society; 1847). Schleiden also discusses his theory of the cell in his *Poetry of the Vegetable World—A Popular Exposition of the Science of Botany and Its Relations to Man* (Cincinnati: Moore, Anderson, Wilstach & Keys; 1853). The development of the cell theory is traced in "The Dawn of the Cell Theory," by John H. Gerould, *Scientific Monthly* (1922). The story of the centenary celebration that misfired, with the papers of Conklin, Woodruff, and Karling, appears in *Biological Symposia*, edited by Jacques Cattell (Lancaster, Pa.: Jacques Cattell Press; 1940).

VI

Many outstanding and authoritative biographies tell of the life and work of Pasteur. Among them are *The Life of Pasteur*, by René Vallery-Radot, Pasteur's son-in-law (London: Constable and Company; 1906); *History of a Mind* by Emile Duclaux, Pasteur's close associate (Philadelphia: W. B. Saunders Company; 1920); *Louis Pasteur: Free Lance of Science*, by René J. Dubos (Boston: Little, Brown & Co.; 1950); and *Louis Pasteur*, by Pasteur Vallery-Radot, Pasteur's grandson (New York: Alfred A. Knopf; 1958). The following works of Pasteur pertain to the subjects discussed in this chapter: *Oeuvres de Pasteur réunis par Pasteur Vallery-Radot*, Vols. 1–5 (Paris: Masson et Cie.; 1922–8); *Etudes sur la Bière* (1876) *La Maladie des Vers à Soie* (1870), and *Etudes sur le Vinaigre* (1868), all published in Paris by Gauthier-Villars; and *Etude sur le Vin* (Paris: F. Savy; 1873). Two of the Harvard Case

Histories in Experimental Science appraise the work of Pasteur in the light of contemporary knowledge and procedures: *Pasteur's and Tyndall's Study of Spontaneous Generation* (1952) and *Pasteur's Study of Fermentation* (1953), both edited by James Bryant Conant and published at Cambridge by the Harvard University Press.

VII

A thorough, expert, and readable summary of Fischer's work is made by Martin Onslow Forster in the Fischer Memorial Lecture, *Journal of the Chemical Society* (Great Britain), Vol. 117, Pt. II, p. 1157 (1920), and in an article in *Nature*, Vol. 106, p. 326 (November 4, 1920). Other biographical materials appear in "Obituary Notices of Deceased Fellows," *Proceedings of the Royal Society*, Vol. 98A (1921); *Eminent Chemists of Our Time*, by Benjamin Harrow (New York: D. Van Nostrand Company; 1927); and *The Nobel Prize Winners*, by T. W. MacCallum (Zurich: Central European Times Publishing Co.; 1936).

Accounts of Buchner's life and work are given in *Journal of Chemical Education*, Vol. 6, No. 2, p. 1849 (November 1929), and in MacCallum's *The Nobel Prize Winners*. René J. Dubos, in his book on Pasteur, writes extensively of the work of Buchner.

VIII

The work of both Roux and Driesch is presented in Driesch's *The History and Theory of Vitalism* (London: Macmillan and Co.; 1914) and *The Science and Philosophy of the Organism* (London: A. and C. Black; 1929). Their work is considered also in *Man a Machine*, by Joseph Needham (New York: W. W. Norton & Company; 1928), and *Embryos and Ancestors*, by G. R. DeBeer (Oxford: At the Clarendon Press; 1940).

IX

De Vries summarizes his vast work on mutations in his two-volume *The Mutation Theory* (1909) and *Species and Varieties* (1905), both published in Chicago by the Open Court Publishing Co.

A translation of Mendel's famous papers is provided in *Mendel's Principles of Heredity*, by William Bateson (Cambridge: At the University Press; 1909). Hugo Iltis, a fellow townsman of Mendel, spent many years preparing his *Life of Mendel* (London: George Allen and Unwin; 1932). A recent biography, particularly directed to young students, is *Gregor Mendel*, by Harry Sootin (New York: The Vanguard Press; 1959).

X

Morgan and the scientists who worked with him on the famous studies of the fruit fly wrote many books and articles. Among them are: *Drosophila simulans and Drosophila melanogaster* (Washington: Carnegie Institution; 1929); *Heredity and Sex* (New York: Columbia University Press; 1913); *The Mechanism of Mendelian Heredity* (London: Constable & Co.; 1915); and *The Physical Basis of Heredity* (Philadelphia: J. B. Lippincott Company; 1919). An important early paper is "Sex Limited Inheritance in Drosophila," in *Science*, Vol. 35 (June 22, 1910). A biography and a review of Morgan's work, written by his associate A. H. Sturtevant, are in *Biographical Memoirs of the National Academy of Sciences*, Vol. 33 (1959). R. A. Fisher wrote the article in *Obituary Notices of Fellows of the Royal Society*, Vol. 5, No. 15 (February 1947).

XI

Muller made his first major report on the production of mutations by X rays in "Artificial Transmutation of the Gene," *Science*, Vol. 66, p. 84 (July 22, 1927). Other publications include: *Heritable Variations* (Washington: Smithsonian Institution Annual Report; 1930: *Genetics, Medicine and Men* (Ithaca: Cornell University Press; 1947); "The Development of the Gene Theory," in *Genetics in the Twentieth Century* (New York: The Macmillan Company; 1951); Pilgrim Trust Lecture, "The Gene," *Proceedings of the Royal Society*, Series B, Vol. 134, No. 1 (November 1, 1945); and a summary of proceedings in *Cold Spring Harbor Symposia on Quantitative Biology*, Vol. 9 (1941).

XII

The first scientific reports on Beadle's and Tatum's discoveries in their work with Neurospora appeared in *Proceedings of the National Academy of Sciences*, Vol. 27, p. 499 (1941), and Vol. 28, p. 234 (1942). Other publications include "The Gene," R. A. F. Penrose Jr. Memorial Lecture, *Proceedings of the American Philosophical Society*, Vol. 90, p. 5 (December 1946); *Genetic Control of Developmental Reactions* (*Biological Symposia*, Lancaster, Pa.: Jacques Cattell Press; 1941); and "Genes and the Chemistry of the Organism," *Science in Progress*, Vol. 5, p. 166 (1947). A more popular presentation was made in "The Genes of Men and Molds," *Scientific American*, Vol. 30 (September 1948). The scientists discuss their work in the Nobel Prize addresses: Beadle's, "Genes and Chemical Reactions in Neurospora," appeared in *Science*, Vol. 129, No. 3365, p. 1715 (June 26, 1959), and Tatum's, "A Case History in Biological Research," in the same issue, p. 1711. Beadle was the subject of a "cover story" in *Time*, Vol. 72, p. 50 (July 14, 1958). Announcement of the awarding of the Nobel Prize and biographies of the two scientists appeared in *The New York Times*, October 31, 1958.

XIII

Two symposia, since published in book form, gave leading scientists an opportunity to present and discuss the new findings about DNA and RNA. These are *The Chemical Basis of Heredity*, edited by William D. McElroy and Bentley Glass (Baltimore: Johns Hopkins Press; 1957), and *Cellular Biology, Nucleic Acids and Viruses* (New York Academy of Sciences, Special Publications, No. 5). In addition, the following articles and books report some of the key work of the scientists named: Mirsky. "Chromosomes and Nucleoproteins," *Advances in Enzymology*, Vol. 3 (1943); Mirsky and Pollister: "Studies on the Chemistry of Chromatin," *Transactions of the New York Academy of Sciences*, Series II, p. 190 (May 10, 1943).

M. H. F. Wilkins. *Biochemical Society Symposia*, No. 14 (Cambridge, 1956).

Avery *et al. Journal of Experimental Medicine*, Vol. 79, p. 137 (1944).

Caspersson. *Proceedings of the National Academy of Sciences*, Vol. 26, p. 507 (1940), and *Cell Growth and Cell Function* (New York: W. W. Norton; 1950).

Hershey and Chase. *Journal of General Physiology*, Vol. 36, No. 1 (September 20, 1952), and New York Academy of Sciences, Special Publications, No. 5, p. 251 (1957).

XIV

Watson's and Crick's proposals for the structure of the nucleic acids are set forth in the following publications: *Nature*, Vol. 171, p. 737 (April-June 1953a) and p. 964 (May 30, 1953b); *Cold Spring Harbor Symposia on Quantitative Biology*, Vol. 18, p. 123 (1953); *Proceedings of the Royal Society*, Series A, Vol. 223, p. 80 (1954); *Scientific American*, Vol. 191, No. 4 (October 1954), and Vol. 197, No. 3 (September 1957). Also see *The Chemical Basis of Heredity*.

XV

Ochoa and his associates reported their synthesis of RNA in the following papers: "Polynucleotide Synthesis," *Science*, Vol. 122, p. 907 (1955); *Journal of the American Chemical Society*, Vol. 77, Pt. III, p. 3165 (May-June 1955); *Biochimica et Biophysica Acta*, Vol. 20, p. 269 (1956); "Symposium on Nucleic Acids," *Federation Proceedings of American Societies for Experimental Biology*, Vol. 15, p. 832 (July 1956); *The Chemical Basis of Heredity*, p. 615; New York Academy of Sciences, Special Publications, No. 5, p. 191 (1957); *Annual Review of Biochemistry*, Vol. 27 (1958).

Concerning Kornberg, see *Federation Proceedings*, Vol. 15, p. 291 (1956); *Biochimica et Biophysica Acta*, Vol. 21, p. 197 (1956), and Vol. 24, p. 651 (1957); *The Chemical Basis of Heredity*, p. 579; and *Harvey Lectures*, Vol. 53, p. 83 (Harvey Society of New York, 1959).

XVI

Among the outstanding studies that have traced the functioning of DNA and RNA are the following:

Taylor *et al.* "The Organization and Duplication of Genetic Material," *Proceedings of Tenth International Congress on Genetics*, Vol. 1, p. 63 (1958); Chapter 21 in *A Symposium on Molecular Biology*, edited by Raymond E. Zirkle (Chicago: University of Chicago Press; 1959); *Proceedings of the National Academy of Sciences*, Vol. 43, p. 122 (1957); *Scientific American*, Vol. 198, p. 36 (June 1958).

Fraenkel-Conrat *et al. The Chemical Basis of Heredity; Virus Hunters; Journal of the American Chemical Society*, Vol. 78, p. 822 (1956); *Proceedings of the National Academy of Sciences*, Vol. 41, p. 690 (1955).

Gierer and Schramm. *Nature*, Vol. 177, p. 702 (1956).

Lederberg *et al.* "Genetic Transduction," *American Scientist*, Vol. 44, p. 264 (1956); *Bacteriological Reviews*, Vol. 21, p. 133 (1957); *Harvey Lectures*, Vol. 53, p. 69 (1959). Lederberg's Nobel Prize address appeared in *Science*, Vol. 131, No. 3396, p. 269 (January 29, 1960). Zinder and Lederberg also reported on their work with bacterial transduction in *Journal of Cellular and Comparative Physiology*, Vol. 45, Supp. 2, p. 23 (1955), and Zinder wrote a more popular report, well illustrated, in *Scientific American*, Vol. 199, p. 38 (November 1958).

XVII

Sumner. The story of Sumner's discovery is told by John Pfeiffer in *The Physics and Chemistry of Life: A Scientific American Book* (New York: Simon and Schuster; 1955). An account of the dispute that surrounded the finding may be found in *The Enzymes*, edited by Paul D. Boyer, Vol. 1 (Second edition, New York: Academic Press; 1959).

Pauling. The work on the structure of proteins is reported in *Proceedings of the National Academy of Sciences*, Vol. 37, No. 4, p. 205 (April 1951); *Nature*, Vol. 171, No. 4341, p. 59 (January 10, 1953); *Scientific American*, Vol. 191, p. 51 (July 1954).

Sanger. The basic reports on the deciphering of the insulin molecule may be found in the following works: Sanger and Tuppy, *Biochemical Journal*, Vol. 49, p. 463 (1951); *Cold Spring Harbor Symposia*, Vol. 14, p. 153 (1949); and in two articles by E. O. P. Thompson, an associate in the work, in *Biochemical Journal*, Vol. 52, p. 11 (1952), and in *The Physics and Chemistry of Life* (New York: Simon and Schuster; 1954). An account of Sanger's receipt of the Nobel Prize appeared with biographical material in *The New York Times*, October 28, 1958.

XVIII

Ingram. A summary article on the chemistry of the abnormal human haemoglobins appeared in *British Medical Bulletin*, Vol. 15, No. 1, p. 27 (1959). J. A. Hunt and Ingram discuss the genetical control of protein structure in *The Ciba Foundation Symposium on Biochemistry of Human Genetics* (Boston: Little, Brown and Company; 1959), p. 114. A more popular account may be found in *Scientific American*, Vol. 198, p. 68 (January 1958).

Palade. The investigation of mitochondria with the electron microscope is reported in *Ford Symposium*, edited by O. H. Gaebler (New York: Academic Press; 1956).

Crick. For the principal reports on the work with the protein code see "Symposium on the Replication of Macromolecules," *Symposia of the Society for Experimental Biology*, Vol. 12 (1958); *Proceedings of the National Academy of Sciences*, Vol. 43, p. 416 (May 1957); *The Nucleic Acids*, edited by Erwin Chargaff and J. N. Davidson (New York: Academic Press; 1955); "Nucleic Acids," *Scientific American*, Vol. 197, No. 3, p. 188 (September 1957).

Hoagland. *Scientific American*, December 1959, and, for a general discussion of the biosynthesis of protein, Robert B. Loftfield in *Progress in Biophysics and Biophysical Chemistry*, Vol. 8, p. 348 (1957).

XIX

Palade. See *Ford Symposium*.

Green. "Studies in Organized Enzyme Systems," in *Harvey Lectures*,

Vol. 52, p. 177 (1958); *Scientific American,* Vol. 190 (January 1954); *Science,* Vol. 115, p. 3 (January 25, 1952); "The Metabolism of Fats," *Scientific American,* Vol. 190 (January 1954).

Siekevitz. "Powerhouse of the Cell," *Scientific American,* July 1957. Lipmann. *Harvey Lectures,* Vol. 44, p. 165 (1950); *Journal of the American Chemical Society,* Vol. 75, p. 4874 (October 5, 1953).

Krebs. *Chemical Pathways of Metabolism* (New York: Academic Press; 1954); *Harvey Lectures,* Vol. 44, p. 165 (1950). The announcement of the awarding of the Nobel Prize to Krebs and Lipmann and biographies of both appeared in *The New York Times,* October 31, 1953.

XX

Spemann. *Embryonic Development and Induction* (New Haven: Yale University Press; 1938).

Rose. The experiments on the differentiation of cells are reported in *The American Naturalist,* Vol. 86, No. 831, p. 337 (November-December 1952); *Annals of the New York Academy of Sciences,* Vol. 60, p. 1136 (June 2, 1955); *Scientific American,* December 1958.

Moscona. "The Compounding of Complex Macromolecules and Cellular Units in Tissue Fabrics," *Proceedings of the National Academy of Sciences,* Vol. 42, No. 11, p. 819 (November 1956); *Scientific American,* Vol. 200, p. 40 (May 1959).

XXI

Szent-Györgyi. The basic studies in the contraction of muscle may be found in his *The Chemistry of Muscular Contraction,* second edition (New York: Academic Press; 1951).

H. E. Huxley. *Journal of Biophysical and Biochemical Cytology,* Vol. 3, No. 5, p. 631 (September 25, 1957); *Scientific American,* November 1958; Jean Hanson and H. E. Huxley, *Symposia of the Society for Experimental Biology,* Vol. 9 (Cambridge: At the University Press; 1955).

A. F. Huxley. *Progress in Biophysics and Biophysical Chemistry,* Vol. 7, p. 255 (1957).

INDEX

A NOTE ABOUT THE AUTHOR

RUTH MOORE was born in St. Louis, Missouri, and received her A.B. and A.M. degrees from Washington University there. She has worked as a reporter on the St. Louis *Star-Times*, as Washington correspondent for the *Chicago Sun*, as assistant editor of the *Kiplinger Magazine*. She is now again in Chicago on the *Sun-Times*, where science feature stories are one of her specialties.

The author of such valuable books as *The Earth We Live On: The Story of Geological Discovery* (1956), *Man, Time, and Fossils: The Story of Evolution* (1953), and *Charles Darwin: A Great Life in Brief* (1955) has, in *The Coil of Life*, achieved another tour de force of science reporting: the story of the two-century search for the source of life itself, the most awe-inspiring success story of them all.

December 1960

A NOTE ON THE TYPE

The text of this book is set in Caledonia, a Linotype face designed by W. A. Dwiggins. This type belongs to the family of printing types called "modern face" by printers—a term used to mark the change in style of type-letters that occurred about 1800. Caledonia borders on the general design of Scotch Modern, but is more freely drawn than that letter.

The book was composed, printed, and bound by Kingsport Press, Inc., Kingsport, Tennessee. Typography and binding designs based on originals by W. A. Dwiggins.